Analysing English in a Global Context

Analysing English in a Global Context offers a global perspective on the changing uses and forms of English and develops the skills needed to analyse these forms. It presents English language teaching in a variety of specific institutional, geographic, and cultural contexts.

This Reader addresses key contemporary issues in English language teaching and applied linguistics. The articles – a range of classic and specially commissioned pieces – have been carefully chosen and edited, and together they provide an overview of the rapid growth and spread of English in its many varieties worldwide. A general introduction outlines the approach, organization, and different perspectives of the collection.

Up-to-date and fully international, the Reader foregrounds some of the most challenging questions for future developments in English language teaching worldwide. Topics include: the internationalization of English; the status of the non-native English teacher; the recognition of language variation; the debate on standard versus non-standard varieties.

Articles by: Vijay K. Bhatia; Anne Burns; Caroline Coffin; David Crystal; Beverly Derewianka; Eleanor Er; David Graddol; M.A.K. Halliday; Rick Iedema; Braj B. Kachru; J.R. Martin; Denise E. Murray; Cecil L. Nelson; Clare Painter; Alastair Pennycook; Maree Stenglin.

Anne Burns is a senior lecturer and Head of the Division of Linguistics and Psychology at Macquarie University, Sydney. **Caroline Coffin** is a lecturer in the Centre for Language and Communications at the Open University, UK.

Companion volumes

The companion volumes in this series are:

English Language Teaching in its Social Context edited by Christopher N. Candlin and Neil Mercer

Innovation in English Language Teaching edited by David R. Hall and Ann Hewings

These three readers are part of a scheme of study jointly developed by Macquarie University, Sydney, Australia and the Open University, United Kingdom. At the Open University, the three readers are part of a single course, *Teaching English to Speakers of Other Languages Worldwide* which forms part of the Open University MA in Education (Applied Linguistics) and Advanced Diploma in Teaching English to Speakers of Other Languages. At Macquarie University, the three readers are each attached to single study units, which form part of the Postgraduate Diploma and Master of Applied Linguistics programmes.

The Open University MA in Education is now established as the most popular postgraduate degree for UK education professionals, with over 3,500 students registering each year. From 2001 it will also be available worldwide. The MA in Education is designed particularly for those with experience in teaching, educational administration or allied fields. The MA is a modular degree and students are free to select, from a range of options, the programme that best fits in with their interests and professional goals. The MA in Education programme provides great flexibility. Students study at their own pace and in their own time. They receive specially prepared study materials, and are supported by a personal tutor. (Successful completion of the MA in Education (Applied Linguistics) entitles students to apply for entry to the Open University Doctorate in Education (Ed.D.) programme.)

The Professional Development in Education prospectus contains further information and application forms. To find out more about the Open University and request your copy please write to the Course Reservations and Sales Centre, The Open University, PO Box 724, Walton Hall, Milton Keynes MK7 6ZW, or e-mail ces-gen@open.ac.uk, or telephone +44 (0) 1908 653231 or visit the website *www.open.ac.uk*. For more information on the MA in Education (Applied Linguistics) visit *www.open.ac.uk/applied-linguistics*.

Macquarie University introduced distance versions of its influential on-campus degrees in 1994 and now has students in over thirty countries. Both the Postgraduate Diploma and the Masters are offered in three versions: Applied Linguistics, Applied Linguistics (TESOL) and Applied Linguistics (Literacy). Credits are freely transferable between the Diploma and the Masters and between the three versions, and students may change between distance and on-campus modes or mix modes if desired. Students study at their own pace, with specially developed materials and with support and feedback provided directly from lecturers in the Linguistics Department through e-mail, web, fax, phone and post, and a specialised library service provided through the Resources Centre of the National Centre for English Language Teaching and Research (NCELTR). External doctoral programmes are also available.

Information about the Macquarie programmes and application forms are available on *www.ling.mq.edu.au* or by writing to the Linguistics Postgraduate Office, Macquarie University, NSW 2109, Australia (tel: +61 2 9850 9243; fax +61 2 9850 9352; e-mail: lingdl@ling.mq.edu.au).

Analysing English in a Global Context

'This volume fills a gap that has been missing in the literature used in many TESOL/ TEFL courses. The uniqueness of this collection of papers is not just the presentation of English in different cultural and social contexts but also in the foregrounding of language as an analytical tool in order to examine language itself.' *Joseph A. Foley, Southeast Asia Ministers of Education Organisation, Regional Centre, Singapore*

'This Reader offers key texts from many of the most interesting authors who consider teaching English to be part of a social and political process, not merely a psycholinguistic one.' *Euan Reid, Institute of Education, University of London*

Teaching English Language Worldwide

A selection of readers' comments on the series:

'This three-part series offers a map to ELT research and practice . . . it represents the best that ELT, as an Anglo-Saxon institution, has developed over the last thirty years for the teaching of English around the world . . . Readers will find in this series the Who's Who guide to this dynamic and expanding community.' *Claire Kramsch, University of California, Berkeley, California*

'Experienced English language instructors seeking to deepen their knowledge and abilities will find this series forms a coherent basis to develop their understanding of current trends, sociocultural diversity, and topical interests in teaching English as a second or foreign language around the world. All three volumes provide ample flexibility for discussion, interpretation, and adaptation in local settings.' *Alister Cumming, Ontario Institute for Studies in Education, University of Toronto*

'This series provides a collection of essential readings which will not only provide the TEFL/TESOL student and teacher with access to the most up-to-date thinking and approaches to the subject but will give any person interested in the subject an overview of the phenomenon of the use and usage of English in the modern world. Perhaps more importantly, this series will be crucial to those students who do not have available to them articles that provide both a wide spectrum of information and the necessary analytical tools to investigate the language further.' *Joseph A. Foley, Southeast Asia Ministers of Education Organisation, Regional Language Centre, Singapore*

'The strong representation of the seminal Anglo-Australian development of the European functional tradition in the study of language and language education makes this a refreshingly bracing series, which should be widely used in teacher education for English language teaching.' *Euan Reid, Institute of Education, University of London*

'In a principled and accessible manner, these three volumes bring together major writings on essential topics in the study of English language teaching. They provide broad coverage of current thinking and debate on major issues, providing an invaluable resource for the contemporary postgraduate student.' *Guy Cook, University of Reading*

Analysing English in a Global Context

A Reader

Edited by

Anne Burns and Caroline Coffin

London and New York
in association with Macquarie University
and The Open University

First published 2001
by Routledge
2 Park Square, Milton Park, Abingdon, Oxon, OX14 4RN

Simultaneously published in the USA and Canada
by Routledge
270 Madison Avenue, New York, NY 10016

Reprinted 2003, 2005, 2006

Routledge is an imprint of the Taylor & Francis Group

Typeset in Perpetua and Bell Gothic
by Keystroke, Jacaranda Lodge, Wolverhampton
Printed and bound in Great Britain
by TJ International Ltd, Padstow, Cornwall

British Library Cataloguing in Publication Data
A catalogue record for this book is available from the British Library

Library of Congress Cataloging in Publication Data
Analysing English in a global context : a reader / edited by Anne Burns and Caroline Coffin.
    p. cm.—(Teaching English language worldwide)
  Includes bibliographical references and index.
    1. English language—Study and teaching—Foreign speakers. 2. English
language—Foreign countries. 3. English language—Variation. 4. Communication,
International. 5. Intercultural communication. 6. Languages in contact. I. Burns, Anne,
1945– II. Coffin, Caroline, 1958– III. Series.

  PE1128.A2 A534 2000
  428'.0071—dc21   00-059193

ISBN 0–415–24115–4 (hbk)
ISBN 0–415–24116–2 (pbk)

Contents

List of illustrations   ix
List of acknowledgements   xi

Anne Burns and Caroline Coffin
INTRODUCTION   1

PART ONE
English in the world: change and variety

Braj B. Kachru and Cecil L. Nelson
1   WORLD ENGLISHES   9

David Graddol
2   ENGLISH IN THE FUTURE   26

Denise E. Murray
3   NEW TECHNOLOGY: NEW LANGUAGE AT WORK?   38

PART TWO
The globalisation of English: opportunities and constraints

David Crystal
4   THE FUTURE OF ENGLISHES   53

Vijay K. Bhatia
5   THE POWER AND POLITICS OF GENRE   65

Alastair Pennycook
6   ENGLISH IN THE WORLD/THE WORLD IN ENGLISH   78

PART THREE
Analysing English: a text perspective

Caroline Coffin
7 THEORETICAL APPROACHES TO WRITTEN
LANGUAGE – A TESOL PERSPECTIVE   93

Anne Burns
8 ANALYSING SPOKEN DISCOURSE: IMPLICATIONS
FOR TESOL   123

J.R. Martin
9 LANGUAGE, REGISTER AND GENRE   149

Clare Painter
10 UNDERSTANDING GENRE AND REGISTER: IMPLICATIONS
FOR LANGUAGE TEACHING   167

M.A.K. Halliday
11 LITERACY AND LINGUISTICS: RELATIONSHIPS BETWEEN
SPOKEN AND WRITTEN LANGUAGE   181

Maree Stenglin and Rick Iedema
12 HOW TO ANALYSE VISUAL IMAGES: A GUIDE FOR
TESOL TEACHERS   194

PART FOUR
Analysing English: a clause perspective

J.R. Martin
13 TECHNICALITY AND ABSTRACTION: LANGUAGE FOR
THE CREATION OF SPECIALIZED TEXTS   211

Eleanor Er
14 TEXT ANALYSIS AND DIAGNOSTIC ASSESSMENT   229

Beverly Derewianka
15 PEDAGOGICAL GRAMMARS: THEIR ROLE IN ENGLISH
LANGUAGE TEACHING   240

Index   270

Illustrations

Figures

2.1	The world language hierarchy in 2050?	32
2.2	Estimates of first-language speakers of English from 1950 to 2050 as calculated by the engco model	33
7.1	Dimensions of discourse and discourse analysis	100
7.2	Story genres in school English	111
8.1	Dimensions of tenor	128
8.2	A typology of spoken interactions	128
9.1	Systemic functional linguistics	150
9.2	Language, register and genre	156
9.3	The effect of different channels on communication	158
9.4	Action/reflection scale	159
10.1	The relation of context and metafunction	178
12.1	Framing and order	196
12.2	The iMac installation text	between pages 196 and 197
12.3	Reading path	198
13.1	English systems for tense and voice	212
13.2	Common-sense taxonomy of diseases	213
13.3	Medical taxonomy of diseases	214
13.4	Taxonomy of ecosystems	215
13.5	Taxonomy of conservers: cacti	216
13.6	Taxonomy of desert landforms	217
14.1	Text 1: Sample of student writing from review writing genre	230
14.2	Text 2: Clause breakdown of student writing sample	231
14.3	Thematic progression	232
14.4	Progression of ideas	232
14.5	Theme–Rheme structure	233
14.6	Reference chains	236
15.1	Tree diagram of sentence	252
15.2	A Hallidayan model of language	257

Tables

1.1	Countries in which English has official status	11
2.1	'Global influence' of major languages according to the engco model	31
8.1	Generic structure of story-telling genres	127
8.2	Analysis of text 2	130
8.3	A framework for analysing spoken discourse	142
10.1	The metafunctions of English	177
12.1	Meanings of visual space	196
12.2	Summary of meanings made in the written and visual modes	201
15.1	Parsed sentence	246
15.2	Sentence broken down into its parts	249
15.3	Pattern drills	250
15.4	Diagrammatic analysis of sentence	260
15.5	Key features of grammatical paradigms	264–5

Acknowledgements

The editors and publishers would like to thank the following for permission to use copyright material:

Vijay K. Bhatia and Blackwell Publishers for 'The power and politics of genre', in *World Englishes* 16:3, 1997.

Blackwell Publishers for an extract from Y. Kachru, 'Cultural meaning and contrastive rhetoric in English education', *World Englishes*, 1997.

David Crystal and Cambridge University Press for 'The future of Englishes', in *English Today* 15: 2, 1999.

Hunter Freeman for the six illustrations from Apple's iMac set up instructions.

David Graddol and the British Council for Chapter 5 from *The Future of English*, 1997.

M.A.K. Halliday for extracts from 'Literacy and linguistics: a functional perspective', in R. Hasan and G. Williams, *Literacy in Society*, Addison Wesley Longman Limited 1996. Reprinted by permission of Pearson Education Limited.

B.B. Kachru, C.L. Nelson and Cambridge University Press for 'World Englishes', in S.L. McKay and N. Hornberger, *Sociolinguistics and Language Teaching*, 1996.

J.R. Martin and Deakin University for 'Language, register and genre', in *Children Writing, Reader*, 1984.

J.R. Martin and Taylor & Francis for 'Technicality and abstraction: language for the creation of specialised texts', in M.A.K. Halliday and J.R. Martin, *Writing Science*, Falmer Press 1993.

Multilingual Matters Ltd for extracts from R. Clark and R. Ivanič, Editorial, *Language Awareness* 8:2, 1999.

Denise Murray for 'The computer at work', in *Knowledge Machines: Language and information in a technological society*, Longman Group Limited 1995, Reprinted by permission of Pearson Education Limited.

New South Wales Adult Migrant English Service for an extract from Helen Joyce, *Workplace Texts in the Language Classroom*, 1992.

Open University Press for extracts from 'Critical social literacy for the classroom', in Colin Lankshear, *Changing Literacies*, 1997.

Alastair Pennycook and Cambridge University Press for 'English in the world/The world in English', in J.W. Tollefson, *Power and Inequality in Language Education*, 1995.

The University of Michigan Press for an extract from J.M. Swales and C.B. Feak, *Academic Writing for Graduate Students: Essential tasks and skills*, 1994.

Text on page 229–39 reprinted from *Text Analysis and Diagnostic Assessment* by Eleanor Er in *Prospect* 8.3: 63–77 with permission from the National Centre for English Language Teaching and Research (NCELTR), Australia. © Macquarie University.

While the publishers and editors have made every effort to contact authors and copyright holders of works reprinted in *Analysing English in a Global Context*, this has not been possible in every case. They would welcome correspondence from individuals or companies they have been unable to trace.

We would like to thank the authors who contributed their chapters, as well as colleagues within and outside The Open University and Macquarie University who gave advice on the contents. Special thanks are due to the following people for their assistance in the production of this book.

Helen Boyce (course manager)
Pam Burns and Libby Brill (course secretaries)
Liz Freeman (Copublishing)
Nanette Reynolds, Frances Wilson and the staff of the Resource Centre of the National Centre for English Language Teaching and Research, Macquarie University.

Critical readers

Professor Vijay K. Bhatia (Department of English, City University, Hong Kong)
Geoff Thompson (Applied English Language Studies Unit, Liverpool University, UK)
Professor Leo van Lier (Educational Linguistics, University of Monterey, USA).

External assessor

Professor Ronald Carter (Department of English Studies, Nottingham University, UK).

Developmental testers

Ilona Cziraky (Italy)
Eladyr Maria Norberto da Silva (Brazil)
Chitrita Mukerjee (Australia)
Dorien Gonzales (UK)
Patricia Williams (Denmark)

We have reproduced all original papers and chapters as faithfully as we have been able, given the inevitable restrictions of space and the need to produce a coherent and readable collection for readers worldwide. Where we have had to shorten original material substantially, these chapters are marked as adapted. Ellipses within square brackets mark text that has been omitted from the original. Individual referencing styles have been retained as in the original texts.

Introduction

Anne Burns and Caroline Coffin

WHEN MACQUARIE UNIVERSITY IN SYDNEY, Australia, and The Open University in the UK decided to collaborate on the development of new curriculum materials for study at Masters level, the partnership brought together the considerable experience and expertise of the two universities in open and distance learning, applied linguistics and language education. The collection of articles in this book and the two companion volumes are a result of that collaboration. While the edited collections have been designed as one part of an overall study programme, they stand alone as extensive yet focused collections of articles which address key contemporary issues in English language teaching and applied linguistics.

A major concern in editing these three volumes has been the desire to present English language teaching (ELT) in a variety of specific institutional, geographic and cultural contexts. Hence, as far as possible across the three volumes, we have attempted to highlight debate, discussion and illustration of current issues from different parts of the English-speaking and English-using world, including those where English is not learned as a first language. In doing this we recognize that English language teaching comprises a global community of teachers and learners in a range of social contexts.

The articles in this volume have been selected to fulfil a dual purpose: to overview the rapid growth and spread of English in its many varieties worldwide, and to present linguistic tools which can be used for the analysis of language in all its different cultural and social contexts. This is both an ambitious and challenging goal for one volume, and inevitably selections have been made. In making selections, theoretical inclinations and predilections come into play, and readers will find in this volume an approach which is primarily oriented towards the sociological and sociolinguistic, the discoursal and functional. In taking a sweep across key authors publishing works from this perspective, we have attempted to draw from different parts of the world, including the United States, the United Kingdom, Hong Kong and Australia.

The selections also, naturally, reflect our own academic backgrounds, preferences, and theoretical and practical experiences, currently, although by no means exclusively, within the British and Australian language-teaching contexts. Thus, the chapters on language analysis draw substantially on socio-semiotic approaches, specifically systemic functional linguistics. The origins of this linguistic theory are to be found in the European rather than the North American linguistic traditions; since the arrival of Michael Halliday as Professor of Linguistics at the University of Sydney in the 1970s, systemic functional linguistics has found a particularly strong representation as an underpinning for developments in language and literacy pedagogy in Australia, as it had earlier, but perhaps to a lesser extent, in the UK. Over the last ten years, however, this approach to language description and analysis has had a growing influence in many other parts of the world, as its relevance and application to language teaching have been more widely acknowledged. However, a collection of articles such as these (some of them published for the first time) bringing this work into a relationship with sociolinguistic debates on world Englishes is rare. In this respect, the volume makes a distinctive contribution to the field of English language.

In ordering and setting out the selections for the volume, one heuristic we have found productive is the concept of refocusing. Beginning with the macro-perspective of World Englishes in the first chapter by Kachru and Nelson, the chapters continually refocus the lens through which the role and nature of the English language can be viewed, towards the micro-perspective of the chapters in Part Four, by Martin, Er and Derewianka, which are concerned with the resources of grammar. These various perspectives on the English language are organized into four sections, each dealing with a different orientation to its analysis and teaching.

The first two parts of the volume – representing in particular the macro aspects – are linked through their common focus on the global spread and diffusion of English, the resulting changes to the language and its use, as well as the impact this development has had on other languages and cultures. Part One, 'English in the world: change and variety', highlights the concept of World Englishes, the very 'pluricentricity' of this term (Kachru, 1996) highlighting the realities of a gradual shift away from the traditional centres of British and American English and the emergence of multidimensional locations and uses. Chapter 1, by Kachru and Nelson draws out the meanings and implications of the emergence of World Englishes, outlining this diffusion through Kachru's model of inner, outer and expanding circles of international English users. Changes in the demographics of English uses have, of course, raised new issues over the last half-century in relation to what we can now understand by the term 'native speaker', how we should conceive of a universal 'standard' for English, and the disadvantages, rather than advantages, of being a monolingual English speaker – a minority group in global terms – particularly when it comes to the teaching of English.

Questions surrounding past and current movements in English in the world raise issues about the possibilities for its future. David Graddol's chapter summarizes research themes from his book, *The Future of English?*. This publication was originally commissioned by The British Council to forecast social and economic trends in the twenty-first century, in which English will be bound up as an international language. The question of a single world standard for English is juxtaposed with debates about the potential status and role of rival languages such as Spanish, Mandarin and Hindi. In assessing the future role of English, questions are raised about whether its current success and spread is unassailable or whether English is 'a transitional phenomenon'. In a volatile global community with unstable patterns of social and economic development, it is by no means pre-ordained that the demand for English will remain paramount. At the beginning of the twenty-first century, discussion about change and variety in English cannot, either, overlook the continuing impact of new technologies, both on communicative and pedagogical practices. Denise Murray's article (Chapter 3) refocuses the lens to explore this particular phenomenon, not so much in relation to World English, but language variations – those that are emerging in the location where technology has perhaps had the greatest impact so far: the world of work. The title of her chapter, 'New technology: new language in the workplace?', highlights the duality of meanings in this discussion.

No changes in a world language of such a momentous nature as those foregrounded in Part One can take place as a neutral process. The shifts and movements of World Englishes offer both potential and threat; they raise questions about who gains and who loses in the current rush to learn English and to hail it as an international lingua franca. These issues are the focus of Part Two, 'The globalisation of English: opportunities and constraints'. David Crystal reminds us in Chapter 4 that language diversity and hybridity are intricately bound up with questions of human behaviour and identity. English as a lingua franca means both accommodation and resistance, as speakers, both native and non-native, pull in different discoursal, structural, lexical and phonological directions. How then are we to perceive of the notion of international standards and norms of English, and to which varieties should English teachers look for pedagogical practices from their various settings around the world?

Bhatia (Chapter 5) argues that the potential for change comes through the creative actions of individuals who will reshape the English language to reflect their own cultural concepts. He explores this argument further from the perspective of genre structure, arguing, with reference to the academic community, that creativity, hybridity and 'genre mixing' are first founded on 'genre standardisation', and drawing out the implications both politically and pedagogically. Pennycook (Chapter 6) takes a different position; he argues that an over-reliance, in the applied linguistics literature and in many English language teaching contexts, on debating the issue of standard English norms has diverted attention away from more critical questions surrounding the political dimensions of English language teaching. He suggests that dominant western-based models of ELT are both constraining of language pedagogy and hegemonic in their impact on classroom practice. He argues for a politically active role for the language teacher in opposing this trend and developing a counter-discourse.

In Part Three, 'Analysing English: a text perspective', the focus shifts yet again. This time the functional and structural properties of English are under examination. The goal here, as in Part Four, is to provide language-teaching practitioners with theoretical and practical tools for analysis that build on other approaches to language analysis – traditional, structural and pedagogical. Maintaining the primarily social orientation of this volume as well as the accompanying volumes in this series, discourse and text-linguistics provide the major motivational standpoint for the discussions presented in these chapters. Further-more, while the two introductory chapters in Part Three by Coffin (Chapter 7) and Burns (Chapter 8) present overviews of different theoretical approaches to analysing written and spoken discourse respectively, a sustained discussion of one major theoretical perspective, systemic functional linguistics (SFL), is the common thread that binds these two parts. The Coffin and Burns chapters aim, in the meantime, to provide the framing perspectives for SFL by locating it in relation to other current analytical approaches, linguistic, sociological and philosophical.

The two chapters by Martin (Chapter 9) and Painter (Chapter 10) set out major constructs of text analysis within systemic functional theory. Martin's discussion of register and genre is first framed by his sketch of the theoretical antecedents of SFL and its juxta-position with other more dominant contemporary linguistic approaches. He then treats in detail the specific system of both register and genre, noting that each is in its own way 'a parasite' that can only be given life by making use of the semiotic of language. Painter's chapter on genre and register provides a complementary opportunity for readers to review their understandings of these concepts, this time with detailed illustration of how to analyse a particular genre. The implications for language teaching and the way in which genre and register analysis can potentially be used in language teaching are well drawn out in this discussion.

There is now a growing body of literature on the nature of the differences and similarities between spoken and written texts, assisted substantially by the technological developments which have allowed for the construction of corpora of spoken as well as written samples of natural discourse. Systemic functional theory has made a significant contribution to analysis of the relationships between spoken and written discourse, and has provided valuable insights into the nature of the textual and grammatical structures of these two modes. Chapter 11 by Michael Halliday overviews some of the typifying features, and makes the important point that an understanding of written and spoken modes is essential if language teachers are to develop their students' ability to read and write effectively.

Many language teachers are aware of the increasingly complex integration of multi-media resources in their teaching. Visual images are widely used in texts and on computer screens, both in everyday life and in teaching and learning materials. Analytical tools are therefore needed for reading the semiotics of images and for assisting students to understand their meanings. Chapter 12 by Stenglin and Iedema makes this point when they argue that visual images are socially and culturally constructed products which have a culturally specific grammar of their own. They provide tools, drawing again on SFL, for the analysis of a computer manual that realizes its meanings almost exclusively through a series of visual images.

All three chapters in Part Four, 'Analysing English: a clause perspective', refocus the analysis on to the grammatical resources of English. Readers concerned with the teaching of subject-specific texts through the medium of English will find Jim Martin's discussion of technicality and abstraction (Chapter 13) revealing. Technical terms and abstract language of the sort found in scientific texts can sometimes appear to be intended only to baffle the uninitiated reader. Martin argues that these forms of language have a significant role in the creation of specialized texts, particularly in their capacity to build taxonomies of rela-tionships between technical and scientific phenomena. Essentially, what Martin is arguing is that language teaching is strengthened in its pedagogical effectiveness when practitioners have a heightened awareness of the functionality of grammatical resources. Such awareness allows for more effective diagnosis of student writing, which is particularly important when students are working towards 'high stakes' outcomes, such as success in public examinations. Er takes up this theme in Chapter 14, illustrating, from her own point of view as a practising teacher, how she utilizes her understanding of functional grammar to assist the writing development of adult learners of English. Her discussion also reveals how grammatical analysis enabled her to reflect on further teaching strategies to reach her pedagogical goals.

The final chapter, by Beverly Derewianka, aims both to sharpen the focus on SFL and to round off the discussion of grammatical analysis. Derewianka tracks the changing paradigms of grammatical analysis that have been used in language pedagogy, reflects on the specific features that distinguish them one from another, and examines how English language teaching has drawn on these paradigms at different points in its recent history. To some extent her chapter is also by way of explicating the pre-eminence in this volume of systemic functional models and uncovering for readers the reasons for the growing impact of this theory within educational contexts.

The selection of papers in this volume is designed to scan some of the current territory of English in the world and to focus on its use and varieties. The arguments aim to stimulate and expand the conceptual repertoires of all those interested in current debates in English language teaching. For some readers, the selections may be a source of dissatisfaction in their self-confessed disposition towards social and critical approaches to English language spread and analysis. However, we would defend our choices by claiming that they represent an up-to-date set of readings that foreground some of the most challenging questions for future developments in English language teaching worldwide – the internationalization of English, the status of the non-native English teacher, the recognition of language variation, the question of standard versus non-standard varieties, and the need for a reinstatement of knowledge and awareness about language in English language teaching. We do not pretend that this volume contains all the answers, but our hope is that it provides points of reference for thinking about these challenges.

References

Kachru, B.B. (1996) 'World Englishes: agony and ecstasy', *Journal of Aesthetic Education*, 30, 2: 135–55.

PART ONE

English in the world: change and variety

Chapter 1

Braj B. Kachru and Cecil L. Nelson

WORLD ENGLISHES

Introduction

THIS CHAPTER PROVIDES AN OVERVIEW of the topics and relationships of sociolinguistics, world Englishes and language teaching. Although the more specific teaching as a second language (TESL) cannot be equated with the more general enterprise of language teaching, still there is undoubtedly more international teaching, materials production, and published thought in TESL than in any language of wider communication, such as Arabic, French, Hindi, or Spanish. Language teachers can readily generalize from research in and hypotheses about TESL. And similarly, although no one would want to make a comparison between what is going on with and what is studied about English and the field of sociolinguistics, the language has rightly been called "the great laboratory of today's sociolinguist" (Kahane and Kahane, 1986, p. 495). That is, what applies to global English is most often found to apply to other language situations involving languages of wider communication.

In this chapter, then, we will usually refer to *world Englishes* and the *teaching of English*; it should, however, be understood that the observations and analyses here will have relevance to sociolinguistics and to teachers of language of wider communication. All these languages (e.g. Arabic, French Hindi, or Spanish) have more than one accepted standard and set of norms for creativity, and thus are termed *pluricentric languages*. Because the term *world Englishes*, and its meaning, may not be familiar or transparent, its sources and features will be briefly described.

The global spread of English

There is little question that English is the most widely taught, read, and spoken language that the world has ever known. It may seem strange, on some moments' reflection, that the native language of a relatively small island nation could have developed and spread to this status. Its path was foreseen, however, by John Adams, who, in the late eighteenth century, made the following insightful prophesy (cited by Kachru, 1992a, p. 2): 'English will be the most respectable language in the world and the most universally read and spoken in the next century, if not before the close of this one.'

The global spread of English has been viewed as two diasporas (see e.g. Kachru, 1992d). The first diaspora involved migrations of substantial numbers of English speakers from the present British Isles to, for example, Australia, New Zealand, and North America. Those English users who left the old country for new ones brought with them the resource of language and its potentials for change which are always with us, though we are not often called upon to contemplate them explicitly. The language that they brought with them changed over time, to be sure, but no more or less substantially or rapidly than the language "at home," for all languages evolve in the natural course of time and use.[1]

The second diaspora of English, in the colonial contexts of Asia and Africa, entailed transportation of the language, but only to a small extent transportation of English-speaking people. Thus, the language was brought into new sociocultural contexts by a very small number of users; nevertheless, English became extremely important and useful to the much larger local populations, who have continued to expand the roles of English, often with greater vigor in postcolonial times.

Along with the mere numbers, it is important to note that these language-contact situations involved English and genetically unrelated and widely divergent Asian and African languages and, concomitantly, their cultures, both of which were far removed from the experience and common presuppositions of the native English speakers. These contact situations have had striking and lasting effects on English in these regions, so that although these contemporary Englishes have much in common, they are also unique in their grammatical innovations and tolerances, lexis, pronunciations, idioms, and discourse.[2]

Characteristics of world Englishes

Everyone is cognizant of the notion of *dialects* of languages, including English. Dialects are characterized by identifiable differences *vis-à-vis* other dialects, in pronunciation, lexical choice or usage, grammar, and so on; we speak easily of *southern English, New England English, American English,* and *British English*. These are all dialects: types of English that are identified with the residents of particular places. There are also age, gender, and other sorts of group-related dialects — as is so often the case with language-involved issues, the label depends upon the question that is being addressed. Any speaker can be said to speak various dialects, depending upon the circumstances of a discussion: in terms of geography, one of the authors grew up speaking southern American English; in terms of profession and education, both authors speak standard English; and so on.

The well-known national dialects are not usually referred to as such, for the term *dialect* has acquired various sorts of stigmatized baggage over the years. In some speakers' minds, to say that people speak a dialect is tantamount to saying that they are provincial, perhaps not well educated — though this is neither a necessary nor a proper connotation of dialect in its technical meaning. However, because of these negative associations, most people nowadays — especially in the United States — use *variety* to refer to a subtype of a language, for example, the American and British varieties of English.

Still, the substitution of one term for another is just that, and "my variety versus yours" can still be a point of contention. The implications for attitudes about control of the language are extremely hard to overcome. The concept *standard English* has been defined in various ways, as exemplified in the writing of two major scholars described in the next passages.

The British phonetician David Abercrombie (1951) wrote of the social barrier (in this case, "bar") represented by *Received Pronunciation* (RP), the variety traditionally used at and associated with the universities of Oxford and Cambridge in Britain:

> [V]ery often the first judgement made on a stranger's speech is the answer to the question: which side of the accent-bar is he? . . . The accent-bar is a little like a colour-bar – to many people, on the right side of the bar, it appears eminently reasonable. It is very difficult to believe, if you talk R.P. yourself, that it is not intrinsically superior to other accents.
>
> (p. 15)

Abercrombie's association of language-based prejudice with racial prejudice clearly makes the point that such language attitudes are undemocratic. He points out that RP speakers are "outnumbered these days by the undoubtedly educated people who do not talk RP" (p. 15). In fact, as McArthur (1992) notes, "It has always been a minority accent, unlikely ever to have been spoken by more than 3–4% of the British population" (p. 851). In this position of minority presence but widespread and important influence, RP constituted a kind of attitudinal despotism, not unlike the cross-cultural one which allows users of native varieties of English to look down on users of non-native varieties.

[. . .]

Commonly accepted varieties of English today include American and British, of course, and also Australian, Canadian, and New Zealand. No one would argue with the first two. The last three might cause some controversy in certain quarters; this matter will not be discussed here. There are many national varieties of English in the world today; a sense of their extent and distribution can be gained by reviewing a list of countries in which English is an official language. Refer to Table 1.1, which is not intended to be an exhaustive

Table 1.1 Countries in which English has official status

Antigua and Barbuda	Irish Republic	St Vincent and the Grenadines
Australia	Jamaica	Seychelles
Bahamas	Kenya	Sierra Leone
Barbados	Lesotho	Singapore
Botswana	Liberia	Tamil
Brunei	Malawi	South Africa
Cameroon	Malta	Surinam
Canada	Mauritius	Swaziland
Dominica	New Zealand	Tanzania
Fiji	Nigeria	Trinidad and Tobago
Gambia	Papua New Guinea	Uganda
Ghana	Philippines	United Kingdom
Grenada	Puerto Rico	United States of America
Guyana	St Christopher and Nevis	Zambia
India	St Lucia	Zimbabwe

Source: Adapted from Crystal (1987), p. 357

list. English may be a co-official language, or it may be, as in the United States, the official language in fact though not in law. A more comprehensive list of "territories for which English is a significant language" is given in McArthur (1992, pp. xxviii–xxix).

When you hear someone speak, you perhaps first identify their variety in terms of their pronunciation or accent. American speakers say "path" and British speakers say "pahth," Americans say "Jag-uar" and "Nicara-gua," and British say "Jag-u-ar" and "Nicarag-u-a," and so on.

In assessing written text, one can notice word choice or *lexis*, preferred word combinations or *collocations*, and grammar.[3] If a text contains the subject-verb combination *the public are . . .* , for example, we can guess that it is probably British; if it refers to parts of a car as *hood* and *trunk*, it is probably American, for the British would be *bonnet* and *boot*. Current BBC usage allows use of the verb *agree* without a preposition (*on* or *upon*), as in "a trade pact has been agreed between the two parties"; informal polls of students indicate that this usage is not widely current in the United States. One can make great lists of lexical and other differences between such major varieties, to say nothing of regional differences within each variety (evident in the various readily available dialect atlases), but when all that is said, it is still apparent that American and British speakers watch each others' movies and news broadcasts and read each others' newspapers and novels without any serious impediments.

If you glance at the front pages of, say, the *New York Times*, the London *Times*, the *Times of India*, and Singapore's *The Straits Times*, you will probably notice more similarities than differences; that is, you will have little trouble reading and understanding the headlines and news stories before you. In fact, the front pages of major English-language dailies in other parts of the world bear striking resemblances to one another, although close reading may reveal some unfamiliar features, depending upon the reader's origin. Consider, then, the following sample, taken more or less at random, from the front page of *The Nation* (6 January 1989), an English language daily newspaper published in Lahore, Pakistan:

> Islamabad, Jan. 5: Yuli [*sic*] Vorontsov, the Soviet Deputy Foreign Minister, currently shuttling in the region to find a solution to the Afghan problem, met Sahabzada Yaqub Khan this morning for about 45 minutes. . . . [S]ources at Pakistan's Foreign Office are adamantly evasive to comment on the progress made so far. . . .
>
> Implying that it must pressurise the Seven-Party Alliance to withdraw some of their demands blocking the inclusion of Afghan Communists . . . .'

At a glance, the text is in English; any reader of this chapter can make out the information in the passage. At the same time, there are features that mark it as not American and not British. In lexis, the American or British reader will be struck by *adamantly* as a modifier of *evasive*, requiring some extension of the adverb's meaning, and by the use of *pressurise* (in its apparently intended sense) instead of *pressure*. In grammar, the use of *shuttling* without something like *back and forth between* may seem unusual, and *evasive to comment* will probably not be considered happily parallel to, say, *eager to comment*.

[. . .]

It is imperative that teachers and students be aware of the sort of presence that English has in the world today, in order to keep the divergences among the extant varieties in a reasonable context. That is, that there are differences does not automatically imply that someone is wrong. The concept of monolithic English as the exponent of culture and communication in all-English-using countries has been a convenient working fiction that is now becoming harder and harder to maintain. What we now have in reality is English languages and English literatures – a much more insightful posture for research. And we believe that this insight has theoretical and pedagogical significance, for both describing and teaching varieties of English and their literatures. To understand the pluralism of English, it is therefore vital to see its spread, uses, and users in sociolinguistic contexts.

Issues

It is now generally recognized that, for purposes of rational analysis, descriptive characterizations of language provide the most positive opportunities for cogent insight into the way language actually works, as opposed to prescriptive declarations of the way one or another group or individual wishes language to work. Descriptive analyses of linguistic phenomena can even inform our notions of *standard* and *model*, allowing us to see clearly what are traditional, learned conventions (which certainly have their place in standard usage).

In the same spirit, the descriptive approach should be applied to world Englishes. No other language even comes close to English in terms of the extent of its usage. What might be seen as a weakness in the sense that there are many varieties of English is actually a clear indication of the importance and status of English in the world today. There is a great range of proficiency evidenced by the users of English in every country, from Asia to the New World. Even people who have very little proficiency in English use it in their daily business or personal lives.

[. . .]

Types of variation and types of users

The uses and users of English internationally have been discussed profitably in terms of three concentric circles.[4] Briefly, the circles model captures the global situation of English in the following way.

The *inner circle* comprises the old-variety English-using countries, where English is the first or dominant language: the United States, Britain, Canada, Australia, and New Zealand. In these countries, though other languages are surely spoken, there is seldom if ever a question of any language other than English being used in an extensive sense in any public discourse (e.g. in media, government, education, and creative writing).

[. . .]

The *outer circle* comprises countries where English has a long history of institutionalized functions and standing as a language of wide and important roles in education, governance, literary creativity, and popular culture, such as India, Nigeria, Pakistan, Singapore, South Africa, and Zambia.

The *expanding circle* countries are those in which English has various roles and is widely studied but for more specific purposes than in the outer circle, including (but certainly not limited to) reading knowledge for scientific and technical purposes; such countries currently include China, Indonesia, Iran, Japan, Korea, and Nepal. However, it must be remembered that languages have life cycles, particularly in multilingual societies, and thus the status of a language is not necessarily permanent.

Some examination of the various situations and case studies of English around the world, and of the history of the spread of English, will convince the reader that the circles model is valid in the senses of earlier historical and political contexts, the dynamic advance of English around the world, and the functions and standards to which its users relate English in its many current global incarnations.

It is telling, for example, that English is the associate official language or an official language in India, Nigeria, and various other countries of the outer circle (see Table 1.1). The sheer numbers of English users worldwide are almost unimaginable to the mono-lingual, monocultural English teacher. But it is difficult to define an English user in terms of either amount of use or degree of proficiency. Freshman composition students at United States universities, for example, may be monolingual speakers of English, yet it is not uncommon – indeed, it is quite usual – to hear their professors complaining that they "can't write," "have limited vocabularies," "have no sense of idiom," and so on. Indeed, a number of committees and commissions have been set up in the United States and Britain to address precisely these sorts of concerns. Being labeled a native speaker is of no particular a priori significance, in terms of measuring facility with the language.[5]

Thus, we believe that deciding who will be labeled an English user is not so straight-forward as might be imagined. However, accepting even cautious estimates, there must be at least three non-native users of English for every old-country native user. At the other end of the caution scale, perhaps a third of the world knows and uses English; see Crystal (1985), who concluded, "I am happy to settle for a billion [English users worldwide]" (p. 9). Such considerations should arouse some interest in a re-examination of our axioms and postulates regarding the basic matter of our English language teaching.

The concept of English in its inner, outer, and expanding circles is only superficially equivalent to *native*, *ESL*, and *EFL*. In thinking of a country as an ESL country or of a person as an ESL speaker, for example, we perpetuate the dichotomy of native versus non-native, "us versus them."

[. . .]

Range and depth

An important first step toward being able to discuss English in its global context is to overcome a quite natural or intuitive (i.e. a priori and unexamined) concept of the owner-ship of language. Hymes (1967, pp. 4–5) wrote that we have always typically thought of any given social group as:

> [A]n "ethnolinguistic" unit, that is, the boundaries of a language, a culture, and a people were seen as identical. One spoke typically of one people, one culture, and one language by one name: the Crow, Crow culture, the Crow language.

In contrast to this "mono" view, over the years we have been obliged to broaden our associations of people and places with English, from the British Isles to the new worlds of North America and Australia. But we did not, perhaps, conceptualize those forms as different in kind; we still think of these native English speakers as Anglo-Saxon in some sense. (For example, the term *Anglo* is used, in various contexts and sorts of reference, to apply to white Americans.) This association of language and peoples cannot be fruitfully examined merely in terms of form (i.e. in terms of words and grammatical rules). It is necessary, therefore, to establish a relationship between a language or language variety and its functions.

The term *range* refers to the contexts or domains in which English functions (law, education, business, and popular culture), and *depth* refers to the extent of use of English in the various levels of society. For example, in India or Singapore, use of English ranges from personal domains, with or without mixing, to business, education, administration, creative writing, and journalism. The result is that English has social penetration, that is, depth, that varies in its manifestations from educated to mixed varieties and to what is locally called *basilect*. In Nigeria, the situation is essentially the same, with the locally marked variety termed *Nigerian pidgin*. These situations contrast with that in Egypt or Japan, where the use of English is highly restricted as to range, and so it has not attained a similar degree of depth.

The native speaker

The often-mentioned term *native speaker* is usually taken to refer to someone who learned a language in a natural setting from childhood as first or sole language. This casual labeling, which used to be so comfortably available as a demarcation line between this and that type or group of users of English, must now be called into serious question (see Paikeday, 1985). It cannot be overemphasized that both attitudes toward English and the degree and types of input that learners receive may vary significantly from place to place. *Input* is used here to refer not only to English as it is taught to people in formal schooling but also as it is available in media such as newspapers and in elements of popular culture such as creative writing.

Attitudes toward varieties in the two diaspora areas can be quite distinct. Standard British and American users, on the whole, are expected to be rather tolerant of each others' English but are likely to be intolerant of the usage of South Asians, Southeast Asians, West Africans, or East Africans. On the other hand, it is likely that users of the second diaspora area will look up to the usage of someone from Britain or North America, without ever considering whether that variety is actually very much used or usable in their own contexts. The attitudinal situation is complicated in outer circle countries by the inescapable fact that English is a colonial legacy that has prompted continual cries for the minimization or elimination of its use in favor of the promotion of an indigenous language. Often, English is settled on in an uneasy compromise, for it is no one's first language and thus confers no real or imagined advantage to one group over another.

Part of the unease stems from the fact that, by and large, these countries have always looked to external reference points (i.e. British and, to a lesser extent, American) for their norms, so that, for example, in Singapore, where English has been used as the language of industry and business for a long time, British English continues to be looked upon by many as the standard of good use. Such attitudinal schizophrenia is yet another cause of complexities in the larger English-using world.

Speech community

A vital sociolinguistic concept relevant to English teaching is that of the *speech community*, the body of speakers who share a language as well as its interrelated social rules of use, its standards and its norms.

Without tracing its origins to the Germanic languages on the European continent, we can agree that English originated (as English) in the British Isles and that its standard form arose from the usage of educated people – basically, those who could read and write and were close to the royal court (see Kachru, 1992c). In the absence of any official policy, the standard was largely a matter of loose convention. The lack of official blessing did not, however, lessen its reality as a concept, a shibboleth, a marker of the "right sort of person." When English spread to the New World, beginning in the sixteenth century, those at home in England – still the seat of religious, educational, and legal authority – clearly thought of the language as remaining the same in its various geographical incarnations. Differences were attributed to improper learning and regarded as errors.

The long-standing debate, even now not wholly laid to rest, over which language is better, that of Britain or of the United States, has had all sorts of effects over the decades, from establishment of literary canon to what pronunciations and usages are correct and should, therefore, be taught.

[. . .]

As English spread across many borders and people began to worry about differences in forms of English, some way of accommodating the differences had to be found, to maintain the convenient fiction that we all speak the same language. Such attempts were mostly rather unconvincing, consisting mainly of passing off differences as "minor," "insignificant," or "just a matter of vocabulary." At times, of course, this position has been attacked, as by Bernard Shaw's famous depiction of the United States and Britain as "two peoples separated by a common language." But basically, there have been two groups or schools of thought: one that underemphasized the differences between American and British English, and one that overemphasized them.

Standards and codification

It is worth noting that English-using countries in the inner circle have never had any sort of codifier, like the French Academy, which was founded in 1635 with the express purpose "to labour with all possible care and diligence to give definite rules to our language, and to render it pure, eloquent, and capable of treating the arts and sciences" (Crystal, 1987, p. 4). One might well wonder, then, what the codifying agencies of English have been. The codification has been a matter of convention, and perpetuation of convention, through dictionaries, grammars, rhetoric handbooks, and pressures of various other types – the makers of all of these being unwilling to stretch very far beyond the reach of their immediate predecessors in what they deemed acceptable form and usage – and through the newspapers and other widely disseminated popular media that use those sources for their style sheets and usage manuals. Further, to these tangible influences the extremely powerful agencies of social and psychological pressures of various sorts must certainly be added. This codification has taken place almost exclusively in the inner circle countries; this has made it necessary for the outer and expanding circles to look to these sources when in need of citable authority, and it has functioned as a deterrent to their setting up authorities of their own.

There are certainly relationships between use and many facets of language, all of them the topic of much previous discussion and all warranting further investigation. Among them are the relationships (possibly also differences) between use and acceptance, standard, institutionalization (in grammars and dictionaries, for example), and normative reference points in education and in society at large.

Observing the different attitudes toward possible norms of English around the world prompts the notion of *pluralistic* centers of reference for norms and standards; if there are two – the United States and Britain – why not three? If three, why not a dozen? It is all too easy to step back from the world and pronounce upon this or that as "should be done otherwise." The sort of pseudotheory that Mencken (1936) refers to as practiced by "cloistered" scholars and having no grounding in real-world data and experience, is especially to be avoided in an endeavor which is essentially sociolinguistic and therefore gets at the heart of communicative ability among and between people.

Monolingual attitudes and bilinguals' creativity

Though it has until relatively recently gone unnoticed by "mainstream" English studies, bodies of literature in English have existed in West and East Africa and in South and East Asia for almost a hundred years. A key observation in an examination of global English literature is that English is used by writers who are multilingual and who do not belong culturally to what may be broadly termed the *Judeo-Christian tradition*. Clearly, English is used in a complete range of interactional contexts across entire cultures, including spoken and written media. The question has been raised: What are the linguistic, cultural, and social characteristics reflected in the writings of such users of English? Defining these characteristics leads to an examination of the concept of the *bilinguals' creativity*. Such creativity is clearly demonstrated in the many works by writers such as Wole Soyinka of West Africa, who won the Nobel Prize for Literature in 1986, and Anita Desai and Raja Rao of India.

A short example such as the following, from Mukherjee's *Jasmine* (1989, p. 68), illustrates this point:

> The next morning I packed my brothers' tiffin carriers more indulgently than usual – extra dal, extra chapatis . . . – and slipped in my most important question: "The friend who came over, not the Sardarji, does he speak English?" I couldn't marry a man who didn't speak English. To want English was to want more than you had been given at birth.

This passage contains not only variety-specific lexical items (*tiffin carriers, dal, chapatis, Sardarji*) but also the culturally defined family interaction (the narrator packs her brothers' lunches for them) and, not incidentally for our topic, a direct reference to the importance of English in the outer circle, at least to some people: "To want English was to want more than you had been given at birth."

Language teachers can use such examples to illustrate bilingual writers' creativity in English including paradigm examples of stylistic experimentation, mixing of codes, and acculturation of English in various other cultural settings. Interpretations of such literary work that is based in the old canons as reference points and in old paradigms as analytical devices cannot account for the great cultural and social diversities that readers will encounter in these literatures. To dismiss them because they do not fit the old paradigms is, to say the least, unscientific.[6]

[. . .]

In the same way that inner circle writers have available to them a range of speech and speaker types, from dialectal-informal (e.g. southern American "y' all") to standard formal, so outer circle creative writers have access to a broad range of English usages, including restricted pidgin or basilect, localized forms (which may or may not be mixed varieties), and acrolectal forms that would be considered non-localized international standard English. Certainly many authors may choose to write in a non-regional or non-national idiom in one work, whereas in another they may cast their characters in markedly local voices (compare, for example, Raja Rao, 1988 with 1963). This versatility available to the multilingual user of English may include sorts of options that are not available to the American or British creative writer.

[. . .]

Teaching English across the world: types of input

Monolingual English teachers with little if any cross-cultural experience may have to stop and think about the situations in which English is acquired across the world. In most cases it is taught to non-native speakers by non-native speakers, neither teachers nor students (who themselves become the next generation of teachers) ever having any contact with a native user. The Nigerian linguist Bamgbose (1982, pp. 99–100), for example, draws our attention to this point when he writes that:

> One noticeable effect of the refusal to accept the existence of a Nigerian English is the perpetuation of the myth that the English taught in Nigerian schools is just the same as, say, British English. . . . In our teaching and examinations we concentrate on drilling and testing out of existence forms of speech that even the teachers will use freely when they do not have their textbooks open before them.

That is, people do not always speak the way they think they do, and linguistic insecurity is perhaps one of the chief motivations for linguistic prescriptivism. What Bamgbose has written about Nigerian English can be said, with appropriate adjustments of references to language and setting, about any institutionalized variety of English.

This issue of the types of input available to learners in the outer and expanding circles is at the core of any pragmatic view of models and standards of English for users in the included countries. It may be seen as bound up with another issue, that of identity: If a typical American has no wish to speak like or be labeled as a British user of English, why should a Nigerian, an Indian, or a Singaporean user feel any differently?

In terms of identity, it is probably a truism to point out that people's language affiliations are a significant part of themselves, and of their images of themselves. Crystal (1987) notes: "More than anything else, language shows we 'belong'; providing the most natural badge, or symbol, of public and private identity" (p. 18). In more specific terms, he says that "language can become . . . a source of pleasure, pride, anxiety, offence, anger and even violence." Compare also the preceding discussion on available English input: Nigerians teach Nigerians and Indians teach Indians, just as North Americans teach North Americans. There is no a priori reason to think that the development of one variety is any stranger than the other. In any case, most learners of English in outer circle and expanding circle contexts never have any serious contact with an inner circle speaker; and, as anyone who has ever tried it can testify, it is not possible, in any complete and active sense, to learn a language from a book.

Communicative competence

The substantive issue of language identity becomes bound up with the new pairing of a language and a culture that yields a distinctive communicative competence for the speakers of, for example, a new English.

It is confusing sometimes, because of the broad concept that "we all speak English," but it is nonetheless true that the rules of speaking change with time and place – just as they might be expected to do, if we think about the development of any language. If we take a comparative stance, then we construe differences as mistakes in the variety that we are investigating (see Nelson, 1992).

In terms of teaching methodology, the concerns and discussion in this chapter make it clear that range and depth can best be explained if a *functional* view of language is adopted. Such a view will provide a theoretical backdrop for both the learner and the teacher of English. Saville-Troike (1996) has discussed the *ethnography of communication* in detail (with reference to Hymes's use of the term). That, of course, is one functional approach. Another functional approach worth exploring is that of M. A. K. Halliday, applications of which occur in several studies done on world Englishes.[7]

The main point that Halliday's research emphasizes is the functional nature of language. His interpretation of language function is that every text created by a language user involves interpersonal, ideational, and textual functions (see e.g. Halliday, 1970). These functions have to do, respectively, with social relationships and individual identity, meaning potential (what the speaker can say in a situation), and the ability to construct recognizable and situationally appropriate discourse. Halliday puts these functional components of the underlying language system at the heart of the interpretation of how language works.

Language usage by a group or by an individual is not innate – rather, it is brought about and formed over time by its very use. As discussed throughout this chapter, if this is true within a variety, and easily seen across major varieties such as American and British English, then there is no reason to suppose that it is or should be otherwise across varieties that include newer ones, as in India and Nigeria. No one can deny that a part of learning different American dialects and registers, say, is the learning of the social rules of when to speak and to be silent, and so forth.

[. . .]

The key element in communicative competence is just these sorts of considerations of *appropriateness* in all facets of language, including rate of speech and level or register of lexis. It is easily understood that what appropriate for a situation in one culture may not be so in another; indeed, it is important to recognize the different sorts of situations that exist across cultures, which, although they may be similar in terms of kind and function to situations in other cultures, are yet unique.

Such cultural-situational distinctiveness is evident in examples in the literature of cross-cultural English studies. In a study of simple request behavior, for example, it as been shown that 76 percent of Indian speakers (of various first languages) "used indirect questions involving permission, ability, or willingness, much like native speakers would use. . . . However, as many as [20 percent] used imperatives or desideratives, reflecting Indian language conventions" (Sridhar, 1989, pp. 104–105).

Simple greeting exchanges in world Englishes can provide readily accessible examples. "I see you've put on weight" may be the equivalent of "You're looking well," an interpretation quite different from the one a typical American speaker would assign to the statement, as has been shown in Berns's (1990, pp. 35–36) report and analysis of her encounter with a Zambian English speaker. One must be familiar with the context in which the utterances are produced – not merely the immediate conversational context but the broader sociocultural context underlying it. It is not reasonable to think that English, or any pluricentric language, can in itself have such force as to establish identical situational interpretations across cultural boundaries.

These sociolinguistic considerations cannot but change the perceptions of one who has been operating with the notions of deficit linguistics as background. Either we admit to creating and accepting a linguistic caste system, under which a person is born into one or another group and can never really rise out of it (or fall, for that matter), whether by effort, marriage, or emigration, or we must agree that the old speech community notions are no longer relevant. As long as the old-fashioned English speech community continues to be the paradigm of reference, a monolingual, monocultural way of looking at the linguistic world is unavoidable. For all that it sounds egalitarian and inclusive, it continues, for the sorts of reasons outlined, to be oppressive and divisive. "Black" or "Hispanic" – any labeled English – is only with difficulty seen as merely nonstandard, with no attendant negative judgments of correctness, worth, and goodness.

These sorts of considerations have wide implications, both in terms of theory and of application. They open the door to almost endless series of questions about how people perceive themselves and others in terms of and by means of language. In applied terms, more and more questions are arising in areas such as language policy and planning. Should the United States officially adopt English as its single language of government and law? What should the statutory place of English be in highly multilingual settings such as South Asia and West Africa? Matters of personal and literary style are natural connections to investigations of language identity. All these areas are cast into new light in view of the unique geographical and cultural spread of world Englishes.

Intelligibility

A major fear expressed by those concerned with standards and correctness has been that English is crumbling at its edges, becoming less and less English in the mouths – and from the pens – of those who (it is claimed) do not so much use it as abuse it. Drawing on the concept that is the source of a definition of *dialect* versus *language*, namely that dialects are mutually intelligible variants of a given language, speakers and writers have voiced the fear that the varieties of English will become mutually unintelligible, and so undeserving of the label *English*.

These concerns about the decay of English must be studied, analyzed, and contrasted by any teacher of English. An abundance of insights that aid in understanding sociolinguistic attitudes, notions of correctness, and linguistic control can be found in the body of literature discussing this topic. A good example is Quirk (1985), who writes of "the diaspora of English into several mutually incomprehensible languages" (p. 3). In the face of the large quantity of well-attested scholarly literature showing large ranges and depths for the use of English, Quirk asserts that "the relatively narrow range of purposes for which the non-native needs to use English . . . is arguably well catered for by a single mono-chrome standard form that looks as good on paper as it sounds in speech" (p. 6). He wants all English-using countries to accede to "a form of English that is both understood and respected in every corner of the globe where any knowledge of any variety of English exists" (p. 6). Although Quirk never says explicitly that we should all be learning British standard English, his very lack of identification of the "single monochrome standard form" leaves the reader in little doubt of what his choice would be.[8]

The best responses to this notion of "dissolution" have been articulated with clear empirical support by Larry Smith, in his own work and with co-authors (see e.g. Smith, 1988; Smith and Nelson, 1985; Smith and Rafiqzad, 1983). First, Smith points out that the most common situation of English use in the outer circle is that of non-natives using it to communicate with non-natives, as already mentioned in this chapter. Further, Smith proposes the idea that any text is received by a reader or hearer on three levels – intelligibility, comprehensibility, and interpretability. Each level is more comprehensive than the preceding one and may comprise its information, although it does not necessarily rely upon it. Briefly, the levels can be described as follows.

In its narrow sense, *intelligibility* consists of word-level recognition. If you recognize that you are hearing (or reading) English, then the language is intelligible to you, according to this technical definition of the term. Smith and Rafiqzad (1983), for example, asked subjects to fill in the blanks in a written cloze passage matching an audiotaped reading of the passage by English speakers from various countries. To the degree that the subjects were successful, the passage was judged as more or less intelligible to them.

Interpretation of this sort of data – as indeed of any linguistic interaction – absolutely requires consideration of both the producer and the receiver of the text in question and, in any broader, real-world test, would require consideration of the circumstances under which the text was produced – what J. R. Firth called the *context of situation* (see Kachru, 1986, p. 106).

To the degree that a recipient finds a text meaningful, it has *comprehensibility*. If someone says, "Please open the door," and if the words are intelligible to you and you can assign referential meaning to them (you understand *please* as a polite request opener, *open* as referring to a particular activity, *door* as having a certain concrete referent in the immediate environment, and so on), then that bit of text is comprehensible to you. Further, if you interpret the utterance "Please open the door" as a request for a particular activity which you may carry out, ignore, object to, or otherwise react to in ways that will, in their turn, elicit another round of interpretation and response from the other participants in the situation, it is comprehensible to you.

Although the preceding example seems straightforward, it is easy to find examples of English text that are not readily intelligible or comprehensible to a receiver. For instance, consider Indian matrimonial advertisements such as the following (cited in Kachru, 1992b, p. 311). The first, from the English language daily *The Hindu* (Madras, India), contains, within its English matrix, terms that would be transparently obvious to the readers of the newspaper but which are probably opaque to most of the readers of this chapter:

> Non-Koundanya well qualified prospective bridegroom . . . for graduate Iyangar girl. . . . Mirugaservsham No dosham. Average complexion. Reply with horoscope.

The code-mixed items (e.g. *Mirugaservsham*, "birth star," and *dosham*, "a flaw in one's horoscope," are not italicized or otherwise specially marked; they are an integral part of the text for the intended readership, who will recognize their meanings, uses, and importance.

[. . .]

Interpretability refers to the apprehension of intent, purpose, or meaning behind an utterance. It is the capacity to take "Gee, it's hot in here" as the equivalent, as far as appropriate response is concerned, of the direct request "Please open the window." Smith (1988) points out very insightfully that, contrary to what we might think initially, certainly contrary to what we teach students from grammar textbooks, "interpretability is at the core of communication and is more important than mere intelligibility or comprehensibility" (p. 274). A few moments' consideration will bear out this observation. What makes grunts, sighs, and non-referential word utterances such as "Well . . .," and "Rats!" so communicatively effective is their contextual interpretability.

Perhaps the most startling point that emerges from the evidence of Smith's investigations concerns the role of native speakers and the relationship of inner circle English to other Englishes; as Smith and Rafiqzad (1983) write: '[T]he native speaker was always found to be among the least intelligible speakers [in the study] . . . (average of 55 per cent [only the speaker from Hong Kong was lower, at 44 per cent])' (p. 52). Although the focus at the time was intelligibility, the same may be said for inner circle *vis-à-vis* outer circle speakers at the levels of comprehensibility and interpretability as well. (This finding of the non-primacy of native-variety English worldwide has been replicated; see e.g. Smith, 1988.)

Startling may be too mild a word for the effect of this discovery on the practice and practitioners of English teaching. It has always been an axiom that native-speaker English was the best, therefore certainly the most widely usable in any circumstance, and if people couldn't understand you, it was their fault (the value judgment inescapable), because their English wasn't "good enough." This conceptualization of English on its own terms in its various contexts is quite different from the monomodel, a priori importance that many have attached to inner circle English in the past; it is more explanatorily powerful, and it is empirically verifiable.

[. . .]

Conclusion

We believe that world Englishes provide paradigm examples of the relationships between linguistic and language-teaching theory, methodology, and application. The preceding sections have shown that anecdotal statements regarding the global spread of English are not empirically sound or functionally valid. The spread of English provides a language teacher with an abundance of data for relating second language issues to pedagogical concerns. This can be done in several ways: through the study of variation, the pragmatics of variation, varieties and culture, and varieties and creativity. These assumptions reflect at least three most powerful sets of pedagogical tools: curriculum, testing, and resource materials.

For achieving positive goals, however, it is most important in teacher training to create teacher awareness of the status and functions of Englishes in the world today and in the future.

Notes

1   See Kachru, 1992d, p. 231.
2   For more information on the historical-chronological aspects of the diasporas of English, see Kachru (1992d) for a quick digest; 1965 and 1966 for early treatments; and 1994b and 1997 for recent summations.
3   Discourse characteristics are, of course, also markers of national and regional varieties. By its nature, discourse requires longer passages for exemplification, and so will not be treated here. See the subsequent discussion, and also Larry Smith (Ed.) (1987) *Discourse Across Cultures: Strategies in World Englishes.*
4   See Kachru, 1985, 1992d, 1994a, b.
5   It must be said that overtones of racism, explicit or implied, conscious or unintentional, may intrude into such attitudinally loaded areas. We may recall, for illustration, the ugly words of Pap Finn's infamous "I'll never vote ag'in" speech (Mark Twain, *The Adventures of Huckleberry Finn*, 1985, p. 30): "There was a free nigger there from Ohio . . ., most as white as a white man. . . . And what do you think? They said he was a p'fessor in a college, and could talk all kinds of languages, and knowed everything. . . . [W]hy, he wouldn't give me the road if I hadn't shoved him out o' the way. . . ." It may be that judgments other than linguistic or educational overshadow assessments of "good" or "poor" English.
6   See, for example, the papers in the "Symposium on speech acts in world Englishes", edited by Y. Kachru (1991) including "Speech acts in world Englishes: toward a framework for research" by Y. Kachru, "Discourse markers in Indian English" by T. Valentine, and "Multi-ethnic literature in the classroom: whose standards?" by S. Tawake.
7   See e.g. Halliday, 1970, 1973, 1975.
8   Graeme Kennedy, as a commentator for Quirk's paper (Quirk and Widdowson, 1985), writes: "There is a delicious irony in Professor Quirk's . . . paper . . . [It] reflects, in many respects, the position Prator [1968] advocated, namely the desirability of a global standard. However, since the orthodoxy has changed, it might be argued that Professor Quirk articulates a new British heresy. You simply cannot win" (p. 7).

References

Abercrombie, D. (1951). R. P. and local accent. *The Listener*, 6. (Reprinted in D. Abercrombie, *Studies in Phonetics and Linguistics*. London: Oxford University Press.

Bamgbose, A. (1982). Standard Nigerian English: issues of identification. In B. Kachru (ed.) (1992). *The Other Tongue: English Across Cultures* (2nd edn, pp. 99–111). Urbana: University of Illinois Press.

Berns, M. (1990). *Contexts of Competence: Social and Cultural Considerations in Communicative Language Teaching.* New York: Plenum Press.

Crystal, D. (1985). How many millions? The statistics of English today. *English Today*, 1, 7–9.

Crystal, D. (1987). *The Cambridge Encyclopedia of Language.* Cambridge: Cambridge University Press.

Halliday, M. A. K. (1970). Language structure and language function. In J. Lyons (ed.) *New Horizons in Linguistics*. Harmondsworth: Penguin Books.

Halliday, M. A. K. (1973). *Explorations in the Functions of Language.* London: Edward Arnold.

Halliday, M. A. K. (1975). *Learning How to Mean.* London: Edward Arnold.

Hymes, D. (1967). The anthropology of communication. In F. E. X. Dance (ed.) *Human Communication Theory: Original Essays*. New York: Holt, Rinehart and Winston.

Kachru, B. B. (1965). The *Indianness* in Indian English. *Word*, 21, 391–410. [Revised version in B. Kachru (1983). *The Indianization of English: The English Language in India* (pp. 128–144). Delhi: Oxford University Press.]

Kachru, B. B. (1966). Indian English: a study in contextualization. In C. E. Bazell, J. C. Catford, M. A. K. Halliday, and R. H. Robins (eds) *In Memory of J. R. Firth*. London: Longman. [Revised version in Kachru (1983). *The Indianization of English: The English Language in India* (pp. 99–127). Delhi: Oxford University Press.]

Kachru, B. B. (1983). *The Indianization of English: The English Language in India*. Delhi: Oxford University Press.

Kachru, B. B. (1985). Standards, codification, and sociolinguistic realism: the English language in the outer circle. In R. Quirk and H. Widdowson (eds) *English in the World: Teaching and Learning the Language and Literatures* (pp. 11–30). Cambridge: Cambridge University Press.

Kachru, B. B. (1986). *The Alchemy of English: The Spread, Functions and Models of Non-native Englishes*. Oxford: Pergamon Press.

Kachru, B. B. (1992a). Introduction: The other side of English. In B. Kachru (ed.) *The Other Tongue: English Across Cultures* (pp. 1–15). Urbana: University of Illinois Press.

Kachru, B. B. (1992b). Meaning in deviation: toward understanding non-native English texts. In B. Kachru (ed.) *The Other Tongue: English Across Cultures* (pp. 301–326). Urbana: University of Illinois Press.

Kachru, B. B. (1992c). Models for non-native Englishes. In B. Kachru (ed.) *The Other Tongue: English Across Cultures* (pp. 48–74). Urbana: University of Illinois Press.

Kachru, B. B. (1992d). The second diaspora of English. In T. W. Machan and C. T. Scott (eds) *English in its Social Contexts: Essays in Historical Socio-Linguistics* (pp. 230–252). New York: Oxford University Press.

Kachru, B. B. (1994a). The paradigms of marginality. Plenary address at International TESOL. Baltimore, MD. [Published (1996) in *World Englishes*, 15(3), 241–255.]

Kachru, B. B. (1994b). The speaking tree: A medium of plural canons. In J. E. Alatis (ed.) *Educational Linguistics, Cross-cultural Communication and Global Interdependence* (pp. 1–17). Georgetown University Roundtable, 1994. Washington, DC: Georgetown University Press.

Kachru, B. B. (1997). World Englishes 2000: resources for research and teaching. In L. E. Smith and M. L. Forman (eds) *World Englishes 2000 Literary Studies East and West* (pp. 14, 209–251). University of Hawaii Press.

Kachru, Y. (ed.) (1991). Symposium on speech acts in world Englishes. *World Englishes* 10(3), 295–304.

Kahane, H. and Kahane, R. (1986). A typology of the prestige language. *Language* 62, 495–508.

Kennedy, G. (1985). Commentator 1. In R. Quirk and H. Widdowson (eds) *English in the World: Teaching and Learning the Language and Literatures* (pp. 7–8). Cambridge: Cambridge University Press.

McArthur, T. (ed.) (1992). *The Oxford Companion to the English Language*. Oxford: Oxford University Press.

Mencken, H. L. (1936). *The American Language: An Inquiry into the Development of English in the United States* (4th edn). New York: Knopf.

Mukherjee, B. (1989). *Jasmine*. New York: Grove Weidenfeld.

Nelson, C. L. (1992) Bilingual writing for the monolingual reader: blowing up the canon. *World Englishes*, 11(2/3), 271–275.

Paikeday, T. M. (1985). *The Native Speaker is Dead!* Toronto: Paikeday Publications.

Quirk, R. (1985). *The English Language in a Global Context*. In R. Quirk and H. Widdowson (eds) *English in the World: Teaching and Learning the Language and Literature* (pp. 1–6). Cambridge: Cambridge University Press.

Quirk, R. and Widdowson, H. (eds) (1985). *English in the World: Teaching and Learning the Language and Literatures*. Cambridge: Cambridge University Press.

Rao, R. (1963). *Kanthapura*. London: Allen and Unwin. [Originally published in 1938.]

Rao, R. (1988). *The Chessmaster and his Moves*. New Delhi: Vision Books.

Saville-Troike, M. (1996). The ethnography of communication. In S. L. McKay and N. H. Hornberger (eds) *Sociolinguistics and Language Teaching*. New York: Cambridge University Press.

Smith, L. E. (Ed.) (1987). *Discourse Across Cultures: Strategies in World Englishes*. London: Prentice-Hall.

Smith, L. E. (1988). Language spread and issues of intelligibility. In P. Lowenberg (ed.) *Language Spread and Language Policy: Issues, Implications, and Case Studies* (pp. 265–282). Georgetown University Roundtable on Languages and Linguistics 1987. Washington, DC: Georgetown University Press.

Smith, L. E. and Nelson, C. L. (1985). International intelligibility of English: directions and resources. *World Englishes*, 4(3), 333–342.

Smith, L. E. and Rafiqzad, K. (1983). English for cross-cultural communication: the question of intelligibility. In L. Smith (ed.) *Readings in English as an International Language* (pp. 49–58). Oxford: Pergamon.

Sridhar, K. K. (1989). *English in Indian Bilingualism*. New Delhi: Manohar.

Twain, M. (1985 [1885]). *The Adventures of Huckleberry Finn*. London: Penguin Books.

Chapter 2

David Graddol

ENGLISH IN THE FUTURE

T HE BOOK FROM WHICH THIS chapter is drawn (Graddol, 1997) tries to establish a new agenda for debate, not simply on the future of the English language in the twenty-first century, but also on the role of its native speakers, their institutions and their global enterprises.

This chapter brings together some of the arguments put forward in the book and shows how they might help address key questions about the future of English. The "rush" to English around the world may, for example, prove to be a temporary phenomenon which cannot be sustained indefinitely. Languages other than English are likely to achieve regional importance while changed economic relations between native-speaking English countries and other parts of the world will alter the rationale for learning and speaking English.

The English Language Teaching (ELT) industry may also find itself vulnerable to shifts in public opinion, like other global business enterprises now experiencing "nasty surprises" in their world markets. An increasing concern for social equity rather than excessive benefit for the few is one expected social value shift which is likely to inform both public policy decisions and personal life-choices and this will have unpredictable consequences for the popularity of learning English as a foreign language.

The English language nevertheless seems set to play an ever more important role in world communications, international business, and social and cultural affairs. But it may not be the native-speaking countries which most benefit.

WORLD ENGLISH

Will a single world standard for English develop?

One question which arises in any discussion of global English is whether a single world standard English will develop, forming a supranational variety which must be learned by global citizens of the twenty-first century. Like most questions raised in this chapter, this demands a more complicated answer than those who ask probably desire.

There are, for example, at least two dimensions to the question: the first is whether English will fragment into many mutually unintelligible local forms; the second is whether the current "national" standards of English (particularly US and British) will continue to compete as models of correctness for world usage, or whether some new world standard will arise which supersedes national models for the purposes of international communication and teaching.

The widespread use of English as a language of wider communication will continue to exert pressure towards global uniformity as well as give rise to anxieties about "declining" standards, language change and the loss of geolinguistic diversity. But as English shifts from foreign-language to second-language status for an increasing number of people, we can also expect to see English develop a larger number of local varieties.

These contradictory tensions arise because English has two main functions in the world: it provides a vehicular language for international communication and it forms the basis for constructing cultural identities. The former function requires mutual intelligibility and common standards. The latter encourages the development of local forms and hybrid varieties. As English plays an ever more important role in the first of these functions, it simultaneously finds itself acting as a language of identity for larger numbers of people around the world. There is no need to fear, however, that trends towards fragmentation will necessarily threaten the role of English as a lingua franca. There have, since the first records of the language, been major differences between varieties of English.

The mechanisms which have helped maintain standard usage in the past may not, however, continue to serve this function in the future. Two major technologies have helped develop national, standard-language forms. The first was printing, the invention of which provided a "fixity" in communication by means of printed books. According to scholars such as Anderson (1983), such fixity was a necessary requirement for the "imagined communities" of modern nation states. But with increasing use of electronic communication much of the social and cultural effect of the stability of print has already been lost, along with central "gatekeeping" agents such as editors and publishers who maintain consistent, standardised forms of language.

The second technology has been provided by broadcasting, which in many ways became more import than print in the socially mobile communities of the twentieth century. But trends in global media suggest that broadcasting will not necessarily play an important role in establishing and maintaining a global standard. Indeed, the patterns of fragmentation and localisation, which are significant trends in satellite broadcasting, mean that television is no longer able to serve such a function. How can there be such a thing as "network English" in a world in which centralised networks have all but disappeared?

Meanwhile, new forms of computer-mediated communication are closing the gap between spoken and written English which has been constructed laboriously over centuries. And cultural trends encourage the use of informal and more conversational language, a greater tolerance of diversity and individual style, and a lessening deference to authority. These trends, taken together, suggest that a weakening of the institutions and practices which maintained national standard languages is taking place: that the native-speaking countries are experiencing a "destandardisation" of English.

The ELT industry, however, may play an important role in maintaining an international standard, as Strevens (1992, p. 39) suggested:

> There exists an unspoken mechanism, operated through the global industry of ELT teaching, which has the effect of preserving the unity of English in spite of its great diversity. For throughout the world, regardless of whether the norm is native-speaker or non-native speaker variety, irrespective of whether English is a foreign or

second language, two components of English are taught and learned without variation: these are its grammar and its core vocabulary . . . the grammar and vocabulary
of English are taught and learned virtually without variation throughout the world.

However, second-language countries are likely to develop their own curricula,
materials and teaching resources which they will seek to export to neighbouring countries.
In some parts of the world, this may help bring new, non-native models of English –
supported by dictionaries and pedagogic materials – into competition with the older
standard varieties. There is no reason why, say, an Asian standard English may not gain
currency.

Smith (1992) carried out an experiment using speakers of nine "national varieties"
of English – China, India, Indonesia, Japan, Papua New Guinea, the Philippines, Taiwan, the
United Kingdom and the United States – in order to discover whether "the spread of English
is creating greater problems of understanding across cultures" (Smith, 1992, p. 88). He
concluded that there was no evidence of a breakdown in the functioning of English as an
international lingua franca but that, interestingly, "native speakers (from Britain and the US)
were not found to be the most easily understood, nor were they, as subjects, found to be the
best able to understand the different varieties of English" (Smith, 1992, p. 88).

Since the ELT publishers from native-speaking countries are likely to follow markets
– most of the large publishers already provide materials in several standards – it will
be non-native speakers who decide whether a US model, a British one, or one based on a
second-language variety will be taught, learned and used. At the very least, English textbooks in countries where English is spoken as a second language are likely to pay much
more attention to local varieties of English and to localise their product by incorporating
materials in local varieties of English.

The most likely scenario thus seems to be a continued "polycentrism" for English –
that is, a number of standards which compete. It will be worth monitoring the global ELT
market for signs of shifting popularity between textbooks published in different standards.

Will English give Britain a special economic advantage?

It has been suggested that the English language will provide the key to Britain's economic
prosperity in the future. After all, if much of the world's business is conducted in English,
this surely will be of advantage to native speakers. Graddol (1997) presents arguments
which challenge this idea and suggests that in future Britain's monolingualism may become
a liability which offsets any economic advantage gained from possessing extensive native-
speaker resources in the global language.

There are several reasons why monolingualism may not be the most advantageous
strategy in a world that increasingly is bilingual and multilingual, and trade is significant
among them. A greater volume of trade will occur within Europe in a context where
trilingual competence (in English, French and German), or at least bilingual competence,
is widely regarded as necessary, especially for trade with peripheral countries. As the "core"
of Europe moves eastwards, there is a danger that Britain's peripheral position will be felt
more acutely and its monolingual status may become an economic liability. In other regions
of the world, regional languages may become important in business – such as Chinese in
East and South-east Asia, and Spanish in the Americas. The inability to field staff competent

in these languages in addition to English may prove a hindrance as markets become more competitive. The likelihood is that English may be so prevalent in the world that Britain obtains no special benefit in having so many native speakers: the advantage may shift more clearly towards bilingualism.

At present, the English language helps make Britain attractive to Asian companies wishing to invest in factories with direct access to European markets, since many Asian countries use English as their international lingua franca. But if a country such as The Netherlands can provide English, German and Dutch-speaking employees, why establish an enterprise within a monolingual English-speaking area which is peripheral geographi-cally, politically and economically? Britain's linguistic advantage in attracting investment from Asia may decrease as English becomes more widely used in other European countries.

English will no doubt remain an important asset to Britain in terms of the production and marketing of intellectual property; English language materials will continue to be important economic resources for native speakers. But intellectual property in English will become more widely produced and marketed in other parts of the world.

The global ELT market, similarly, is likely to become more complex. As in other global industries, the strategic importance of alliances and cooperative ventures will grow. International networks of language schools may take an increasing market share. Competitors to Britain will arise in Europe, some of whom will employ British native speakers on a contract basis, while others will establish offices in Britain. These trends may make it less easy to identify distinctively British goods and services.

There is also a likelihood that new ELT providers based in European and Asian second-language areas may prove more attractive to some clients than native-speaker institutions. There is a rising demand for courses, materials and teachers which cater for the needs and experiences of second-language users. Non-native-speaking teachers are not necessarily regarded as "second best" any more. More people are asking, "How can monolingual British teachers best understand the needs of second-language users of English?"

Such developments make it difficult to argue that Britain will have an intrinsic economic advantage based on language. If Britain retains an edge with regard to the English language, it will be largely because of wider cultural associations and its international "brand image".

[. . .]

RIVAL LANGUAGES

Which languages may rival English as a world lingua franca in the twenty-first century?

There is no reason to believe that any other language will appear within the next fifty years to replace English as the global lingua franca. The position of English has arisen from a particular history which no other language can, in the changed world of the twenty-first century, repeat.

We have argued, however, that no single language will occupy the monopolistic position in the twenty-first century which English has – almost – achieved by the end of the twentieth century. It is more likely that a small number of world languages will form an "oligopoly", each with particular spheres of influence and regional bases.

As trade, people movement and communication between neighbouring countries in Asia and South America become more important than flows between such regions and Europe and North America, so we can expect languages which serve regional communication to rise in popularity. But it is actually very difficult to foresee more precisely what will occur.

For example, we have noted that economic activity, telecommunications traffic and air travel between Asian countries will greatly increase. But there are at least three possible linguistic scenarios which may develop from this. One is that English will remain the preferred language of international communication within Asia, since the investment in English may be regarded as too great to throw away, or the social elites who have benefited from English in the past may be reluctant to let their privileged position become threatened. Or it may simply be the most common shared language. A second scenario is that Mandarin becomes regionally more important, beginning as a lingua franca within Greater China (for communication between the regions of Hong Kong, Beijing, Shanghai and Taiwan) and building on increased business communication between the overseas Chinese in South-east Asia.

The third scenario is that no single language will emerge as a dominant lingua franca in Asia and a greater number of regional languages will be learned as foreign languages. If intraregional trade is greatest between adjacent countries, then there is likely to be an increased demand for neighbouring languages. In this case the pattern of demand for foreign languages will look different in each country.

The position of Russian in Central and North Asia is subject to similar problems of prediction. But it does seem clear that the global fortunes of Spanish are rising quite rapidly. Indeed, the trading areas of the south (Mercosur, Safta) are expected to merge with Nafta in the first decade of the new millennium. This, taken together with the expected increase in the Hispanic population in the US, may ensure that the Americas emerge as a bilingual English-Spanish zone.

[. . .]

What gives a language global influence and makes it a "world language"?

No one has satisfactorily answered the question of what makes a language a "world" language. Sheer numbers of native speakers do not in themselves explain the privileged position of some languages.

David Crystal suggests that "a language becomes an international language for one chief reason: the political power of its people – especially their military power" (Crystal, 1997, p. 7). Historically that may have be true: in the future, it will be less clearly military power which provides the international backing for languages, because of changes in the nature of national power, in the way that cultural values are projected and in the way markets are opened for the circulation of goods and services.

What we need is some sense of what makes a language attractive to learners, so that we can identify languages which newly meet such criteria in the future. This would also allow us to chart and ideally anticipate the decline of erstwhile popular languages.

In Graddol (1997) we have focused on economic and demographic factors. Some combination of these might usefully form a starting point for an understanding of what makes a language acquire importance. The engco model[1] provides an illustration of the kind of approach that can be taken. The model calculates an index of "global influence" taking into account various economic factors which have been discussed earlier, including Gross Language Product and openness to world trade (Traded Gross Language Product). The model also includes demographic factors, such as the numbers of young speakers and rates of urbanisation. Finally, it takes into account the human development index (HDI) for different countries. This is a composite figure produced by the UN, which combines measures of quality of life with those for literacy and educational provision. In this way, HDI provides an indicator of the proportion of native speakers who are literate and capable of generating intellectual resources in the language.

The engco model of global influence thus generates a new kind of league table among languages, which weights languages not only by the number and wealth of their speakers, but also by the likelihood that these speakers will enter social networks which extend beyond their locality: they are the people with the wherewithal and ambition to "go about" in the world, influence it and to have others seek to influence them. The calculations for the mid-1990s for the "basket" of languages we have surveyed are as shown in Table 2.1.

No strong claims are made for the validity of this index, but it does seem to capture something of the relative relations between world languages which other indices, based crudely on economic factors or numbers of native speakers, do not convey. It shows that English is, on some criteria at least, a long way ahead of all other languages, including Chinese.

The advantage of the engco index is the way it can be used to generate projections. As the model is refined and the full demographic and economic projections for the countries concerned are taken into account, league tables will be published for the decades up to 2050. Preliminary results indicate that on this basis Spanish is one of the languages which will rise most quickly. The nearest rivals to English – German, French and Japanese – will grow much more slowly. The relative positions of the "top six" are likely to change during the coming decades, but it is unlikely that any other language will overtake English.

Table 2.1 "Global influence" of major languages according to the engco model. An index score of 100 represents the position of English in 1995

1	English	100
2	German	42
3	French	33
4	Japanese	32
5	Spanish	31
6	Chinese	22
7	Arabic	8
8	Portuguese	5
9	Malay	4
10	Russian	3
11	Hindi/Urdu	0.4
12	Bengali	0.09

Source: The engco model

The changing status of languages will create a new language hierarchy for the world. Figure 2.1 shows how this might look in the middle of the twenty-first century, taking into account economic and demographic developments as well as potential language shift. In comparison with the present-day hierarchy there are more languages in the top layer. Chinese, Hindi/Urdu, Spanish and Arabic may join English. French and other OECD languages (German, Japanese) are likely to decline in status. But the biggest difference between the present-day language hierarchies and those of the future will result from the loss of several thousand of the world's languages. Hence there may be a group of languages at the apex, but there will be less linguistic variety at the base. The shift from linguistic monopoly to oligopoly brings pluralism in one sense, but huge loss of diversity in another. This will be offset only in part by an increasing number of new hybrid language varieties, many arising from contact with English.

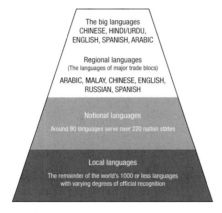

Figure 2.1 The world language hierarchy in 2050?

ENGLISH AS A TRANSITIONAL PHENOMENON

Will the demand for English in the world continue to rise at its present rate?

Although the position of English seems entrenched, it is possible that the extraordinary interest in the language in recent years will prove to be a temporary phenomenon associated with the "first-wave" effects in a period of global change: the transitional nature of a global economy, the current state of telecommunications networks, the immaturity of satellite television markets, and educational curricula which lag behind the needs of workers and employers. These pages examine why the current global wave of English may lose momentum.

Figure 2.2 shows the projections made by the engco model for speakers of English to 2050. The dotted lines represent speculative curves for second-language and foreign-language speakers. There is, as yet, no basis for estimating these groups safely – although it is these communities which will in practice determine the future of global English. Nevertheless, the curves are located approximately correctly for the present time (the vertical dashed line) and the speculative curves demonstrate some ideas developed in Graddol (1997).

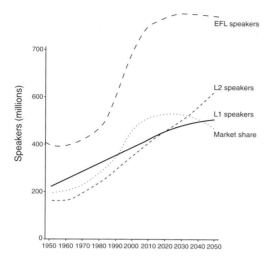

Figure 2.2 Estimates of first-language speakers of English from 1950 to 2050 as calculated by the engco model, together with speculations regarding L2 and EFL communities

Source: The engco model

First, L1 speakers of English will soon form a minority group. Second, at some point the increase in people learning English as a foreign language will level out. This is a demographic necessity, but may be hastened by a "leakage" of EFL speakers to L2 status. The key question is, at what point will the numbers of learners decline?

The dotted line, "market share", indicates a speculative projection of the global ELT market open to the ELT industries of native-speaking countries, which currently dominate global ELT provision. The curve begins with a notional 50 per cent share, which takes account of the present closed nature of many national textbook markets. The actual share of the market taken by publishers and educational providers from Britain, Ireland, US, Canada, Australia and New Zealand is at present impossible to estimate – but it is the shape of the curve which is important. Here it shows a declining market share, as providers from L2 territories become more active. That British and other native-speaking ELT providers will find the global market much more competitive, will lose market share and may even experience a decline, is entirely compatible with the idea that more people in the world are learning and using English.

[. . .]

Will English continue to be associated with leading-edge technology?

Leading-edge technology, particularly computers and information technology, has been largely English based in several respects. First, its research and development is focused in the US, though often in close collaboration with Japanese transnational companies (TNCs). Second, the literature and conferences in which research findings are reported and through which researchers keep up to date with developments elsewhere, are English based. Third, communications technology and document-handling software have developed around the English language. Indeed, the notorious history of the ascii coding set which has plagued the use of computer systems for non-English languages for many years, is one example. Fourth, the installed user base of new technology is primarily located in the US, resulting in support manuals, help lines, on-screen menu systems and so on, appearing first in English.

The close association between English and information technology may prove a temporary phenomenon. As software and technology become more sophisticated, they support other languages much better. Desktop publishing and laser printing are now capable of handling hundreds of lesser used languages and a wide range of scripts and writing systems. Computer operating systems and software are now routinely versioned for many languages. In many cases the user can further customise the product, allowing even very small languages, unknown to the manufacturers, to be accommodated. So whereas English speakers used to enjoy the best and latest technology, this is no longer so true.

Will economic modernisation continue to require English for technology and skills transfer?

Currently, English is to be found at the leading edge of economic modernisation and industrial development. The typical pattern of economic modernisation involves technology and skills transfer from the Big Three regions (North America, Europe and Japan) as a result of investment by TNCs, often via joint-venture companies: a process associated closely with English.

But as countries benefit from such transfer and "come up to speed", there develop local networks of small companies supplying the large TNC enterprises. Since many such suppliers use local employment, this secondary economic activity does not stimulate English to the same degree as the primary activity around TNCs.

There is yet a third wave to be expected in economic development. Just as the Big Three TNCs transfer technology, not simply to produce goods more cheaply but also to create new markets, so countries like Thailand and Malaysia are looking towards their neighbours, including Vietnam, Laos and Cambodia, as future trading partners. The development of such regional trade, in which no Big Three country is directly involved, may diminish the primacy of English as the language of technology transfer: the necessary level of expertise can be obtained closer to home and more cheaply. Sources of management and technology transfer in Asia now include Singapore, Hong Kong, Taiwan, Korea, Malaysia and Thailand. This third-wave technology transfer – often associated with less than leading-edge technology – may be less reliant on English. But it is equally possible that English provides the means for such countries to extend into regional markets.

There is no doubt that it would be extremely helpful to have a better understanding of how the next phases of globalisation will affect the use of English.

What impact will the Internet have on the global use of English?

The Internet epitomises the information society, allowing the transfer of services, expertise and intellectual capital across the world cheaply, rapidly and apparently without pollution or environmental damage. At present 90 per cent of Internet hosts are based in English-speaking countries. It is not surprising, therefore, that the majority of traffic and the majority of websites are based in English, and that those users based in other countries and who normally work in other languages find they have to communicate with others in the cyberspace community through the medium of English.

Many studies, however, have shown how well the Internet supports minority and diasporic affinity groups. Although early studies of "nationally oriented" Internet news-groups (containing discussions of national or regional culture and language) seemed to indicate a preference for using English (for example, soc.culture.punjabi), others which have become more recently active (such as soc.culture.vietnamese) extensively use the national language. It is not yet clear why some groups use English less than others, but an overall trend away from the hegemony of English in such groups is visible and often surfaces as an explicit topic of discussion.

One reason may be that the Internet user base is developing rapidly in Asia and non-English-speaking countries. And software technology, such as browser and HTML standards (which govern the HyperText Mark-up Language in which Web pages are written), now also supports multilingual browsing.

The quantity of Internet materials in languages other than English is set to expand dramatically in the next decade. English will remain pre-eminent for some time, but it will eventually become one language among many. It is therefore misleading to suggest English is somehow the native language of the Internet. It will be used in cyberspace in the same way as it is deployed elsewhere: in international forums, for the dissemination of scientific and technical knowledge, in advertising, for the promotion of consumer goods and for after-sales services.

In the meantime, local communication on the Internet is expected to grow significantly. This, and the increasing use of e-mail for social and family communication, will encourage the use of a wider variety of languages. English is said to have accounted for 80 per cent of computer-based communication in the 1990s. That proportion is expected to fall to around 40 per cent in the next decade.

MANAGING THE FUTURE

[. . .]

The need for an ethical framework for ELT

There is a growing appreciation that the business environment of the next century will require global enterprises to meet three "bottom lines": economic prosperity, environmental protection and social equity. Public trust in the institutions and organisations which provide goods and services may in the future represent a more important component of brand image than the quality of the product itself. Hence ethical, as well as environmental, values are likely to come under increasing public scrutiny and significantly influence customer loyalty.

However, one of the problems facing the proponents of an ethical approach to English teaching is that no one is sure where the moral high ground lies when it comes to the export of ELT goods and services. English has for long been seen as a "clean" and safe export, one without some of the complex moral implications associated with the sale of products such as weapons or military vehicles. The ELT industry has been portrayed as one which benefits both producer and consumer and both exporting and importing countries. It has been a major component in overseas aid as well as a commercial enterprise.

How, then, can the teaching of English be brought within a more ethical framework? What social responsibilities are associated with the promotion and teaching of English? There is a growing concern about endangered languages but very little debate about the management of large languages, of which English is the largest.

A more sensitive approach will be needed in the future, which recognises that English is not a universal panacea for social, economic and political ills and that teaching methods and materials, and educational policies, need to be adapted for local contexts. The world is becoming aware of the fate of endangered languages and more anxious over the long-term impact of English on world cultures, national institutions and local ways of life. Perhaps a combination of circumstances – such as shifting public values, changed economic priorities and regional political expediency – could bring about a serious reversal for British ELT providers at some point in the future. . . .

Whether such a discussion is held in terms of global "brand management", the need to adapt to a changing business environment, or a moral requirement to work within an ethical framework, the ELT industry will have to respond to changing international social values. This would bring a major exporting activity into the same framework which is now expected to regulate trading relations with other countries and would help to ensure that the reputation of Britain, of the British people and their language, is enhanced rather than diminished in the coming century.

Note

1   The engco model
     The engco forecasting model has been designed by The English Company (UK) Ltd as a means of examining the relative status of world languages and making forecasts of the numbers of speakers of different languages based on demographic, human development and economic data. The figures reported in this document are based on demographic projections from *World Population Prospects 1950–2050 (1996 Revision)* and *Sex and Age Quinquennial 1950–2050 (1996 Revision)* in machine-readable data sets made available by the United Nations in 1997, on economic data for 1994 from the World Bank, and from estimates of proportions of national populations speaking different languages taken from national census data and a variety of reference sources.

     The main purpose of the model is to explore the potential impact of urbanisation and economic development on the global linguistic landscape of the twenty-first century. A more detailed explanation of the assumptions made by the engco model can be found on The English Company (UK) Ltd's Internet site (http://www.english.co.uk) along with details of any other reports and revised projections which may become available from time to time.

References

Anderson, B. (1983) *Imagined Communities*. London: Verso.

Crystal, D. (1997) *English as a Global Language*. Cambridge: Cambridge University Press.

Graddol, D. (1997) *The Future of English?* London: British Council.

Smith, L.E. (1992) Spread of English and matters of intelligibility. In B.B. Kachru (ed.) *The Other Tongue: English Across Cultures*. Urbana: University of Illinois Press.

Strevens, P. (1992) English as an international language: directions in the 1990s. In B.B. Kachru (ed.) *The Other Tongue: English Across Cultures*. Urbana: University of Illinois Press.

Chapter 3

Denise E. Murray

NEW TECHNOLOGY: NEW LANGUAGE AT WORK?

IT IS IN THE WORKPLACE that people first come in contact with explicit computer technology. Their livelihood so often depends on how they adapt to the technology; rarely is the technology adapted to them. According to Brod (1984), information technology operates in two zones – the private, for conducting our personal lives (e.g. banking, mail ordering) and the production, "where we depend on computers to perform our work".

[. . .]

This chapter will focus on the way computers in the workplace affect human–machine and human–human communication.

The computer interface

Most people have experienced the blank screen of a computer, a screen that gives no indication of what the user should do. . . . Most users have no understanding of the internal workings of either the hardware or software – nor do they want it. It is not only the blank screen that is perplexing. Even with a manual, system commands are not intuitive. In early machines, users had to learn arcane key combinations to get the computer to do what they wanted. . . . Interestingly, many of the early terms for interacting with the computer drew on military metaphors, perhaps largely because the military funded much of the computer research and was the largest purchaser of computer systems in the United States. Thus, we have terms such as "command", "abort", "escape", "crash", and "kill the program".

> A well-known computer company decided to redesign its computer keyboard. To test the design, they had many people use the keyboard, adapting it until it was user friendly. When the keyboard became a product and was used by customers and internally within the company, users complained bitterly about the complex key combinations they had to use to perform even the most basic commands, such as clear screen, move to bottom of the screen, etc. The company had used data entry clerks to test the keyboard. Thus, the keyboard was designed to have single key-strokes for their tasks, not for word processing or programming, the functions used by most users.

Xerox was the first company to try to implement a more effective system, one with easy-to-use commands and "obvious" visual displays. Xerox's hardware, however, could not keep up with the software, resulting in unacceptable time lags between asking the computer to perform a function and its actual performance. It was Apple Computer that took many of these basic breakthroughs (e.g. the mouse, visual displays), tried it on the unsuccessful Lisa and then on the Macintosh, leading to the window and pull-down menu interface so familiar today. Certainly these approaches were a breakthrough from blank screen or a non-intuitive command sequence such as Ctrl-Alt-Del to reboot the system. However, despite advertisements to the contrary, the interface is not necessarily natural and intuitive. Who has not tried to perform some simple word-processing function, only to find it impossible to work out how to do it without both manual *and* knowledge of the name of the function. Who would automatically look up "hanging indent" when wanting to have the first line flush with the margin and the second indented (especially used in typing references)? . . . Currently, the two primary modes for choosing a function on a computer are keyboard commands or pointing to an icon. The first is limited by the number of keys on the keyboard; the second by the number of universal, intuitively understood icons. . . .

Even more importantly, we have exchanged the military metaphor for one of a desktop. For those of us familiar with office work, the desktop is a robust metaphor, with its file folders, telephones, rolodexes, and cut and paste. However, if the computer is to be the universal machine, the metaphor must be accessible to all, not just office workers. . . .

Airline reservations automated

> A grandmother, wanting to fly out to visit her son and his family for a couple of weeks' vacation, calls Alligator Airlines and asks the fare for flights from San Francisco to New York. The first question the reservation agent asks is "When are you travelling?" Since the grandmother is looking for the cheapest fare and date of travel is irrelevant, she just nominates a month – "Oh, probably May." The reservation agent then asks, "What date in May?" Again, the grandmother doesn't care; she wants the cheapest fare. So the agent checks midweek fares and finds that if she leaves midweek and returns midweek, the fare is cheaper. So the agent selects a midweek date in May (the 16th) and tells the grandmother, "There are two non-stop flights that day, 10:00 a.m. and 6:00 p.m. Which would you prefer?" The grandmother asks what time each arrives, and decides that the 10:00 a.m. is more convenient. So the agent then says, "OK, then, I'll book you on the 10:00 a.m. flight on 16 May. What's your name? Now, for your return. How long do you want to stay?" By now, the grandmother is confused since she never had a particular date in mind. So, she tells the agent she'll have to check dates with her son and call back.

This scenario illustrates the implementation of computer monitoring on the discourse style and conversational moves of these airline employees. . . . The case of Alligator (aka American) Airlines illustrates how communication gets redefined when efficiency experts apply the rules for streamlining manufacturing to service industries. Time-and-motion studies applied to manufacturing in the nineteenth century are now being applied to office work; only now they are aided by the computer as the monitoring device *par excellence*. . . . The workers first get new tools to improve the speed of their routine tasks and then, since the next step is to automate these tasks, they have machines perform them instead of people. Leaving aside issues of quality and of human alienation, such rationalization usually did produce more products in manufacturing industries – more cars, more cans, more computer chips – at lower prices. Just as the industrial revolution extended human physical capabilities, the information revolution will extend human mental capabilities, it is believed. But, when applied to service (and other) industries where human communication is the core of the job, the very nature of the job changes.

American Airlines decided to rationalize their reservation agents' jobs. First, they identified two general types of calls: action and potential. An action call is where the customer knows where and when she is travelling and asks for reservations. A potential call is from someone like the grandmother in the scenario above. The sign of a good reservation agent is that he can convert the potential call into an action call.

To determine how this could be achieved most efficiently, American then broke down the conversations between agent and customer into modules. Each speech act of the agent was identified – acts such as opening, probe, sales pitch, close, address; each speech act of the customer was identified – acts such as resist. Agents were trained to use certain types of presupposition questions rather than yes/no questions in the probe. Thus, in the scenario above, the agent asks the grandmother, "Which would you prefer, the 10:00 a.m. or the 6:00 p.m.?" Here, the presupposition is that the listener wants one of these. A yes/no question such as "Do you want to book?" on the other hand has no such presupposition. They were trained to try to close, that is, ask for the person's name so they can start the booking process. In addition to standardizing the conversations between reservation agents and customers, American uses the computers to monitor these conversations. Supervisors on site and at company headquarters listen in to conversations and report on whether the agent probed or used the caller's name. The computer also tracks the talk time, the amount of time the agent is actually plugged in, the time spent making the reservation online after the end of the phone call, and the conversions (the enquiries "converted" into bookings). Pay rises depend on these statistics. However, American found that their customers complained that the reservation agents were too aggressive and many of the conversions never actually boarded the plane – presumably people made the reservation just to get off the phone! Thus, American has instituted a new rating system where the subjective qualities (such as politeness or consideration of the customer) of the conversation are used, as well as the talk time and boarding, rather than conversion. However, the standardized conversation is still in place – it is only that one aspect of monitoring that has changed.

American Airlines is a case study of the belief in perfect technical control of the workplace, with its monitoring and emphasis on quantity over quality. But what has happened to the conversation of our grandmother? Her wishes and language have been manipulated to get a sale. Thus, she ends with three alternatives: hang up and try again, take the reservation being offered by the agent, or visit a travel agent who will access the same computer as the reservation agent, but who will discuss different schedules, different fares, etc. While airlines have attempted to standardize telephone call conversations, no one has standardized face-to-face conversations in such encounters. Another alternative exists – online reservations from home. Through one such computer service I am able to check airline schedules, fares, food, aircraft, and so on, online. I can even make the reservation online or I can use this information to call the airlines as an action call.

But, for those of us who must interact with pre-programmed clerks, the interaction is at best efficient, at worst a disaster. Since the clerks are pre-programmed, they do not listen to any hidden meanings (implicatures) in our conversation – they are only cuing on the keywords of place, time, etc. This is a virtual conversation and perhaps will be better when it is automated, for then customers will not expect real communication from real people; but that would lead to loss of jobs.

What has happened to the interaction reservation which agents had with each other? Now, every keystroke is counted; every break is noted. Since work occupies most of our waking time, for most people it is more than a place to work – it is a place to make friends, to socialize, to discuss ideas about the job and about life in general. . . . Many times, informal chatting about work or non-work can result in serendipitous leads to new ideas and new ways of seeing our work. To stay creative, we need to explore ideas with others and within ourselves.

[. . .]

Sportswriting automated

Read each of the following introductions to published stories about the same basketball game. One was written by a human sportswriter, one by a computer program. Which is which?

Story no. 1

Golden State's Latrell Sprewell scored twenty-six points and had two key steals in the last two minutes as the Warriors rallied to beat San Antonio Spurs 106–101 Tuesday at San Antonio.

The warriors had led by 22 with 5:22 left in the second quarter in a win carried by a strong first quarter.

[. . .]

Story no. 2

Hail fell, the roof leaked, the Warriors swooned, Chris Webber arrived, Byson Houston left, Coach Don Nelson followed and the Warriors somehow recovered.

Or, to put it more simply, so many dramatic events took place in the Alamodome on Tuesday night that Dennis Rodman almost looked ordinary.

(Ochwat, 1994, pp. 1F, 6F, 7F)

Yes, the first story was written by a computer. . . . It works and is read in isolation as a "real", not a "virtual" sports story *because* the programmer has analysed the essential content features of a sports story: key events, quotations, team statistics, names of players and coaches. The program, *Sportswriter*, was written by a sportswriter and so the shell into which the data are plugged fits the style of sports stories: short, punchy sentences, past tense, direct speech, action verbs. . . .

What trips the program up is unexpected events like the rain and hail that happened during half-time and caused the second half to be delayed. To accommodate this, the program "wrote" "In the final half, the game was delayed for 12 minutes . . . " (p. 6F). The program is used extensively for high school sports, allowing many events and schools to be covered by small, poor, local newspapers. However, even the writer of the program is refusing to market it for fear it will erode jobs. Like all other forms of automation, it could result in workers using lower level functions, but . . . a human still has to do the final editing, and editing is a higher level skill.

[. . .]

Pedagogy automated?

> A gifted teacher of history stands in a classroom in California and teaches her 12th grade class about the American Civil War. The lesson is videotaped and beamed to a hundred other schools across the nation. Students at the sites have a teacher's aide, video cameras, computers, and telephones. The technology allows the students to "talk" with the teacher – by telephone or by computer. The video cameras allow the teacher to "see" the students at any site she chooses. Once the lesson is over, the teacher's aide helps the students at their site with questions and to study for the upcoming test. The teacher's aide can introduce computer programs on the Civil War for students to use. With a CD ROM, students can see pictures and movies about the period.

This scenario is not possible now for schools, but has been trialled in high-tech companies to deliver their own training. It could be possible if the Information Superhighway had all the necessary features. Distance learning of this sort is expected to make learning more equitable – children from the poorest areas could have access to the best teachers. However, this scenario makes some fundamental assumptions both about learning and the role of teachers. It assumes that students learn by having material presented to them. However, research shows that teachers are most successful, and most learning takes place when teachers tap into the knowledge and schemata children bring with them to the classroom (Bell and Stern, 1994). . . . Such distance learning projects are often promoted to decrease costs. However, if they are to be implemented in pedagogically sound ways they are very expensive, requiring not only technology, but also teachers skilled at using it and incorporating it effectively in their own syllabus. . . .

This scenario also illustrates the role of teachers. The gifted teacher in this case is seen merely as the deliverer of information. The aides, who would in fact be providing the most instruction, are limited by the technology. They (and current teachers) do not have the time to spend on curriculum development to incorporate technology meaningfully into their lessons. So, pressed for time, they accept pre-packaged software, frequently written by programmers rather than educators. . . . Teachers become unskilled aides, implementing someone else's educational plan for their pupils.

[. . .]

Technology can be useful in education, but education should not be designed around the technology. Rather, the technology should be chosen because it fits the curriculum and fits the way students learn.

[. . .]

Electronic mail in the workplace

Electronic mail (e-mail) has begun to replace the water cooler or coffee machine as the hub for chatting. Within IBM more than 200,000 employees use VNET (the electronic mail system). William H. Gates, Chairman of Microsoft Corporation, runs his company largely through e-mail, used by most of the 5,000 employees. Decisions about products, vacation policy and so on are discussed, debated, and announced online. Gates himself receives and sends hundreds of e-mail notes a day, from employees at all levels and from all sectors of the company. . . . These computer networks become speech communities, linking people hundreds or thousands of miles apart. Lines of communication are restructured, as in the example of Microsoft, where Gates talks with any employee via e-mail.

Control

However, the question of control becomes crucial. Although companies tell employees not to use telephones for personal communication they cannot enforce this rule easily, especially in the United States, where telephone surveillance is illegal. So the use of e-mail becomes attractive. . . . But, even more importantly, e-mail surveillance is both easy and legal. This control raises the important issue of what language and information are public and what private. . . . Let me give an example of software designed to help control workplace communications, one that illustrates the tension between the employee wanting more efficiency in electronic communication and wanting to choose when she says what to whom and how.

The Coordinator: an example of control

A computer system called The Coordinator supports interactive work in organizations (especially by managers, whose major function is to get work done through discourse). . . . Based on . . . the Winograd and Flores (1986) model of conversation for action, the system requires that the sender define what type of communication the e-mail is – request, decline, promise, and so on. If the sender makes a request, the system prompts for a "respond-by" date, a "complete-by" date, and an "alert" date. The system keeps track of the conversation so that, at any time, one of the participants can check what requests they have asked that have not been fulfilled, or what promises they have made that they have not yet fulfilled. . . . While the program is based on sound design principles and an adequate theory of the way discourse works in an office environment, does it truly "allow work to flow more smoothly"? Many users have found it actually hampers their communication work.

The system also includes a "free-form" e-mail, where the sender does not have to identify what type of communication she is carrying out. . . . In initial implementations of the system, many people overwhelmingly used free-form since they did no want to go through the rigmarole of making choices or felt constrained by doing so. In Flores' interpretation of conversation for action, information does not exist – most workplace conversation is or the purpose of getting something done. . . . In more recent implementations, The Coordinator, while still including free-form, also includes "Conversation for Possibilities". This recognizes the serendipitous nature of conversation I alluded to earlier. Often, our initial e-mail may be "for your information", but the information may lead to some conversation for action with requests and so on at a later date. So what are the problems associated with this application?

1   Although based on both a study of conversation in the workplace, and on a principled theory of language use, Flores' system has not gained wide acceptance and has met with initial hostility from many users. The issue here is not whether the model is appropriate (it clearly is) but whether explicitly identifying speech acts is appropriate. . . . It is ambiguity that so often leads to new possibilities, as well as to miscommunications.

2   Online conversations, like face-to-face conversations, are embedded within other conversations; utterances often carry more than one speech act or instances of a speech act (e.g. a request); several requests (or promises, etc.) are made in one e-mail message. The Coordinator does not accommodate this type of conversation very easily. Thus I could not promise to send a colleague a paper she has requested and in the same e-mail ask her to write me a letter of recommendation. . . .

    To use The Coordinator, users face restrictions on what they can say when and how; but they also gain the ability to track their conversations, overcoming a major drawback of most e-mail systems . . . . Thus the issue here is how much restriction and change are worth the pay-off in enhanced organization of email?

3   Winograd and Flores (1986) themselves argue that there is no objective world that can be measured; the world is created through the language we use to communicate. They believe that making the actions in conversation transparent to the participants helps focus the commitment to action required for business interaction. However, The Coordinator also falls into the trap of hiding its biases through language. By objectifying the speech acts in conversations for action, it hides the other types of interactions that take place in the work environment. Although workers may be exhorted not to gossip in company time, much gossip can become the basis for innovative, creative new work. Flores and his colleagues claim that these non-conversations for action should perhaps take place in face-to-face conversations around the coffee pot or in chance encounters . . . . As Flores admits, The Co-ordinator (and any other technology) is a form of intervention – the question will always be to what extent does the intervention facilitate human–human interaction and to what extent does it interfere?

Automating the office

Office work was the first information domain to be automated, especially with the introduction of word processors. Companies use one of three basic strategies for implementing the new technology – centralization, autonomy, and work council. The first two are by far the most prevalent, especially in the United States. Centralization involves central planning, central control, with the system distributed down through the hierarchy. In addition to producing worker alienation, this type of implementation results in individual departments not having the system adapted to their specific needs. Autonomy (this is most prevalent in universities) occurs where individual departments are left free to introduce their own automation systems.

    While this provides flexibility, it results in lack of compatibility, and inefficiency. One department cannot talk to another through a network; files cannot be transferred;

expertise and experience with a system cannot be shared. The third implementation through work councils (done primarily in Europe) is what is often called participatory design, which emphasizes extensive prototyping and user involvement in the entire design and development process. Participatory design began because unions, seeing the possibility of lay-offs resulting from computerization, demanded that they be part of the introduction of any new technology. Thus workers, managers and systems analysts all contribute to the design and testing of any new systems. . . .

In a detailed study of *Managing Organizational Innovation: The Evolution from Word Processing to Office Information Systems*, Johnson and Rice (1987) use the effects of the introduction of word processing as indicative of the effects of other information systems. After examining nearly two hundred organizations, they developed the following principles:

1   Involve members in changing the technology and social system jointly to accomplish organizational mission.
2   Provide experiences for continuous learning.
3   Encourage experimentation; systems evolve, and managers must continuously attend to adaptation.
4   Design work units to promote communication.
5   Promote self-regulation of work groups through autonomy; locate the decision-making at the task requiring the decision.
6   Design jobs so that people can perceive and complete a whole task.
7   Administer policies with flexibility.
8   Design jobs for upward mobility.
9   Establish boundaries so that recognizable success can lead to claims of expertise and authority.
10   Attend to the environment outside the boundaries.

It is clear from these recommendations that centralized introduction of new technologies is unlikely to provide such an environment since workers would not be involved in decisions about initial implementation or ongoing adaptation; nor is an autonomous system since it does not have permeable boundaries – a worker is unlikely to be able to move to another department since he would probably have to learn a new system. Like participatory design, this model calls for an increase in the communication between knowledge worker, manager and systems experts. Isolating workers with small tasks is bound to fail. Thus discourse and interaction are essential to the successful introduction of information systems into the office.

"Real executives don't use computers"

. . . In my own observations (and Brod (1984) also notes this), I have noted that many top-level executives consider typing a secretarial function and do not wish to be seen doing it. Others, like the general public and their own workers, are frightened they will make mistakes and be shown to be incompetent.

Face-saving

A perhaps apocryphal tale runs like this. Before the advent of personal computers, individual workers had terminals in their offices that were linked directly to the mainframe computers in a large, air-conditioned computer room. . . . In this particular large computer company, upper-level management never used the terminals in their offices. Instead, they relied on secretaries to type their memos, access information and so on. Despite all attempts to get these managers to use the new technology, they resisted – and no one knew why. After all, these were intelligent people *and* in a company that made its living selling computers!

Then came the personal computer. Each manager had a computer in his or her office. . . . Suddenly, typing could be heard coming from behind the closed office doors. In a relatively short time, these former Luddites (or at least that is what the "techies" thought they were) began using electronic mail, typing their own documents, filling out forms online and so on. They did so largely because they were able to learn how to use the computer in a completely face-saving environment. Previously, when everything they did on the terminal was immediately relayed to the mainframe computer, they were afraid they would make fools of themselves in front of the technical people. Indeed, most people who first use a computer blame themselves for every problem – not the manuals, not the program, not the hardware. For example, once when I was using a terminal during my research study and made a careless mistake, the whole computer system crashed. I immediately ran to the computer room to ask what I had done wrong. Of course, I had not caused the crash – my error and the computer failure just happened to occur at the same time. With personal computers, the managers could make mistakes without anyone knowing.

Unmet needs

. . . For most executives, the information technology just does not meet their needs. Executives can use information technology for three major purposes: as a word processor, as a communication channel, and as information broker . . . . Many executives use the computer as a word processor and communication vehicle; few use it to access information and support their decision-making. Why? To answer this question, we first need to ask why the adoption of such technology is promoted. What are its perceived advantages by its creators and marketers? In general terms, a new technology is adopted if it improves technical efficiency and contributes to institutional stature. In other words, the company gains a competitive advantage.

Does information technology improve the *technical efficiency* of executives? Not very much. The most commonly proposed information technology for management is one that facilitates decision-making. These decision-support systems assume that "preferences are stable, problems and premises preceded solutions and conclusions, information is neutral and managers make decisions by considering alternatives in terms of their anticipated consequences for prior objectives" (March and Sproull, 1990, p. 150). Human information processing is far less structured. For example, imagine a decision-support system that controls managers' calendars. The manager provides the information for the programmer: times when she has regularly scheduled meetings or other engagements; a priority list of preferred times for meetings, for seeing individuals; a priority list of people; a priority list of projects/topics; the time length of different meeting types. An employee can log straight into the manager's calendar and attempt to set up a time to drop by. The program can even prompt the employee to name the topic to be discussed. The manager's secretary can do the same – but she has access to the calendars of other people and so can schedule a meeting without ever talking to any of the principals. This sounds efficient, but what if the topic is delicate and cannot be captured well in a few words in the topic space? What about the employee who is ranked at the bottom of the list? He will soon find out when he keeps trying to make an appointment with the manager and finds there is never any time to see him. The manager may never know the employee has been trying to see him until it is too late. Certain conventions of face-to-face and telephone conversations are broken. Our cultural convention is to give an excuse when refusing an offer or request. So, instead of the usual polite excuse (even if untrue), the employee gets shut out of the calendar. Another convention, that of serendipitous meetings, is flouted. . . .

Decision-support systems have been fairly unsuccessful, largely because of the changing information needs and decision criteria of executives. Executives have a great need for information on which to base their decisions. This information is gathered through their staff and middle management, both through direct requests and serendipitously. Why can a computer decision-support tool not provide such information? First, the information the manager needs changes daily, and her preferences change with altering information and situations. To program a computer to support a calendar is relatively trivial; to program one to constantly change the information base and the decision-making criteria is (certainly at present) impossible. Even more fundamentally, decision-support programs have been built on a biased set of information. Such a system (if possible) would dramatically alter the balance of power in the executive suite. Staff (and especially bureaucrats) use their knowledge to exert influence. Often the request for information that an executive makes is ill-formed, vague. The staff person is then able to mould the reply such that it meets the request but also gives him power in the decision-making process. . . . Further, it is the knowledge of the system that they control that may be invaluable to the decision-making process. Thus, if the programmer receives expert advice only from the executive, a large part of the necessary information base will be missing.

The other reason for adoption of a new technology is if it contributes to *institutional stature*. Does the calendar system enhance the manager's prestige and thus the image of his company? Not necessarily. While it may be viewed as efficient, it is probably also viewed as cold and inhuman. The executive has lost some of her "charm" and "people skills". . . . Executives do not need help with decision-making; they need help with gathering information. This could happen if executives used Computer-mediated Communication (CmC) to gather information from a broad base of employees (as Bill Gates of Microsoft does), and if they used appropriate information retrieval systems. But, as I showed above, these information systems may not provide the filtered and processed information the executive really needs.

So it seems clear why executives have not rapidly adopted information technology for their own use, relying on their staff to access databases, to test ideas on computer simulations or through decision-support systems. They keep for themselves the role of accessible leader and expert decision-maker.

What skills for future workers?

Many commentators on the information age and its effects on the workplace have focused on the need for workers who are more knowledgeable, have more skills and adaptability. They claim we will need a more educated workforce, not a less educated one.

[. . .]

Fewer skills required

Interestingly, the example of the airline agents counters this trend to more knowledgeable workers who can access required information. Their entire job has been redefined by technology. They do need to be able to access the computer for information on schedules, fares, etc., but they no longer need to have this information in their head as they did years ago. . . .

An even better example of workers needing less knowledge and skill can be seen when visiting a local McDonald's. The cash register, instead of having numbers on it, has symbols representing the various products. Thus the server need only press the correct symbols and the price will appear. Similarly, even the chefs' duties are controlled by computers that assess the time to fry the french fries or the time to grill the meat patties. The chefs need make no judgements at all.

Greater skills required

At the other end of the scale are jobs that require literacy and understanding of the relationship between the computer and the product. We see the ever-increasing need for computer programmers, electronic engineers and systems analysts. The principles set out by Johnson and Rice (1987) show that more communication and skill at understanding one's job and articulating needs, problems and solutions are vital for successful information technologies. We can no longer afford to let systems be designed solely by systems analysts and implemented solely by management. We need to ensure that the technology fits well with the way people communicate and process information.

[. . .]

Because of this frequent lack of fit of computer technology in the workplace, William W. Winspisinger, President of the International Association of Machinists and Aerospace Works, has suggested that there be a Technology Bill of Rights. It says:

1   New technology must be used in a way that creates and maintains jobs and promotes full employment.
2   New technology must be used to improve the conditions of work.
3   New technology must be used to develop the industrial base.
4   Workers and their trade unions must have a role in the decision-making processes with respect to the design, deployment, and use of new technology.

(McCorduck, 1985, pp. 211–212)

References

Bell, P. and Stern, J. (1994) NII in education: access isn't enough. *The CPSR Newsletter*, Spring, 4–5.

Brod, C. (1984) *Technostress: The Human Cost of the Computer Revolution*. Reading, MA: Addison Wesley.

Johnson, B. M. and Rice, D. E. (1987) *Managing Organizational Innovation: The Evolution from Word Processing to Office Information Systems*. New York: Columbia University Press.

McCorduck, P. (1985) *The Universal Machine*. New York: McGraw-Hill.

March, J. G. and Sproull, L. S. (1990) Technology, management and competitive advantage. In P. S. Goodman, L. S. Sproull and associates (eds) *Technology and Organizations*. San Francisco, CA: Josey-Bass.

Ochwat, J. (1994) Reporters, who needs reporters? *San Jose Mercury News*, 8 May, IF, 6F, 7F.

Winograd, T. and Flores, F. (1986) *Understanding Computers and Cognition*. Norwood, NJ: Ablex.

PART TWO

The globalisation of English: opportunities and constraints

Chapter 4

David Crystal

THE FUTURE OF ENGLISHES

DOES AN INCREASING AWARENESS OF THE SHEER INTERNATIONAL VARIETY IN THE ENGLISH LANGUAGE COMPLEX NECESSITATE A NEW PEDAGOGY FOR A NEW CENTURY?

THE PACE IS HOTTING UP. Reluctant as I have been to be swayed by the fashionable neologizing of recent years, my title shows capitulation. Like many since the early 1970s I have become used to the steady pluralization of the noun *English*, in such phrases as 'new Englishes' or the journal title 'World Englishes'. Associated locutions, such as 'an English' and 'each English' are also now routine. 'The English languages' is a phrase which has been used for over a decade, most recently by Tom McArthur as the title of his book for Cambridge University Press's Canto series (1998). 'Is English really a family of languages?' was the title of an article in the *International Herald Tribune* a few years ago (Rosen, 1994). And I have no doubt that we shall soon hear all the jargon of comparative philology turning up in the domain of ELT – daughter languages, sister languages, and the like. The question we all have to face, of course, is how a concept of 'best practice' survives in the face of such massive and unprecedented innovation. . . . explorations are likely to succeed only if we are clear in our theoretical thinking about what might be going on, and are clear about the facts of language change which motivate that thinking. Both levels of clarity are in short supply at the moment.

Part 1 Language matters

Intelligibility and identity

I begin by exploring the metaphor of 'family' a little. What could an English 'family' of languages possibly mean? The term 'family', of course, arose with reference to such domains as 'Indo-European', 'Romance' and 'Slavic' – domains where there exists a clearly identifiable set of entities whose mutual unintelligibility would allow them to be uncontroversially classified as different languages. Intelligibility is the traditional criterion, and when that has been applied to the case of English, there has hitherto been little justification for the notion of an English language family. Although there are several well-known instances of English regional accents and dialects causing problems of intelligibility to people from a different dialect background, especially when encountered at rapid conversational speed – in Britain, Cockney (London), Geordie (Newcastle), Scouse (Liverpool) and Glaswegian (Glasgow) are among the most commonly cited cases – the problems largely resolve when the speaker slows down, or they reduce to difficulties over isolated lexical items. This makes regional varieties of English no more problematic for linguistic theory than, say, occupational varieties such as legal or scientific. It is no more illuminating to call Cockney or Scouse 'different English languages' than it would be to call Legal or Scientific by such a name, and anyone who chooses to extend the application of the term 'language' in this way finds a slippery slope which eventually leads to the blurring of the potentially useful distinctions between 'language', 'variety', and 'dialect'.

The intelligibility criterion has traditionally provided little support for an English language family (whether it will continue to do so I shall discuss below). But we have learned from sociolinguistics in recent decades that this criterion is by no means an adequate explanation for the language nomenclature of the world, as it leaves out of consideration linguistic attitudes, and in particular the criterion of identity. If intelligibility were the only criterion, then we would have to say that people from Norway, Sweden and Denmark spoke a single language – 'Scandinavian', perhaps – with several regional varieties. The socio-political history of these nations, of course, disallows any such option. Swedes speak Swedish, Norwegians Norwegian, and Danes Danish – or at least (as a Dane glumly remarked to me the other day), they do when they are not speaking English. Or, to take a more recent example of how language nomenclature can change (and rapidly): at the beginning of the 1990s, the populations of Croatia, Bosnia, and Serbia would all be described as speaking varieties of Serbo-Croatian. Today, the situation has polarized, with Croatians considering the language they speak to be Croatian, and Serbs Serbian, and efforts being made to maximize the regional differences between them. The 'Croatian variety of Serbo-Croatian' has become 'the Croatian language'. A similar story can be found in any part of the world where language is an emergent index of socio-political identity.

That is the point: if a community wishes its way of speaking to be considered a 'language', and if they have the political power to support their decision, who would be able to stop them doing so? The present-day ethos is to allow communities to deal with their own internal policies themselves, as long as these are not perceived as being a threat to others. However, to promote an autonomous language policy, two criteria need to be satisfied. The first is to have a community with a single mind about the matter, and the second is to have a community which has enough political-economic clout to make its decision respected by outsiders with whom it is in regular contact. When these criteria are lacking, the movement is doomed.

[. . .]

The changing situation

English is now spoken by more people (as a first, second, or foreign language) than any other language and is recognized by more countries as a desirable lingua franca than any other language. This is not the place to recapitulate the relevant statistics, insofar as they can be established: this information is available elsewhere (for my own estimates, see

Crystal, 1995, 1997; see also Graddol, 1997). But it is important to recognize that the unprecedented scale of the growth in usage (approaching a quarter of the world's population) has resulted in an unprecedented growth in regional varieties.

Variation, of course, has always been part of the language, given that Angles, Saxons, and Jutes must have spoken different Germanic dialects. The emergence of Scots can be traced back to the beginning of the Middle English period. In the eighteenth century, Noah Webster was one of many who argued the need to recognize a distinct American (as opposed to British) tongue. And the issue of identity has been central to debate about the nature of creole and pidgin Englishes around the world. But it is only in recent decades (chiefly, since the independence era of the 1960s) that the diversity has become so dramatic, generating a huge literature on 'world Englishes' and raising the question of linguistic identity in fresh and intriguing ways.

Hybrids

The chief aim of McArthur's book *The English Language* (1998) is to draw attention to the remarkable 'messiness' which characterizes the current world English situation, especially in second-language contexts. Typically, a 'new English' is not a homogeneous entity, with clear-cut boundaries, and an easily definable phonology, grammar, and lexicon. On the contrary, communities which are putting English to use are doing so in several different ways. As McArthur puts it (p. 2), 'stability and flux go side by side, centripetal and centrifugal forces operating at one and the same time.' And when actual examples of language in use are analysed, in such multilingual settings as Malaysia and Singapore, all kinds of unusual hybrids come to light.

Different degrees of language mixing are apparent: at one extreme, a sentence might be used which is indistinguishable from Standard English. At the other extreme a sentence might use so many words and constructions from a contact language that it becomes unintelligible to those outside a particular community. In between, there are varying degrees of hybridization, ranging from the use of a single lexical borrowing within a sentence to several borrowings, and from the addition of a single borrowed syntactic construction (such as a tag question) to a reworking of an entire sentence structure. In addition, of course, the pronunciation shows similar degrees of variation, from a standard British or American accent to an accent which diverges widely from such standards both in segmental and nonsegmental (intonational, rhythmical) ways (Crystal, 1996).

For example, within a few lines from less than half-a-minute of Malaysian conversation, we can extract the following utterances (for the original conversation, see Baskaran, 1994). At the top of the list is a sentence which could be called Standard Colloquial English; below it are other sentences which show increasing degrees of departure from this norm, grammatically and lexically. At the bottom is a sentence (in this English dialogue) which is entirely Colloquial Malay.

> *Standard colloquial English*
> Might as well go window-shopping a bit, at least.
> *Grammatical hybrids*
> My case going to be adjourned anyway.
>   [auxiliary verb omitted]
> Okay, okay, at about twelve, can or not?

[distinctive tag question in English]

You were saying you wanted to go shopping,
    nak perga tak? [addition and tag question in Malay 'Want to go, not?']

Can lah, no problem one! ['I can'; *lah* is an emphatic particle]

Lexical hybrids

No chance to ronda otherwise. [Malay 'loaf']

You were saying, that day, you wanted to beli some barang-barang. [Malay 'buy . . . things']

But if anything to do with their stuff – golf or snooker or whatever, then dia pun boleh sabar one. [Malay 'he too can be patient']

Colloquial Malay

Betul juga. ['True also']

Continua of this kind have long been recognized in creole language studies. What is novel, as McArthur points out, is the way phenomena of this kind have become so widespread, happening simultaneously in communities all over the world. After reviewing several speech situations, he concludes (p. 22):

> Worldwide communication centres on Standard English, which however radiates out into many kinds of English and many other languages, producing clarity here, confusion there, and novelties and nonsenses everywhere. The result can be – often is – chaotic, but despite the blurred edges, this latter-day Babel manages to work.

[. . .]

Hybridization has been a feature of English since Anglo-Saxon times. Any history of English shows that the language has always been something of a 'vacuum-cleaner', sucking in words and expressions from the other languages with which it has come into contact. . . . But today, with more contact being made with other languages than ever before, the scale of the borrowing is much greater than it has been in the past. A wider range of languages is involved: there are over 350 modern languages listed in the etymology files of the *Oxford English Dictionary*. And the borrowing is now found in all varieties of English, and not just in the more academic or professional domains.

Novel developments

Linguistic change has in store for us many novel kinds of hybrid. Consider, for example, the situation which is appearing with increasing frequency around the world in regions where there are high immigration or 'guestworker' populations. A man and a woman from different first-language backgrounds meet, fall in love, and get married, using the English they learned as a foreign or second language as their only lingua franca. They then have a baby, who learns from them – what, exactly? The child will hear English as a foreign language from its parents, but will learn this as its mother tongue. What form will this take? Will there be a linguistic growth analogous to that which takes place when a pidgin becomes a creole – though beginning, one imagines, at a much more advanced level of structural development? What kind of English will be the outcome? We are faced with the notion of foreign-language (or second-language) English as a mother tongue. Our nice models of World English – for example, in terms of concentric circles – will need some radical overhaul to cope with this.

Or, to take another example: the corridors of power in such multinational settings as Brussels. Although several languages are co-official in the European Union, pragmatic linguistic realities result in English being the most widely used language in these corridors. But what kind of common English emerges, when Germans, French, Greeks, and others come into contact, each using English with its own pattern of interference from the mother tongue? There will be the usual sociolinguistic accommodation, and the result will be a novel variety of 'Euro-English' – a term which has been used for over a decade with reference to the distinctive vocabulary of the Union (with its *Eurofighters, Eurodollars, Euro-sceptics,* and so on: for a few recent examples using the *Euro*-prefix, see Knowles (1997); for earlier examples, Mort (1986)), but which must now be extended to include the various hybrid accents, grammatical constructions, and discourse patterns encountered there.

On several occasions, English-as-a-first-language politicians, diplomats, and civil servants working in Brussels have told me how they have felt their own English being pulled in the direction of these foreign-language patterns. A common feature, evidently, is to accommodate to an increasingly syllable-timed rhythm. Others include the use of simplified sentence constructions, and the avoidance of idioms and colloquial vocabulary, a slower rate of speech, and the use of clearer patterns of articulation (avoiding some of the assimilations and elisions which would be natural in a first-language setting). It is important to stress that this is not the 'foreigner talk' reported in an earlier ELT era. My British informants (I have no information on what their US counterparts do) were not 'talking down' to their colleagues, or consciously adopting simpler expressions: this was unconscious accommodation, which they were able to reflect upon only after considerable probing on my part.

WSPE and WSSE

A philosophy of diversity, recognizing the importance of hybridization, does not exclude the notion of a standard, of course. This is a point which the oversimplifying prescriptive pundits of the world consistently get wrong: in honeyed tones, they think that a focus on diversity must mean a dismissing of standards. On the contrary: the need to maintain international intelligibility demands the recognition of a standard variety of English, at the same time as the need to maintain local identity demands the recognition of local varieties of English. My fundamental principle is that we need both in a linguistically healthy world. And our theoretical as well as pedagogical models need to allow for the complementarity of these two functions of language.

There are two complications which we need to anticipate. First, the emergence of new varieties is very likely going to increase the pace of change in what counts as standard usage. It would be surprising if, at least at a spoken level, the trends which we see taking place simultaneously all over the English-speaking world did not at some point merge, like separate drops of oil, to produce an appreciable normative shift. What long-term chance has the tag question got, for example, in its full array of grammatical concord, faced with the simplifying tendencies which can be heard everywhere – and which have their ana- logues in such first-language contexts as Estuary English (*right?*) or Anglo-Welsh English (*te?*). Would you place good euros on the long-term survival of interdental fricatives in standard English, in a world where there will be five times as many English speakers for whom *th* is a pain as those for whom it is a blessing?

The second complication is that we seem to be moving towards a global situation in which English speakers will have to operate with *two* levels of spoken standard. This is not something which people have had to cope with before. Standard English, as it currently exists, is a global reality only with reference to the written language: it might more accurately be called World Standard Printed English (WSPE). The comparison of international written varieties in *The Cambridge Encyclopedia of the English Language* (Crystal, 1995: 300ff.) showed WSPE to be pretty well the same wherever it is encountered. This is what one would expect. That is what a standard is for. It would not be able to fulfil its role as an international (written) lingua franca if it were riddled with regional idiosyncrasies. And, apart from a few instances of literature and humour involving the representation of regional dialect, and the occasional US/UK spelling variation, WSPE has no regional manifestations.

But if a spoken equivalent to WSPE develops – World Standard Spoken English (WSSE), as I have elsewhere called it (Crystal, 1997), a regionally neutral international spoken standard, acting as a stabilizing force on global spoken diversity – this situation will change. I have drawn attention to its emergence elsewhere (Crystal 1998), having encountered international gatherings where people are using English as their spoken lingua franca, while trying to avoid the idiosyncrasies associated with national varieties of expression. At one international seminar, for example, a casual use of a baseball idiom (*out in left field*) by an American led to the temporary disruption of the meeting (as non-Americans debated what it meant) and resulted in the self-conscious side-stepping of further regional expressions by all the participants. It might not have gone that way, of course. On another occasion, the participants might have decided to adopt the US idiom – using it back to the American, and – by definition – turning what was an Americanism into a global usage. That has been the predominant practice in the past. Whether WSSE will prove to be predominantly American in its historical origins, in the long term, or whether other varieties from around the world will 'gang up' on American English, swamping it by weight of numbers, is currently unclear. But some sort of WSSE, I have no doubt, will emerge.

An international norm

Whatever the eventual character of WSSE, it will occupy a world which, as far as its use of English as a spoken lingua franca is concerned, will be a multidialectal one. Many of us will have three dialects at our disposal, and – unlike the WSPE situation – two of these will have status as educated standards. Using myself as an example, I already have my original Welsh/ Scouse mix functioning as a marker of local identity, and my educated (Standard) British English functioning both as a means of national communication within Britain and as a marker of national identity outside. The scenario I have outlined suggests that one day there will additionally be an international standard of spoken English, to be used as a means of international communication in an increasingly diversified world (as well as, possibly, a marker of Earthly identity, once we have a community presence on other planets). In further due course, the different kinds of standard may evolve their written equivalents, and we will end up with two educated standards in writing as well. To call this situation a kind of diglossia (or triglossia) is probably not too misleading, although the kind of functional distinctions involved are not really the same as the 'High' vs 'Low' functionality seen in the case of such languages as Greek or Arabic. It anticipates a day when learners will have to adapt their British Standard English to an international norm – or perhaps vice versa, learning an international norm first, and modifying it to British (or US, etc.)

English. The situation may not be unlike the kinds of shift which learners have to make these days when they visit Britain, and find that the Standard British English they have been taught needs adaptation if it is to work to best effect in, say, Scotland or in Wales. But a world in which there are two educated standards of spoken English seems inevitable.

Part 2   Teaching matters

Much of the evidence presented in this paper is anecdotal. It can do little more than provide motivation for hypotheses. There is a real need for empirical research into these hybrid language situations. But it is plain that the emergence of hybrid trends and varieties raises all kinds of theoretical and pedagogical questions:

- They blur the long-standing distinctions between 'first', 'second' and 'foreign' language.
- They make us reconsider the notion of 'standard', especially when we find such hybrids being used confidently and fluently by groups of people who have education and influence in their own regional setting.
- They present the traditionally clear-cut notion of 'translation' with all kinds of fresh problems, for (to go back to the Malaysian example) at what point in a conversation should we say that a notion of translation is relevant, as we move from 'understanding' to 'understanding most of the utterance precisely' to 'understanding little of the utterance precisely ("getting the drift" or "gist")' to 'understanding none of the utterance, despite its containing several features of English'?
- And, to move into the sociolinguistic dimension, hybrids give us new challenges in relation to language attitudes: for example, at what point would our insistence on the need for translation cause an adverse reaction from the participants, who might maintain they are 'speaking English', even though we cannot understand them?

Towards a new pedagogy

'O brave new world, That has such people in't.' Miranda's exclamation (from *The Tempest*, V. i. 88) is apposite. It is a brave new world, indeed; and those who have to be bravest of all are the teachers of English. I am never sure whether to call language teaching or translating the most difficult of all the language tasks; both are undeniably highly demanding and professional activities (and it is one of the world's greatest scandals that such professions can be so badly paid). But in a world where traditional models and values are changing so rapidly, the task facing the teacher, in particular, is immense. Keeping abreast of all that is taking place is a nightmare in itself. Deciding what to teach, given the proliferation of new and competing models, requires metaphors which go beyond nightmares. Is there any consensus emerging about what a teacher should do in such circumstances?

My impression, as I travel around and listen to people reporting on their experiences, is that this situation – one of rapid linguistic transition – is demanding an increased recognition of the fundamental importance of distinguishing between production and reception skills in language teaching.

From a production point of view, there is a strong case for pedagogical conservatism. If one is used to teaching Standard English and an RP (received pronunciation) accent, this argument goes, then one should continue to do so, for a whole range of familiar reasons – the linguistic knowledge base is there in the various analyses and descriptions, there are copious course-books and materials, and there is a well-understood correspondence between the norms of spoken and written expression (important for examination purposes as well as for reading literature). In short, there is a general familiarity with this variety which must breed a modicum of content.

But from the viewpoint of listening comprehension, there is an equally strong case for pedagogical innovation. It is a fact that RP is changing (to be precise, continuing to change), and that many forms of 'regionally modified RP' are now to be heard among educated people in Britain and abroad. It is a fact that several regional accents (e.g. Edinburgh Scots, Yorkshire) are now more prestigious than they used to be, and are being used in settings which would have been inconceivable twenty years ago – such as by presenters on radio and television, or by switchboard operators in the rapidly growing domain of telemarketing. . . . It is a fact that new regional first-language standards, in dialect as well as accent, are emerging in such countries as Australia and South Africa.

It is a fact that new regional second-language standards are emerging in such areas as West Africa and the subcontinent of India though less obvious how far these are country-restricted: see Crystal (1995: 358ff.). And it is a fact that there are new hybrids emerging in foreign-language contexts all over the English-speaking world.

Flexibility and variety

If this is the case, teachers need to prepare their students for a world of staggering linguistic diversity. Somehow, they need to expose them to as many varieties of English as possible, especially those which they are most likely to encounter in their own locale. And above all, teachers need to develop a truly flexible attitude towards principles of usage. The absolutist concept of 'proper English' or 'correct English', which is so widespread, needs to be replaced by relativistic models in which literary and educated norms are seen to maintain their place alongside other norms, some of which depart radically from what was once recognized as 'correct'.

Yes, familiarity breeds content – but also contempt, when it fails to keep pace with social realities. All over the world there are people losing patience with what they perceive to be an irrational traditionalism. You will all have your own stories of the uncertainties and embarrassments generated when accepted local usages come into conflict with traditional standards. While there are still some parts of the world where there is a reverential attitude towards British English in general, and RP in particular, this attitude is rapidly being replaced by a dynamic pragmatism. If people in a country increasingly observe their own high-ranking, highly educated people using hybrid forms, if they increasingly hear linguistic diversity on the World Service of the BBC and other channels, if they find themselves being taught by mother-tongue speakers who themselves reflect current trends in their regionally tinged speech, then who can blame them if they begin to be critical of teaching perspectives which reflect nothing but a parochial past?

The new reality

[. . .]

The emphasis has got to move away from 'British English' or, at least, to a revised concept of British English which has variety at the core. For what is British English today? The spoken British English of Britain is already a mass of hybrid forms, with Celtic and immigrant language backgrounds a major presence. Accent variation is always the clearest index of diversity, because it is a symbol of identity: What we might call 'classical' RP (as described by Gimson *et al.*) is probably down to about 2 per cent of the population now; and modified forms of RP are increasingly the norm, and regional accents, as we have seen, are increasingly accepted in educated contexts which would have rejected them a generation ago.

If you want to hear good classical RP spoken by whole communities, you will more likely find it in Moscow or Copenhagen than in Manchester or Reading. In Britain itself, diversity is the reality. 'Real Britannia: What Does it Mean to be British?' shouts a headline in the *Independent* earlier this week, and the author Suzanne Moore comments, towards the end of a piece in which 'a nation in search of an identity' is the theme:

> The question, then, is how do we create a modern version of Britishness that is inclusive rather than exclusive, that is based in the present rather than in the past, that is urban rather than rural, that is genuinely multicultural, that does not reside in 'middle England' but amongst a society of hybrids and mongrels.

Linguistic diversity and language health

Our linguistic past has been shaped by recognizing the value of linguistic diversity; and I believe the same should be true for our linguistic future. ELT policy-making, accordingly, should make diversity its central principle – removing it from the periphery to which it has hitherto largely been assigned. No country has dared do this yet. . . . But to do so may make many feel uncomfortable. . . .

Even a statement recognizing the value of competing linguistic standards is too much for some. I was a member of the panel which discussed English language issues at the British Council's launch of David Graddol's book *The Future of English?* (1997), and I hinted at this view in a contribution I made there. Afterwards, at the buffet, someone came up and asked me if my notion of linguistic tolerance of English diversity extended to such things as the errors foreigners made. I said it all depended on what you mean by an error. *I am knowing*, for example, is not allowed in traditional Standard English, but it is normal in some parts of the world, such as the Indian subcontinent (and also, incidentally, in some British dialects). Would you correct a Frenchman who said *I am knowing*, then, he asked? It all depends, I said. Not if he was learning Indian English. My interlocutor's face told me that the concept of a Frenchman wanting to learn Indian English was, at the very least, novel.

There was a pause. Then he said, 'Are you saying that, in the British Council, we should be letting our teachers teach Indian English, and not British English?'

'If the occasion warranted it, yes,' I said.

'I don't like the sound of that,' he said, and he literally fled from me, upsetting a glass of wine in the process. He didn't hear me add: 'Or even other languages.'

For in some parts of the world, the wisest advice would be to recommend that we divert some of our resources to maintaining the life of minority languages. Identity and intelligibility are both needed for a healthy linguistic life. And the responsibility of doing something to try to minimize the ongoing damage to the world's ecolinguistic environment – with a language dying somewhere in the world, on average, every fortnight or so – belongs to everyone, whether they are ELT specialists or not.

A change in mindset

There is indeed a radical change of mindset here. To go back to the example of RP. Even abroad, the many cases of successfully acquired RP – where the influence of the mother-tongue is negligibly present in a person's speech – are far outnumbered, these days, by the cases where the RP is being filtered through an overlay of local segmental phonology and syllable-timed prosody.

This overlay, as we all know, can be so dominant that it can make a person's speech unintelligible to outsiders. And here we face the crux of the matter. If we observe a group of well-educated people from Ghana, or India, or Japan, talking happily together in their country in English, and we find we can understand little of it, what are we to say? Are we to blame the teaching methods, the educational system, the motivation of the learners? Do we continue trying to make their speech improve towards the standard British model (or US, or Australian, or whatever model we are using)? Or do we recognize the possibility that here we may have a new variety of English which has achieved some viability? If this happened in Britain – we arrive in a Glasgow pub, shall we say, and find we are unable to follow the speech of a group at the next table – do we turn to them with a beatific ELT smile, and ask them to speak more clearly? We all know what is likely to happen.

The assumption, of course, is that if my Glaswegian group were to achieve higher levels of education, their speech would in the process become more diglossic – they would acquire a more standard kind of spoken English, alongside their original dialect. But in the Ghanaian type of case, the higher levels of education are *already* present in the speakers. Any motivation to change must therefore come from their felt need to make themselves understood to outsiders: if – to put it succinctly – they need us more than we need them, then there is such a motivation – and this has traditionally been the case, with the centre of economic and political power lying outside their country.

But we know from the predictions of David Graddol and others that power centres are ever-changing – and in fifty years' time, who knows whether we will not want them more than they want us? In which case, maybe we will have to take pains to accommodate to their dialect (or, of course, language), if we want to make inroads into their markets. It will never be a simple question of code-switching – I chose the word 'accommodation' carefully. There will, I imagine, be give and take on both sides. Trade – whether in products or ideas – is a double-sided notion. But we need to begin now thinking about how such scenarios of mutual respect would relate to our current teaching models and policies. At present I do not think they do at all. I am quite sure that most people still feel that, in the Ghanaian-type case, there is blame to be assigned; that the teaching has been unsuccessful.

'Best practice' in a new century

I am aware that this kind of talk is controversial, but we have to address these issues. They will not go away. We cannot stick our heads into the sand, and pretend they are not there. Everywhere is in the same boat. Or, to be more accurate, they are all in their own boats, each taking on board the waters of diversification and hybridization at its own rate.

American English, with over 350 significant foreign language inputs (according to the last census), is at a particularly waterlogged stage, with over a million people now panicking for the *US English* lifeboat (Crystal, 1997: Ch. 5); the past decade has seen unprecedented amounts of water slopping into the Australian English boat; and other first-language areas are beginning to find the waters choppy. So indeed are second-language areas. There is no longer (if there ever was) a nice, neat variety called Singapore English. The only reason we ever got the opposite impression is that, when linguists first began to describe these new Englishes, they were working with individual informants, and their descriptions inevitably presented a monolithic picture. As the linguistic viewpoint widens, following more empirical research, diversity gradually comes into focus.

In my view, the chief task facing ELT is how to devise pedagogical policies and practices in which the need to maintain an international standard of intelligibility, in both speech and writing, can be made to comfortably exist alongside the need to recognize the importance of international diversity, as a reflection of identity, chiefly in speech and eventually perhaps also in writing.

English (as opposed to French, Spanish, etc.) language teaching is in the best position to do this. We have an advantage in that our language has been coping with diversity for centuries. It is difficult to talk about languages as *langues* (as collective community aware-nesses); but the vacuum-cleaner analogy I used earlier gives a hint about one feature of the English language which must somehow be present in the subconscious of each of us – a readiness to assimilate new forms. It is a thousand years since the publication of the first ELT conversation – the *Colloquy* of Aelfric, in *c*. 1000 – and already by that stage English had readily borrowed hundreds of words from other languages, chiefly Latin and Norse. This readiness has been with us ever since. It is a readiness which is conspicuously lacking in, say, the modern French *langue* – at least, as it has developed over the past 200 years. But English has it strongly – and perhaps this feature has been an element in its global growth. As has often been observed, people who have learned English as a foreign language have been known to comment on the way in which they were helped by the presence in English of words which they already recognized as deriving from their own.

Any move to a new mindset is never easy, and some will not wish to make it, for old habits die hard. We should perhaps bring to mind the wise words of Igor Stravinsky, in his *Poetics of Music* (Ch. 5): 'A renewal is fruitful only when it goes hand in hand with tradition.' But there is no doubt in my mind that the concept of 'best practice' for the next century will need to be grounded in a dynamic linguistic relativism, recognizing as axiomatic the notions of variation and change. This is the chief challenge facing ELT specialists.

References

Baskaran, Loga. 1994. 'The Malaysian English mosaic.' In *ET* 37, 27–32.

Crystal, David. 1995. *The Cambridge Encyclopedia of the English Language*. Cambridge: University Press.

——. 1996. 'The past, present and future of English rhythm.' In M. Vaughan-Rees, *Changes in Pronunciation*, Summer 1996 issue of the Newsletter of the IATEFL Pronunciation Special Interest Group, 8–13. Whitstable: IATEFL.

——. 1997. *English as a Global Language*. Cambridge: University Press.

——. 1998. 'The future of English: where unity and diversity meet.' Keynote address to TESOL Arabia, Al Ayn, March.

Graddol, David. 1997. *The Future of English*. London: The British Council.

Knowles, Elizabeth, ed. 1997. *The Oxford Dictionary of New Words*. Oxford: University Press.

McArthur, Tom. 1998. *The English Languages*. Cambridge: University Press.

Moore, Suzanne. 1998. 'Real Britannia: what does it mean to be British?' In the *Independent* (*Monday Review*), 20 July.

Mort, Simon. ed. 1986. *Longman Guardian New Words*. London: Longman.

Rosen, Barbara. 1994. 'Is English really a family of languages?' In the *International Herald Tribune*, 15 October.

Chapter 5

Vijay K. Bhatia

THE POWER AND POLITICS OF GENRE

Introduction

ALL DISCOURSE FORMS, especially those used in institutionalized contexts, are socially negotiated. At the very heart of most frameworks for the analysis of discourse, especially as genre, is the belief that there is nothing like a universal form of discourse for structuring knowledge. There can only be a 'consensus or an agreement' (Bruffee, 1986: 777) among the members of specific disciplinary communities to express their concerns in specific discursive forms. Most institutionalized forms of discourse, therefore, are socially constructed, interpreted and used. Goodrich (1987) explains this institutionalization of discoursal practices in terms of 'social authorship' as against the more familiar subjective authorship.

> The right to a discourse is organized and restricted by a wide variety of means, to particular roles, statuses, professions and so on. Similarly the institutionalisation of discourse is limited in terms of its legitimate appropriation, and the restrictive situations of its reception – church, court, school, hustings and so on.

[. . .]

Like other forms of discourse, genres are also socially constructed and are even more intimately controlled by social practices. Genres are the media through which members of professional or academic communities communicate with each other. They are, as Berkenkotter and Huckin (1995) point out, 'intimately linked to a discipline's methodology, and they package information in ways that conform to a discipline's norms, values and ideology.' Myers (1995: 5) also points out,

> Disciplines are like cultures in that their members have shared, taken for granted beliefs; these beliefs can be mutually incomprehensible between cultures; these beliefs are encoded in a language; they are embodied in practices; new members are brought into culture through rituals.

The consensus is arrived at and negotiated through professional conversations and practices amongst the informed and practising members of a professional community. Interactions and conversations enable consensus, on the one hand, and have a regulatory or limiting effect on the other, as to what should or should not be admitted into a community's body of knowledge. Genres, in other words, are socially authorized through conventions, which, in turn, are embedded in the discursive practices of members of specific disciplinary cultures. These discursive practices, to a large extent, reflect not only conventions used by specific disciplinary communities, but also social conventions, including social changes, social institutions and social knowledge, all of which, in a way, could be seen as significantly contributing to what in genre theory is regarded as 'genre knowledge'. Genres, in whatever manner one may identify them, whether as a *typification of rhetorical action* (as in Miller (1984), and more recently, Berkenkotter and Huckin (1995)) as a *staged, goal-oriented social process* (as in Martin (1993)), or as *shared communicative purposes* (as in Swales (1990) and Bhatia (1993)), are products of an understanding or a prior knowledge of generic conventions. These generic conventions are responsible for regulating generic constructs, giving them internal ordering, which in discourse literature, for various reasons, has been given different names, some of which include discourse structuring, staging of discourse and generic structure potential (GSP).

Complexity of generic forms

Although generic forms are products of conventional knowledge embedded in disciplinary cultures, they are dynamic constructs. Typical realizations of these institutionalized forms are often characterized by their generic integrity, on the one hand, and their propensity for innovation, on the other (see Bhatia, 1993, 1995). These two aspects of genre may appear to be somewhat contradictory at first, but as we shall soon discover, these two characteristics are complementary to each other. In fact, it will not be inaccurate to suggest that one is, in a way, an essential prerequisite to the other. Generic integrity is the product of the conventional features of a specific generic construct. Although these conventions are embedded in the rhetorical context, they often constrain the use of linguistic resources (lexico-grammatical as well as discoursal), and are frequently invoked to arrive at a reasonable interpretation of the genre or even determine the choice of the genre to suit a particular context. Within generic boundaries, experienced users of genre often manage to exercise considerable freedom to manipulate generic conventions to respond to novel situations, to mix what Bhatia (1993) calls 'private intentions' with socially recognized communicative purposes, and even to produce new forms of discourse. Therefore the tension between conformity and creativity, so often made an issue of in applied discourse studies, is not necessarily real. As Dubrow (1982: 39) points out, 'a concern for generic traditions, far from precluding originality, often helps to produce it.' . . . In fact, a subtle exploitation of a certain aspect of generic construct is always seen as tactically superior and effective. It is almost like the advertiser's exploitation of the cliché *the shape of things to come* in the following opening headline of an advertisement for a car.

The shape of things to come: Mitsubishi Cordia

Or, the use of the famous statement about the British colonial empire in the Lufthansa advertisement, *The sun never sets on Lufthansa territory*, or in the following slogan for energy conservation, which says, *Don't be fuelish*, where the whole idea of waste of energy is lost unless it is associated with 'Don't be foolish'. The whole point about such associations is that they communicate best in the context of what is already familiar. In such contexts, words on their own carry no meanings; it is the experience which gives them the desired effect. Therefore, if one is not familiar with the original, the value of the novel expression is undermined. Just as the advertiser makes use of the well-known and the familiar in existing knowledge, a clever genre writer makes use of what is conventionally available to a discourse community to further his or her own subtle ends. The innovation, the creativity or the exploitation becomes effective only in the context of the already available and familiar. The main focus of this paper is on these two interrelated aspects of genre theory, i.e. the constraints on generic construction, a pre-knowledge of which gives power to insiders in specific discourse communities, and the exploitation of this power by experienced and expert members of such disciplinary cultures to achieve their 'private intentions' within 'socially recognized communicative purposes'.

Organizational preferences and generic controls

The other interesting area of generic variation, although within a restricted range, one finds in organizational preferences. In the case of academic publications, we often come across what we commonly refer to as housestyles. Although every single journal claims to have its own style sheet, most of them can be characterized more by their overlap rather than variation.

Similarly, in the case of newspaper genres, especially the news reports and the editorials, we find an unmistakable 'generic identity' (Bhatia, 1993) in almost all of the exploits of these genres from various newspapers, although all of them have their own preferences in terms of style, stance and substance. Some may be more objective, while others more interpretative; some more socially responsible, while others more sensational. In spite of all these differences, most of them display common characteristics in terms of their use of generic resources, in terms of their structure, interpretation and communication of intentions. These somewhat different orientations to the events of the day do not make their stories very different in terms of their generic form.

Even in the case of business communities, we often find different organizations displaying their unique identities through their organizational preferences in the matters of their choice of generic forms, but the broad range of genres they tend to exploit to further their organizational objectives show remarkable similarities rather than differences. All these areas of generic use indicate that although their preferred generic forms show a subtle degree of variation for what could be seen as 'tactical advantage', they never disregard some of the basic features of individual generic constructs, which give these genres their essential identities.

The power of genre

There is no better illustration of the saying 'knowledge is power' than the one in the case of generic power. Power to use, interpret, exploit and innovate novel generic forms is the function of generic knowledge which is accessible only to the members of disciplinary communities.

How do these disciplinary communities maintain what we have called generic integrity in their discursive practices? Let us look at this phenomenon by looking at the academic community.

Maintaining generic integrity: editorial intervention

In some forms of academic discourse, especially the research articles, one can see generally two kinds of mechanism in place to ensure generic integrity: the peer review process, and editorial intervention. Both these mechanisms, though operating at different levels, are actively invoked to ensure that all accounts of new knowledge conform to the standards of institutionalized behaviour that is expected by a community of established peers in a specific discipline. Although individual judgements can vary within the membership of specific disciplinary communities, a high degree of consensus is often ensured by selecting like-minded scholars from within well-defined disciplinary boundaries.

[. . .]

After peer review, the second most important intervention comes from the editors, who enjoy all the power one can imagine to maintain the identity and integrity of the research article genre. Berkenkotter and Huckin (1995) document an in-depth and fascinating study of this kind of editorial control to maintain generic integrity. They point out that for the construction and dissemination of knowledge 'textual activity' is as important as 'scientific activity'.

Generic conventions as authority: the case of citations and references

The power of genre is nowhere better illustrated than in the publication of research articles. Swales in his research report *Aspects of Research Article Introductions* (1981) was the first one to point out the importance of the description of previous research on the rhetorical activity of knowledge dissemination as distinct from knowledge creation. In order to become acceptable to the specialist community of fellow researchers, one must relate his or her knowledge claims to the accumulated knowledge of the discipline, without which his or her claims in the field are unlikely to find recognition through publication. In this context it is hardly surprising that the literature review occupies an important place in the researcher's repertoire of skills in most academic disciplines. Referring to the importance of citation in scientific research activity, Amsterdamska and Leydesdorff (1989: 451) point out,

> In a scientific article 'the new encounters the old' for the first time. This encounter has a double significance since articles not only justify the new by showing that the result is warranted by experiment or observation or previous theory, but also place and integrate innovations into the context of 'old' and accepted knowledge. . . . References which appear in the text are the most explicit manner in which the arguments presented in the article are portrayed as linked to other texts, and thus also to [a] particular body of knowledge.

Power to innovate (mixing and embedding)

Although the pressure for the 'democratisation' (Fairclough, 1992) of discourse is becoming increasingly intense in some countries, especially in the USA, it is unlikely to make a significant dent in the so-called integrity of professional genres, at least not in the foreseeable future. However, one can see an increasing 'fragmentation of discursive norms and conventions' (Fairclough, 1992: 221), often leading to genre-mixing and embedding . . . on the one hand, and creation of new genres, on the other. To a large extent, these changes in discursive practices are making professional genres increasingly dynamic and complex.

The dynamic complexity of academic and professional communication is further increased by the role of multimedia, the explosion of information technology, the multi-disciplinary contexts of the world of work, the increasingly competitive professional environment, and above all, the overwhelmingly compulsive nature of promotional and advertising activities, so much so that our present-day world of work is being increasingly identified as a 'consumer culture' (Featherstone, 1991). The inevitable result of this is that many of the institutionalized genres, whether they are social, professional or academic, are seen as incorporating elements of promotion. . . . Referring to such changes in discourse practices, Fairclough (1993: 141) points out,

> there is an extensive restructuring of boundaries between orders of discourse and between discursive practices, for example, the genre of consumer advertising has been colonising professional and public service orders of discourse on a massive scale, generating many new hybrid partly promotional genres.

As an instance of such a hybrid genre, Fairclough (1993) discusses the case of contemporary university prospectuses, where he highlights an increasing tendency towards marketization of the discursive practices of British universities. Bhatia (1995), in his discussion of genre-mixing in professional discourse, gives examples from several settings, where genre-mixing and embedding is becoming increasingly common. He also mentions several instances where one may find an increasing use of promotional strategies in genres which are traditionally considered non-promotional in intent, especially academic introductions, including book introductions, forewords, prefaces of various kinds, which are becoming increasingly difficult to distinguish from publishers' blurbs.

Shared knowledge – privileged access / insider information

If generic conventions, on the one hand, give suitable expression to the communicative intentions of genre writers (who are members of a particular discourse community), on the other hand, they also match their intentions against their intended reader's expectations. This is possible only when all the participants share, not only the code, but also the knowledge of the genre, which includes the knowledge of its construction, interpretation and use. A necessary implication of this shared genre knowledge is that it is not routinely available to the outsiders, which creates a kind of social distance between the legitimate members of a discourse community and those who are considered outsiders. Although this creates conditions of homogeneity between the insiders, at the same time it also increases social distance between them and the outsiders, sometimes resulting in disastrous consequences for the one who does not have access to such shared knowledge. This shared knowledge could be in the form of linguistic resources used to construct a generic form, or it could be in the awareness of the rules of language use, some of which are socially learnt, as the ones associated with classroom discourse and academic genres, while others can be legally enforced, such as the ones associated with courtroom procedures. Allen and Guy (1989), based on a personal communication from Worthington (1984: personal communication), report an excellent example of the lack of shared knowledge from the account of the courtroom interaction.

An off-duty policeman in a store had shot and killed an intruder. Investigation had shown a set of burglar tools at the back of the store. The prosecutor was trying to show that there was no ground for presuming criminal intent, and that this was cold-blooded murder. The victim's wife was testifying for the prosecution. Here she is being cross-examined by the defense.

Defense Lawyer: Could you tell the court and the jury what your husband's occupation was?
Wife: He was a burglar.

This supported the defense's contention of criminal intent, and secured acquittal for the policeman.

If the wife had been slightly more familiar with the conventions of the courtroom examination, the task of the defence lawyer would not have become that easy.

Another example of the use of insider information to get access to information can be illustrated by the following headline from an advertisement for 'The Schroder Singapore Trust,' which reads,

The Schroder Singapore Trust Has Grown Over 60% In 3 Years

The information being given here can be extremely misleading, except to those who are well aware of the discursive practices of the professional community of financial managers. Anybody trying to make sense of this statement should know that this 60 per cent growth in three years on its face value could be misleading, to say the least. Although it carries the usual statutory disclaimer in the form of a note in small print saying, 'Past performance is not necessarily a guide to future performance, the price of units may fall as well as rise and cannot be guaranteed', a lay person might still be led to think that his investment will probably get him close to a 60 per cent return. The fact, on the other hand, could be that the unit value might have declined by 100 per cent in the past one year or so, and may still be showing the downward trend at the time of the advertisement. There could be several other possible scenarios which will be accessible only to those with inside knowledge of the way these genres function.

Maintaining solidarity within a professional community

One of the most noticeable characteristics of any professional or academic discourse community is the availability and typical use of a range of appropriate genres, which their members think serve the goals of their community. The recurrent use of such discoursal forms create solidarity within its membership giving them their most powerful weapon to keep the outsiders at a safe distance. Hudson (1979: 1) rightly claims, 'If one wished to kill a profession, to remove its cohesion and its strength, the most effective way would be to forbid the use of its characteristic language.' In this context, it is hardly surprising that most of the attempts by the powerful reformist lobbies in many Western democracies to introduce plain English in legislative contexts are seen as an imposition from outside and have been firmly rejected by the professional legal community.

The main purpose of legislation, as Bhatia (1993) points out, is to govern the behaviour of individuals and institutions in society through the use of rules and regulations. In order to keep control firmly in the hands of the legislature rather than the judiciary in a parliamentary democracy, statutory acts are written not only clearly, precisely and unambiguously but all-inclusively too. This rigour and adequate specification of scope in legislation helps the legislature to control a totally subjective and idiosyncratic interpretation of the statute book.

All attempts to reform legislative language, including those by the plain English campaign (see Thomas, 1985; Eagleson, 1988; Kelly, 1988), have to a large extent met with very limited success, for the simple reason that they are seen as a transgression of the generic integrity of the whole tradition in the legislative process. Although the plain English movement has been quite effective in influencing the redrafting of general commercial and administrative documents, including insurance policies, residential leases, tax return forms, social benefit claim forms and other papers for better *accessibility* and *usability* by a larger section of society, when it comes to legislative provisions, it has not been able to soften the attitude of the parliamentary draftsmen significantly in many of the Commonwealth countries. The other argument for the preservation of these generic characteristics of legislative discourse is that the real legislative power in all parliamentary democracies must rest with the legislature and not with the judiciary. This is one of the most important reasons why clarity, precision, unambiguity and all-inclusiveness are so highly prized in British legislative discourse, which gives a relatively high degree of transparency to legislative intentions.

Power and control in legislative context

Writing legislative discourse in terms of simple principles without adequate specification of the required scope, on the other hand, means giving wider powers to the judges and the courts to interpret the intentions of the legislature, which is not considered highly desirable in parliamentary democracies.

We find an excellent illustration of this point in the Basic Law drafted by the People's Republic of China. It is meant to be a mini-constitution for post-1997 Hong Kong based on the Sino-British Joint Declaration of 1978. It is written in the form of very simple principles and guidelines, a generic form, which can be seen as almost exactly the opposite of what we find in a typical legislative discourse from any of the countries of the Commonwealth. It is written in the form of basic principles on which there can hardly be any disagreement, lacking very significantly in details of all kinds. One of the important issues raised there is that of status of the laws previously in force in Hong Kong. Article 8 of the Basic Law states,

> The laws previously in force in Hong Kong, that is, the common law, rules of equity, ordinances, subordinate legislation and customary law shall be maintained, except for any that contravene this law, and subject to any amendment by the legislature of the Hong Kong special Administrative Region.

As one may see, like the other Articles of the Basic Law, this one too is expressed in terms of somewhat universal principles which are applicable to everything one could think of in the context of pre-existing legislative machinery. One may be tempted to point out that there should be no serious problem in expressing legislation in terms of general principles. There are several legal systems which adopt such a strategy. The French legislative system is a good example of this. However, problems have occurred in this context, primarily because the transition of power has still some way to go. A number of issues are still unresolved and to make it worse, all this is happening in the context where two very different systems are in operation, the most elaborate and exhaustive legislative style used in the UK and their extremely diluted plain English versions captured in the Basic Law. Every time a new ordinance is considered or promulgated in Hong Kong, it becomes a matter of fresh negotiation between the two governments.

Obviously, this generic form of writing gives maximum power to the one who has the authority to interpret it. Since the Basic Law is meant to take effect only after 1 July 1997, after the territory is handed over to China, the eventual control over its interpretation will be concentrated in the hands of the future SAR government of the PRC. However, in the intervening period leading up to the hand-over, the interpretations of many of its sections have been disputed by both sides, for the simple reason that the genre in which it is written allows maximum power to interpret it to those who have the power to do it, which for the time being is shared by the two parties.

The power and politics of genre are the two sides of the same coin. In one context, it can be seen as a legitimate force often used to maintain solidarity within a disciplinary community, whereas on the other hand, it is used to keep outsiders at a respectable distance. On the one hand, it empowers some people, the insiders, while at the same time, it tends to silence others, especially the outsiders. That is what I meant by the power and politics of genre. We have see the power of genre, let's turn to its politics now.

The politics of genre

Exploitation, innovation and manipulation of generic conventions

I have tried to present genre as a dynamic rather than a static construct. I have also tried to maintain that it has a propensity for innovation, exploitation and manipulation. I would now like to take this argument further to discuss the nature of this exploitation or manipulation and constraints on such exploitation.

Genres are dynamic constructs, even though they are essentially seen as embedded in conventions associated with typical instances of language use in social, academic or professional settings. An understanding or a prior knowledge of conventions is considered essential for its identification, construction, interpretation, use and ultimate exploitation by members of specific professional communities to achieve socially recognized goals with some degree of pragmatic success.

The nature of genre manipulation is invariably realized within the broad limits of specific genres and is often very subtle. This can only be handled within the concept of genre because such liberties, innovations, creativities, exploitations, whatever one may choose to call them, are invariably realized within rather than outside the generic boundaries. . . . The moment it becomes a free-for-all kind of activity, communication itself will become more of a problem. The reason is that the flouting of generic conventions leads to the opting out of the genre altogether and is noticed by the members of the concerned disciplinary community as being odd. Any attempt, therefore, to overlook, ignore or undermine the power of conventions at this stage can result in disastrous consequences.

Although a good understanding of genre knowledge is a prerequisite to any manipulation of generic resources, it is by no means sufficient to get such innovations and exploitations accepted in a disciplinary community. Kress (1987: 42) mentions two significant ways in which generic innovations are accepted: either they are backed by a stable social occasion or by authority.

> Unless . . . there is a change in the social structures – and in the kinds of social occasions in which texts are produced – the new generic forms are unlikely to succeed. That is why childish innovations fail; not because they do not constitute perfectly plausible solutions to particular textual/cognitive problems, but because they are supported neither by a stable social occasion, nor by 'authority.' This latter is of course the case where a writer of 'authority' creates a new generic form, which, seemingly because of the writer's authority alone, succeeds in establishing a new generic convention.

Gate-keeping function of discourse communities

Berkenkotter and Huckin (1995: 102) in their study of gate-keeping at an academic con-vention, i.e. the study of abstracts submitted for the Conference on College Composition and Communication (CCCC), discuss an interesting instance of the power of generic control in well-defined contexts. On the basis of their analysis of the process of selection of papers for the CCCC convention, they claim that:

1. The high-rated abstracts all addressed topics of current *interest to active, experienced members of the rhetoric and composition community*; the low-rated abstracts often did not.
2. Almost all of the high-rated abstracts *clearly defined a problem*; the low-rated abstracts often did not.
3. The high-rated abstracts all *discussed this problem in a way that would be seen by experienced insiders as novel and therefore interesting*, whereas virtually none of the low-rated abstracts did.
4. The high-rated abstracts usually *projected more of an insider ethos* through the use of terminology, special topoi, and/or explicit or implicit references to the scholarly literature of the field than did the low-rated abstracts.

(Emphasis added)

They also point out that often 'the genre was shaped significantly by the interests of the program chair'. This is generally done through the theme statement issued when papers are invited for the convention. Depending upon the interests of the program chair or of the discourse community he/she represents, the emphasis can shift from one year to the other. Based on their study of CCCC abstracts for four years between 1988 and 1992, they find two main levels of gate-keeping (1995: 115):

> (a) the external reviewers and (b) the program chair. We have observed many cases where the reviewers rated an abstract Excellent and yet it was not included in the

program. Presumably, the chair disagreed with the reviewers' judgements. . . . In short, each convention bears the stamp of its principal gatekeeper.

They further point out (1995: 115) that:

> In one particularly unfortunate case, a very interesting abstract was submitted to the Technical Communication area one year, where it received an Excellent rating from a reviewer and the program chair but was not included in the program (presumably because of a bad 'fit'). It was revised slightly and resubmitted the following year to the Discourse Analysis area. Again it received an Excellent rating, but again it was not included in the program. The author of this abstract probably never knew that she had written an outstanding abstract. All she would have been told was that her paper had been rejected for the program.

Another interesting case of such a gate-keeping encounter, though of a slightly different nature, between two different discourse groups was recently referred to by William Bright (1996). Giving his view of thirty years of American linguistics, he referred to the following extract from a letter written by Chomsky:

> the level of rumour-mongering and of personal hostility . . . outright falsification so scandalous that they raise serious questions about the integrity of the field . . . I do not want to be associated with a journal . . . which publishes flat lies . . . couched in rhetoric of a sort that might be appropriate to some criminal, but that one is surprised to find in a scholarly journal.

No wonder Chomsky never published in the journal, not because he was kept out, but he decided to keep himself out. Gate-keeping can obviously work both ways.

Hegemony and world Englishes – generic variation and control

Another important aspect of generic control raises the issue of hegemonic attitude to maintain generic standards, which in much of contemporary discourse and genre studies are dominated and even determined by essentially Western conventions. Although it is true that English is the most dominant and widely used global language for academic as well as professional purposes, it is no longer the sole property of any one community of people, be they English, American, Australian or any other. Like cricket, English has also become more universal not only in usage but also in its character. True to the reality of present-day variation in English, one needs to think in terms of world Englishes, rather than English as a single monolithic variety of English (for a detailed discussion and references see Kachru (1986, 1994 and 1996)). This variation in the use of English across the globe is getting increasing recognition in the sociolinguistic literature in the last decade or so; however, in some of the genres, especially used in the academia, the power to control and maintain generic standards can be, and often is, interpreted in terms of the dominant community, which undoubtedly happens to be a Western community. Anything which appears to be different from the norms set by the dominant community is viewed as deficient and in need of correction.

In some areas, genre writers have become increasingly sensitive to local knowledge, and have started constructing, interpreting and using genres in forms which display such sensitivities, especially in the case of advertising and some other business genres, where it has become an established practice now to develop local teams to act alongside the expatriates in most of the multinational advertising companies. The reason for such sensitivities is also not difficult to understand. In the case of academic genres, especially in research publications, the politics is still controlled by those who have the power. Much of the academic discourse still fails to acknowledge the sources of variations, especially those of marginality and exclusion, giving the impression that there is, or should be, no variation in the way genres are constructed, interpreted and used.

Implications for language teaching and learning

What are the implications of all this for language teaching? Applied genre analysis, unlike many other analytical frameworks, is neither static nor prescriptive. Potentially, it is dynamic and explanatory. It is for the language teacher to use it the way one would like to use it, for innovative exploitation of generic resources or for a limited exposure to standardized generic contexts. Although it is essential for the learner to be familiar with specific generic conventions associated with a particular professional setting, it is neither necessary nor desirable to restrict the experience of linguistic behaviour to just the conventionalized and standardized aspects of genre construction and use.

How can one bring in creativity in genre-based language teaching and learning? Since genre analysis gives a grounded description of linguistic behaviour in professional settings, it is possible to bring in a fair amount of creativity in language teaching by adjusting communicative purposes, the nature of participation in a particular communicative setting, the social and professional relationship between the participants taking part in a particular genre-construction exercise, and above all, by bringing in variability in the use of generic strategies to achieve the same communicative purposes.

There are two schools of thought, I should say. Those who believe in the explicit teaching of genres, especially the regularities of textual form and typifications, and others who see this as too constraining and advocate free expression. The truth, however, rests somewhere in the middle. All genres, primary as well as secondary, involve regularities and, hence, these regularities must be learnt by anyone who has even the slightest ambition of being part of any specialist disciplinary community. As Bakhtin (1986: 80) points out, 'genres must be fully mastered to be used creatively.'

However, in order to make this happen, the first prerequisite is to have an awareness of the conventional knowledge that is situated within a specific disciplinary genre or a 'system of genres'.

Bazerman (1993: viii) attempts to resolve this tension between institutionalized expression and individual expression when he points out,

> the individual learns to express the self against the compulsive society. . . . We are not ourselves because we set ourselves apart from each other. We become ourselves as we realize ourselves in relation to each other. The social is everything we do with each other and what we become as we do it. We individuate by identifying ourselves on a social landscape, a landscape we come to know as we interact with it. We discover and create ourselves and others by what we do with each other.

There are at least three things which stand out clearly from the foregoing discussion. First, language learners need to become aware of the conversations of the disciplinary community to which they aspire to be members, which could be done through 'centripetal participation in the learning curriculum of the ambient community' (Lave and Wenger, 1991: 100). Second, acquisition of genre knowledge, which leads to an understanding of generic integrity, is necessary but not sufficient for any subsequent exploitation or manipulation of generic conventions. And, finally, genre knowledge should be best viewed as a resource to exploit generic conventions to respond to recurrent and not so recurrent rhetorical situations, rather than a blueprint for replication.

References

Allen, Donald E. and Guy, Rebecca F. (1989) Non-routine conversation in operational crisis. In *Working with Language: A Multidisciplinary Consideration of Language Use in Work Contexts*, edited by Hywel Coleman. Berlin, New York: Mouton de Gruyter.

Amsterdamska, O. and Leydesdorff, L. (1989) Citations: indicators of significance? *Scientometrics*, **15**, 449–71.

Bakhtin, M. (1986) The problem of speech genres. In *Speech Genres and Other Late Essays*, edited by C. Emerson M. Holquist, trans. V. W. McGhee. Austin: University of Texas Press, pp. 60–102.

Bazerman, Charles (1993) Foreword to *Professional Communication: The Social Perspective*, edited by Nancy Roundy Blyler and Charlotte Thralls. London: Sage, pp. VII–VIII.

Berkenkotter, C. and Huckin, Thomas N. (1995) *Genre Knowledge in Disciplinary Communication – Cognition / Culture / Power*. New Jersey: Lawrence Erlbaum Associates.

Bhatia, V. K. (1993) *Analysing Genre – Language Use in Professional Settings*. London: Longman.

Bhatia, V. K. (1995) Genre-mixing and in professional communication: the case of 'private intentions' v. 'socially recognized purposes'. In *Explorations in English for Professional Communication*, edited by Paul Bruthiaux, T. Boswood and B. Bertha. Hong Kong: Department of English, City University of Hong Kong.

Bright, William (1996) The view from the editor's desk: 30 years of American Linguistics. A talk given at the City University of Hong Kong.

Bruffee, K. A. (1986) Social construction, language and the authority of knowledge: a bibliographical essay. *College Composition*, **48**, December, 730–90.

Dubrow, Heather (1982) *Genre*. London: Methuen & Co. Ltd.

Eagleson, R. D. (1988) Efficiency in legal drafting. In *Essays on Legislative Drafting: In Honour of J Q Ewens, CMG, CBE, QC*, edited by D. Kelly. Adelaide: University of Adelaide, The Adelaide Law Review Association Law School, pp. 13–27.

Fairclough, N. (1992) *Discourse and Social Change*. London: Polity.

Fairclough, N. (1993) Critical discourse analysis and the marketization of public discourse: the universities. *Discourse & Society*, **4**(2), 133–68.

Featherstone, M. (1991) *Consumer Culture and Postmodernism*. London: Sage.

Freedman, Aviva and Medway, Peter (eds) (1994) *Genre and the New Rhetoric*. London: Taylor & Francis.

Goodrich, P. (1987) *Legal Discourse*. London: Macmillan.

Hudson, Kenneth (1979) *The Jargon of the Professions*. London: Macmillan.

Kachru, Braj B. (1986) The power and politics of English. *World Englishes*, **5**(2–3), 121–40.

Kachru, Braj B. (1994) World Englishes: approaches, issues and resources. In *Readings on Second Language Acquisition*, edited by D. Brown and S. Gonzo. New York: Prentice-Hall. (An earlier version in *Language Teaching: The International Abstracting Journal of Language Teachers and Applied Linguistics*. January, 1992. Cambridge: Cambridge University Press, pp. 1–14.

Kachru, Braj B. (1996) The paradigms of marginality. *World Englishes*, **15**(3), 241–55.

Kelly, D. L. (ed.) (1988) *Essays on Legislative Drafting: In Honour of J Q Ewens, CMG, CBE, QC*. University of Adelaide, The Adelaide Law Review Association, Law School.

Kress, Gunther (1987) Genre in a social theory of language: a reply to John Dixon. In *The Place of Genre in Learning: Current Debates*, edited by I. Reid. Geelong, Australia: Deakin University Press.

Lave, J. and Wagner, E. (1991) *Situated Learning: Legitimate Peripheral Participation*. Cambridge, MA: Cambridge University Press.

Martin, J. R. (1993) *A Contextual Theory of Language. In The Powers of Literacy – A Genre Approach to Teaching Writing*. Pittsburg, PA: University of Pittsburgh Press, pp. 116–36.

Miller, C. R. (1984) Genre as social action. *Quarterly Journal of Speech*, **70**, 151–67.

Myers, Greg (1995) Disciplines, departments, and differences. In *Writing in Academic Contexts*, edited by Britt-Louise Gunnarsson and Ingegerdy Backlund. Uppsala Universitet. pp. 3–11.

Swales, John M. (1981) *Aspects of Article Introductions*. LSU Research Report. University of Aston in Birmingham.

Swales, John M. (1990) *Genre Analysis – English in Academic and Research Settings*. Cambridge: Cambridge University Press.

Thomas, R. (1985) Plain English and the law. *Statute Law Review*, **9**(3), 144.

Chapter 6

Alastair Pennycook

ENGLISH IN THE WORLD/THE WORLD IN ENGLISH

[. . .]

WHAT I WOULD LIKE TO explore in this chapter is the *worldliness* (cf. Said 1983) of English. I want to maintain the ambiguity of this term — worldliness in the sense of being in the world and worldliness in the sense of being global — and to argue that English is inextricably bound up with the world: English is in the world and the world is in English. Following Said's (1983: 35) question as to whether there is a way to deal fairly with a text without either on the one hand reducing it to its worldly circumstances or on the other leaving it as a hermetic textual cosmos, I want to ask how we can understand the relationship between the English language and its position in the world in such a way that neither reduces it to a simple correspondence with its worldly circumstances nor refuses this relationship by considering language to be a hermetic structural system unconnected to social, cultural and political concerns.

This chapter, therefore, will seek to draw relations between global inequalities and the English language. I will also be trying to work out ways of thinking about this relationship that avoid the pitfalls of structuralist determinism. I think it is of great importance in looking at questions of language, power and inequality that we examine very carefully the critical frameworks we employ. In the next sections I shall review the predominant paradigm of writing on English as an International Language (EIL) before discussing more critical work that has raised numerous questions about the global spread of English. This will be followed by a discussion of . . . how we can conceptualize the question of the world being in English, and also of how opposition to the power of English and Western discourses can be formed.

The predominant paradigm

Otto Jespersen ([1938] 1968) estimated speakers of English to have numbered 4 million in 1500, 6 million in 1600, 8.5 million in 1700, between 20 and 40 million in 1800, and between 116 and 123 million in 1900. . . . Today, rough agreement can be found on figures that put the total number of speakers of English at between 700 million and 1 billion. This figure can be divided into three roughly equal groups: native speakers of English, speakers of English as a second (or intranational) language, and speakers of English as a foreign (or international) language. It is this last group that is the hardest to estimate but clearly the fastest-growing section of world speakers of English.

[. . .]

There seems to be fairly broad agreement on the reasons for and the implications of this spread. Although perhaps not all would agree with Hindmarsh's (1978) bland optimism that "the world has opted for English, and the world knows what it wants, what will satisfy its needs" (p. 42), this view is nevertheless not too distant from the predominant view. Although few today would overtly cling to the common nineteenth-century arguments that England and the English language were superior and thus intrinsically worthy of their growing pre-eminence, the spread of English is today commonly justified by recourse to a functionalist perspective, which stresses choice and the usefulness of English, and suggests that the global spread of English is natural (although its spread was initiated by colonialism, since then it has been an accidental by-product of global forces), neutral (unlike other, local languages, English is unconnected to cultural and political issues), and beneficial (people can only benefit by gaining access to English and the world it opens up). Platt *et al.* (1984), for example, introducing the question of the "new Englishes", deal with the spread of English thus: "Many of the New Nations which were once British colonies have realised the importance of English not only as a language of commerce, science and technology but also as an international language of communication" (p. 1). Similarly, Kachru (1986: 8–9) argues that

> English does have one clear advantage, attitudinally and linguistically: it has acquired a *neutrality* in a linguistic context where native languages, dialects, and styles sometimes have acquired undesirable connotations. . . . It was originally the foreign (alien) ruler's language, but that drawback is often overshadowed by what it can do for its users. True, English is associated with a small and elite group; but it is in their role that the *neutrality* of a language becomes vital.

He goes on to suggest that "whatever the reasons for the earlier spread of English, we should now consider it a positive development in the twentieth-century world context" (p. 51).

The main issue of debate is whether efforts should be made to maintain a central standard of English or whether the different varieties of English should be acknowledged as legitimate forms in their own right. The popular view, according to Crystal (1988), is that "while all mother-tongue speakers inevitably feel a modicum of pride (and relief) that it is their language which is succeeding, there is also an element of concern, as they see what happens to the language as it spreads around the world. . . . Changes are perceived as instances of deterioration in standards" (p. 10). . . . In academic circles, the two leading figures in this debate have been Kachru (e.g. 1985) and Quirk (e.g. 1985), the former arguing, for example, that "native speakers of this language seem to have lost the exclusive prerogative to control its standardization" (p. 30), and the latter maintaining, for example, that "the existence of standards . . . is an endemic feature of our mortal condition and that people feel alienated and disorientated if a standard seems to be missing in any of these areas" (pp. 5–6).

Apart from some work on the sociological and social psychological implications of the spread of English (see Fishman *et al.* 1977), which has also suggested that English is a neutral tool of international communication, the principal focus of work on EIL has been on questions of standards or on descriptions of varieties of English. The key issues, then, as represented in Kachru's important edited volume, *The Other Tongue: English Across Cultures*, are questions of models, standards, and intelligibility (e.g., Kachru 1982a, 1982b; Nelson 1982), and descriptions of the new forms of English: Nigerian English (Bamgbose 1982), Kenyan English (Zuengler 1982), Singapore English (Richards 1982), and so on.

The view that the spread of English is natural, neutral and beneficial also seems to hold sway for many people more directly involved in English language teaching. Naysmith (1987) suggests that there is a "cosy, rather self-satisfied assumption prevalent at successive national and international conferences that ELT [English Language Teaching] is somehow a 'good' thing, a positive force by its very nature in the search for international peace and understanding" (p. 3). With the extent of the debate on the role of English in the world being between a conservative view on standards and a more liberal pluralist concept of variety, and with the primary concerns being those of intelligibility and description, most people in English language teaching have been poorly served by academic work that fails to address a far more diverse range of questions that might encourage a reassessment of our role as teachers of English in the world. It is to some of the critical work that has sought to address these issues that I shall turn in the next section.

Critical views on English in the world

What I think is sorely lacking from the predominant paradigm of investigation into English as an international language is a broad range of social, historical, cultural and political relationships. There is a failure to problematize the notion of choice and an assumption that individuals and countries are somehow free of economic, political and ideological con-straints; there is a lack of historical analysis that would raise many more questions about the supposed naturalness of the spread of English during both the colonial and neo-colonial eras; there is a view of language that suggests that it can be free of cultural and political influences and therefore neutral. . . .

As I have argued elsewhere (Pennycook 1989a, 1990), this divorce of language from broader questions has had major implications for teaching practice and research.

[. . .]

English language teachers have been poorly served by the limited analysis of EIL provided by mainstream applied linguistics. There has been little opportunity to speculate on questions other than structural varieties of English. As Phillipson (1988) suggests, the "professional training of ELT people concentrates on linguistics, psychology and education in a restricted sense. It pays little attention to international relations, development studies, theories of culture or intercultural contact, or the politics or sociology of language or education" (p. 348). . . .

Cooke (1988) has described English as a Trojan horse, arguing that it is a language of imperialism and of particular class interests. Both he and Judd (1983) draw attention to the moral and political implications of English teaching around the globe in terms of the threat it poses to indigenous languages and the role it plays as a gatekeeper to better jobs in many societies. First of all then, English poses a threat to other languages. This is what Day (1980, 1985) has called linguistic genocide. In his study of the gradual replacement of Chamorro in Guam and the North Marianas, Day (1985) concludes pessimistically that "as long as the Marianas remain under the control of the United States, the English language will continue to replace Chamorro until there are no native speakers left. This has been American policy and practice elsewhere, and there is no reason to believe that Guam and the North Marianas will be an exception" (p. 180). Although this may seem to be an extreme case, we should nevertheless acknowledge the widespread threat that English presents. If it is not posing such a threat to first languages, as a universal second language it is constantly replacing other languages in daily use and school curricula. In bilingual or multilingual societies, for example, the prevalence of English can easily lead to the disregarding of one or more other languages.

The second major issue raised here is the extent to which English functions as a gatekeeper to positions of prestige in society. With English taking up such an important position in many educational systems around the world, it has become one of the most powerful means of inclusion into or exclusion from further education, employment, or social positions. In many countries, particularly former colonies of Britain, small English-speaking elites have continued the same policies of the former colonizers, using access to English language education as a crucial distributor of social prestige and wealth. Ngugi (1985) describes his experiences in Kenya, where not only was his native language proscribed with humiliating punishments (similar punishments and proscriptions were also the norm in schools for Canada's Aboriginal peoples) but English became "*the* main determinant of a child's progress up the ladder of formal education" (p. 115):

> [N]obody could go on to wear the undergraduate red gown, no matter how brilliantly they had performed in all the papers in all other subjects, unless they had a *credit* (not even a simple pass!) in English. Thus the most coveted place in the pyramid and in the system was only available to holders of an English-language credit card. English was the official vehicle and the magic formula to colonial elitedom.

[. . .]

The extent to which English is involved in the political, educational, social and economic life of a country is clearly a result of both the historical legacy of colonialism and of the varying success of countries since independence in warding off the threats of neo-colonialism. The different roles of English and Swahili in Kenya and Tanzania, for example, need to be seen with respect to both their colonial pasts and the different educational and development policies in the two countries (Zuengler 1985). In Tanzania, Swahili has become widely used as the national and official language due in no small part to Nyerere's insistence on "education for self-reliance", a policy that emphasized the need for each stage of schooling to be complete in itself and to prepare Tanzanians to participate in the socialist development of the country. In Kenya, by contrast, although Swahili is also the official national language, English remains the dominant language of Kenya's economic and legal spheres as it is the dominant language of much schooling, especially in Nairobi, within an educational system that has sought more to prepare an elite few for higher education than to educate a citizenry capable of maintaining a policy of socialist self-reliance.

If English thus operates as a major means by which social, political and economic inequalities are maintained within many countries, it also plays a significant role as a gatekeeper for movement between countries, especially for refugees hoping to move to the English-speaking countries. In his extensive studies of the English language programmes in the Southeast Asian refugee processing centres, Tollefson (1988, 1989) has suggested that they "continue to limit refugees' improvement in English language proficiency, capacity for cultural adaptation and preemployment skills, thereby contributing to the covert goal of ensuring that most refugees will only be able to compete effectively for minimum-wage employment" (1988: 39). These programmes then, although ostensibly providing immigrants with English language education to prepare them for their immigration to the United States, serve as centres for the preparation of a workforce to suit the US economy. They are constantly oriented towards the Americanization of immigrants, a process that assumes that American society has little or nothing to learn from immigrants' cultures and that "immigrants' primary civic responsibility is to transform themselves by adopting that society's dominant values, attitudes, and behaviors" (1989: 58).

The central belief here is that the cultures of immigrant peoples are the principal hindrance to their future prospects in North America, and that the American ideologies of individualism, self-sufficiency and hard work as a guarantor of success need to be inculcated in these future citizens of the United States before their arrival. . . . This discussion starts to raise questions not only about the connections between English in the world and social and economic power but also about the relationship between English and various cultural forms.

Ndebele (1987: 4) suggests that "the spread of English went parallel with the spread of the culture of international business and technological standardization". . . . Most important is the dominance of English in the domains of business, popular culture and international academic relations. As Flaitz (1988) has shown, it is through popular music that English is making a major incursion into French culture. . . .

In international academic relations, the predominance of English has profound consequences. A large proportion of textbooks in the world are published in English and designed either for the internal English-speaking market (United Kingdom, United States, Australia and so forth) or for an international market. In both cases, students around the world are not only obliged to reach a high level of competence in English to pursue their studies, but they are also dependent on forms of Western knowledge that are often of limited value and extreme inappropriacy to the local context. . . . Altbach (1981), for example, argues that much technological expertise in India has been inappropriate because "much of Indian science is oriented toward metropolitan models, because of the use of English, because of the prestige of Western science, and because of the foreign training of many key Indian researchers" (p. 613).

Other writers have claimed an even more fundamental role of English in the (re)production of global inequalities. Naysmith (1987), for example, suggests that English language teaching "has become part of the process whereby one part of the world has become politically, economically and culturally dominated by another" (p. 3). The core of this process, he argues, is the "central place the English language has taken as *the* language of international capitalism" (ibid.). Such a position, which suggests that English is an integral part of the global structures of dependency, has been explored at length by Robert Phillipson. He argues that *linguicism* — "the ideologies and structures which are used to legitimate, effectuate and reproduce an unequal division of power and resources (both material and non-material) between groups which are defined on the basis of their language (i.e., of their mother tongue)" (1988: 339) — is best seen within the broader context of *linguistic imperialism*, "an essential constituent of imperialism as a global phenomenon involving structural relations between rich and poor countries in a world characterised by inequality and injustice" (ibid.).

Most significantly, Phillipson's work demonstrates the limitations of arguments that suggest that the current position of English in the world is an accidental or natural result of world forces. Rather, through his analysis of the British Council and other organizations, Phillipson makes it clear that it has been deliberate government policy in English-speaking countries to promote the worldwide use of English for economic and political purposes. The British Council report for 1960–61, for example, draws a direct parallel between the advantages of encouraging the world to speak English (with the help of American power) and the history of US internal policies for its immigrant population: "Teaching the world English may appear not unlike an extension of the task which America faced in establishing English as a common national language among its own immigrant population" (cited in Phillipson 1988: 346). Ndebele (1987) also suggests that "The British Council . . . continues to be untiring in its efforts to keep the world speaking English. In this regard, teaching English as a second or foreign language is not only good business, in terms of the production of teaching materials of all kinds. . . . but also it is good politics" (p. 63). Given the connections outlined in this section between English and the export of certain forms of culture and knowledge, and between English and the maintenance of social, economic, and political elites, it is evident that the promotion of English around the world may bring very real economic and political advantages to the promoters of that spread. Indeed, Skutnabb-Kangas and Phillipson (1989) conclude that "it has been British and American government policy since the mid-1950s to establish English as a universal 'second language', so as to protect and promote capitalist interests" (p. 63).

Of primary importance to those of us working in English language teaching is the connection between our work and this global spread of English. Phillipson (1986) states that a primary purpose of his work is to gauge "the contribution of applied linguists and English Language Teaching Experts in helping to legitimate the contemporary capitalist world order" (p. 127). As I have suggested elsewhere (Pennycook 1990), it is incumbent on applied linguists to explore the interests served by our work. If we start to accept some of the critical perspectives outlined here, we must surely start to raise profound questions about our own practices. Certainly, these perspectives suggest that we must be highly suspicious of claims that the spread of English is natural, neutral, or beneficial.

[. . .]

Discourse, counter-discourse and the world in English

Of significance to the issues I wish to address in this chapter are, on the one hand, the continued acknowledgement of inequalities and dependencies between First and Third World countries, and on the other, an attempt to conceptualize these relationships in a way that avoids the reductionist and deterministic tendencies inherent in looking pre-dominantly at socioeconomic relationships. Of fundamental importance is the elevation of notions of culture and discourse as principal factors in our understanding of the world. Although not belittling the importance of economic and material inequalities, I would argue that it is also crucial to understand how discourses construct and regulate our realities and operate through a diverse range of international institutions. Once we move beyond a view of the world as made up of competing states or as reducible to a set of socio-economic relations, in favour of a view that also tries to account for diverse cultures and discourses constituting our subjectivities, then it also starts to become clear that language, and especially any international language, may play a far greater role in the world than had heretofore been considered. Importantly, too, this view suggests that people around the world are not merely passive consumers of culture and knowledge but active creators. In this section I shall explore the relationship between international discourses and English, and I shall discuss the importance of counter-discourses formed in English.

. . . First although I want to acknowledge the very great importance of work such as Phillipson's in its description of the structures of global language inequality, I also want to avoid what seems to be a foreclosure of discussion and possibilities by naming the spread of English as linguistic imperialism.

Phillipson describes a massive structure of linguistic imperialism and suggests ways of trying to counter this through language-planning policies. My position, however, is that we cannot reduce language spread to an imperialism parallel to economic or military imperialism. What I want to examine are the *effects* of the spread of English, how people take up English in their daily lives, what is done with "the world language which history has forced down our throats" (Achebe 1975:220). By taking up the concept of discourse I am suggesting that the implications of the spread of English may be even greater than suggested in structuralist analyses because of the connection between English and international discourses, and that it may be almost impossible to solve these problems through language-planning policies since, as Luke, McHoul and Mey (1990) argue, "while language . . . can be 'planned', discourse cannot". And yet I also want to suggest that the concept of discourse allows for the construction of counter-discourses in English and may offer remarkable potential for change.

Language plays a central role in how we understand ourselves and the world, and thus all questions of language control and standardization have major implications for social relations and the distribution of power. . . . Once we start to deal with language as always political, never neutral, its relationship to other forms of power becomes easier to perceive.

Kachru (1986) quotes the Nigerian novelist Chinua Achebe (1975) in support of his arguments for the legitimation of the new Englishes. Achebe argues that it is neither necessary nor desirable for an African writer to be able to use English like a native speaker. Rather, he argues that English "will be able to carry the weight of my African experience. But it will have to be a new English, still in communion with its ancestral home but altered to suit its new African surroundings" (p. 223). But what do we mean when we talk about a new English? I want to argue that this is a far more complex question than simply a case of new words, new syntax or new phonology, that Achebe is concerned not so much with the structural diversity of English as with the cultural politics of new meanings, the struggle to claim and to create meanings in the political arenas of language and discourse. Significantly, Achebe's remark follows a quotation from the African-America writer James Baldwin, who argues that

> My quarrel with English has been that the language reflected none of my experience. But now I began to see the matter in quite another way. . . .Perhaps the language was not my own because I had never attempted to use it, had only learned to imitate it. If this were so, then it might be made to bear the burden of my experience if I could find the stamina to challenge it, and me, to such a test.
>
> (Cited in Achebe 1975: 223)

Achebe and Baldwin are referring to a political struggle over meaning, and it is in this domain that the notion of new Englishes becomes interesting. As Mazrui (1975) demonstrates, the relationship between English and politics is always complex. Although English has been one of the major languages of colonialism and neo-colonialism in Africa, a language linked to oppression, racism and cultural imperialism it was also the language through which opposition to the colonizers was formed. "Among the functions of the English language in the Commonwealth must indeed be included a function which is unifying. What are often overlooked are some of the *anti*-Commonwealth tendencies which are also part of the English language" (1975: 191). On the eve of an election in Nairobi, Mazrui relates, the Kenyan political leader Tom Mboya stood in front of a vast crowd and recited the poem "If" by Rudyard Kipling. What are we to make of the use of a poem by one of the great apologists of imperialism in a political speech by a vehement opponent of imperialism and colonialism? According to Mazrui (1975: 209),

> The cultural penetration of the English language was manifesting its comprehensiveness. That was in part a form of colonization of the African mind. But when Rudyard Kipling is being called upon to serve the purposes of the Africans themselves, the phenomenon we are witnessing may also amount to a decolonizing of Rudyard Kipling.

What starts to emerge from these instances is a sense that language is a site of struggle, that meanings are always in flux and in contention. The process of using language against the grain, of the empire writing back to the centre (see Ashcroft, Griffiths and Tiffin 1989), of using English to express the lived experiences of the colonized and to oppose the central meanings of the colonizers, is a crucial aspect of global language use. . . .

In looking at postcolonial literature, at forms of "writing back" in the language of the colonizers, I wish to avoid the same liberal pluralism of the writing on the new Englishes that we looked at earlier and that takes as its central concerns a notion of diversity and the legitimation of other standards. I am not here concerned with legitimating other forms of Commonwealth literature or "New literatures in English" so that they can be incorporated into the canon of English. Rather, I am interested in the ways in which these literatures in English are rich in struggles over meaning and opposition to the central definitions. As Ashcroft *et al.* (1989: 189) suggest, "A canon is not a body of texts *per se*, but rather a set of reading practices." Thus, the question is not so much one of replacing, validating or incorporating new forms of English language or literature, but rather of rethinking our understanding of language practices.

[. . .]

Discourses and languages can both facilitate and restrict the production of meanings. When we look at the history and present conjunction of English and many discourses of global power, it seems certain that those discourses have been facilitative of the spread of English and that the spread of English has facilitated the spread of those discourses. It is in this sense that the world is in English. The potential meanings that can be articulated in English are interlinked with the discourses of development, democracy, capitalism, modernization, and so on. And if we accept the argument that subjectivities are constructed in discourse (see e.g. Weedon 1987), then we can see how the spread of English is not only a structural *reproducer* of global inequalities, but also *produces* inequality by creating subject positions that contribute to their own subjectification. But it is also at this point that possibilities for resistance present themselves in alternative readings of Rudyard Kipling, postcolonial struggles in English, and the formation of counter-discourses.

[. . .]

I have been trying to suggest in this section, then, that if we elevate language, culture and discourse to a central role in the (re)production of global inequalities, the relationship between English and these inequalities becomes on the one hand stronger but on the other more open to resistance. If we see the relationship between power/knowledge in discourse and the power inscribed in words and produced in the struggle over meaning, we can start to understand not only the extent to which English is in the world and the extent to which it appears to run parallel to many forms of global oppression, but also the ways in which the world is in English, the ways in which the history of conjunctions between various discourses and English creates the conditions for people's complying with their own subjugation. . . . In the final section I shall try to suggest what implications such a view holds for teaching English around the world.

English teachers and the worldliness of English

I have suggested that the predominant paradigms of analysis of the spread of English around the world have by and large failed to problematize the causes and implications of this spread. They have dealt primarily with descriptions of varieties of English and have paused only to debate the questions of standardization and intelligibility. The spread of English is taken to be natural, neutral and beneficial. English language teachers, therefore, have been poorly served by a body of knowledge that fails to address the cultural and political implications of the spread of English. More critical analyses, however, show that English threatens other languages, acts as a gatekeeper to positions of wealth and prestige both within and between nations, and is the language through which much of the unequal distribution of wealth, resources and knowledge operates. Furthermore, its spread has not been the coincidental by-product of changing global relations but rather the deliberate policy of English-speaking countries protecting and promoting their economic and political interests. Thus, I have argued, English is in the world and plays an important role in the reproduction of global inequalities.

I have also suggested that when we consider the importance of language, culture and discourse in how we make sense of the world (and how the world makes sense of us), another aspect of the worldliness of English emerges: the extent to which the world is in English. By considering the relationship between language and discourse, it is possible to go beyond an understanding of the structural concordance of English and forms of global inequality to understand how people's subjectivities and identities are constituted and how people may comply with their own oppression. This, however, is by no means a deterministic thesis; it is not the structure of English that is important here but the politics of representation. And it is in this locus of struggle over meaning that counter-discourses can be formulated.

[. . .]

What, then, are the implications of all this for teachers and applied linguists? Rogers (1982) argues that, given the falsity of the hopes that English teaching provides, we should try to discourage the teaching of English. As the responses to Rogers' article rightly suggest, however, to deny people access to English is an even more problematic solution (Abbott 1984; Prodromou 1988). Although I think we should support language-planning policies aimed at maintaining languages other than English, there are also limits to the effectiveness of such policies. Phillipson's (1988: 353) "anti-linguicist strategies" may only be part of the picture. As long as English remains intimately linked to the discourses that ensure the continued domination of some parts of the globe by others, an oppositional programme other than one that seeks only to limit access to English will be necessary.

Elsewhere (Pennycook 1989b), I have argued that local forms of opposition can indeed be taken up. Following Foucault's (1980: 81) formulation, I suggested that by asking what forms of knowledge have been disqualified and subjugated by the dominant discourses, we could attempt to bring about the "insurrection of subjugated knowledges". More generally, I would suggest that counter-discourses can indeed be formed in English and that one of the principal roles of English teachers is to help this formulation. Thus, as applied linguists and English language teachers we should become political actors engaged in a critical pedagogical project to use English to oppose the dominant discourses of the West and to help the articulation of counter-discourses in English. At the very least, intimately involved as we are with the spread of English, we should be acutely aware of the implications of this spread for the reproduction and production of global inequalities.

References

Abbott, G. 1984. Should we start digging new holes? *ELT Journal* 38(2): 98–102.

Achebe, C. 1975. English and the African writer. In A. Mazrui, *The Political Sociology of the English Language* (Appendix B, pp. 216–23). The Hague/Paris: Mouton.

Altbach, P. G. 1981. The university as center and periphery. *Teachers College Record* 82(4): 601–22.

Ashcroft, B., Griffiths, G. and Tiffin, H. 1989. *The Empire Writes Back: Theory and Practice in Post-colonial Literatures*. London and New York: Routledge.

Bamgbose, A. 1982. Standard Nigerian English: issues of identification. In B. J. Kachru (ed.), *The Other Tongue: English Across Cultures* (pp. 99–111). Urbana: University of Illinois Press.

Cooke, D. 1988. Ties that constrict: English as a Trojan horse. In A. Cumming, A. Gagne and J. Dawson (eds), *Awarenesses: Proceedings of the 1987 TESL Ontario Conference* (pp. 56–62). Toronto: TESL Ontario.

Crystal, D. 1988. *The English Language*. Harmondsworth: Penguin.

Day, R. 1980. ESL: a factor in linguistic genocide? In J. C. Fisher, M. A. Clarke and J. Schachter (eds), *On TESOL '80. Building Bridges: Research and Practice in Teaching English as a Second Language*. Washington, DC: TESOL.

—— 1985. The ultimate inequality: linguistic genocide. In N. Wolfson and J. Manes (eds), *Language of Inequality* (pp. 163–81). Berlin: Mouton.

Fishman, J. A., Cooper, R. L. and Rosenbaum, Y. 1977. English around the world. In J. A. Fishman, R. W. Cooper and A. W. Conrad (eds), *The Spread of English* (pp. 77–107). Rowley, MA: Newbury House.

Flaitz, J. 1988. *The Ideology of English: French Perceptions of English as a World Language*. Berlin/New York/Amsterdam: Mouton de Gruyter.

Foucault, M. 1980. *Power/Knowledge: Selected Interviews and Other Writings, 1972–1977*, edited by Colin Gordon. New York: Pantheon.

Hindmarsh, R. X. 1978. English as an international language. *ELT Documents: English as an International Language* 102: 40–3.

Jespersen, O. [1938] 1968. *Growth and Structure of the English Language*. Toronto: Collier-Macmillan.

Judd, E. L. 1983. TESOL as a political act: a moral question. In J. Handscombe, R. A. Orem and B. P. Taylor (eds), *On TESOL '83* (pp. 265–73). Washington, DC: TESOL.

Kachru, B. 1982a. Introduction: The other side of English. In B. J. Kachru (ed.), *The Other Tongue: English Across Cultures*. Urbana: University of Illinois Press.

—— 1982b. Models for non-native Englishes. In B. J. Kachru (ed.), *The Other Tongue: English Across Cultures* (pp. 31–57). Urbana: University of Illinois Press.

—— 1985. Standards, codification and sociolinguistic realism: the English language in the outer circle. In R. Quirk and H. G. Widdowson (eds), *English in the World*. Cambridge: Cambridge University Press.

—— 1986. *The Alchemy of English: The Spread, Functions and Models of Non-native Englishes.* Oxford: Pergamon.

Luke, A., McHoul, A. and Mey, J. L. 1990. On the limits of language planning: class, state and power. In R. B. Baldauf, Jr. and A. Luke (eds), *Language Planning and Education in Australasia and the South Pacific* (pp. 25–44). Clevedon: Multilingual Matters.

Mazrui, A. 1975. *The Political Sociology of the English Language.* The Hague/Paris: Mouton.

Naysmith, J. 1987. English as imperialism? *Language Issues* 1(2): 3–5.

Ndebele, N. S. 1987. The English language and social change in South Africa. *The English Academy Review* 4: 1–16.

Nelson, C. 1982. Intelligibility and non-native varieties of English. In B. J. Kachru (ed.), *The Other Tongue: English Across Cultures* (pp. 58–73). Urbana: University of Illinois Press.

Ngugi wa Thiong'o. 1985. The language of African literature. *New Left Review* 150 (March/April): 109–27.

Pennycook, A. 1989a. The concept of method, interested knowledge, and the politics of language teaching. *TESOL Quarterly* 23(4): 589–618.

—— 1989b. *English as an International Language and the Insurrection of Subjugated Knowledges.* Paper presented at the Fifth International Conference of the Institute of Language in Education, Hong Kong, 13 December 1989: "LULTAC '89".

—— 1990. Towards a critical applied linguistics for the 1990s. *Issues in Applied Linguistics* 1(1): 9–29.

Phillipson, R. 1986. English rules: a study of language pedagogy and imperialism. In R. Phillipson and T. Skutnabb-Kangas (eds), *Linguicism Rules in Education* (pp. 124–343). Roskilde University Centre, Denmark.

—— 1988. Linguicism: structures and ideologies in linguistic imperialism. In J. Cummins and T. Skutnabb-Kangas (eds), *Minority Education: From Shame to Struggle.* Avon: Multilingual Matters.

Platt, J., Weber, H. and Ho, M. L. 1984. *The New Englishes.* London: Routledge and Kegan Paul.

Prodromou, L. 1988. English as cultural action. *ELT Journal* 42(2): 73–83.

Quirk, R. 1985. The English language in a global context. In R. Quirk and H. G. Widdowson (eds), *English in the World.* Cambridge: Cambridge University Press.

Richards, J. C. 1982. Singapore English: rhetorical and communicative styles. In B. J. Kachru (ed.), *The Other Tongue: English Across Cultures* (pp. 154–67). Urbana: University of Illinois Press.

Rogers, J. 1982. The world for sick proper. *ELT Journal* 36(3): 144–51.

Said, E. 1983. *The World, the Text and the Critic.* Cambridge, MA: Harvard University Press.

Skutnabb-Kangas, T. and Phillipson, R. 1989. Wanted! Linguistic human rights. *Rolig Papir.* (Roskilde Universitetscenter) 44.

Tollofson, J. W. 1988. Covert policy in the United States refugee program in Southeast Asia. *Language Problems and Language Planning* 12(1): 30–42.

—— 1989. *Alien Winds: The Reeducation of America's Indochinese Refugees*. New York: Praeger.

Weedon, C. 1987. *Feminist Practice and Poststructuralist Theory*. Oxford: Blackwell.

Zuengler, J. E. 1982. Kenyan English. In B. J. Kachru (ed.), *The Other Tongue: English Across Cultures* (pp. 112–24). Urbana: University of Illinois Press.

—— 1985. English, Swahili, or other languages? The relationship of educational development goals to language of instruction in Kenya and Tanzania. In N. Wolfson and J. Manes (eds), *Language of Inequality* (pp. 241–54). Berlin: Mouton.

PART THREE

Analysing English: a text perspective

Chapter 7

Caroline Coffin

THEORETICAL APPROACHES TO WRITTEN LANGUAGE – A TESOL PERSPECTIVE

A focus on text and discourse can help us to notice and analyse aspects of usage which have previously gone unnoticed and untaught – the better a text analyst the teacher can be, the better equipped – all other things being equal – his or her students are likely to be in using the language appropriately.

(McCarthy and Carter, 1994, p. xii)

Introduction

WITHIN THE DISCIPLINE OF LINGUISTICS, as well as in newly evolving fields of study such as the "New Literacy" and the "New Rhetoric" studies, different ways of examining written language have been proposed. Written language in contemporary linguistic and literacy theory is generally examined in terms of stretches of language rather than just at the sentence level. Typically, the terms "text" or "discourse" are used to refer to such stretches of language. In this chapter I look at different theoretical approaches to analysing discourse which are particularly relevant to educational applications within the field of teaching English to speakers of other languages (TESOL). The areas of study listed below have all made valuable contributions:

- Systemic functional linguistics
- Critical discourse analysis
- Literacy studies (including Critical Literacy and the "New Literacy Studies")
- Genre approaches (including the "New Rhetoric")
- Contrastive rhetoric.

Apart from providing different theoretical models for examining written texts or discourse, the various approaches listed above have influenced the pedagogical treatment of written language. In this chapter, therefore, not only are the main orientations and theoretical principles of the different approaches considered but also their implications for the teaching and learning of English.

Before beginning this overview it is important to point out that, although for the purposes of this chapter, each approach has been treated in a relatively discrete way, there are, in fact, many shared characteristics across the different frameworks. Fundamentally, all the approaches acknowledge the cultural and social aspects of written text and in terms of the analytical tools they use there is often overlap. Thus, some critical literacy theorists incorporate critical discourse analysis into their methodological framework and, in turn, critical discourse analysts may make use of systemic functional linguistics. In addition, many of the approaches have educational applications as an explicit part of their agenda. For this reason issues of an applied nature as well as concerns for theoretical integrity have influenced their design and development. Many approaches, for example, share the aim of developing in learners a critical orientation towards discourse.

Systemic functional linguistics

The main aims of systemic functional linguistics

Systemic functional linguistics (SFL) is primarily a linguistic theory. However, anthropology has played an important role in its conceptualisation. Therefore, unlike some linguistic theories, the social and cultural role of language is a central concern.

Rather than just focusing on how a specific language such as English works, SFL is a theory of how language works generally. The chief "architect" of SFL is Michael Halliday, formerly Professor Emeritus of Linguistics at the University of Sydney, Australia (see Chapter 11, this volume). As a teacher of Chinese at an earlier stage of his career, Halliday became particularly interested in linguistics as a means of solving problems confronted by language teachers. These problems, he believed, were often inadequately dealt with in existing grammars and linguistic theories which focused on language structure rather than language function and sentence rather than text level analysis. Halliday was also motivated by the desire to develop a theory of language that would give value to kinds, or varieties, of language that had traditionally been ignored; for example, spoken as opposed to written language and non-standard dialects as opposed to standard languages.

One of the main purposes for Halliday, therefore, in developing SFL has been to create a theory for solving a range of problems faced by potential "consumers" of linguistics. This is an aim shared by another influential "architect" of SFL, Jim Martin, who, in particular, has ensured that the design of SFL takes into account educational concerns. Martin (see Chapters 9 and 13, this volume) has also been inspired by the notion of critical linguistics – a linguistics "which 'deconstructs' texts – with a view to critically evaluating the ideologies they construe" (Martin, 1992, p. 2).

Outline of theoretical approach

Orientation to both text and clause

SFL has developed analytical tools for looking at spoken and written language both in terms of how sentences or clauses are organised and how sentences combine to create whole texts. At the level of whole text, genre is a particularly influential tool in educational contexts (e.g. Coffin, 1996; Derewianka, 1990; Feez, 1998; Rothery, 1994). The concept of genre (which has also been developed within other theories) is examined under the heading 'Genre approaches' on p. 108.

At the level of clause, SFL has developed tools for looking at how the structure or grammar of a clause can be interpreted from a functional perspective. Thus clauses can be analysed to see how their grammatical patterning simultaneously:

- builds a picture of the world (experiential grammar)
- creates point of view and exchanges information (interpersonal grammar)
- organises and makes coherent a message (textual grammar).

Some methods of discourse analysis do not include a consideration of grammatical patterning. Halliday, however, argues that grammar which is semantically or meaning oriented has a central place in the interpretation of a text (Halliday, 1994, p. xvii). He claims that:

> A discourse analysis that is not based on grammar is not an analysis at all, but simply a running commentary on a text . . . the exercise remains a private one in which one explanation is as good or as bad as another.
>
> (Halliday, 1994, pp. xvi–xvii)

Relationship between context and language

One of the most important features of SFL is the way its theoretical framework is designed to explain the interrelationships between culture, society and language use. One of its central tenets is that behaviours, beliefs and values within a particular cultural and social environment influence and shape both the overall language system (such as English) and language "instances", the way people use language in everyday interactions. Equally, it asserts that everyday language use plays an active role in shaping the social and cultural context in which it operates.

The concepts of "context of culture", "context of situation" and "register" (comprising "field", "tenor" and "mode") are used in systemics to explain this relationship. They will not be elaborated here since they are discussed in Martin's and Painter's chapters (Chapters 9 and 10) in this volume.

It is important to emphasise that SFL, unlike many theories of language, looks at language from the "outside" as well as the "inside". That is, it asks questions that traditionally would be seen as belonging to the domains of sociology or anthropology such as "What is the role of language in creating social identity?", "How is language used for purposes of propaganda?", "How do the 'below the surface' patterns of grammar construct particular ideologies?" It also asks questions that are the traditional concern of linguists, for example, "What is the structure of a noun or verbal group?", "What are the types of relationship that exist between clauses?"

System and instance

In systemic functional theory both the system of language (the overall set of meanings that a language such as English makes available) and the instances of language (the particular utterances that are produced or "chosen" by speakers and writers in everyday interactions) are given equal emphasis. This dual focus is what distinguishes the SFL approach to language from other approaches, and therefore it is worthwhile elaborating this theoretical principle by drawing on Halliday's analogy of the climate and the weather (Halliday and Matthiesson, 1999, p. 328).

Climate and weather, following Halliday, need to be seen as two different ways of looking at the same phenomenon rather than as distinct phenomena. Whereas weather is an immediate and direct experience of "rain falling" or "the sun shining", climate is based on the observation and modelling of long-term, and possibly quantitative, patterns of hours of sunshine and measurement of rainfall. Language, according to Halliday, needs to be similarly conceptualised. It too can be seen as a kind of weather event, with words unfolding in a particular context. But, equally, we can stand back and look at it from the perspective of climate and thereby see the whole system of meanings or resources that are available to speakers of a particular language.

To fully understand and make useful observations about language, Halliday argues that we need to look at language from both ends (that is, take both a "weather" and a "climate" perspective). In other words, rather than treating the language system as one phenomenon and focusing on instances of language as another, we need to always bring both halves of the picture together.

Language as resource

Overall the focus of SFL is on semantics – how people use language to make meaning; and functionality – how people use language in order to get on with their lives. This semantic and functional orientation leads to the conceptualisation of language as a resource, or a cultural tool, rather than a set of rules. This is a rather different orientation to other linguistically and grammatically based approaches to analysing language. Many approaches to written language, for example, focus on grammatical correctness, treating language as a set of rules. For example: "A preposition is something you should never end a sentence *with*. . . . It is quite wrong to *carelessly* split infinitives" (Martin and Rothery, 1993, p. 141).

Systemic functional grammar, in contrast, is interested in looking at the potential of the language system in terms of all the different kinds of meanings from which speakers of the language can choose.

Focus on spoken and written language

SFL is a general theory of language and is therefore equally interested in written and spoken usage. Unlike some other theories, however, it argues that spoken language is not merely an imperfect or ungrammatical form of language or that written language is simply spoken language written down. Rather, it argues that spoken and written language have different grammars because they have evolved to carry out different social and cultural purposes (Halliday explores these ideas in Chapter 11 of this volume).

The value of SFL for analysing written language: a TESOL perspective

SFL is currently used in educational contexts in many parts of the world. However, it is an approach that is best known in Australia, and much of the research and development has occurred there. For example, many Australian primary and secondary school syllabi have been influenced by SFL both within the subject area of English and across other curriculum areas, including science and mathematics. In ESL (English as a second language) and EFL (English as a foreign language) contexts, both within and beyond primary and secondary education, SFL is drawn on in a variety of ways. In English for academic purposes (EAP) programmes, for example, the tools of SFL have been used to assess language learners, particularly their control of written text (e.g. Drury and Gollin, 1986). More broadly they have been used to conduct needs analyses, and to design courses (e.g Murison and Webb, 1991). In the Australian Adult Migrant English Program (AMEP), many language teachers are involved in English settlement programmes for newly arrived immigrants. Such programmes, which prepare learners for community access, further study or employment, draw extensively on the tools of SFL in relation to syllabus design (e.g. Feez, 1998), teaching and learning methodologies (e.g. Hood, Solomon and Burns,1996) and assessment practices (e.g. within the Certificates in Spoken and Written English, NSW AMES, 1995).

The extract below is an example of how SFL has influenced the design of materials for adult learners of English following an English in the workplace (EWP) programme (based in Australia). EWP is designed to provide students with the language needed for effective participation in a range of work situations. In the example here, language activities are based around a text – "Lifting" (reproduced below). Lifting is an example of a procedure "genre", in this case a safety procedure. A procedure is a genre whose social purpose is to tell its readers how to carry out a particular task. Each suggested activity focuses on a different dimension of language use; for example, the text's social context and purpose (as embodied in the structure of the text or its "schematic structure") as well as its particular patterns of language choices (such as its use of imperative verbs).

Focal text:

LIFTING

Check the weight of the load

Put one foot in front of the other

Bend your knees

Hold the load firmly

Keep arms close to the body

Lift the load

Keep your back straight

Hold the load close to the body as you walk

Materials

Still picture of person lifting a heavy load
Procedural text on OHT and individual copies for students
A range of different text types

Activities

1   Discussion of lifting
     Teacher shows class a picture of someone lifting a heavy load and the class discusses the picture.

2   Demonstrating the procedure
     As the teacher rereads the text she demonstrates the procedure.
3   Reading the lifting procedure
     The class reads the text with the teacher.
4   Instructing the teacher
     The students instruct the teacher how to lift a load as she follows their instructions.
5   Revision of schematic structure of procedural text
     Teacher revises modelling of schematic structure of procedural texts.
     Could ask students to sequence the procedural text.
6   Categorising texts
     Teacher gives students a range of text types including some procedural texts.
     Students in pairs or in groups pick out the procedural texts.
7   Modelling imperative structure
     Teacher explains the imperative structure to the students showing them where the
     action verbs are located in the lifting text.
8.   Highlighting action verbs
     Students highlight action verbs in the emergency text which they have dealt with
     earlier.
9   Cloze activity
     Teacher omits action verbs from text and class complete cloze on OHT.

Assessment checklist

•   students able to recognise schematic structure
•   students able to relate text to context
•   students able to sequence oral instructions
•   students able to distinguish procedural texts from other text types
•   students able to recognise imperative structure
•   students able to recognise action verbs.

(Joyce, 1992, p. 83)

Educational applications of SFL are generally designed to teach students how to operate in social contexts relevant to their educational, social and cultural needs. Thus, in an EWP programme, there is a focus on the language of workplace texts, and the teaching and learning activities aim to develop students' understanding of how workplace texts function in particular institutions as well as society at large; how workplace discourse relates to the English language as a whole; and how contextually sensitive are the linguistic structures of workplace discourse. The ideological dimension of workplace texts may also be integrated into the activities.

In sum, theoretical developments in SFL provide both teachers and students with tools for analysing how texts are structured and grammatically patterned as well as for critically examining how they function in the wider social and cultural context. SFL is not restricted to developing students' control of written text, although written rather than spoken discourse has tended to be the main focus of research and materials development (see Burns, Chapter 8, this volume, for applications of SFL to spoken discourse).

Critical discourse analysis

The main aims of critical discourse analysis

Critical discourse analysis (CDA) is closely associated with, and has its origins in, critical linguistics. It is essentially an approach to language analysis which concerns itself with issues of language, power and ideology. One of its main aims is to highlight how language serves to construct particular ideological positions which entail unequal relations of power. CDA therefore has a strong political agenda in addition to its linguistic dimension. As Widdowson (1998, p. 136) points out:

> What is most plainly distinctive about critical discourse analysis is its sense of responsibility and its commitment to social justice. This is linguistics with a conscience and a cause, one which seeks to reveal how language is used and abused in the exercise of power and the suppression of human rights.

One of the most influential developers of CDA, Norman Fairclough (1995, p. 219), states:

> The issue of language and power in education is just a part of the more general social problematic of language and power, and ought not in my view to be isolated from it. At least in developed capitalist countries, we live in an age in which power is predominantly exercised through the generation of consent rather than through coercion, through ideology rather than through physical force, through the inculcation of self disciplining practices rather than through the breaking of skulls. . . . Part of this development is an enhanced role for language in the exercise of power: it is mainly in discourse that consent is achieved, ideologies are transmitted, and practices, meanings, values and identities are taught and learnt.

CDA is an approach to language analysis which has been used to examine spoken (see Burns, Chapter 8, this volume) as well as written language.

Outline of theoretical approach

The relationship between language, power and ideology

In CDA, the relationship between language and social dimensions is the central area of exploration. Fairclough (1989, p. 166) states that "there is no rule of thumb determining how far one should extend one's analysis into sociological aspects of the institution and the society." Generally, in CDA, the social *dimension* is seen as having three levels, all of which need to be explored to understand the connections between language, power and ideology: "Both social effects of discourse and social determinants of discourse should be investigated at three levels of social organisation, the societal level, the institutional level, and the situational level" (Fairclough, 1989, p. 163).

Processes of production and interpretation

In its examination of written text, CDA gives attention to the dynamic interplay between text production, the text itself, and text interpretation or consumption (see Figure 7.2).

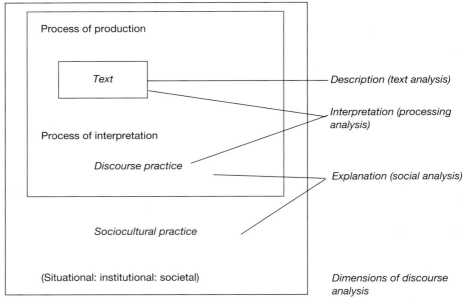

Figure 7.1 Dimensions of discourse and discourse analysis
Source: Fairclough (1995, p. 98)

Fairclough (1989, pp. 10–11) explains that:

> The relationship between social action and text is mediated by interaction: that is, the nature of the interaction, how texts are produced and interpreted, depends upon the social action in which they are embedded; and the nature of the text, its formal and stylistic properties, on the one hand depends upon and constitutes "traces" of its process of production, and on the other hand constitutes "cues" for its interpretation.

Orders of discourse

Unlike SFL, CDA does not theorise about language as a system or about the nature of grammatical structures. Rather, drawing on social theorists such as Foucault (e.g. 1979, 1980), the main theoretical focus is on "discourse" or "orders of discourse". Orders of discourse refer to the different ways of talking and writing which occur in particular institutional settings, such as school, church or family. Each "order of discourse" is made up of discourse types. In the institutional setting of a school, for example, discourse types would include teacher-to-student talk, school authorities' communication with teachers, playground talk and the specialised language of different curriculum areas. Each discourse type displays different grammatical patterning in the various texts and thus linguistic features are drawn on (often using the framework of SFL) as a means of identifying and distinguishing discourse types.

The value of CDA for analysing written language: a TESOL perspective

CDA has been found to be a beneficial tool in a range of TESOL contexts around the world. Educational applications of CDA are usually referred to as critical language awareness (CLA). In South Africa, Hilary Janks (1993, 1996) has done a great deal of work in applying CDA to language classrooms, arguing that an understanding of the relationship between language and power should be taught at all levels of education. In English for academic purposes (EAP) programmes, South African teachers such as Bock (1998) and Thesen (1998) have used CDA to underpin materials design and teaching-learning activities. Bock (1998, p. 63) argues:

> In both critical linguistics and stylistics, the study of texts draws on and develops students' knowledge of language in interesting ways. Students learn to notice features of language because they are stylistically foregrounded or socially relevant.

Clark and Ivanič, UK academics, have also incorporated CLA into courses on academic writing (e.g. Clark and Ivanič, 1991, 1997a, 1997b). These courses, rather than being exclusively focused on the needs of second language learners, target undergraduate and postgraduate students more generally. Clark and Ivanič summarise the CLA pedagogy they have developed in this context as follows:

- *Socially situated learning*
  That the teaching and learning of academic literacy practices in higher education must be firmly located within the departments to which students belong, so that language can be discussed in relation to real social contexts.

- *Mainstreaming*
  That CLA work must be made available to all students, not only special groups such as those for whom English is an additional language, or those identified as having "problems".

- *A questioning approach*
  Constantly answering the questions: "Why are conventions/practices the way they are?", "In whose interests do they operate?", "What views of knowledge and representations of the world do they perpetuate?", "What are the possible alternatives?"
  (Clark and Ivanič, 1999, p. 66)

CDA has also been applied in the contexts of general English language programmes in both EFL and ESL settings. The focus here has been on the teaching of critical reading. Wallace (1992, p. 61), for example, has used CDA to fill what she perceives to be a gap in EFL textbooks where she argues that readings are:

> not generally selected for their potential to challenge. They are more frequently seen as either vehicles for linguistic structure, as general interest material usually of a fairly safe, bland kind or as functional survival material.

Wallace has developed a reading methodology which addresses ideological assumptions as well as developing general reading comprehension. Key dimensions of the methodology include:

1   Encouragement of reflective critical reading rather than a focus on right or wrong, comprehensive style questions.
2   Extension of a "pre-reading"/"while reading"/"post-reading" procedure. Following this procedure students are set tasks at all three stages of the reading process which include a critical dimension.

The main aim of Wallace's approach is to encourage students to move away from focusing on form for its own sake, as in many traditional language and reading exercises, and instead to use language to explore, and provide evidence of, the text's ideological positioning (Wallace, 1992, pp. 61–70).

Literacy studies (including critical literacy and the "new literacy studies")

The main aims of literacy studies

In recent years there has been increased interest in the study of literacy whereby researchers investigate how members of a culture use written texts and engage in written practices as part of their social lives as well as for their educational development. This work extends more traditional concerns with literacy which have focused on the encoding and decoding skills necessary for producing and reading written symbols.

Two main branches can be identified: critical literacy (CL) and the new literacy studies (NLS). Neither of these branches has developed in isolation from the other and they have many shared characteristics. These include an interest in the social dimension of literacy and a belief that literacy is best understood as consisting of many distinct "literacies", thus challenging the traditional view that literacy is a single, uniform skill. In other words, literacy can be seen as being made up of many different types of reading and writing practices which vary across social and cultural contexts. Another characteristic which is shared by both CL and NLS is their critical and questioning approach to the description of literacy practices and their acknowledgement of its ideological dimension.

Similarly there is considerable dialogue and overlap between researchers and writers associated with CL and those associated with CDA and SFL. For example, the need for a form of linguistic micro-analysis (focusing on clause level grammar) to complement other types of broader analysis (such as the nature of the social institution in which the language occurs) has been advocated by Lee (1996, p. 227) and Luke (1995, pp. 3–47) among others. Not surprisingly, therefore, many researchers cannot easily be placed as belonging to a single tradition.

Critical literacy

The main aim of critical literacy studies

Critical literacy includes a range of contemporary educational theories concerned both with the nature of writing and written text and with developing appropriate pedagogies for reading and writing. According to Lankshear et al. (1997, p. 44), the aim of critical literacy is any or all of the following:

- knowing literacy in general or particular literacies, critically; that is, having a critical perspective on literacy or literacies *per se*
- having a critical perspective on particular texts
- having a critical perspective on – i.e. being able to make "critical readings" of – wider social practices, arrangements, relations, allocations, procedures, etc. which are mediated by, made possible, and partially sustained through reading, writing, viewing, transmitting, etc. texts.

Generally, CL is an approach to analysing written text which includes an understanding of how different positions are taken in texts and an analysis of, and challenge to, the ways texts shape and are shaped by social and political relations in society.

As in the case of CDA, therefore, a political agenda is an integral component of CL. As Gilbert argues:

> To work with a commitment to critical literacy, therefore, will inevitably necessitate an engagement with the politics of language practices. . . . To explore the social context of language practices is . . . to explore . . . networks of power that are sustained and brought into existence by such practices.
>
> (Gilbert, 1993, pp. 324–5)

Outline of theoretical approach

Literacy as social practice

CL takes a sociocultural view of literacy, being informed by perspectives from the disciplines of sociology, educational philosophy, cultural theory and social cognition:

> On the traditional view, literacy is seen as a largely psychological ability – something to do with our "heads". We, on the other hand, see literacy as a matter of social practices – something to do with social, institutional, and cultural relationships.
>
> (Gee *et al.*, 1996, p. 1)

This *sociocultural* view extends earlier ethnographic work on language as social practice (e.g. Hymes, 1972) by contextualising it within a political framework of power and political resistance.

Discourse and the positioning of human subjects

Drawing on the work of the French social theorist, Michel Foucault (e.g. 1979, 1980), a central thesis of CL is that discourse defines, constructs and positions human subjects. CL theorists argue that, depending on participants' control of different types of discourse, they are positioned differently within the hierarchical structure of society and have different degrees of access to social goods (i.e. money, power and status). Not only do CL theorists posit in general terms that there is a relationship between social power, identity and discourse types but researchers such as Gilbert (1993) and Lee (1996) have investigated, in particular, relationships of gender and discourse.

Tools of analysis

The approach to analysing discourse adopted by CL theorists often focuses on the more global or macro level of literacy practices, typically examining, in sociological terms, how such practices contribute to the differential production of power. At the level of language, there is no unified approach to analysing text or grammar. As Luke points out, there is "difficulty in bridging what we might broadly term 'macro' approaches to discourse with more micro analytic text analyses" (Luke, 1995, p. 10). He argues that a central task is to

> theorise and study the micropolitics of discourse, to examine actual patterns of language use with some degree of detail and explicitness but in ways that reconnect instances of local discourse with salient political, economic and cultural formations.
> (Luke, 1995, p. 11)

The value of CL for analysing written language: a TESOL perspective

Much of the work in CL has been designed for educational contexts with multicultural student groups, particularly at the level of primary and secondary schooling, with the main focus being on critical reading rather than writing. Pennycook (e.g. 1994) has proposed that such work could profitably be taken up in EFL practices. He argues that a critical pedagogy for EFL students should encourage students "to use English in their own way, to appropriate English for their own ends" (1994, pp. 315–16) (in addition to developing standard forms of the language relevant to their needs).

CL pedagogies have also been developed in the context of adult ESL where the focus has been to develop problem-posing curricula, designed to increase critical consciousness of issues around student lives, particularly first generation immigrants to English-speaking countries (e.g. Auerbach, 1993; Auerbach and Wallerstein, 1987). Much of this work is inspired by the ideas of Paolo Freire (e.g. 1974, 1985). Freire's main concern was to emancipate disempowered members of a culture rather than to develop methods for analysing written text (for this reason his work is not described as part of this overview).

In the section below, some of the classroom practices underpinned by CL are presented. These practices, developed by Lankshear (much influenced by Freire) and Knobel (1997, pp. 53–62), were designed for use in multicultural secondary school contexts. The ideas and methods reported on could, however, be equally well applied in EFL and EAP contexts.

Media texts and interdisciplinary critique

In the following report we see how a media text can be used to teach critical literacy. First, Lankshear describes the media text and accompanying photograph that he and Knobel chose:

_____

The starting point is a front page story from an Australian daily newspaper, "The Face of Starving Africa". The story is dominated by a 22 cm by 16 cm black and white photograph . . . of a young unclad Somali boy sitting in the dust. The child is starving, almost to the point of death – he is literally skin and bone and his face is etched with the pain of starvation. The photograph, a study in pathos, carries the byline of Phoebe Fraser, daughter of a former Australian prime minister. In addition to this front page story, the same issue of the newspaper carried further coverage on page 7, dealing with specific aspects of the drought in Somalia. "The Face of Starving Africa" pointed readers to these additional stories.

The Face of Starving Africa

A Somali boy, one of 30 million Africans suffering from the effects of drought – Picture: Phoebe Fraser.

AFRICA today. A starving child waits to die in the dust of Somalia.

Hundreds of Somalis collapse every day, unwilling and unable to live any longer in the worst drought to grip their continent for 100 years.

More than 30 million Africans, from Ethiopia to Mozambique, have left their villages in search of food and water.

This photograph was taken by Care Australia's program officer, Ms Phoebe Fraser, the daughter of former prime minister, Mr Malcolm Fraser, who is president of Care.

'Somalia is desperate,' she says. 'In a country where hundreds of bodies line the streets, most of them children, you can only hope the world is watching.'

Yesterday, the United Nations said it would send 500 armed soldiers to protect aid supplies to Somalia, which has been ravaged by drought and civil war, following agreement by warring faction to allow the safe delivery of aid.

The Australian's readers have helped raise thousands of dollars to buy food and medicine by sending donations to the addresses of aid agencies alongside articles on Africa's heartbreaking story.

Aid should be sent to: Care Australia, GPO Box 9977, in your capital city; World Vision, GPO Box 9944, in your capital city; Red Cross, GPO Box 9949, in your capital city; Save the Children's Fund, GPO Box 9912, in your capital city; Austcare Africa Appeal, PO Locked Bag 15, Camperdown NSW 2050; Community Aid Abroad, GPO Box 9920, in your capital city.

(*The Australian*, Friday 14 August 1992, p. 1)

Lankshear's report next shows how students can be taught to "break texts open" by using techniques similar to those used in CLA. A preliminary "opening up" of the text provides a basis for exploring its discursive and ideological implications. Thus, a text analysis exercise such as the one reproduced below would encourage students to explore how there are multiple and diverse ways in which the reality in Somalia might have been represented or constructed textually.

Text analysis exercise

Read "The Face of Starving Africa", and explore the following questions:

1   What version of events/reality is foregrounded here?
2   Whose version is this? From whose perspective is it constructed?
3   What other (possible) versions are excluded?

4   Whose/what interests are served by this representation?
5   By what means – lexical, syntactic, etc. – does this text construct (its) reality?
6   How does this text position the reader? What assumptions about readers are reflected in the text? What beliefs, assumptions, expectations (ideological baggage) do readers have to entertain in order to make meaning from the text?

Lankshear suggests the kinds of responses that such an exercise might generate:

A possible (sample) response to text analysis exercise

Construction of reality

Those people starving in Somalia – and, indeed, the 30 million Africans from Ethiopia to Mozambique – are suffering from the effects of drought.

This drought is the worst in 100 years.

Somalia is also ravaged by civil war, which contributes to starvation.

The situation is so desperate the only hope is international sympathy and goodwill (aid).

Readers have contributed money to aid agencies.

Aid agencies address the situation in Somalia.

Six agencies are named, to whom donations should be sent.

Putting these elements together, we find a construction of the Somalia reality in terms of an extreme drought happening in a setting where there is also a war. In such circumstances, aid agencies coordinate relief. The role for ordinary people is to donate aid. The action is undertaken by the aid agencies, with assistance from some (special) history-making individuals like the Frasers. Aid agencies exist to respond to calamitous happenings like droughts.

Lankshear suggests that, ideally, text analysis needs to be extended by exploring related texts which put forward alternative perspectives, in terms of their underlying theories, questions, assumptions and overall standpoint. The aim is to reveal aspects that may have been left out or distorted in the original media story and initial text analysis exercise. For example, texts which present a geographical or historical perspective can be located and used as stimuli for the following questions:

Geography exercise 1
1   In which countries do famines mainly occur?
2   Which social groups do they affect most?
3   Are famines *natural* disasters?
4   Find texts that provide significantly different accounts of particular famines.

Modern history exercise 1
1   Identify some countries that have been badly affected by famine.
2   In which cases was "political instability" a factor?

3   In those instances where it was a factor, what different accounts are provided of the causes of the "instability"?
4   In the different accounts, who is seen to "be behind", or benefit from, the factors causing instability? How do these interests differ according to the accounts provided?

Having explored the issue of famine from these other perspectives, students can then reassess their responses to the initial text analysis.

Perhaps more importantly, however, Lankshear asks the question "To what extent might we have here the potential for some larger and more embodied critique of discursive practice in the real world of human actors?" In other words, how can the newspaper article be used to critique a more general style of news reporting that positions us to see events and the world in a particular way? He argues that

> "The Face of Starving Africa" can be seen as involved in the discursive production of unduly passive and underinformed citizens. To be sure, they play an important role in helping mobilize essential material resources (aid) in moments of human catastrophe, and that fact must not be overlooked, downplayed or trivialised. At the same time, to the extent that they channel us toward passive "curative" and poorly informed approaches to addressing global and local challenges crucial to the survival and thriving of the human race, they are part of the "problem logics" that contribute to creating social disasters in the first place.

Lankshear suggests that extended critique of the global discursive practices which surround texts such as "The Face of Starving Africa" will develop the necessary conscious thought and action that can evaluate and transform such discourse. This step extends the territory of many CLA practices, aiming to produce citizens who can take the initiative:

> to transform school and society away from authoritarian relations and the undemocratic, unequal distribution of power; taking part in and initiating social change projects; overcoming the induced anti-intellectualism of mass education.
>
> (Shor, 1993, pp. 32–3)

New literacy studies

New literacy studies (NLS) follows many of the precepts proposed by critical literacy theorists. For example, it acknowledges the socially embedded nature of literacy practices as well as their political and ideological role. Street's (1984, 1995) work in literacy, for example, emphasises the notion of a multiplicity of literacies where the meaning and uses of literacy practices are related to specific cultural contexts. Street views such practices not simply as neutral "technologies", but as associated with relations of power and ideology.

In theoretical terms, NLS, rather than emerging from sociology and philosophy, as is generally the case with CL, has it basis in anthropology and sociolinguistics. Barton (1994, p. 7) argues that literacy is best understood as "a set of *practices* which people use in literacy events". Such a definition follows an anthropological and ethnographic tradition of examining language and literacy practices, often documenting those considered to be "non-mainstream" (see e.g. Barton and Hamilton, 1998; Heath, 1983).

Much of the work of the NLS, therefore, provides fine-grained accounts of the social uses and meanings of literacy as embedded in specific cultural and social contexts. Street cites an example from the South Africa context:

> the uses of documents and print in squatter settlements by political activists who may not be able to pass formal tests of literacy but who have successfully incorporated documentation in their presentations of cases to committees and politicians.
>
> (Street, 1996, p. 3)

The documentation of literacy practices occurring in informal and unacknowledged ways is, according to NLS researchers, a rich base for planning educational programs. Street, referring to case studies of the literacy practices of Black South Africans, argues that the researchers:

> link the account of everyday literacy practices in South Africa to contemporary theories regarding the New Literacy Studies, discourse and power on the one hand and to precise policy outcomes regarding apprenticeship, mediation and non-formal education in the design of literacy programmes on the other.
>
> (Street, 1996, p. 3)

Barton (1999) also makes the point that NLS is a theory that acts as

> a lens enabling teachers to see literacy and language in a different way. There is a whole set of issues of relevance to the learning of reading and writing which a social view of literacy highlights, including changes in the social role of the written word, and in the relation of spoken and written language to each other and to other media. There are also changes in English and its role throughout the world and changing interrelationships between languages.

Using as a case study a UK-based English language class with a group of twelve Japanese students, Barton argues that a more concrete use of NLS theory is the re-examination of the classroom as "a textually mediated world". The insights into classroom interaction emerging from this particular study were threefold: "that literacy was used to create time and space; that the texts had other uses beyond being read; and that the talk around texts was central to the classroom activities" (Barton, 1999).

Thus, although NLS does not necessarily have an educational agenda, much of its research has potential for educational applications. Other examples include research into adult literacy (e.g. Barton, 1994; Barton and Hamilton, 1998) and ESL at secondary school level (e.g. Moll, 1990). In sum its premise, like that of CL, is that learning to engage with texts and discourses entails far more than language development or skill acquisition *per se*. NLS classroom applications therefore necessarily share CL's aim of deconstructing hegemonic "truths" about social life, political values and cultural practices (cf. Luke, 1995, p. 37).

Genre approaches

Although traditionally a literary construct, over the past twenty years genre has been developed as a means for examining non-literary texts. In broad terms, genre can be defined as rhetorical actions or responses to recurring situations or contexts. It is a construct that has been developed (in educationally relevant ways) within the contexts of SFL, New Rhetoric and a specialised area of English language teaching, referred to as English for specific purposes (ESP). Each of these developments is discussed in turn in order to draw out the differences and similarities across the three approaches.

Systemic functional linguistics and the concept of genre

The main aim of the SFL concept of genre

In SFL, the concept of genre, primarily developed by Martin together with Rothery (e.g. 1980, 1981, 1986) can be seen as an enhancement of Halliday's theory of the relationship between form, function and context. That is, the relationship of language and its cultural context can be further examined by analysing how written and spoken texts are structured and shaped in order to achieve the goals and purposes of a particular culture: "As a level of context, genre represents the system of staged goal oriented social processes through which social subjects in a given culture live their lives" (Martin, 1997, p. 13).

Within educational contexts, SFL work in genre can be seen as motivated by the recognition that students need to acquire control over the kinds of texts that are relevant to their educational and wider social needs, particularly those texts that can be considered as institutionally powerful. In particular, SFL-based genre research and educational applications have been motivated by the needs of economically and socially disadvantaged groups, including both first and second language speakers. It is argued that explicit teaching of genres increases the opportunities of such groups to extend their repertoire of institutionally valued linguistic resources and texts. Martin states:

> It is the view of genre-based researchers and teacher trainers that subjectivity changes by evolution, not revolution, and that teaching powerful discourse expands a student's meaning potential . . . powerful discourses are not regarded as so ineffable that they cannot be taught.
>
> (1993, p. 161)

Outline of theoretical approach

Essentially, SFL genre theory has been developed as a means of examining how cultures draw on different kinds of written and spoken texts to get different things done, for example, recording personal experiences, giving instructions, having a casual conversation. In the 1990s, genre description became more fine-tuned by describing text structures occurring in specific social contexts and institutions (see Christie and Martin, 1997). Genre theory has not been developed exclusively as an educational tool although, like SFL, the insights it provides into language structure and function have many useful educational applications.

Schematic structure

The SFL approach to genre proposes that, depending on a speaker or writer's overall social purpose, language is shaped and organised to form different types of texts in which "beginnings", "middles" and "ends" have distinct functions. The structures which shape and organise a text are typically referred to as "schematic structures".

Schematic structure specifies the structural possibilities for a particular genre – what elements must or may occur as well as their ordering. Individual texts are classified as members of a particular genre when their structure instantiates a particular configuration of elements or "stages". For example, a recount genre has the obligatory stages of orientation and record of events as well as the optional stage of personal evaluation. These stages are instantiated in the text – Visit to the Brewery – below (written by an adult ESL learner), which can therefore be classified as belonging to the recount genre:

> **Visit to the Brewery**
> *Orientation*
> Ian and Lucy asked us to visit the brewery.
>
> *Record of events*
> Firstly we met at the big wheel on the corner of Bellevue Street and Milton Road, five minutes before the tour began.
>   Then we divided into three groups and went into the brewery in different ways. During the tour we saw how the machines made the beer from beginning to end.
>   After this, we went to the bar to watch the video about the brewery's history while we drank beer.
>   Finally we asked our guides some questions. Before we left two of our classmates thanked them for their attention and help. Then we left to go to our homes.
>
> *Personal evaluation*
> We had a wonderful day.
>
> (Hammond et al., 1992, p. 89)

The role of lexico grammatical analysis

One of the ways in which the different approaches to genre diverge turns on the degree of delicacy in analysing the grammatical constitution of the stages in a structure. The current tendency of SFL, as noted above, is to analyse texts or genres operating within particular contexts of use. An example would be the genre functioning to report on a newsworthy event within the institutional setting of the print media. As a result, the linguistic analysis carried out as a basis for making decisions about generic structure takes into account the specific social setting and tends to reach greater degrees of grammatical delicacy than analyses carried out within the ESP tradition. Within junior secondary school English, for example, Rothery (1994) has shown how the story-telling genre is best conceptualised as a set of subtypes (a "typology"), each with a different textual structure and grammatical patterning – the exemplum, the anecdote, personal recount, etc. Rothery points out how different subtypes are typically taken up by students at different points in their learning (see Figure 7.2).

Genre as probabilistic rather than deterministic

SFL-based genre theory recognises that real-life texts are not necessarily clear-cut, straightforward instances of canonical genres. For example, a text may appear to have

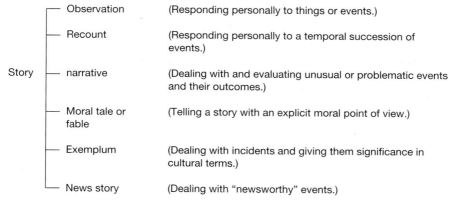

	Observation	(Responding personally to things or events.)
	Recount	(Responding personally to a temporal succession of events.)
Story	narrative	(Dealing with and evaluating unusual or problematic events and their outcomes.)
	Moral tale or fable	(Telling a story with an explicit moral point of view.)
	Exemplum	(Dealing with incidents and giving them significance in cultural terms.)
	News story	(Dealing with "newsworthy" events.)

Figure 7.2 Story genres in school English

Source: Rothery (1994)

many of the characteristics of a narrative genre but might omit the "Resolution" stage, or it may draw on language that is uncharacteristic of the genre. Thus a narrative may lack evaluative or affectual language and appear rather "flat". This issue of a text not exhibiting all the defining features of a genre category can be handled by applying the notion of prototype. The concept of prototype suggests a way of categorising which accounts for the fuzziness and blurred edges of category boundaries. As Paltridge (1995, p. 30) notes, "prototypes have a common core at the centre and fade off at the edges" (see Paltridge (1995) for further elaboration).

SFL genre theorists therefore think of genre descriptions as probabilistic rather than deterministic (cf. Halliday, 1991; Nesbitt and Plum, 1988), as descriptions of staging and linguistic patterning typically drawn on to achieve particular social goals, rather than as rule-governed structures. The theory also takes into account that genres can vary from one culture to another, that the way they are structured may depend on the cultural context in which they operate and that they will often evolve over time, as the original purpose they were established to achieve develops and changes within a culture.

The new rhetoric studies

The main aim of the new rhetoric studies

In the New Rhetoric Studies (NRS), sometimes referred to as the North American school (due to the geographical location of many of its theorists and researchers), the concept of genre largely evolved in the 1980s within the fields of composition studies, rhetoric and professional writing. Compared to the SFL approach to genre, the New Rhetoric "places far less emphasis on explicating textual features, its main goal being to unpack complex relations between text and context" (Freedman and Medway, 1994, p. 9). Unpacking these relations, according to Miller (1994, pp. 38–9) provides "the keys to understanding how to participate in the actions of a community". Although some educational applications of the NRS are recognised, many of the researchers in this tradition are theoretically and research oriented.

Outline of theoretical approach

Genre and context

The focus in NRS is on the functional and contextual aspects of genres and on under-standing their use by particular communities. Miller argues that "a rhetorically sound definition of genre must be centred not on the substance or form of discourse but on the action it is used to accomplish" (Miller, 1984, p. 151).

Genres as provisional

Schryer (e.g. 1994) draws attention to the underpinning theoretical assumption of the New Rhetoric school – that genres are provisional and represent "stabilized-for-now" or "stabilized-enough sites of social and ideological action". The main claim here is that genres are sensitive to contestation and struggle and that there is always the possibility of "play".

Analytical tools

Within the New Rhetoric tradition, ethnographic rather than linguistic methods are employed as a means of analysing texts (e.g. Bazerman, 1988; Schryer, 1994). Such methods "offer thick descriptions of academic and professional contexts surrounding genres and the actions texts perform within these situations" (Hyon, 1996, p. 696). Berkenkotter and Huckin (e.g. 1995), in addition to ethnographic techniques, employ discourse analysis and cognitively based rhetorical analysis forming what they refer to as "a sociocognitive theory of genre" (Berkenkotter and Huckin, 1995, p. xi).

ESP

The main aim of the ESP concept of genre

Within the field of applied linguistics, a body of literature focusing on text structure and generally referred to in terms of genre has been built up in the area of English for specific purposes (ESP) and English for academic purposes (EAP). Generally, this literature is concerned with researching and describing the structure and stylistic features of texts that are seen as pivotal either in the workplace or else in undergraduate and postgraduate study. Such descriptions underpin curriculum and materials design within these specialised language-teaching programmes. The goal of genre theory in this tradition, therefore, is largely educational with one of the main target audiences being non-native speakers of English.

Outline of theoretical approach

Genre and communicative purpose

Within the ESP/EAP tradition the main proponents of genre, Swales (1990), Bhatia (1993) and Dudley-Evans (1994), make communicative purpose the central criterion for genre identification. Text structure and grammar, however, unlike in the NRS tradition, are also recognised as defining features.

As in the case of both SFL and NRS, the social context of genre is likewise emphasised – theorists recognise that texts are constructed and interpreted within particular contexts of culture and that learning the discourse and texts of a particular discipline area or domain of work constitutes an important part of apprenticeship into a new community or "discourse community" (Swales, 1990, p. 3).

Analytical tools

In terms of the method of textual analysis employed by applied linguists such as Swales and Bhatia, approaches are similar to those of SFL. That is, a text is broken down into a linear sequence of constituents (usually referred to as "moves"), each of which is identified by reference to its perceived communicative functionality. For example, Bhatia (1993, p. 165) analyses persuasive academic writing as using a generalisable structure of four moves:

- Presenting the case
- Offering the argument
- Reaching the verdict
- Recommending action.

Researchers in the ESP/EAP tradition may also take into account grammar, usually focusing on particular features such as verb tense, hedges and passive voice (see Swales and Feak, 1994).

The value of a genre approach to analysing written language: a TESOL perspective

Pedagogical applications of genre theory have been developed more extensively in the SFL and ESP/EAP traditions than in the New Rhetoric school. In fact, the new rhetoricians are generally opposed to what they perceive to be the unnecessary explicitness and "authoritarianism" in genre pedagogy (Freedman, 1994, p. 192). They argue that learning a new genre is not a conscious process and that genres are generated in response to a task. Thus rather than explicitly teaching students the "schematic structure" or "moves" of a genre, they assert that students acquire new genres in the process of struggling to solve a problem:

> critical consciousness [of genre structure] becomes possible only through the performance: full genre knowledge (in all its subtlety and complexity) only becomes available as a result of having written. First comes the achievement of performance, with the tacit knowledge implied, and then, through that, the meta awareness which can flower into conscious reflexive knowledge.
>
> (Freedman, 1994, p. 206)

In contrast, both SFL theorists and applied linguists working in the fields of ESP and EAP believe that the explicit teaching of generic structures and their associated grammatical features can help learners (particularly non-native speakers of English) to master the functions and linguistic conventions of texts necessary for successful participation in a range of disciplines and professions.

The most extensively used genre-based pedagogy in the Australian context is a three-phase model of intervention whereby teachers model target genres and then jointly construct them with learners as a basis for learners' independent constructions. The model is designed to develop both control as well as critical reflection on the genres that are relevant to student needs (see e.g. Hammond *et al.* (1992) for a version of this model).

In the context of applied linguistic work in EAP and ESP, rather than follow an overall teaching-learning model, various pedagogic strategies have been developed as a means of teaching genre. In the section below, some sample tasks illustrate the approach taken in this tradition. They form part of a section in a "self-help" book by John Swales and Christine Feak aimed at helping non-native students write a research paper in English. The specific extract is designed to help non-native speaker postgraduate students to write the introductory section to a research article.

Creating a research space
In summary, then, the Introduction sections of RPs [research papers] typically follow the pattern in table 21 in response to two kinds of competition: competition for research space and competition for readers. We can call this rhetorical pattern the Create-a-Research-Space (or CARS) model.

TABLE 21.   Moves in Research Paper Introductions

Move 1   Establishing research territory
        a   by showing that the general research area is important, central, interesting, problematic, or relevant in some way. (optional)
        b   by introducing and reviewing items of previous research in the area. (obligatory)

Move 2   Establishing a niche[a]
        a   by indicating a gap in the previous research, raising a question about it, or extending previous knowledge in some way. (obligatory)

Move 3   Occupying the niche
        a   by outlining purposes or stating the nature of the present research. (obligatory)
        b   by announcing principal findings. (optional)
        c   by indicating the structure of the RP. (optional)

a In ecology, a niche is a particular micro environment where a particular organism can thrive. In our case, a niche is a context where a particular piece of research makes particularly good sense.

Task one
Read our draft Introduction to our mini-RP [The Position of Sentence Connectors in Academic English] and carry out the tasks that follow.

The Position of Sentence Connectors in Academic English
C. B. Feak and J. M. Swales

(Draft) Introduction

1 Many commentators have noted that sentence connectors (e.g., however) are an important and useful element in expository and argumentative writing. 2 Frequency studies of their occurrence in academic English extend at least as far back as Huddleston (1971). 3 ESL writing textbooks have for many years regularly included chapters on sentence connectors (e.g., Herbert, 1965). 4 Most reference grammars deal with their grammatical status, classification, meaning, and use. 5 Some attention has also been given to the position of sentence connectors in clauses and sentences. 6 Quirk and Greenbaum (1973) observe (a) that the normal position is initial; (b) that certain connectors, such as hence and overall, "are restricted, or virtually restricted, to initial position" (p.248); and (c) that medial positions are rare for most connectors, and final positions even rarer. 7 The only attempt known to us to explain differences in position on semantic grounds is an unpublished paper by Salera (1976) discussed in Celce-Murcia and Larsen-Freeman (1983). 8 The Salera paper deals only with adversatives like however and suggests that initial position reflects something contrary to expectation, while medial position reflects a contrast that is not necessarily unexpected. 9 However, neither of these studies provides any descriptive evidence of the actual positions of sentence connectors in academic texts. 10 In the present paper, we report on a preliminary study of sentence-connector position in a sample of twelve published articles.

1 Divide the text into the three basic moves.
2 Look at table 21 again. Where in our Introduction would you divide Move 1 into 1a and 1b?
3 What kind of Move 2 do we use?
4 What kind of Move 3a do we use?
5 Underline or highlight any words or expressions in sentences 1 through 3 used to establish a research territory.
6 List the six citations used in our draft introduction. (Salera is cited twice.) Do you have criticism of our review of the previous literature?
7 Where do these six citations occur in the sentence? What does this tell us?

(Swales and Feak, 1994, pp. 174–6)

Contrastive rhetoric

The main aim of contrastive rhetoric

A central aim of contrastive rhetoric (CR) is to explore how the organisation of texts, particularly expository and argumentative texts, varies across cultures and languages. Recent studies have also focused on the way in which distinct rhetorical forms have developed within different varieties of English. These studies show how the institutionalised varieties of English used in the countries of the Outer Circle (see Kachru and Nelson, Chapter 1, this volume) have their own "nativised" rhetorical organisation. The focus of CR is almost exclusively written rather than spoken text.

Although originally motivated by pedagogical concerns related to ESL writing (e.g. Kaplan, 1966), CR's current concerns extend beyond issues of teaching and learning.

Outline of theoretical approach

CR was first developed in the 1960s (e.g. Kaplan, 1966) as an area of research primarily concerned with second-language acquisition, specifically second-language writing. At that time the main theoretical underpinning was classical rhetoric. More recently the new extended paradigm of contrastive rhetoric takes a broader, more communicative view and is influenced by a range of theories and areas of study, including those of text linguistics, genre, composition and translation. Context, text and grammatical features are therefore all of interest in this tradition.

Methods of analysis

In terms of examining textual features a variety of discourse analysis methods are employed, particularly those that focus on cohesion, coherence and patterns of information flow. In terms of "top-level" discourse structures, several approaches have been advanced, including Hoey's problem-solution text patterns (1986), Tirkkonen-Condit's superstructure of argument (1985) and genre analyses (see Connor (1996, pp. 158–60) for further discussion of these different approaches).

In terms of examining context and context-text relations, systemic linguistics may be drawn on by CR researchers. Kachru, for example (e.g. 1995, 1997), draws on the notion of "meaning potential" and "context of culture" and "context of situation" as a framework for considering the following:

- There may be genres which are unique to a language and culture. For example, the Anglo-American genres of written recipes, instructions (for knitting, or assembling pieces of furniture, etc.) have no parallel in the traditional Indian context.
- Identical speech situations (e.g. ceremonies) may call for distinct genres in different sociocultural contexts. Thus, in the Indian context, a written invitation has to be preceded by an oral face-to-face invitation, or where great distances are involved, a personal letter apologising or extending invitation through the written medium only.
- There may be different rhetorical patterns associated with different genres. For example, whereas Hindi appears to favour a spiral rhetorical pattern in expository prose, the Anglo-American expectation is a straight linear pattern of organisation.

(Kachru, 1997, pp. 340–1)

The value of contrastive rhetoric for analysing written language: a TESOL perspective

The findings of CR have various pedagogical implications. First, the diverse approaches to writing taken by different cultures explain preferences in writing styles in terms of cultural formations. Second, English language teachers who are aware of differences in rhetorical styles can make these differences explicit particularly in a context where students are from a single native language and educational background.

The main pedagogical innovation rising from CR studies is to teach explicitly rhetorical modes of English relevant to the needs of learners. This kind of pedagogic intervention is premised on the belief that learning standard rhetorical patterns and the sociolinguistic constraints associated with them (across English-speaking contexts) is essential for access to scientific, technical and other types of information disseminated in English throughout the world.

Another school of thought argues that an equally important pedagogic goal of CR should be not only to raise the consciousness of non-native speakers of English *vis-à-vis* English rhetorical patterns, but also to raise the consciousness of native English speakers *vis-à-vis* the existence of other rhetorical traditions and conventions (Kachru, 1995, p. 29). In particular, Kachru (1995) argues that editors, publishers, academics and teachers should be aware of different rhetorical styles. She asserts that this would prevent the exclusion of non-native speakers (who are unwilling or unable to conform to Western rhetoric) from contributing to the world's knowledge base.

In the extract below, Kachru's analysis of an essay, written by a second-year BA degree student at an Indian college, illustrates the approach to written text carried out within a CR framework. Such an analysis and accompanying commentary shows how CR can provide both teachers and students with insights into distinctive rhetorical patterns which appear to be culturally based. For example, Kachru argues that her analysis of the essay, "Dowry system" provides evidence of a non-confrontational mode of argumentation characteristic of the rhetorical traditions of Hindi and other modern Indian languages. She notes that "the order in which the arguments are presented is the opposite of what is preferred in the 'direct, linear' tradition of academic writing emphasised in the Inner Circle of English" (Kachru, 1997, p. 341).

Text Analysis and Commentary
[Essay 28: Grade A-]

Dowry system: a curse on the Indian society

(1) Since the very ancient times the Indian society has been burdened by a series of orthodox traditions which in due course of time proved to be much accused social evils. (2) Dowry, of course, is one of those social ills.

(3) In the ancient Indian society, i.e. during the period of great rishis or sages, it was a custom that every new [*sic*] married couple was gifted with some amount in cash or kind from the parents of the bride. (4) This practice finds its reference in the Vedas also. (5) Even from the modern standards, this practice in its preliminary form seems justified, as every new couple needs some sound economy for a nice beginning. (6) But, then this practice was totally voluntary. (7) It was on the bride's parents whether to give such gifts to their daughter and son-in-law for a fresh start. (8) But in due course of time, this practice developed roots and found <u>a strong establishment in the Indian soil fertile for such orthodox beliefs</u>. (9) Now-a-days when the world is gearing up for the 21st century, most of the Indian natives are suffering from this much detested system. (10) The most affected are the females, who are still thought an inferior race in India. (11) Almost everyday a news-item announcing a dowry-death finds its appearance in the dailies.

(12) Dowry has become a matter of resentment among the Indian women. (13) They are now rising against this evil. (14) With the spread of modern education in the Indian villages, <u>a consciousness is being aroused</u> in the hearts of orthodox Indians. (15) We are quite hopefull [*sic*] that with the lapse of time <u>this sin will finally be wiped out of our society</u>.

(16)   The most possible remedies can be:

    (i)   The spread of co-education
    (ii)   Permission of love-marriages
    (iii)   Promotion of self-sufficiency among Indian youths.

Although the text does not strictly conform to the argumentative text structure proposed in Tirkkonen-Condit (1985) and modified in Teo (1995), it has the essential components of problem–solution structure. The first paragraph and the first six sentences of the second paragraph exemplify the initiation component, although there are many lexical indicators of the problem – dowry – is characterised as one of the social evils in sentence 1, and a social ill in sentence 2.12 Sentences 3–7 continue the initiation act, giving further background information. For the first time, in the 8th sentence, the current problem begins to be articulated, again implicitly, and only in the 11th sentence do we have a crucial piece of information, namely, dowry-death. Nowhere is the topic, or the problem – the socially undesirable nature of the dowry system – explicitly expressed.

The next paragraph illustrates the elaboration act (sentences 12–14); sentence 15 marks a transition toward a solution. The final paragraph, sentence 16, expresses the solution component, which suggests a set of solutions to the problem. It represents the conclusion act.

The essay does not conform to the model outlined in Tirkkonen-Condit (1985).* That there is a problem with dowry is lexically expressed several times, mainly with attributive phrases (much detested system, a matter of resentment) and much more strongly, with evaluative nouns (curse, evil, ill, sin, etc.); the problem of dowry and its undesirable consequences for the society are never explicitly stated as the topic of the composition.

Sentences 4–7 are of interest from the point of view of the Indian tradition of discussion from a variety of perspectives. Dowry system is looked at from the point of view of a scripturally sanctioned system (S4), and a socially justifiable system (S5). The subsequent sentence pair (S6 and S7) state the grounds on which the system is justifiable. Thus, all facets of dowry are made apparent before the discussion proceeds.

Sentence 8 contains only an implicit statement of the problem. Sentences 9–11 continue in the same vein. Sentences 12–14 represent the elaboration component. Sentence 15 does not suggest or assert a solution; it merely expresses a wish on the part of the writer. Sentence 16 contains the suggestions for a solution.

---

* The model suggested in Tirkkonen-Condit (1985) consists of three modes of analysis; problem–solution analysis, illocutionary and interactional analysis, and macrostructure analysis. The first two modes are relevant for the analysis of argumentative text structure and will be summarized here (the third is useful in translation across languages and thus is not of immediate relevance). For problem–solution analysis, a text is considered a hierarchical structure with complexes of sequences called minitexts. A minitext is a unit which is recursive and is characterized by a problem– solution structure. The three global units of initiation, elaboration and conclusion that characterize an argumentative text are minitexts which, in turn, are composed of other minitexts. In addition to the global units, a sequence of structural units of situation, problem, solution and evaluation can be identified in an argumentative text. These are specific slots in the text for the initial, undesirable state – the problem – and for the final, desirable state – the solution. The evaluation slot is reserved for the evaluation of the conjectured outcome of the suggested solution. The situation slot is reserved for background material, i.e. facts and views intended for the orientation of H [hearer] to the problem area (Tirkkonen-Condit, 1985, p. 30).

(Kachru, 1997, p. 342: edited version)

According to Kachru, the essay also illustrates a characteristic of the Indian writing tradition referred to as "the culture of sound", whereby language is used as a form of incantation and rhetorical flourish. The underlined parts of the essay contribute to this feature.

Summary

The theoretical approaches to discourse as outlined above demonstrate that written text can be analysed from a number of perspectives. Each of these perspectives provides insight into the nature of written language, such as the way in which it is related to social and cultural contexts, its principles of text organisation and its varying lexical and grammatical patterning. In addition, the ideological implications of literacy and literacy practices are emphasised in many of the approaches.

The different sets of insights and understandings about the nature of written language deriving from each theoretical perspective have led to a variety of pedagogical approaches, many of which have shared characteristics such as a concern that students approach language and text critically and that they understand how texts function in a variety of cultural and social situations. In addition, many of the approaches advocate that students develop an explicit understanding of how written text works. These pedagogical innovations suggest that acquiring the tools of discourse analysis is a valuable enterprise for English language teachers. This is particularly the case in an age where the globalisation of English is leading to increased diversity in the cultural and social contexts in which it is used. This situation requires greater teacher and student awareness and understanding of the different forms and functions of written practices and texts, both locally and internationally.

References

Auerbach, E. (1993) "Re-examining English Only in the ESL classroom", *TESOL Quarterly*, 27(1), pp. 9–32.

Auerbach, E. and Wallerstein, N. (1987) *English for Action*. New York: Addison-Wesley.

Barton, D. (1994) *Literacy: An Introduction to the Ecology of Written Language*. Oxford: Blackwell.

Barton, D. (1999) "Literacy practices in and out of the classroom". Paper presented at Conference on Second language teaching: reading, writing, discourse, Hong Kong/ Guangzhou, June.

Barton, D. and Hamilton, M. (1998) *Local Literacies*. London: Routledge.

Bazerman, C. (1988) *Shaping Written Knowledge: The Genre and Activity of the Experimental Article in Science*. Madison: University of Wisconsin Press.

Berkenkotter, C. and Huckin, T. (1995) *Genre Knowledge in Disciplinary Communication*. Hove, Sussex: Lawrence Erlbaum.

Bhatia, V.K. (1993) *Analysing Genre: Language Use in Professional Settings*. London: Longman.

Bock, M. (1998) "Teaching grammar in context", in S. Angelil-Carter (ed.) *Access to Success: Academic Literacy in Higher Education*. Cape Town, SA: University of Cape Town.

Christie, F. and Martin, J.R. (1997) *Genres and Institutions: Social Processes in the Workplace and School*. London: Pinter.

Clark, R. and Ivanič, R. (1991) "Consciousness-raising about the writing process", in P. Garrett and C. James (eds) *Language Awareness in the Classroom*. London: Longman.

Clark, R. and Ivanič, R. (1997a) *The Politics of Writing*. London: Routledge.

Clark, R. and Ivanič, R. (1997b) "Critical discourse analysis and educational change", in L. van Lier (ed.) *Encyclopedia of Language and Education*, Vol. 6: *Knowledge about Language*. Dordrecht: Kluwer.

Clark, R. and Ivanič, R. (1999) "Raising critical awareness of language: a curriculum aim for the new millennium", editorial in *Language Awareness, Special Issue — Critical Language Awareness*, 8(2), pp. 67–70.

Coffin, C.J. (1996) *Exploring Literacy in School History*. Sydney: Disadvantaged Schools Program, Metropolitan East Region.

Connor, U. (1996) *Contrastive Rhetoric: Cross-cultural Aspect of Second-language Writing*. Harvard, MA: Cambridge University Press.

Connor, U. and Kaplan, R. (1987) *Writing Across Languages: Analysis of L2 Text*. Reading, MA: Addison-Wesley.

Cope, B. and Kalantzis, M. (eds) (1993) *The Powers of Literacy: a Genre Approach to Teaching Writing*. London: Falmer Press.

Derewianka, B. (1990) *Exploring How Texts Work*. Sydney: PETA.

Drury, H. and Gollin, S. (1986) *The Use of Systemic Functional Linguistics in the Analysis of ESL Student Writing and Recommendations for the Teaching Situation*. ALAA, Occasional Papers 9, pp. 209–36.

Dudley-Evans, T. (1994) "Genre analysis: an approach to text analysis for ESP", in M. Coulthard (ed.) *Advances in Text Analysis*. London: Routledge, pp. 219–28.

Eggington, W.G. (1987) "Written academic discourse in Korean: implications for effective communication", in U. Connor and R. Kaplan (eds) *Writing Across Languages: Analysis of L2 Text*. Reading, MA: Addison-Wesley.

Fairclough, N. (1989) *Language and Power*. Language in Social Life Series, ed. C. Candlin. London: Longman.

Fairclough, N. (1992) *A Critical Language Awareness*. Singapore: Longman.

Fairclough, N. (1995) *Critical Discourse Analysis: The Critical Study of Language*. Language in Social Life Series, ed. C. Candlin. London: Longman.

Feez, S. (1998) *Text-based Syllabus Design*. Sydney: NCELTR , Macquarie University.

Foucault, M. (1979) *Discipline and Punishment* (A Sheridan translation). New York: Harper.

Foucault, M. (1980) *Truth and Power* (A Sheridan translation). New York: Harper.

Freedman, A. (1994) "Do as I say": the relationship between teaching and learning new genres", in A. Freedman and P. Medway (eds) *Genre and the New Rhetoric*. London: Taylor & Francis.

Freedman, A. and Medway, P. (1994) "Locating genre studies: antecedents and prospects", in A. Freedman and P. Medway (eds) *Genre and the New Rhetoric*. London, Taylor & Francis.

Freire, P. (1974) *Education for Critical Consciousness*. London: Sheed and Ward.

Freire, P. (1985) *The Politics of Education*. London: Macmillan.

Gee, J.P., Hull, G. and Lankshear C. (1996) *The New Work Order: Behind the Language of the New Capitalism*. Sydney and Boulder, CO: Allen and Unwin and Westview Press.

Gilbert, P. (1993) "(Sub)version: using sexist language practices to explore critical literacy", *Australian Journal of Language and Literacy*, 16 (4), pp. 323–32.

Halliday, M.A.K. (1991) "Towards probabilistic interpretations", in E. Ventola (ed.) *Functional and Systemic Linguistics: Approaches and Uses*. Berlin: Mouton de Gruyter.

Halliday, M.A.K. (1994) *An Introduction to Functional Grammar*. London: Edward Arnold (2nd edn).

Halliday, M.A.K. and Matthiesson, C.M.I.M. (1999) *Construing Experience through Meaning: A Language Based Approach to Cognition*. London: Cassell.

Hammond, J., Burns, A., Joyce, H., Brosnan, D. and Gerot, L. (1992) *English for Social Purposes*. Sydney: NCELTR, Macquarie University.

Heath, S.B. (1983) *Ways with Words: Language, Life and Work in Communities and Classroom*. Cambridge: Cambridge University Press.

Hoey, M. (1986) "Overlapping patterns of discourse organisation and their implications for clause relational analysis in problem–solution texts", in C.R. Cooper and S. Greenbaum (eds) *Studying Writing: Linguistic Approaches*. Newbury Park, CA: Sage.

Hood, S., Solomon, N. and Burns, A. (1996) *Focus on Reading*. Sydney: NCELTR.

Hymes, D. (1972) "Models of interaction and social life", in J. Gumperz and D. Hymes (eds) *Directions in Sociolinguistics: The Ethnography of Communication*. New York: Holt-Rinehart.

Hyon, S. (1996) "Genre in three traditions: implications for ESL", *TESOL Quarterly*, 30 (4), pp. 693–721.

Janks, H. (1993) *Language and Position*. London: Hodder and Stoughton, in association with Witwatersrand University Press.

Janks, H. (1996) *Why We Still Need Critical Language Awareness in South Africa*. Spil Plus: University of Stellenbosch.

Joyce, H. (1992) *Workplace Texts in the Language Classroom*. Sydney: AMES.

Kachru, Y. (1995) "Contrastive rhetoric in World Englishes", *English Today*, 41 (11), pp. 21–31.

Kachru, Y. (1997) "Cultural meaning and contrastive rhetoric in English Education", *World Englishes*, 16 (3), pp. 337–50.

Kaplan, R. (1966) "Cultural thought patterns in intercultural education", *Language Learning*, 16, pp. 1–20.

Lankshear, C. with Gee, J.P., Knobel, M. and Searle, C. (1997) *Changing Literacies*. Buckingham: Open University Press.

Lee, A. (1996) *Gender, Literacy, Curriculum*. London: Taylor & Francis.

Luke, A. (1995) "Text and discourse in education: an introduction to critical discourse analysis", *Review of Research in Education*, 21, pp. 3–47.

McCarthy, M. and Carter, R. (1994) *Language as Discourse: Perspectives for Language Teaching*. Harlow: Longman.

Martin, J.R. (1992) *English Text: System and Structure*. Amsterdam: Benjamins.

Martin, J.R. (1993) "Genre and literacy – modelling context in educational linguistics", *Annual Review of Applied Linguistics*, 13, pp. 141–72.

Martin, J.R. (1997) "Analysing genre: functional parameters", in F. Christie and J.R. Martin (eds) *Genre and Institutions*. London: Cassell.

Martin, J.R. and Rothery, J. (1980, 1981, 1986) *Writing Project Report, Nos. 1, 2 and 4*. Sydney: Department of Linguistics, University of Sydney.

Martin, J.R. and Rothery, J. (1993) "Grammar: making meaning in writing", in B. Cope and M. Kalantzis (eds) *The Powers of Literacy*. Bristol, PA: Falmer Press.

Miller, C. (1984) "Genre as social action", *Quarterly Journal of Speech*, 70, pp. 151–67.

Miller, C.R. (1994) "Genre as social action", in A. Freedman and P. Medway (eds) *Genre and the New Rhetoric*. London: Taylor & Francis.

Moll, L. (1990) "Literacy research in communities and classrooms: a socio-cultural approach". Paper presented at the Conference on Multidisciplinary Perspectives on Research Methodology in Language Arts, National Conference on Research in English, Chicago, Illinois.

Murison, E. and Webb, C. (1991) *Writing a Research Paper*. Learning Assistance Centre, University of Sydney, Australia.

Muspratt, S., Luke, A. and Freebody, P. (eds) (1997) *Constructing Critical Literacies: Teaching and Learning Textual Practices*. Sydney: Allen and Unwin.

Nesbitt, C. and Plum, G. (1988) "Probabilities in a systemic grammar: the clause complex in English", in R. Fawcett and D. Young (eds) *New Developments in Systemic Linguistics*, Vol. 2: *Theory and Application*. London: Pinter, pp. 6–38.

NSW AMES (1995) *Certificates in Spoken and Written English*. Sydney: NSW AMES.

Paltridge, B. (1995) "Genre and the notion of prototype", *Prospect*, 10 (3), pp. 28–34.

Pennycook, A. (1994) *The Cultural Politics of English as an International Language*. Harlow: Longman.

Prinsloo, M. and Breier, M. (eds) (1996) *The Social Uses of Literacy*. Bertsham, SA: Sached Books, and Amsterdam, The Netherlands: John Benjamin's Publishing Company.

Rothery, J. (1994) *Exploring Literacy in School English, Write it Right: Resources for Literacy and Learning*. Sydney: Disadvantaged Schools Program, Metropolitan East Region.

Schryer, C.F. (1994) "The lab versus the clinic: sites of competing genres", in A. Freedman and P. Medway (eds) *Genre and the New Rhetoric*. London: Taylor & Francis.

Shor, I. (1993) "Education is politics: Paolo Freire's critical pedagogy", in P. Mclaren and P. Leonard (eds) *Paulo Freire: A Critical Encounter*. London: Routledge.

Street, B. (1984) *Literacy in Theory and Practice*. Cambridge: Cambridge University Press.

Street, B. (1993) *Cross-cultural Approaches to Literacy*. Cambridge: Cambridge University Press.

Street, B. (1995) *Social Literacies: Critical Approaches to Literacy in Development, Ethnography and Education*. London: Longman.

Street, B. (1996) "Preface", in M. Prinsloo and M. Breier (eds) *The Social Uses of Literacy*. Bertsham, SA: Sached Books, and Amsterdam, The Netherlands: John Benjamin's Publishing Company.

Swales, J.M. (1990) *Genre Analysis* Cambridge: Cambridge University Press.

Swales, J.M. and Feak, C.B. (1994) *Academic Writing for Graduate Students: A Course for Non-native Speakers of English*. Ann Arbor: University of Michigan Press.

Teo, Adisa (1995) Analysis of Editorials: A Study of Argumentative Text Structure. University of Illinois, Ph.D. Dissertation.

Thesen, L. (1998) "Creating coherence, design and critique of academic literacy materials", in S. Angelil-Carter (ed.) *Context in Access to Success: Academic Literacy in Higher Education*. Cape Town, SA: University of Cape Town.

Tirkkonen-Condit, S. (1985) "Argumentative text structure and translation", *Studia Philological Jyvaskylaensia*, Vol. 18. Jyvaskla, Finland: Kirjapaino Oy, Sisasuomi.

Wallace, C. (1992) "Critical literacy awareness in the EFL classroom", in N. Faircough (ed.) *Critical Language Awareness*. London: Longman.

Widdowson, H. (1998) "The theory and practice of critical discourse", *Analysis in Applied Linguistics*, 19 (1), pp. 136–61.

Wodak, R. (1996) *Disorders of Discourse*. London: Longman.

Chapter 8

Anne Burns

ANALYSING SPOKEN DISCOURSE: IMPLICATIONS FOR TESOL

Introduction

IN MANY CONTEMPORARY LANGUAGE TEACHING contexts one of the main aims is to enable students to engage in successful spoken exchanges with other speakers of the target language. In relation to English language teaching, this aim is inevitable in an increasingly mobile world where native and non-native speakers of the language will need to communicate across national borders in order to do business on a world scale and to develop relationships beyond the confines of a particular culture (see Kachru and Nelson, Chapter 1, and Graddol, Chapter 2, this volume). In this chapter I argue that, with the advent of communicative language teaching, the more conventionally used models of language based on the written mode will no longer suffice as a basis for teaching speaking. Instead, if teachers are to engage students in more authentic language use, they will need greater understanding of the recent insights provided by discourse analysis. I also examine some major approaches to spoken discourse analysis which can be used to inform language teaching.

Discourse analysis is a relatively new discipline where the focus is on examining natural and extended samples of both spoken and written language (see Coffin, Chapter 7, this volume, for an explanation of this term and applications to written discourse). The insights from discourse analysis for spoken text analysis are particularly new, although as early as the 1920s Palmer (e.g. Palmer and Blandford, 1924) stressed that the study of language should be based on conversation, while Firth (1957:32) argued that: 'Neither linguistics nor psychologists have begun the study of conversation, but it is here that we shall find the key to a better understanding of what language really is and how it works.' For many years, however, spoken language was still considered too disorganised, ungrammatical and formless to be analysed systematically. Mitchell (1957:43) reflects the general sentiment when he states: 'It is certainly the common view that the written form is the only one deserving serious attention, study and cultivation.'

It is only more recently that corpora of spoken English and studies focusing on conversational analysis are enabling us to see more clearly the distinctiveness of spoken grammar (Biber, 1995; Biber *et al.*, 1998; Carter and McCarthy, 1997; McCarthy, 1998; McCarthy and Carter, 1994; Ochs *et al.*, 1996; Ono and Thompson, 1995). These studies have, of course, been facilitated by advances in computer and audio technology which allow for the extensive storage, analysis and recording of corpora of spoken language. One key insight from this more recent research is that the kinds of grammatical choices speakers make are highly dependent on contextual features, together with the speakers' moment-by-moment creation of the interaction (Hughes and McCarthy, 1998), a perspective that stands in contrast with traditional prescriptive and sentence-level approaches to grammatical description.

Spoken texts and the language classroom

Despite these advances in applied linguistics, the teaching of speaking in the English language teaching field is still largely based on 'idealised' (Carter, 1997) spoken texts. These are texts designed specifically for the language classroom which are generally in the form of scripted dialogues, usually developed from the writers' intuitions about spoken interaction, and frequently accompanied by audio-cassettes of the dialogue. There are often good reasons for choosing ready scripted materials such as these, especially when dealing with lower level students. They are easily available, and recordings are generally profes-sionally produced and of good quality; they are considered easier for students to process, and provide a sense of teacher and student security.

However, for most students the sense of security evaporates when they are faced with the task of interacting in the target language in authentic social contexts outside the class-room. While they may provide some overall structure and vocabulary, scripted dialogues rarely reflect the unpredictability, the dynamism or the linguistic features and structures of natural spoken discourse. To highlight these differences, let's consider two texts drawn from Australian sources (Gollin, 1994).

Text 1 Making a doctor's appointment

(telephone rings)
Patient: Could I make an appointment to see the doctor please?
Receptionist: Certainly, who do you usually see?
Patient: Doctor Cullen.
Receptionist: I'm sorry but Dr Cullen has got patients all day. Would Dr Maley do?
Patient: Sure.
Receptionist: OK then. When would you like to come?
Patient: Could I come at four o'clock?
Receptionist: Four o'clock? Fine. Could I have your name please?

(Nunan and Lockwood, 1991:56)

Text 2 Confirming an appointment with the doctor

1. *Receptionist*: Doctor's rooms can you hold the line for a moment?
2. *Patient*:   Yes
3. *Receptionist*: Thanks
    (pause)
4. *Receptionist*: Hello
5. *Patient*:   Hello
6. *Receptionist*: Sorry to keep you waiting

7.	*Patient:*	That's all right um I'm just calling to confirm an appointment
8.		with Dr X for the first of October . . .
9.	*Receptionist:*	Oh
10.	*Patient:*	Because it was so far in advance I was told [to . . .
11.	*Receptionist:*	[I see what you
12.		mean, to see if she's going to be in that day
13.	*Patient:*	That's right
14.	*Receptionist:*	Oh we may not know yet
15.	*Patient:*	Oh I see
16.	*Receptionist:*	First of October . . . Edith . . . yes
17.	*Patient:*	Yes
18.	*Receptionist:*	There she is OK you made one. What's your name?
19.	*Patient:*	At nine fift . . .
20.	*Receptionist:*	Got it got it

(Burns *et al.*, 1996:17)

It is not difficult to identify that the second of these two texts is drawn from naturally occurring data. From discourse-based perspective, several observations can be made. The utterances are fragmented, vary in length and cannot be set out as completed sentences. Unpredictable elements occur such as, *can you hold the line for a minute?*, where the patient's purpose for the call is delayed; and there are interruptions (*at nine fift . . .*), and overlaps where the speakers speak at the same time (*I was told to . . . I see what you mean*). There are also hesitations, fillers and pauses which oil the wheels of the interaction as speakers check information or process and think about responses (*Oh; Oh I see*) as well as repetitions (*Got it got it*). The speakers use an informal style and idiomatic language (*I see what you mean; OK you made one*) as well as showing they already have some shared understanding of the context of the interaction (*to see if she's going to be in that day . . .*).

In contrast, Text 1 is a much more idealised version of reality. It represents interaction as smooth, predictable and trouble-free. Utterances are polite and neat and occur as complete sentences; speakers do not interrupt or talk over each other; utterances are short and well formed with standard structures; there is distinct turn-taking as one speaker waits while the other finishes, and there are no hesitations or fillers and very little idiomatic language. Carter *et al.* (1998:69) state that this kind of text represents a 'can-do' and predictable society and that the two texts constitute different orders of reality:

> The scripted text is easier to comprehend, but is unlikely to be produced in actual contexts of use; the unscripted text is real English, but more difficult to comprehend and produce and therefore likely to be considered less appropriate pedagogically.

Students who encounter only scripted spoken language in the classroom have less opportunity to extend their linguistic repertoires in ways that prepare them for unforeseeable interactions outside the classroom. While it is still undoubtedly challenging to introduce authentic spoken texts into the classroom, some – for example, Burns *et al.* (1996), Carter (1997) and Carter *et al.* (1998) – have argued that to withhold such opportunities from students is disempowering and patronising.

How then can English language teachers go about using tools of discourse analysis to underpin communicative language teaching? The following discussion outlines some of these tools and suggests a framework for applying them in language teaching. Analytical

approaches in discourse analysis have been derived from linguistics, philosophy, anthropology and sociology. There is an extensive literature and therefore only a brief overview
can be offered within the scope of this chapter. Five areas of theoretical development in
discourse analysis will be outlined: systemic functional linguistics, exchange structure
analysis, pragmatics, conversation analysis and critical discourse analysis. These areas
provide tools which enable teachers to focus on different features of spoken discourse. The
analyses developed and the degree of delicacy to which teachers take these analyses will
depend on factors such as the purposes to which the analyses will be put, the students'
levels of proficiency, the goals and outcomes towards which students are aiming and the
teacher's and students' time and interest. However, analysing spoken discourse from these
various perspectives provides teachers and students with a richer knowledge of the way
spoken discourse functions as well as an important teaching-learning resource.

Systemic functional linguistics

Coffin (Chapter 7) has already highlighted some of the key theoretical features of systemic
functional linguistics, and other chapters in this volume also take these up in some detail
(see Martin, Chapter 9 and Painter, Chapter 10); only a very brief description will
therefore be outlined here. Systemic functional linguistics (SFL) (e.g. Eggins, 1994; Eggins
and Slade, 1997; Halliday, 1994; Halliday and Hasan, 1976; Martin, 1992) provides insights
into the ways in which language is socially constructed and embedded in culture. It
highlights the functional nature of language and the linguistic differences between, for
example, unplanned conversation and formal written language (see Halliday, Chapter 11).
Genre analysis, within the tradition of SFL, is valuable for highlighting the macro-structure
of text by showing how spoken discourse follows structural conventions; that is, how it
follows various functional sequences (schematic structure) and unfolds in a series of
obligatory or optional stages (for further discussion see Martin, Chapter 9). Slade (1997:
49), for example, supplies generic structures (see Table 8.1) for four of the major genres
of casual conversation: narrative (an entertaining story involving the resolution of some
kind of crisis), anecdote (similar to a narrative, but the crisis is reacted to – amazement,
embarrassment – rather than explicitly resolved), exemplum (the incident is told in order
to make a moral point about how the world should or should not be) and recount (a
retelling of factual events usually concluding with an appraisal of the events; see Coffin
(Chapter 7) for an example of a recount). In Slade's research these 'story-telling' genres
accounted for 43.4 per cent of the casual conversation that occurred in workplace coffee-
breaks, a figure that reflects the importance placed on sharing personal experiences in
everyday social life. She makes the point that such genres are rarely to be found in current
language teaching materials. Slade's research also highlights the way these analysable
generic 'chunks' of language are interspersed with highly interactive sequences of 'chat'
that are unanalysable as genres.

In addition to these large units of discourse, SFL can also help to reveal the micro-
structures of the grammar of texts. Analysis of the register variables of field (the experiential
elements), tenor (the interpersonal elements) and mode (the textual elements) shows
how particular fields are built up through choices of vocabulary (processes, participants)
and expressions of place, time and location (circumstances); how relationships between
interactants are mediated through expressions of attitude (appraisal systems), probability

Table 8.1 Generic structure of story-telling genres

[^ = followed by; ( ) = optional stages]

Genre	Generic structure
Narrative	(Abstract)^(Orientation)^Complication ^Evaluation^ Resolution^(Coda)
Anecdote	(Abstract)^(Orientation)^Remarkable Event^Reaction^(Coda)
Exemplum	(Abstract)^(Orientation)^Incident ^Interpretation^(Coda)
Recount	(Abstract)^Orientation^Record of Events^(Coda)

Source: Slade (1997:49)

(modality) and so on; and how the textual features reflect the immediacy or distance of the events being discussed; that is, the extent to which interactions accompany action, constitute the action, or comment on the action.

A typology of spoken interaction

In terms of their functional motivation, spoken interactions are often identified as falling into one of two major categories (e.g. Brown and Yule, 1983; McCarthy, 1991). *Transactional* interactions are those primarily involving the exchange of some form of good and service (e.g. making an appointment at the dentist), or information (e.g. seeking careers information), while *interactional* interactions primarily involve the creation, maintenance and extension of personal and social relations. It is important to emphasise the word *primarily* here, as in reality many spoken interactions are a mixture of both. Eggins (1990:7) has developed a typology of spoken interactions, using the notion of functional motivation. She uses the terms *pragmatic* to describe transactional encounters and *interpersonal* to define casual conversation. Pragmatic motivation is found in 'interactions which are motivated by the achievement of specific, practical, usually tangible objectives' while interpersonal motivation is present in 'interactions which are motivated by the creation, maintenance or exploration of affective bonds, attitudes, inclinations, obligations'.

In her typology Eggins also draws on Poynton's description of the dimensions of social role relationships related to the register variable of tenor. According to Poynton (1985: 77), social role relationships are mediated by:

1   a social distance or intimacy dimension called CONTACT
2   an attitudinal dimension concerned with attitude or emotion towards addressee (or towards the field of discourse) called AFFECT
3   an authority dimension, which involves force, status or expertise, called POWER.

Poyton argues that these dimensions should also be seen as clines rather than absolutes as in Figure 8.1. Eggins' typology is set out in Figure 8.2.

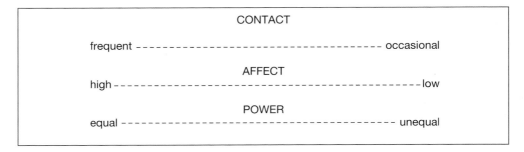

Figure 8.1 Dimensions of tenor

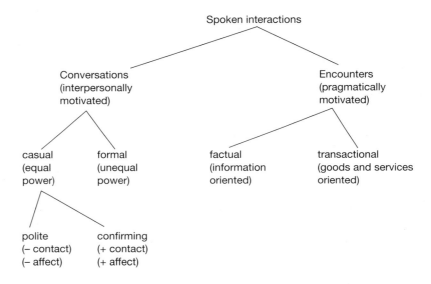

Figure 8.2 A typology of spoken interactions

This typology can be usefully employed in language teaching for classifying different kinds of texts that teachers may wish to introduce or that might be encountered by students.

The contribution of SFL to language teaching

I have outlined very briefly some of the key analytical concepts from systemic functional linguistics and presented a classificatory typology. Together, these tools can provide a useful framework for analysing samples of spoken discourse in order to highlight:

- the functional motivation of the text (e.g. pragmatic)
- the general social purpose of the text (e.g. factual encounter or polite casual conversation)
- the genre and therefore the schematic structure of the text

- how the context and the language work together through the register variables of field, tenor and mode
- how the variables of field, tenor and mode are realised through grammatical and lexical (vocabulary) choices in the text
- the social role relationship dimensions of tenor.

To illustrate how these analytical tools can be put into practice, let us return to Text 2 above and analyse it from an SFL perspective. Table 8.2 on page 130 sets out an analysis undertaken by a group of Australian TESOL teachers.

Exchange structure analysis

One of the criticisms sometimes levelled at SFL is that it is essentially a text-based theory that focuses on the 'finished product' where linguistic choices have already been selected from the grammar and lexical (lexico-grammatical) systems (e.g. Hughes and McCarthy, 1998:264). Exchange structure analysis, an analytical approach sharing a common theoretical origin with systemic functional linguistics, complements SFL by focusing on 'how interactants can keep taking turns' (Eggins and Slade, 1997:44) in the moment-by-moment process of negotiating the interaction and taking into account specific interactional factors in the context. Exchange structure analysis comes out of the work of Sinclair and Coulthard (1975) and Berry (1981) within 'The Birmingham School'. Sinclair and Coulthard analysed classroom interactions, arguing in their analysis that discourse needed to be recognised as a distinct category of analysis from grammar (syntax at sentence level) and phonology (sound and intonation systems). They identified patterns of discourse at different ranks or levels within the classroom, each unit consisting of one or more of the units below. The ranks they identified ranged from act (the smallest unit), to move, to exchange, to transaction to lesson (the largest unit). They also systematically described how each of these units related to the grammatical unit of clause. Our discussion here focuses on the rank of exchange 'two or more utterances' (1975:21) which Sinclair and Coulthard analysed in their classroom data as a three-part (question, answer, comment) structure that typically characterises (traditional) teacher–pupil classroom interaction and which has become known as the IRF structure:

T:	. . . And er, I've got this here. What's that?	
	Trevor.	(initiation)
P:	An axe.	(response)
T:	It's an axe yes. What do I cut with the axe?	(follow-up)/(initiation)
P:	Wood, wood	(response)
T:	Yes I cut wood with the axe . . .	(follow-up)

(Sinclair and Coulthard, 1975:94)

Sinclair and Coulthard's work was taken further by Berry (1981) who, drawing on the anthropological work of Labov (1970), identified a four-part exchange structure. In Berry's framework an exchange involves:

- giving information in a knowledge exchange (these moves are labelled K when analysing the exchange structure)

Table 8.2 Analysis of text 2

Functional motivation	pragmatic (transactional encounter)
Social purpose	to obtain information about services for a medical condition
Genre	confirming appointment for general practitioner consultation
Schematic structure	(Identification 1.1)^(Request 1.1)^Greeting 1.4–5 ^(Apology 1.6–7)^Request for confirmation 1.7–15^ Confirmation of appointment 1.16–29
(Register) Field	Medical setting and activity. Grammatical features: • lexical items related to making a medical appointment by telephone (e.g. *doctor's rooms, line, Dr X, confirm, name*) • verbs related to different schematic stages (e.g. **hold** *the line*, **calling** *to* **confirm**; *know, was, going to be*) • focus on verbs of action in request stages and knowing and being in confirmation stages • circumstances of time and location (*first of October, nine fift . . .*)
(Register) Tenor: social role relationships	Receptionist/patient where there is: • low contact (no indication of personal familiarity) • neutral affect (receptionist polite but neutral towards patient) • unequal power (receptionist in role of knowing and having information)
(Register) Tenor	Grammatical features: • high incidence of personal pronouns (*I, you, she, we*) • some use of modality (*just, may*) • informal lexis related to affect and contact (*sorry to keep you waiting, got it, got it*)
(Register) Mode	• language jointly negotiated in non-face-to-face context • here-and-now, i.e. language accompanies action • references out into context (*there she is*) • ellipsis related to contextual features (*[I'm] sorry to keep you waiting, [I've] got it*)

- giving/accompanying goods and services in an action exchange (these moves are labelled A when analysing the exchange structure).

We will concern ourselves with examining knowledge exchanges (for a detailed account of exchange structure theory see Martin, 1992) which involve the negotiation or transmission of knowledge. They consist of a sequence of four functional slots in which the speaker can take one of two roles:

- the primary knower (K1) who is 'the person who already knows the information' (Berry, 1981:9) and who has the power that comes from being able to display knowledge
- the secondary knower (K2) who is 'the person to whom the information is imparted' (Berry, 1981:10).

Speakers can also make follow-up or feedback moves, labelled *f* when analysing exchanges. The following example, showing K1, K2 and *f* moves is taken from another medical interaction in which the receptionist and caller are negotiating an appointment date for the caller's daughter around her school holidays.

Receptionist (K2):	Because she breaks on the nineteenth, does she?
Parent (K1):	Yes yes
Receptionist (K2):	then she resumes on the fourteenth
Parent (K1):	Yes yes
Receptionist (K2*f*):	Oh
Parent (K1*f*)	Yeah

(Taken from Burns *et al.*, 1996:117)

Feedback moves are not the only moves possible. Changes in this basic pattern indicate that the speaker is using an alternative discourse strategy such as challenging, summarising, clarifying or hypothesising. In the following exchange, concerning membership of an organisation, the enquirer (K2) challenges the information officer (K1) in order to keep the interaction from closure.

Enquirer (K2):	Can you tell me how I would go about applying for new membership then?
Officer (K1):	Well, I'm not sure you're eligible to apply any more. You'll have to write to us. OK? Right?
Enquirer (K2*f*):	Oh . . .
Enquirer (K2*ch*):	I've got one of your brochures in front of me. It says I should be able to get information over the phone. Is that right?

The enquirer's final move in this exchange not only provides K1-type information, but also places a social obligation on the officer to provide an answer. The challenge is a discourse strategy used by the speaker to renegotiate her position within the interaction and to keep the encounter open. It is important to stress that exchange structure analysis is not concerned, as is SFL, with the analysis of texts as a whole; rather, it provides a way of analysing the discourse strategies used by interactants to negotiate meaning *within* the stages of a genre.

Sinclair and Coulthard's and Berry's work has proved useful in capturing the dynamic nature of spoken language. It highlights the move-by-move construction of spoken interactions and shows how each series of moves is organised. However, Berry's work is more suited to pragmatic than interpersonal interactions and its use in the analysis of casual conversation has been limited. Burton (1978, cited in Eggins and Slade, 1997:47) suggested that exchanges in casual conversation are more open-ended and do not follow the 'polite consensus-collaborative model' (Burton, 1978:140) which underpins pragmatic discourse. Burton notes that casual conversation thrives on keeping exchanges open; thus interactants select challenging moves that result in further talk rather than supportive moves which encourage closure (see Eggins and Slade (1997) for further discussion and in-depth analyses of exchanges in casual conversation).

The contribution of exchange structure analysis to language teaching

Language teachers can use insights from exchange structure to help students identify how information is negotiated at each stage of the text. In the first instance, students can observe the basic patterns of unproblematic exchanges with their typical initiation, response, follow-up structure, and note that the follow-up exchanges are often filled by formulaic phrases such as: *oh, yeah, I see, mm, that's interesting* and so on. These kinds of follow-up moves are often absent in English language course books where typically question-answer exchanges predominate. The lack of follow-up moves, however, can make students' conversational attempts seem stilted and distant (McCarthy and Carter (1994:184–93) discuss this issue in some detail). At a later stage, teachers and students can use samples of natural data to discuss the discourse strategies as well as the grammatical structures of moves that enable speakers to expand, challenge, reformulate or summarise. Not only does such analysis potentially increase students' linguistic repertoire, but it also equips them with skills to renegotiate their positions in encounters outside the classroom.

We can turn again to Text 2 above to provide some practical applications of analysis of this type. In this interaction we can see that the receptionist is in the K1 position and the patient in the K2 position. Essentially there are two pieces of information at stake, of which the receptionist is in possession: that the doctor will be on duty and that the appointment has been recorded. Throughout the interaction the patient is in the K2 position because she is unaware of this information. Because of this the receptionist is in the more powerful position, as she is in control of the information and whether it gets released to the patient; we can say that she is in a 'gate-keeping' position, a concept we will return to later in the discussion on critical discourse analysis (p. 138). Interestingly a significant move occurs in lines 14–15 when the receptionist suggests that the information may not be forthcoming: *Oh we may not know yet*. The interaction could potentially have closed at this point had the patient accepted this utterance as final. Instead she says *Oh I see*, using a feedback discourse strategy that encourages the receptionist to continue and to provide her with the information she requires. Observing such strategies and learning the kinds of expressions that can maintain interaction can be very valuable for non-native English speakers, who may otherwise assume that such information is not available.

Conversation analysis

We turn now to another major area of discourse analysis – conversation analysis (CA). CA derives from approaches to discourse analysis known as ethnomethodology and developed in the United States in the 1960s and 1970s by a group of American sociologists. One of the leading theorists was Harold Garfinkel, who was interested in the question of how people interpret everyday life and develop a sense of social order. He was concerned with 'paying to the most commonplace activities of daily life the attention usually accorded extraordinary events' (Garfinkel, 1967:1). A large part of the study of social order centres on how people converse with each other and thus conversation analysis grew out of ethno-methodological approaches, notably through the work of Sacks *et al.* (e.g. 1974), Goffman (e.g. 1967, 1971, 1981) and Atkinson and Heritage (1984). CA focuses on detailed recorded conversations, analysing them for the specific features of their moment-by-moment production, and interpreting the significance of the utterances in the light of their 'environments of action' (Heritage, 1984:292). The relationship between action, meaning and knowledge as it is realised in talk is also a major focus of CA work.

In contrast with SFL, which underpins analyses at both micro- and macro-level, CA with its interest in speaker-by-speaker utterances operates at the micro-level of analysis. Conversation analysts study the smallest units of conversation first. They observe what happens between the participants in conversation and interpret the conversational norms and patterns that emerge as the interaction unfolds. Work in CA has highlighted the nature of various aspects of spoken interaction. An early observation from this approach included the 'grossly apparent facts' (Sacks *et al.*, 1974:700) that speakers take turns in speaking one at a time and that speaker change recurs. From their research with natural data, Sacks *et al.* developed a *turn-taking* system to explain these phenomena. A further question that arose from their observations related to how interactants continue talk and achieve conversational closure. The adjacency pair, which highlights the relatedness of one type of turn to another, provides a further important concept in CA. In the following sections, we will briefly consider these two concepts – turn-taking and turn types – and consider the implications for the teaching of spoken discourse.

Turn-taking

Turn-taking is concerned with when and how speakers take turns and how new speakers are determined. Sacks *et al.* (1974) suggested that at the point of possible turn transfer there are two possibilities: either the next speaker self-selects; or the current speaker selects the next speaker in which case she/he could select her/himself or another speaker. These possibilities are localised not predetermined, which means that speakers must negotiate turns at the end of interaction points, such as a clause or phrase, where the opportunity for transfer exists. Where the interaction is cooperatively negotiated, there is less competition for turns. Overlapping turns may mark areas of disagreement, urgency or annoyance and a high degree of competition for turns.

Pauses convey yet other kinds of meaning negotiation, such as searching for the appropriate response or signalling that an unanticipated response may be forthcoming. Longer turns often signal their endings by pauses, laughter, or fillers such as *anyhow* or *so*.

Turn types

Adjacency pairs are major kinds of turn types, which allow speakers to allocate and give up turns. One of the most common is question/answer, although many others exist such as instruct/receipt, compliment/rejection; challenge/rejection; request/grant; offer/accept;

offer/reject; complaint/denial (Sacks *et al.*, 1974). Adjacency pairs refer to the organised patterns of expected turn types, where speakers can anticipate certain types of forms and meanings from one utterance to the next. A speaker's point of reference in conversation is that the utterance of one speaker is likely to be followed by a particular kind of response (e.g. an offer by an acceptance or a greeting by a greeting). Conversation analysts also iden-tify two possible types of responses: preferred and dispreferred. For example, a request may be followed by an acceptance (the preferred response) or a refusal (the dispreferred response). (Cook (1989:55–7) and Schiffrin (1994:237–8) provide more extensive discussion on turn types.)

We can illustrate how turn-taking and turn types can be analysed in the following data from a pragmatic encounter where a customer and a travel agent are discussing overseas travel arrangements.

Travel agent: Do you want me to hold you some seats?
Customer: (pause)   No . . . I'm just finding out the price. I'm not sure whether I can go yet.

(Author's data)

In this adjacency pair it is the travel agent who takes the initiating turn, which is quickly relinquished to allow the customer to respond. In other words, the travel agent selects the customer as the next speaker. The customer is asked a question and therefore makes a response as would be anticipated in this kind of adjacency pair. However, the question appears to be perceived as a challenge by the customer and she prepares to make a *dispre-ferred* response. This turn is marked as being dispreferred by a slight pause. A dispreferred response is usually accompanied by some kind of justification or explanation, both of which we see in this example: *I'm just finding out the price* (justification); *I'm not sure whether I can go yet* (explanation). Dispreferred responses, with their justifications, explanations or apologies, are usually longer than preferred responses which work towards consensus and compliance to achieve closure and are therefore also usually linguistically simpler.

The contribution of conversation analysis to language teaching

The strength of the analytical tools of conversation analysis is that they have come from research based on meticulously recorded and transcribed samples of natural data. Con-versation analysts reject simulated or 'set-up' interactions from experimental situations. A weakness of conversation analysis resides in the fact that we still do not have precise ways of recognising adjacency pairs. In addition, because it has focused on the micro-structures of talk, it provides powerful accounts of the interactive and dynamic nature of talk but is limited in its ability to account for lengthy and sustained spoken interactions. Never-theless, CA is a very helpful analytical tool in language teaching, enabling the teacher to assist students to observe at a micro-level the turn-taking patterns used to negotiate and renegotiate conversational interaction and the strategies that enable speakers to take on different kinds of roles. In language classrooms, tasks can be developed to explore the following features of authentic talk.

1   Turn-taking organisation and sequencing:
•   discussing speaker roles and rights to turns in spoken interactions (in different cultures, languages and contexts)

- observing and discussing different turn-taking conventions in English (how inter-actants get to keep and retain turns)
- discussing the degree to which overlaps and pauses are tolerated in different cultures and languages
- analysing the degree to which turn-taking is likely to be cooperative as opposed to competitive in different types of interactions
- practising the language that signals one's desire to speak (signals, discourse markers and non-verbal signs that indicate when speakers can gain or give up turns in spoken discourse e.g. paralinguistic (non-verbal) strategies such as eye contact, body posture and position).

2   Turn types:
- observing the nature of preferred and dispreferred responses
- practising the language which typically realises preferred or dispreferred responses
- noting similarities and differences between turn types across different cultures and languages
- analysing the role of feedback turns (*right, ok, uhuh*) and evaluating turns (*really, great*) in maintaining interaction
- analysing the role of different turn types (challenging, rejecting, hypothesising) in renegotiating spoken interactions
- developing strategies for using different turn types (repair – correcting your own or other speaker's meanings; clarification – reformulating the gist or upshot of previous exchanges).

Speech act theory and pragmatics

Speech act theory and pragmatics are analytical areas which share a common concern with how utterances can be interpreted within their settings, rather than how they are produced. Both approaches are therefore philosophical rather than linguistic in their background and orientation. They focus on analysing the meanings and intentions of speakers as they relate to the particular social setting, examining how interactants use and understand the appropriateness of utterances in relation to various situational contexts (e.g. Leech, 1983; Levinson, 1983).

Speech act theory

The work of Austin (1962) and Searle (1969, 1976) was an important contribution to speech analysis. Their central concern was to analyse how speakers' utterances realise or achieve a particular purpose. In other words, what is it that certain pieces of language are doing or performing, for example, apologies (*I'm sorry . . .*), requests (*Would you mind . . .*), promises (*I'll find out for you . . .*), threats (*I'll get you . . .*), acceptances (*I'd love to . . .*), refusals (*I'm not prepared to . . .*), offers (*Would you like . . .*) and so on. The major unit of analysis in speech act theory is the 'illocutionary act'; in other words, the performance of a particular piece of language, which is analysed and given particular forms of meaning in relation to the surrounding situation. Austin and Searle also noted that speech acts may be indirect, and that there is no essential one-to-one correlation between the function (illocutionary force) of an utterance and its form (grammatical structure). For example, in Text 2 above, the receptionist's first utterance includes, *can you hold the line for a moment?* Although this is realised as a question, its illocutionary force is that of command – she is telling the caller to hold the line. Equally she could have expressed this command in a number of ways: *You'll have to hold the line a moment* (declarative); *Hold the line, please* (imperative); *Just a minute, please!* (exclamation).

In the following extract, the utterance *Enquiries* acts to identify the speaker's role but also as an offer of service:

(Service encounter in bureaucratic setting)
A: Hello. Enquiries.
B: Hello. Can I talk to somebody about the sponsorship scheme for migrants?
A: Yes. You can talk to me. What can I help you with?

Here, speaker A gives a *Yes* which responds grammatically to the previous interrogative (adjacency pair of yes/no question and answer) but also responds functionally as an additional identification, *You can talk to me*, as well as a further offer of service: *What can I help you with?* In this instance speaker A's speech act is fulfilling several different speech functions at once, thereby exemplifying what Thompson (1983) calls a complex illocutionary act.

Pragmatics

Pragmatics is mainly derived from the philosophical ideas of H.G. Grice. Grice (1975) proposed that there were distinctions between different types of meaning and that general conversational maxims are based on what he called the 'cooperative principle'. This is the assumption that in any interaction the speaker is potentially obeying four conversational maxims:

- be true (the maxim of quality)
- be brief (the maxim of quantity)
- be relevant (the maxim of relevance)
- be clear (the maxim of manner).

These principles make it possible for conversational partners not only to relate to overt meanings but also to trace possible hidden or indirect meanings. Thus, Gricean pragmatics also proposes that linguistic meanings are distinct from the implied meanings, or 'implicatures' that are present in interactions: 'Implicatures depend on hearers' ability to infer what a speaker intends by drawing upon their knowledge of both linguistic meanings and contexts (including the Cooperative Principle)' (Schiffrin, 1990:5).

More recently, pragmatics theorists such as Sperber and Wilson (1986) have suggested that Grice's four maxims can be placed by a single maxim – be relevant – which can address a central issue in conversation analysis; how it is that one utterance can be seen as a relevant response to another. We can consider how the maxim of relevance works through the following scenario:

I am engaged in conversation with a friend and I ask, *Are you coming to the dinner tonight?* My friend replies, *I must go to the bank.* This response seems odd and disconnected and appears to be in violation of the maxim of relevance. How am I to interpret the intended but hidden meaning of this utterance? I may make the following assumptions about the implicature of this utterance:

- my friend is coming to the dinner, but needs to get some money to cover the cost
- my friend is changing the subject in order to avoid the topic
- my friend has other things on her mind and has not heard the question.

My next utterance is likely to be one that clarifies one of these assumptions, e.g. *OK, so I'll see you later at the dinner, then.* I will then need to judge by my friend's next utterance whether my interpretation of the implicature is correct.

Pragmatists have also explored the conversational principles of politeness (Brown and Levinson, 1978; Lakoff, 1973). The work of Brown and Levinson highlights the way in which cooperation and the maintenance of social relationships acknowledge the 'face' of speech partners in conversational interactions. Pragmatic analysis has frequently been used in the investigation of cross-cultural communicational misunderstandings, assumptions and expectations, as it provides explanations of why communication breakdowns may occur (see e.g. Gumperz *et al.*, 1990; Roberts *et al.*, 1992; Willing, 1992).

The contribution of speech act theory and pragmatics

Like conversation analysis, speech act theory and pragmatics focus on the micro analysis of conversational utterances. However, they have made notable contributions in discourse studies, where the notion of speech acts or illocutionary acts has been used as a major unit of analysis, and the notion of illocutionary force has highlighted the distinctions between form and function. Speech act theory and pragmatics offer teachers the opportunity to highlight for students:

- the 'components' of particular speech acts (how they are composed linguistically)
- the appropriateness of utterances in their situational contexts
- how speakers negotiate certain social situations (e.g. greeting, thanking, accepting/rejecting invitations)
- what roles utterances perform (students could choose speech acts and observe how they are used in natural or pre-recorded settings, such as soap operas or news interviews; see Riggenbach, 1990)
- the performance of certain speech acts (e.g. through classroom role-plays or communicative games).

One of the criticisms sometimes levelled at pragmatic approaches is that the basic assumption is that interaction occurs cooperatively and rests on a state of equality between participants. It fails to account for the disagreement and resistance that often underlies daily interactions, as well as the uneven distributions of power that exist. Eggins and Slade (1997) point out that this view of talk as homogeneous, cooperative, autonomous and equal is hard to sustain when working with authentic samples of discourse. These facets of social interaction have been highlighted by critical discourse approaches and it is to these that we now turn.

Critical discourse analysis

Critical discourse analysis (CDA) was discussed in some detail by Coffin (Chapter 8). I will reiterate briefly here the main tenets of this approach. CDA and its related disciplines of critical linguistics (CL), critical language study (CLS) and critical language awareness (CLA) is a relatively new theoretical approach, emerging in part from the post-structuralist work of social philosophers such as Foucault, Bourdieu and Habermas. While critical discourse analysts often draw on functional approaches such as SFL (cf. Fairclough, 1995; Kress and van Leeuwen, 1996), they examine not only the structures, functions and forms of language in common with text-linguistics, but also the ideological bases of texts, and their uses as media for political or social control and the maintenance of power structures (Fairclough, 1989, 1992a, 1995; Fowler *et al.*, 1979; Kress, 1989; Kress and Hodge, 1979). Their major argument is that language use is not neutral and that language analysis should take account of the way in which linguistic exchanges are mediated by difference and contestation; for example, in worldview, social purpose and intention, age, race and gender. They see all texts as critical sites for the negotiation of power and ideology, even within the most seemingly unremarkable and everyday forms. By 'denaturalising' discourse that may otherwise be seen as taken for granted, critical discourse theorists aim to reveal how particular discourse practices act to the detriment or advantage of certain social groups or individuals.

Work in critical discourse analysis has investigated the power relationships within particular discourse practices in areas such as professional–client interactions (e.g. Mishler, 1984; Wodak, 1996), the law, multicultural and multiracial settings (e.g. Bremer *et al.*, 1996), gender-related differences (e.g. Cameron, 1992; Talbot, 1998) and literacy prac-tices (e.g. Street, 1993; Wallace, 1992). CDA presupposes that language is doing more than merely representing a certain state of affairs, by examining the social power relationships between the interactants and how these affect and motivate choices of linguistic form.

In terms of spoken discourse, CDA theorists such as Fairclough (1995) critique the locally focused, descriptive analyses of a wide range of other approaches – including those of conversation analysts, The Birmingham School and pragmatists – for overlooking how the micro-structures of talk realise and maintain larger social structures. Fairclough (1992b:10) articulates the core of this argument when he states:

> Every discoursal instance has three dimensions; it is a spoken or written language text; it is an interaction between people involving processes of producing and interpreting the text; and it is part of a piece of social action – and in some cases virtually the whole of it.

It is this final dimension – the work that language does in producing and reproducing particular social structures – that is central in CDA approaches. CDA researchers there-fore typically examine how the micro-structures of talk are constitutive of and linked with the macro-structures of the broader discourse community or society.

The contribution of critical discourse analysis to language teaching

Work in critical discourse analysis is part of a broader movement of critical theory to be found, for example, in education, sociology, anthropology and psychology. Unlike other approaches found in these disciplines, however, CDA work encompasses detailed textual analysis and therefore is a useful body of research for language teaching. CDA looks behind the surface structures of texts and asks what social or ideological positions motivate them. This orientation recognises speakers as members of particular cultural, social or professional groups and examines how the forms and functions of the language used take on the discursive practices, histories and ideologies of these groups. The notion of difference and the interactions of different groups is important in CDA analysis. Kress (1989: 12) outlines the nature of difference thus:

> There are likely to be problems at any time, arising out of unresolved differences in the individual's discursive history, the individual's present discursive location and the context of discourses in interactions. That difference is the motor that produces text. Every text arises out of a particular problematic. Texts are therefore manifestations of discourses and the meanings of discourses, and the sites of attempts to resolve particular problems.

Since the early 1980s, an extensive literature drawing on CDA perspectives has emerged and CDA now offers a framework for looking at the ideological basis of talk. It should be stressed, however, that much CDA work has focused on the analysis of written texts (see Coffin, Chapter 8). Recent work on spoken language that employs a CDA perspective includes Eggins and Slade (1997) on analysing genres of casual conversation, such as story-telling and gossip, Coates and Cameron (1988) on the language of all-female groups, and Talbot (1998) on gendered language in spoken interactions between men and women.

In data I collected with other Australian researchers and teachers (see Burns *et al.*, 1996), we noted that in pragmatic encounters speakers such as receptionists and information officers have considerable gate-keeping status in that they often control access and levels of information. They are in powerful positions to decide whether their interlocutors are 'wrong' or 'difficult' categories of enquirer and employ particular discourse strategies to exclude or cut them short. It can be particularly difficult for non-native speakers to renegotiate or contest these strategies in order to keep the interaction open and extend the text towards a satisfactory conclusion. Discussing issues of this kind in the classroom can be very informative for students. In Text 2 above, for example, the receptionist controls the flow of information to the patient, threatening in line 12 to end the interaction by withholding the information the caller seeks. The receptionist also interrupts or cuts off the patient in several places, claiming the right to do so by virtue of her position as a 'gate-keeper' and the fact that she holds a recognised position within a particular type of discourse community. From a CDA point of view, we can make the following observations about Text 2. The receptionist demonstrates her gate-keeping role by:

- keeping the patient waiting
- interrupting the patient's explanations in several exchanges (*I see what you mean*)
- overlapping with the patient (*At nine fift . . .*)
- holding up information about the availability of the doctor (*Oh we may not know yet*).

The patient demonstrates her subordinate role by:

- accepting the receptionist's routine apology (*That's all right*)
- speaking tentatively (e.g using modifiers such as *just*)

- feeling obliged to offer an explanation for her call (*Because it was so far in advance . . .*)
- using a passive voice (*I was told . . .*)
- responding to the receptionist's lack of information with a mild response (*I see . . .*).

Text 2 is not a socially neutral text, but is indicative at a micro-level of patterns of social action which may be realised when people approach companies, bureaucracies or institutions for information or services. People in gate-keeping roles often have well-practised pieces which they rehearse in interactions with their clients. We can see in this text how, although the caller was successful, there are points in the interaction where her enquiry might equally have failed to produce the information she required.

Classroom discussions about power relationships in discourse can empower students who can then prepare themselves with strategies for renegotiating interactions. In a similar pragmatic interaction, for example (Burns *et al.*, 1996:26), where a course information officer at a technical college attempts to get a caller off the line, the caller repositions herself by saying:

> *Yeah, I would be advised to ring up later to ask . . .*

and later:
> *There's not another hobby course at any other tech that you know of . . .?*

and following this:
> *And they might be able to [help] . . .?*

By persistently pursuing her requirements through such discourse strategies, the caller was able to get the information officer to supply her with the information she needed. As Gollin (1994:31) states:

> By bringing these aspects of the interactions to the attention of the learners, they can begin to see that there are a range of spoken language options open to them and that there are specific points in the discourse when they can exercise them. They may or may not choose to be more assertive in a similar situation. This will depend on their own analysis of the relative costs and benefits to themselves but at least they have the power to make more informed choices.

Bringing together analytical tools for language teaching

This chapter has looked only briefly and in a very introductory way at some of the major theories associated with the analysis of spoken discourse. At the basis of this overview is the argument that understanding more about authentic spoken language and exploring and analysing it from a discourse perspective is a worthwhile pursuit for language teachers. Table 8.3 on page 142 aims to bring together the different approaches discussed as a framework for such analysis. The framework assumes that the analysis will derive from natural data and therefore also contains brief guidelines for transcription (see Burns *et al.* (1996:60–3) for further discussion on transcribing data for teaching purposes). However, teachers may wish to work from spoken samples or recordings provided in sources such as

Carter and McCarthy (1997), which provides a good collection and is one of the few books to date aimed at teachers and students which offers extensive natural data.

When using this kind of framework it is not necessary to draw on all tools of analysis, but instead to use those which are relevant to the students and to the types of discourse features the teacher wishes to foreground. In order to illustrate how this framework can be used, consider the analysis of the following text from which you also saw an extract on exchange structure analysis (p. 131).

Text 3 *Making a dentist's appointment*

(R = Ros; E = Emily; [= overlap; . . . = one-second pauses)

1. R: Good morning. Dr Wang's dental surgery. Ros speaking.
2. E: Hi, Ros. It's Emily here.
3. R: How are you Emily?
4. E: Hi. I'm fine.
5. R: That's good.
6. E: I'm ringing to make an appointment for Jennifer to see Wai . . . for a check-up . . .
7. R: [Right
8. E: [. . . during her school holidays.
9. R: When is . . . when is the school . . . first to the thirteenth . . .
10. E: Er no . . . well any day from the twentieth of September.
11. R: Oh, that's nice. Oh . . . no . . . sorry . . . um, we're away.
12. E: Oh.
13. R: Yes.
14. E: That always happens. . . . When are you back?
15. R: We're back on the fourteenth . . .
16. E: [Is that school . . .
17. R: [October . . . um . . . and then school's back, isn't it? Oh well actually that's very interesting. We're away for the whole of the school holidays . . . because she breaks on the nineteenth, does she?
20. E: Yes, yes.
21. R: Then she resumes on the fourteenth.
22. E: Yes . . . yes.
23. R: Oh . . .
24. E: What about the actual fourteenth. I think she might have to go in on the fourteenth . . . on the evening of the fourteenth.
26. R: Oh, on the evening of the fourteenth. Well then that's fine. We could make it on the day. We could make it as early as nine.
28. E: Nine? OK.
29. R: 'Cos you'll be back at work then, won't you?
30. E: Yes, yes.
31. R: Is that a problem for Jennifer?
32. E: Um, that's a thought.
33. R: Do you want to make it after four?
34. E: Well, make it after school, yeah.
35. R: That's not cutting it too fine for you, is it?
36. E: Um . . . yeah . . . that's a problem.
37. R: (laughs) Will you make it here and back home again?

Table 8.3 A framework for analysing spoken discourse

1 Transcribe the recording

- give the text a title
- leave a line between each speaker and number lines for easy reference
- label each speaker using letters, first names or positions (e.g. A, Jo)
- insert contextual information
- retain the wording of the discourse as accurately as possible.

2 Analyse the transcript

- complete a general analysis on a page facing the transcript
- use the following headings to complete the general analysis:

    (i)   Background to the text
          - identify when, how and why the text was produced
          - include relevant social and cultural information.

    (ii) General comments
          - make relevant general comments which will help students understand overall features of the text.

    (iii) Type of interaction
          - identify whether the text is pragmatic or interpersonal.

3 Analyse the discourse and linguistic features of the text

- select the focus of the analysis from the following areas:

    (iv) generic structure analysis
          - identify the social purpose of the text
          - label the stages of the text with functional labels
          - indicate which stages are obligatory and which are optional.

    (v)   register analysis
          - identify the field (topic) of the text
          - identify the tenor (speakers' interpersonal relationships)
          - identify the mode (channel of communication).

    (vi) conversation analysis
          - identify significant adjacency pairs (question–answer)
          - analyse turn-taking patterns and related discourse signals and markers
          - analyse turn types and related strategies.

    (vii) pragmatic analysis
          - identify speech functions
          - analyse how speakers conform to conversational strategies
          - analyse any cross-cultural aspects which may be significant.

    (viii) critical discourse analysis
          - identify any significant aspects of the text in terms of ideology or social power (e.g. bureaucratic gatekeeping).

4 Implications for teaching

- identify significant teaching points arising from the analysis.

38. *E*: Well, how about . . . I could drop her there and she could get herself back home, or she could go out for the day.
40. *R*: Right.
41. *E*: OK, well we'll leave it for the nine . . . er nine o'clock.
42. *R*: Yes, on the fourteenth.
43. *E*: Right. That's Monday isn't it.
44. *R*: Right. Yes.
45. *E*: OK. Good.
46. *R*: Good. Are we going to see you on Saturday? You weren't there last Saturday.
47. *E*: No, er, yes, I will be coming next Saturday.
48. *R*: Good. Even though it was windy, the weather had actually dropped when we were on the courts. It wasn't as bad as I thought it would be.
50. *E*: Oh, really? Actually, that's why I didn't come, because it was so windy and I thought I'd get on with other things.
52. *R*: (laughs) Yes, I was tempted to do the same and Wai said No we're going (laughs).
53. *E*: OK. We'll see you Saturday.
54. *R*: Thank you Emily.
55. *E*: Bye, Ros.

Background to the text

This is a telephone interaction between two Australian women (one of Anglo-Celtic and one of Chinese background). The patient, Emily, is ringing on behalf of her school-aged daughter to make an appointment for a dental check-up. The patient and the receptionist are good friends who play tennis together at the weekend.

General comments

The interaction is a variation on what would normally be expected of an appointment-making interaction. Because of their personal relationship, the receptionist is unusually tolerant of the protracted negotiation that occurs before the appointment is finally fixed. During this negotiation, the receptionist's knowledge of Emily's personal circumstances is also brought to bear.

Type of interaction

This is primarily a pragmatically motivated interaction but it has a strong interpersonal dimension because of the relationship between the two women. The transactional purpose of making the appointment is mixed with confirming casual conversation which occurs when the transactional element is concluded. This type of mixed personal and pragmatic interaction is more common when speakers share long-standing associations or in small communities where people are likely to meet socially as well as professionally. The interaction therefore forms part of the 'discursive history' of the two speakers.

Register analysis

Field: Medical appointment-making. Lexical items are related to field (e.g. recurring references to time and dates), while relational verbs (*is*, *are*) dominate throughout. Material (action) verbs are used to refer to holidays (*breaks*, *resumes*) in transactional (pragmatic) phases, while mental (thinking and perceiving) and verbal (saying) verbs are used in the interactional (interpersonal) phase at the end of the text.

Tenor: Contact is medium to high as there are regular social encounters through the tennis club. In terms of power, the differences have been minimised by the interpersonal relationship, even though Ros is currently in her position as a employee of the dental practice. There is moderately high affect as the speakers clearly feel friendly and cooperative towards each other.

Mode: As this is a telephone call, there is spatial distance and no visual feedback. The feedback moves (*right*, *good*, *OK*, etc.) assure each listener that the exchanges are being attended to as the interaction proceeds.

Conversation analysis

There is a high degree of turn-taking cooperation in this text, with few overlaps or interruptions. In general, the speakers orient well to each other's completion of turns, with interrupted turns such as *Is that school . . .* in line 16–17 being relatively rare. The nature of turn-taking in this interaction is one that reaffirms the warm and non-competitive relationship between the two women. The speakers proceed smoothly primarily through a series of question-answer type exchanges, interspersed with clarifications and explanations. The two speakers do not need to compete to get their points across and the negotiation is not hurried.

Pragmatics

Lines 1–6 are a good example of how interpersonal and pragmatic concerns are mixed in this interaction. If we did not know the background, Emily's response to Ros would appear to infringe Grice's maxims of relevance and quantity. If the interactants did not know each other, using first names and making enquiries about well-being would be inappropriate at this stage. Similarly, questions about school holidays are relevant in this situation. Both speakers infer from their background knowledge to negotiate a successful outcome that satisfies the purpose of the interaction.

Critical discourse

This conversation between two women from a similar cultural and social background and age group reflects social relationships of this type more generally. In this interaction, the potential power of Ros in her role as receptionist is downplayed in order to maintain the positive social relationships that exist between the two women. The negotiation of the appointment is built up patiently and jointly in a text which is unusually protracted for this type of interaction. The language the two women employ works towards their ideological assumptions about how a relationship with medium to high contact is maintained in this cultural setting (e.g. *How are you Emily . . . I'm fine*; the use of *we* (lines 26–7) to express solidarity) through pleasant and polite cooperation.

Possible classroom applications of this text

This text could be used in whole or in part with students at different levels to highlight the following features:

- how spoken texts are frequently a mixture of transactional and interactional
- how aspects of tenor will influence departures from the expected 'script' of a text of this type
- which aspects of the text deal with the obligatory stages of the genre and which with the non-obligatory
- how people address each other through different levels of politeness and familiarity
- ways of giving feedback over the telephone
- the use of modality to express degrees of certainty or probability when negotiating expressions of time
- the extent to which a date or time is open to negotiation.

Final comments

In this chapter, I have attempted to show how discourse-based conceptions of language can begin to frame the teaching of speaking. I would argue that a discourse-based approach to the teaching of speaking is long overdue in language teaching and will become an essential direction for the future of language-teaching pedagogy and research as more and more people find a need to develop strategies for effective interpersonal and intercultural communication, for business negotiation, and for academic participation in tertiary contexts. A passive and idealised representation of spoken interaction, such as exists currently in the majority of language materials, will not suffice to equip non-native speakers with the discourse skills and strategies required in increasingly multicultural and internationalised settings.

However, one major problem for the kind of work I have outlined is that so far the natural language corpora available are primarily based on the discourse of native English speakers from a limited number of cultural and social groups. This raises a number of questions in relation to the concept of teaching English in global contexts, not the least of which is the validity of native speaker discourse as a norm for intercultural communication (see Kachru and Nelson, Chapter 1, Graddol (Chapter 2), and Pennycook (Chapter 6), this volume). Can we assume that the language structures and strategies used by native speakers are those that will be adopted or will wish to be adopted by non-native speakers? If so, which native speaker varieties of English (British, American, Australian, Canadian) are the preferred options from which to derive teaching activities? Are they the most relevant for all learners? Are native speaker varieties adequate for the expression of particular kinds of meanings, values or interpersonal relationships across cultural boundaries? What are the implications for speakers who wish to use English as an alternate or bilingual mode of communication? How does the other language or culture impact on the grammar of English in these situations? How can these alternate forms be represented in the classroom and what choices can be made available to non-native speakers? These are just some of the complex questions that the field of English-language teaching will need to address as it takes up the challenge of teaching English in a globalised world.

Acknowledgements

This chapter draws on material previously written in conjunction with Helen de Silva Joyce and Sandra Gollin. I wish to acknowledge their contributions to the ideas and texts presented.

References

Atkinson, J.M. and Heritage, J. (1984) *Structures of Social Action*. Cambridge: Cambridge University Press.

Austin, J. (1962) *How to do Things with Words*. London: Oxford University Press.

Berry, M. (1981) Systemic linguistics and discourse analysis: a multilayered approach to exchange structure. Mimeo, University of Birmingham.

Biber, D. (1995) *Dimensions of Register Variation*. Cambridge: Cambridge University Press.

Biber, D., Conrad, S. and Reppen, R. (1998) *Corpus Linguistics: Investigating Language Structure and Use*. Cambridge: Cambridge University Press.

Bremer, K., Roberts, C., Vasseur, M., Simonot, M. and Broeder, P. (1996) *Achieving Understanding*. London: Longman.

Brown, G. and Yule, G. (1983) *Discourse Analysis*. Cambridge: Cambridge University Press.

Brown, P. and Levinson, S. (1978) Universals in language use: politeness phenomena. In E. Goody (ed.) *Questions and Politeness: Strategies in Social Interaction*. Cambridge: Cambridge University Press.

Burns, A., Joyce, H. and Gollin, S. (1996) *'I See what you Mean'. Using Spoken Discourse in the Classroom: A Handbook for Teachers*. Sydney: NCELTR.

Burton, D. (1978) Towards an analysis of casual conversation. *Nottingham Linguistics Circular*, 17(2): 131–59.

Cameron, D. (1992) Not gender difference but the difference gender makes: explanation in research in sex and language. *International Journal of the Sociology of Language*, 94: 13–26.

Carter, R. (1997) Speaking Englishes, speaking cultures, using CANCODE. *Prospect*, 12(2): 4–11.

Carter, R. and McCarthy, M. (1995) Grammar and the spoken language. *Applied Linguistics*, 16(2): 141–58.

Carter, R. and McCarthy, M. (1997) *Exploring Spoken English*. Cambridge: Cambridge University Press.

Carter, R., Hughes, R. and McCarthy, M. (1998) Telling tails: grammar, the spoken language and materials development. In B. Tomlinson (ed.) *Materials Development in Language Teaching*. Cambridge: Cambridge University Press.

Coates, J. and Cameron, D. (eds) (1988) *Women in their Speech Communities. New Perspectives on Language and Sex*. London: Longman.

Cook, G. (1989) *Discourse*. Oxford: Oxford University Press.

Eggins, S. (1990) The analysis of spoken discourse. Paper presented at the National Centre for English Language Teaching and Research Spoken Discourse Project Workshop. September, Macquarie University, Sydney.

Eggins, S. (1994) *An Introduction to Systemic Functional Linguistics*. London: Pinter.

Eggins, S. and Slade, D. (1997) *Analysing Casual Conversation*. London: Cassell.

Fairclough, N. (1989) *Language and Power*. London: Longman.

Fairclough, N. (ed.) (1992a) *Discourse and Social Change*. London: Longman.

Fairclough, N. (ed.) (1992b) *Critical Language Awareness*. London: Longman.

Fairclough, N. (1995) *Critical Discourse Analysis*. London: Longman.

Firth, J. (1957) *Papers in Linguistics 1934–51*. Oxford: Oxford University Press.

Fowler, R, Hodge, K., Kress, G. and Trew, T. (1979) *Language and Control*. London: Routledge and Kegan Paul.

Garfinkel, H. (1967) *Studies in Ethnomethodology*. Englewood Cliffs, NJ: Prentice-Hall.

Goffman, E. (1967) *Interaction Ritual: Essays in Face-to-face Behaviour*. Chicago, IL: Aldine.

Goffman, E. (1971) *Relations in Public: Microstudies of the Public Order*. New York: Basic Books.

Goffman, E. (1981) *Forms of Talk*. Oxford: Blackwell.

Gollin, S. (1994) Some insights from the NCELTR spoken discourse project. *Interchange*, Sydney, NSW AMES, 23: 28–31.

Grice, H.G. (1975) Logic and conversation. In P. Cole and J. Morgan (eds) *System and Semantics 3: Speech Acts*. New York: Academic Press.

Gumperz, J., Jupp, T. and Roberts C. (1990) *Crosstalk*. London: NCILT and BBC Education and Training.

Halliday, M.A.K. (1994) *Introduction to Functional Grammar*. (2nd edn). London: Arnold.

Halliday, M.A.K. and Hasan, R. (1976) *Cohesion in English*. London: Longman.

Heritage, J. (1984) *Garfinkel and Ethnomethodology*. Oxford: Blackwell.

Hughes, R. and McCarthy, M. (1998) From sentence to discourse: discourse grammar and English language teaching. *TESOL Quarterly*, 32(2): 263–87.

Ivanič, R. (1997) *Writing and Identity: The Discourse Construction of Identity in Academic Writing*. Amsterdam: Benjamins.

Kress, G. (1989) *Linguistic Processes in Sociocultural Practice*. Oxford: Oxford University Press.

Kress, G. and Hodge, R. (1979) *Language as Ideology*. London: Routledge and Kegan Paul.

Kress, G. and van Leeuwen, T. (1996) *Reading Images: The Grammar of Visual Design*. London: Routledge and Kegan Paul.

Labov, W. (1970) The study of language in its social context. *Studium Generale*, 23: 30–87.

Lakoff, R. (1973) The logic of politeness: Or minding your p's and q's. In Papers from the Ninth Regional Meeting of the Chicago Linguistics Society, Chicago: 292–305.

Leech, G. (1983) *Principles of Pragmatics*. London: Longman.

Levinson, S. (1983) *Pragmatics*. Cambridge: Cambridge University Press.

McCarthy, M. (1991) *Discourse Analysis for Language Teachers*. Cambridge: Cambridge University Press.

McCarthy, M. (1998) *Spoken Language and Applied Linguistics*. Cambridge: Cambridge University Press.

McCarthy, M. and Carter, R. (1994) *Language as Discourse: Perspectives for Language Teachers*. London: Longman.

Martin, J.R. (1992) *English Text: System and Structure*. Amsterdam: Benjamins.

Mishler, E. (1984) *The Discourse of Medicine*. Norwood, NJ: Ablex.

Mitchell, A.G. (1957) *Spoken English*. London: Macmillan.

Nunan, D. and Lockwood, J. (1991) *The Australian English Course*. Cambridge/Sydney: Cambridge University Press.

Ochs, E., Schegloff, E. and Thompson, S. (eds) (1996) *Interaction and Grammar*. Cambridge: Cambridge University Press.

Ono, T. and Thompson S. (1995) What can conversation tell us about syntax? In P. Davis (ed.) *Alternative Linguistics Descriptive and Theoretical Modes*. Amsterdam: Benjamins.

Palmer, H.E. and Blandford, F.G (1924) *A Grammar of Spoken English. First Edition*. (Third edition, revised and rewritten by R. Kingdon.) Cambridge: Heffer.

Poynton, C. (1985) *Language and Gender: Making the Difference*. Geelong, Vic: Deakin University Press.

Riggenbach, H. (1990) Discourse analysis and spoken language instruction. *Annual Review of Applied Linguistics*, 11: 152–63.

Roberts, C., Jupp, T. and Davies, E. (1992) *Language and Discrimination: A Study of Communication in Multi-ethnic Workplaces*. London: Longman.

Sacks, H., Schegloff, E. and Jefferson, G. (1974) A simplest systemic for the organisation of turn-taking for conversation. *Language*, 50: 696–735.

Schiffrin, D. (1990) Conversation analysis. *Annual Review of Applied Linguistics*, 11: 3–16.

Schiffrin, D. (1994) *Approaches to Discourse*. Oxford: Blackwell.

Searle, J. (1969) *Speech Acts: An Essay in the Philosophy of Language*. Cambridge: Cambridge University Press.

Searle, J. (1976) A classification of illocutionary acts. *Language in Society*, 5: 1–23.

Sinclair, J. McH. and and Coulthard, R.M. (1975) *Towards an Analysis of Discourse*. Oxford: Oxford University Press.

Slade, D. (1997) Stories and gossip in English: the macro-structure of casual talk. *Prospect*, 12(2): 43–71.

Sperber, D. and Wilson, D. (1986) *Relevance*. Cambridge, MA: Harvard University Press.

Street, B. (ed.) (1993) *Literacy in Cross-cultural Perspective*. Cambridge: Cambridge University Press.

Talbot, M.M. (1998) *Language and Gender: An Introduction*. London: Polity Press.

Thompson, J. (1983) Cross-cultural pragmatic failure. *Applied Linguistics*, 4(2): 92–112.

Wallace, C. (1992) Critical literary awareness in the EFL Classroom. In N. Fairclough (ed.) *Critical Language Awareness*. London: Longman.

Willing, K. (1992) *Talking it Through: Clarification and Problem Solving in Professional Workplaces*. Sydney: NCELTR.

Wodak, R. (1996) *Disorders of Discourse*. London: Longman.

Chapter 9

J.R. Martin

LANGUAGE, REGISTER AND GENRE

Without thinking

EVERYBODY DOES THINGS WITHOUT THINKING. People learn to talk and walk, drive cars, serve and volley, play instruments, and so on. And the point comes where what was once a slow and painful, often error-prone process becomes automated. It is then simply taken for granted – we forget about it. At least until something goes wrong. If we fall or stutter, have an accident, double fault or play out of tune, we may stop for a moment and think about what we were doing. But for the most part we carry on, functioning as members of our culture, doing what other people accept.

Towards the end of the nineteenth century, three famous scholars became very interested in the unconscious forces that shape our lives. These men, Saussure, Durkheim and Freud, were the founders of what is now known as social science. Saussure is the father of linguistics, Durkheim sociology, and Freud psychiatry. All were concerned with what it is that makes people tick, without their knowing that it does so. They were interested, in other words, not in physical, material things, as in anatomy or astronomy, but in human behaviour – in social facts. Taken together, these social facts constitute a system. These systems are set up to explain why people do what they do without really thinking about what they are doing.

For example, I am writing this paper in English, in English of a particular kind in fact. I am not using slang; I am not using double negatives (I don't write, though many speakers of English might say *I don't use no double negatives*), and I am not writing in French or Tagalog. Why am I doing this? I am not doing it because you cannot write about language, register and genre in French or Tagalog. I am doing it because I want to interact with you the reader. I know that you expect me to use English – that is the language we share. So, by convention, I use English. Or, to take another example, as I sit here writing I am wearing trousers. I am doing so because I am a male, working in Australia, and in winter this is what Australian males wear. I am not necessarily wearing trousers because of the cold. A number of females pass by my window from time to time, and many of them are not wearing trousers, but skirts or dresses. I, like them, am dressing the way I do by convention. I dress, without thinking about it, as people expect. I might at times in my life think about it, and mutter to someone in Tagalog or put on a dress. But if I do, my behaviour will be take as a joke, or considered asocial, perhaps even outrageous. If I break the rules, people will start thinking. Otherwise life simply goes on.

Now, the point of these remarks about the unconscious nature of language and culture is to try and give you an idea of what linguists and sociologists do. Their job is to discover the unconscious rules which govern our behaviour and to make them explicit – to make the invisible visible in other words. In order to do this they develop models for organising these social facts and theories about the best way to build these models (Culler 1976; Saussure 1915/1966).

Let me try and illustrate with regard to a small example the kind of description of human behaviour linguists and sociologists interested in social facts come up with. Imagine that you are an alien, that you have just landed on earth, and are standing at a pedestrian crossing. You notice that there is a set of lights, with green and red pictures of what appear to be men. The lights change in a certain sequence, first a green man, then a flashing red man, and then a red man which does not flash. This goes on repeatedly. You also notice that there are real people crossing the street and that their movements seem to be conditioned by the lights. When the light is green they walk, when the light is flashing red they walk faster or run, and when the light is red they stop and wait for cars to go by. Now, if you were an alien semiotician (a semiotician is someone who is interested in the systems of meaning or social systems which regulate human behaviour) you would jot down in your journal a brief description of the system you have been observing. The system would have three terms or options: 'walk', 'hurry up' and 'stop'. Each of these choices has a meaning: when people choose 'walk' they start to move across the street; if they choose 'hurry up' they start to run or walk more quickly across the street; and if they choose 'stop', they wait on the corner. In addition, each of these options has an expression – a way of communicating its meaning: 'walk' is expressed by (linguists would say 'is realised by') the green man, 'hurry up' by the flashing red man, and 'stop' by the red man.

The notes you have made are in fact a description of the semiotic system of pedestrian crossing lights. The description has three parts: (1) a statement of the meanings, in this case the socially significant human behaviour the system regulates – moving across the street, moving quickly across the street and not moving; (2) the choices themselves – 'walk', 'hurry up' and 'stop'; and (3) the realisation of the choices, in this case the lights – red, flashing red and green. An outline of this little semiotic system is presented in Figure 9.1, as it would be modelled in systemic functional linguistics.

Social behaviour   The system itself   Expression

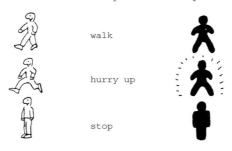

walk

hurry up

stop

Figure 9.1 Systemic functional linguistics

Systemic functional linguistics

Systemic functional linguistics is one of the main functional theories of language which has been developed in the twentieth century. Its major architect is M.A.K. Halliday, formerly

Professor of Linguistics at the University of Sydney (Halliday 1978, 1994); one of his main influences was J.R. Firth, the first Professor of Linguistics in Great Britain, who held the chair at the University of London (Firth 1957a, b). In origin then, the theory is a British one, with much stronger ties to European linguistics than to American approaches. The influence of Saussure (who taught in Geneva), Hjelmslev (who worked in Copenhagen), Malinowski (an anthropologist based in London), linguists of the Prague School and another of Halliday's teachers, the Chinese linguist Wang Li, combine to give the school its distinctive flavour (Hjelmslev 1961; Malinowski 1923, 1935; Mathesius 1964).

How do systemic functional linguists differ from linguists of other schools? First of all, they place considerable emphasis on the idea of choice. They view language as a large network of interrelated options, from which speakers unconsciously select when speaking. In more technical terms, their focus is on paradigmatic relations – on what you say in relation to what you could have said. Other linguists have much stronger syntagmatic perspective – on what you say in relation to what you said before and what you are going to say next. Systemicists formalise these choices by means of systems (thus the name of the theory): for example, singular versus plural, active versus passive, declarative versus interrogative and so on. The way in which these systems bundle together in their grammars gives systemicists an insight into how language is related to the contexts in which it is used; this takes us to the second distinctive feature of systemic linguistics.

Second, then, systemicists, like Firthians before them, have taken a great interest in the relation between language and context. They have always argued, following Malinowski (1923, 1935), that you cannot understand the meaning of what someone says or writes unless you know something about the context in which it is embedded. Or, looking at this the other way round, if you understand what someone says or writes (a text in technical terms), you can also figure out a great deal about the context in which that text occurred (Ure and Ellis 1977). This idea about the relationship between language and context was taken over from Malinowski into linguistics by Firth (1957a, b).

Malinowski was an anthropologist who worked largely in Melanesia, studying the culture of people living on islands to the south and east of Papua New Guinea. Malinowski was what people commonly think of when they hear the word *linguist*: not someone who describes languages, but someone who knows a lot of languages and learns them easily. Malinowski believed that learning the language of the people you were studying was essential for an anthropologist, and he collected a number of texts, taken from many different aspects of the life of the Melanesians he was studying (note that anthropologists like Malinowski are social scientists too, very closely related to sociologists in what they do, though tending to work on more exotic and less familiar cultures). When he was translating these texts into English, for the benefit of his English readers, Malinowski noticed that the translations he was producing did not really make much sense. This was partly because Malinowski was not a linguist in the grammar-describing sense of the term, and tended to give word-for-word translations which exaggerated the differences between Melanesian languages and English. But more importantly, and this was Malinowski's point, no matter how good a translation he made, it still turned out that if you didn't know what the people involved in the text were doing, and didn't understand the culture, then you couldn't make sense of their text. In order to deal with this problem Malinowski introduced the terms 'context of situation' and 'context of culture'.

Let me try and give an example of what Malinowski was on about. Suppose you are sitting in a room, and hear someone yell: 'John, don't do it there mate!' (if you know another language, think about how you would say this in that language). Now, however faithfully you translate this sentence into another language, it will still be the case that unless you know what John was doing, you don't really know what the person talking to him meant. You don't know what John was doing, what he was doing it to, and where he was doing it. If however you had a translation of this sentence, and a description of the context of situation in which it was uttered (say John dumping a load of broken mud bricks into a drainage trough), then you would be able to understand the text. So, in order to explain the meaning of a sentence, you need both a description of that sentence and of the context in which it was used.

But Malinowski believed that even this would not be enough. Alongside a description of the context of situation, you also need a description of the culture in which the utterance is used. Suppose, for example, you are wandering down a corridor at Sydney University and hear someone say 'Okay, now what we have here is a mental process rank-shifted into the Carrier of a relational clause'. (Try translating that into another language if you know one!) Suppose as well that you happen to glance through an open door and see a lecturer talking to a group of students and pointing to the underlined constituent in a clause such as the following written on the blackboard: _what they want is unacceptable_. You have now heard the sentence; if you look closely you can see which part of the clause the Carrier is; and you can see what the lecturer is doing and who he is talking to. But if you are not studying linguistics you will still be at a loss as to what exactly is going on. This is because you have not been socialised into the world where such a sentence makes sense. You are not a member of the subculture which goes around talking about language in his way. This is Malinowski's point about needing a description of the language, the context of situation and the context of culture in which a sentence is used. If you are not a member of the culture, you cannot understand what is meant.

Malinowski's ideas about language in relation to context of situation and context of culture were taken over by Firth and incorporated into linguistic theory. In sharp contrast to the goals of many of his American contemporaries, Firth believed that the purpose of linguistics was to explain meaning (American linguists such as Bloomfield felt that this was a hopelessly complicated goal). Firth did little to flesh out Malinowski's concept of context of culture, but he did take steps to outline those aspects of the context of situation which were relevant to linguistic description. This work was carried on by Firth's students, who adopted the term 'register' for the study of the relation between language and context of situation.

Firth's students were for a time referred to as neo-Firthians (many, following Halliday, would go on to develop systemic linguistics; Bazell _et al._ 1966). They developed a more sophisticated framework than Firth for describing register, making use of three main categories: field, mode and tenor (at first they used the term 'style' for 'tenor', but then, following Gregory, agreed to reserve that term for the study of literary texts; Halliday 1978; Halliday and Hasan 1985). Definitions of these three categories varied slightly over the years (Gregory in fact suggested splitting tenor into personal tenor and functional tenor in 1967 – this will be further discussed below; see Gregory and Carroll 1978); but in general the terms can be understood as follows.

Field refers to what is going on, where what is going on is interpreted institutionally, in terms of some culturally recognised activity (what people are doing with their lives, as it were). Examples of fields are activities such as tennis, opera, linguistics, cooking, building construction, farming, politics, education and so on. When people ask you what you do when first getting to know you, you tend to answer in terms of field (e.g. *Well, I'm a linguist. I play tennis. I'm interested in music* and so on).

Tenor refers to the way you relate to other people when doing what you do. One aspect of this is status. Our society, like all other human societies we know of, is structured in such a way that people have power over one another. This power is of various kinds: mature people tend to dominate younger ones, commanding their respect; bosses dominate employees; teachers dominate students and so on. There is no escaping this, however nice we try to be about it. When you think people are bossy or 'above themselves', it is usually because they are asserting an inordinate amount of power over you. When you think someone is quiet, evasive and looking insecure, it is often because they are being overly deferential to you. And of course you can resist, as when feminists struggle to renovate the power relations between women and men. Renovation is hard work as we all know, and however democratic our ideals, there always seems to be some residue of power, and maybe more, around.

Mode refers to the channel you select to communicate – the choice most commonly presented is between speech and writing. But modern society makes use of many additional channels: e-mail, telephone, radio, television, video, film and so on, each a distinct mode in its own right. It should perhaps be stressed here that writing is a relatively late development in human culture, both in terms of the history of our race and in the life of a child. Writing as we know it was invented just three times in human history – once in China, once in the Middle East (and once in Central America, although this tradition has not survived). In European and Asian contexts writing is only a few thousand years old; many languages still do not use a writing system in day-to-day life, and across cultures children have learned to speak much of their language before they put pen to paper. Interestingly enough, the emergence of writing systems has had a considerable effect on the structure of languages which use them. This is related to why speech and writing differ as they do, and why learning to write involves far more than using squiggles to make meaning instead of sounds. The choices you make from your grammar are themselves very different in speech and writing (see Halliday, Chapter 11, this volume). It is for this reason that learning to write effectively takes so long.

Formalising the relationship of language and culture

In the late 1960s, after working for some years on formalising the choices relevant to clause structure in English, Halliday made a significant breakthrough as far as work on the relationship between language and context is concerned (Halliday 1973). He noted that the register categories of field, mode and tenor that he and his colleagues had developed earlier in the decade had striking parallels in the structure of language itself. What had happened was that as work on formalising clause systems progressed, it became clear that those systems were tending to cluster into three main groups. One bundle of choices was referred to in his early work by Halliday as *transitivity*; this bundle of choices was concerned with the structure of clauses in terms of the way they map reality – the difference between verbs of doing and happening, reacting, thinking and perceiving, saying, and describing and identifying, along with the *voice* (active/passive) potential associated with each. Another bundle he referred to as *mood*, and was concerned with distinguishing statements from questions from commands from exclamations as well as expressing the possibility, probability or certainty of some meaning. The third bundle, called *theme*, has to do with the way in which speakers order constituents in a clause, putting first a theme which connects with the overall development of a paragraph or text, and last something that contains information which is new to the listener. Later, Halliday was to use more semantically oriented terms to generalise these three broad areas of meaning potential: 'ideational' for meaning about the world, 'interpersonal' for intersubjective meaning between speakers, and 'textual' for meanings relating pieces of text to each other and to their context (Halliday 1978, 1994).

Looked at in this way, in terms of the kinds of meaning involved, the three main bundles of systems were seen to match up with register categories in the following way. Field obviously correlated with ideational meaning. There was a connection between the institutional activities in which people engage and what they were talking about. Mode was most clearly related to textual meanings. The channel you choose has a big effect on the relationship between language and its context, and tenor was closely related to interpersonal meaning. Power and solidarity are both implicated in whether you are giving or demanding goods and services or information and how sure you are about what you are doing. This correlation between register categories and functional components in the grammar is very important. It is this that enables systemicists to predict on the basis of context not just what choices a speaker is likely to make, but which areas of the grammar are at stake. Conversely it allows us to look at particular grammatical choices and to understand the contribution they are making to the contextual meaning of a sentence. This makes it possible for systemic linguists to argue on the basis of grammatical evidence about the nature of field, mode and tenor at the same time as it gives them a way of explaining why language has the shape it does in terms of the way in which people use it to live. Systemic grammar is often referred to as systemic functional grammar for this reason (Eggins 1994; Fries and Gregory 1995).

This particular approach to language and context of situation did not have much influence within linguistics proper when it first appeared in the early 1960s. In general, when linguists looked at context at that time they were concerned with phonological and low-level morphological variation, and were studying the difference between the dialects of English spoken by speakers coming from different social backgrounds (sociolinguists inspired by William Labov were the main researchers in this area). But the approach did have obvious implications for applied linguistics and began to be used in work on the teaching of English (both as a mother tongue – the Nuffield Foundation project (Pearce *et al.* 1989), and as a second or foreign language – English for special purposes and functional-notional syllabus research), language development (Halliday 1975; Painter 1984, 1991, 1999), schizophrenic speech (Rochester and Martin 1979), stylistics (Hasan 1985; Birch and O'Toole 1988), ideology (Kress and Hodge 1979) and coding orientation (Bernstein 1973; Hasan 1990, 1996). It was mainly in these applied contexts that register theory continued to evolve (Ghadessy 1988, 1993; Leckie-Tarry 1995; Matthiessen 1993).

Register

The particular model of language and register to be presented here was developed in the applied context of studying the development of children's writing abilities in infants, primary and secondary school (Rothery 1996). One important aspect of the model is the emphasis it places on treating register as a semiotic system. *Semiotic*, as I have already noted, is a term referring to systems that make meanings. *Register*, however, is a semiotic system which differs from semiotic systems such as language, music, dance, image and so on. This is because it is a kind of parasite. It has no phonology of its own. The only way it can make meaning is by using the words and structures of the semiotic we call language. The great Danish linguist Louis Hjelmslev (1961) referred to semiotics like register as connotative semiotics, in order to distinguish them from semiotics like language which can make their own meanings and are not dependent on the resources of another meaning system to express themselves.

What does this mean? For one thing, if register is a semiotic, then it should be possible to work out the choices open to speakers as far as field, mode and tenor are concerned. What exactly is the set of institutions in which we participate? What is the range of roles we can adopt with respect to other speakers? What is the nature of the channels we can use to convey our message? Another consequence of interpreting register as a semiotic system is that you have to be able to say how the different register choices, once selected, are realised. What in other words does it mean as far as language is concerned if the field of discourse is linguistics instead of sociology, tennis instead of cricket, and so on?

Another important aspect of the model is its focus on genre. This in fact goes back to Gregory's (1967) suggestion that tenor be split into personal tenor (concerned with status and formality) and functional tenor (having to do with purpose). The relation of purpose, or what a speaker is trying to accomplish, to register has long been an uneasy one. Over the years Halliday has tended to subsume purpose through his definitions of field, tenor and especially mode (e.g. 1978). We encountered two main problems with this conflation. First of all, it makes the correlation between register categories and functional components of the grammar less clear. Predictions about such and such a register choice being realised in such and such a part of the grammar are weakened. Second, it fails to give a satisfactory account of the goal-oriented beginning-middle-end structure of most texts (for example, the Orientation Complication Evaluation Resolution Coda structure for narrative suggested by Labov and Waletzky (1967)). In our work on children's writing we felt that a clearer relation between register choices and metafunctional components would help us clarify the linguistic reflection of the stages a child goes through in learning to write in different registers. We also felt a need to give some more explicit account of the distinctive beginning-middle-end (or schematic) structures which characterise children's writing in different genres. So we took the step of recognising a third semiotic system, which we called genre, underlying both register and language. Like register it is a parasite – without register and language it would not survive.

In a sense this takes us back to Malinowski, who argued that contexts both of situation and culture were important if we are to fully interpret the meaning of a text. Our level of genre corresponds roughly to context of culture in his sense, our register perhaps to his context of situation. This means we are using the term genre in a far wider sense than that in which it is used in literary studies where it refers to literary text types such as poem, fable, short story or novel. For us, a genre is a staged, goal-oriented, purposeful activity in which speakers engage as members of our culture. Examples of genres are staged activities such as making a dental appointment, buying vegetables, telling a story, writing an essay, applying for a job, writing a letter to the editor, inviting someone for dinner, and so on. Virtually everything you do involves your participating in one or another genre. Culture

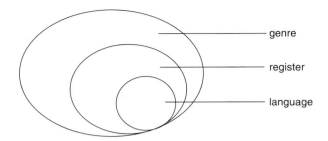

Figure 9.2 Language, register and genre

seen in these terms can be defined as a set of generically interpretable activities. The model of language and its connotative semiotics presented here is outlined in using co-tangential circles in Figure 9.2, where language functions as the phonology of register, and both register and language function as the phonology of genre (Christie and Martin 1997; Eggins and Martin 1997; Martin 1985, 1992; Martin and Veel 1998).

So much for the superstructure. Now let's come back to field, mode and tenor and see what they look like in more detail, given a framework such as this. First of all remember that field, mode and tenor make very general kinds of meaning. Even within language itself, grammatical meanings are more general than lexical ones (the *transitivity* structure Agent Process Goal, which we might gloss as 'X does something to Y', makes a more general meaning than the wordings which might fill its roles, as in *Mary hugged John*, for example). And register meanings are more general still. Interestingly enough, once we leave language, an increase in the generality of the meanings involved does not seem to go hand in hand with invisibility. True, we cannot see them. But speakers are generally more conscious of the meanings associated with register and genre, once you point them out, than they are of grammatical meanings.

Field

This is probably the most daunting of the register variables we have to describe, simply because there are so many things people do. We will probably get a workable description of tenor and mode in our culture long before we produce an encyclopedia of fields. Nevertheless, it is possible to sketch out here something of what we are on about, at least by way of an example. For purposes of illustration, let's consider the set of fields having to do with people in relation to animals. There are really two things to worry about here: first, what do people do with animals (activity focus)? and second, what animals are involved in these activities (object focus)? Fields are about people interacting with their world, so they tend to be characterisable along these two dimensions: what people are doing and what they are doing it to. As a first approximation we might say that there are three main ways in which people are involved with animals: keeping them, using them and observing them. By 'keeping animals' I mean keeping them as pets. The main function of animals in this context is that of companionship. Some people are deeply involved in this field, breeding animals and taking them to shows. By 'using animals' I refer to two main areas: animal husbandry and sport. The main opposition here is between using animals for food and clothing and using them for recreation, hunting and racing being the principal leisure activities in which animals are involved. By 'studying animals' I refer to an interest people take in animals for their own sake. This interest may be focused in different ways: studying animals as a scientist, showing them off at zoos, preserving them in museums or observing them in the wild. This list of animal-related institutions is certainly not exhaustive, but it does serve to illustrate the activities which lie behind what people mean when they say 'I'm a naturalist or biologist (or zoo-keeper/curator/punter/hunter/farmer/dog lover, etc.)'.

The other side of this picture is, of course, the animals themselves. We keep dogs, cats, fish and birds as pets; we farm cows, sheep, pigs and fowl; we hunt with dogs and hawks; we race horses and dogs; we study anything we can lay our hands on. I will not attempt to develop a folk taxonomy of animals here, but note that it is the nature of their involvement with people that shapes a taxonomy of this kind.

As noted above, register categories have no words and structures of their own; so in order to get realised they have to borrow linguistic ones. They do this in two main ways. The first is to make certain linguistic choices much more likely than others. The result of this is that as we listen to a text, certain patterns of choice begin to stand out in a non-random way. These patterns represent a particular register choice telling us it's there. The second way is for register categories to take over a small number of linguistic choices as their own. This type of realisation is indexical rather than probabilistic. The choice then functions as a trigger, giving away the register selection once we hear the word or phrase involved. Obviously only a very small number of language choices can be taken over in this way – otherwise language would cease to exist. The relationship between language and register is much more symbiotic than this.

As far as probabilistic realisation is concerned, field is realised by making certain experiential choices far more likely than others (lexical choices are more noticeable; grammatical choices are too general in meaning to transparently distinguish fields). Thus if you drop in on a conversation, it will take you a moment before you realise what people are talking about. You have to wait until you have heard enough of the mutually expectant lexical items to give away the field. Depending on your familiarity with the field, it may take you more or less time to catch on. When, for example, do you recognise the field of the following string: *boot, menu, algorithm, bit, storing capacity, program*?

The more you know about computers, the quicker you will catch on. Indexical realisations are also found. As far as field is concerned these are words, very technical ones, which tend to be used almost exclusively in a given field. If you understand the word, it almost automatically implicates the field. The word *morphophonemics*, taken from the field of linguistics, is one such indexical trigger.

Note that indexical items and sets of mutually expectant lexical items realise field; they must not be equated with field. Field is a register category, referring to one or another institution. Lexical items are linguistic categories, through which field is realised. At the level of register we are looking at field in terms of what people are doing with their lives. At the level of language we are looking at field in terms of how we know what people are doing. The two perspectives are distinct, associated with different semiotic systems – the one realising the other (Halliday and Martin 1993; Martin and Veel 1998).

Mode

On the surface, choice of mode looks like it could simply be specified in terms of channel: television, telephone, film, letter, notice, e-mail and so on. But it is in fact necessary to go somewhat deeper than this if the effect which mode has on choices within language is to be fully appreciated. The best way to do this is to consider the effect different channels have on communication. One clear effect is that they affect the relation between speaker and listener by placing barriers between them. When compared with face-to-face conversation in this light, different channels can be seen to affect both aural and visual contact. Telephones remove the visual channel, while maintaining aural feedback. Television permits one-way visual contact, but removes aural feedback. Radios take away the visual channel completely. Considered along these lines it is possible to set up a scale ranging from face-to-face dialogue to stream-of-consciousness writing or thinking aloud at the other. At one end, speaker and listener are as close to each other as possible; at the other, the question of audience disappears completely. This scale is outlined in Figure 9.3.

face to face	telephone	TV	radio	letter	book	stream of consciousness
+ aural + visual	+ aural – visual	one way aural & visual	one way aural; – visual	delayed written feedback; – visual	review feedback; – visual (unless illustrated)	audience = self

Figure 9.3 The effect of different channels on communication

The second thing that modes do is affect the relation between language and what it is talking about. This dimension opposes language in action to language as reflection. Consider, for example, a game of cricket. At one end of this scale we have the language of the players and umpire during the game. Next on the scale would be ball-by-ball commentary on the game. This will be somewhat further removed from language in action on radio than on television since on television the commentator and his audience can both see what is going on, but on radio only the commentator can. At a further remove from the action would be an interview with the players after the game, followed by a report of the game in the paper the next day. This is leading us towards the reflective end of the scale, where action is reconstructed, rather than commented on. Next we might place a book about cricket in a given year, then a book about cricket in general. Finally, is an even more abstract text, one which constructs rather than reconstructs reality. An example might be a philosophically oriented treatise on sport, fair play and cricket as symbolising the English way of life (no underarm bowling allowed). What is happening along this scale is that language is becoming further and further removed from what it is actually talking about, not simply in terms of temporal distance (distance from the scene of the crime as it were), but eventually in terms of abstraction as well. Abstract writing is not really about anything you can touch, taste, hear, see or smell, though of course, in the end, if what we write is in any sense material, it must connect with observable facts of some kind or other. This action/reflection scale is outlined in Figure 9.4.

Like field, mode has both indexical and probabilistic realisations. Unlike field, it is realised for the most part through textual systems. One clear set of indexical realisations occurs in greeting sequences at the beginning of texts: reciprocal *Hi – Hi* signals face-to-face dialogue; phone conversations begin with *Hello*, followed by *Hi* or some other greeting, and possibly some form of identification; newsreaders begin with a more formal greeting, to which there is of course no reply; letters begin with *Dear X*; books with a

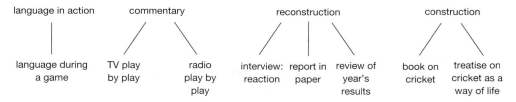

Figure 9.4 Action/reflection scale

preface or acknowledgements, and so on. (Note that it is not the formality of the greeting which is important here, but rather the form of the greeting and its relation to a response if there is one. The formality of greetings is a feature of tenor.) Probabilistic realisations of mode focus largely on deixis, where this is interpreted broadly to encompass *tense*, *identification* and *theme*. Choice of present tense (*am doing*), first person (*I, we*), demonstratives pointing to the nonverbal context (*this, here, now*) and the selection of first or second person (*I, we, you*) theme produces a pattern indicative of language in action/ dialogue mode. Language which reconstructs events on the other hand prefers past tense and remote demonstratives (*there, then, that*). And reflective language often selects a simple generic present tense (*Braking distance varies with speed*), generic reference to whole classes (*Whales are mammals*), and favours abstract lexical items as theme.

There is a great deal more to be said about the realisation of mode, based on knowledge about the grammar and discourse structure of English which cannot be assumed here. What all the different realisations reflect is the general concept of contextual dependency. Are the meanings of the text largely implicit, in the sense that unless we can see what the participants are doing we can't really understand what is going on? Or is the text explicit, independent of context, so that simply by reading the text we can understand what the text is about (assuming we know enough about the field that technicality is not a problem)? The more speakers are doing things together and engaging in dialogue, the more they can take for granted. As language moves away from the events it describes, and the possibility of feedback is removed, more and more of the meanings a text is making must be rendered explicit in that text if they are to be recovered by a reader, no matter how well informed (Biber 1988; Halliday 1985, Halliday and Martin 1993).

Tenor

Tenor was discussed above with regard to status and formality; but it is actually a more complex issue than that. Alongside status, our relations with others are shaped by another factor: contact. This has to do with our feelings towards others – whether or not we like them, love them or hate them. These feelings themselves are somewhat volatile, depending in part on our emotions from moment to moment. We all have a tendency to treat our lovers as enemies after banging our heads or watching them break a prized possession. Alongside these dispositions is the question of how often we run into the people we are talking to. There are many people we meet quite frequently – for example, administrators, colleagues, newsagents, sandwich counter attendants and sales clerk – without necessarily feeling much of an emotional bond with them.

This gives us two dimensions to worry about when considering tenor: status, which focuses on power relations (dominant or deferential roles); and contact, which focuses on our alignment and affinity with others (close and distant roles). It is always important to consider a text from both perspectives, since power and solidarity shape all the social relations we enact.

Tenor is for the most part realised through interpersonal systems. One of the clearest indexical realisations of tenor is found in the choice of vocatives or address terms. Reciprocal use of first names (*John/Bill*) signals solidarity, while non-reciprocal (*John/Prof. Brown*) is the sign of power. Similarly, *my little darling* indexes love, and contrasts with *you fucking bastard* which does not. In addition, there are many probabilistic realisations of tenor. Indeed, English is probably at one extreme in this respect. Many languages structure tenor much more fully into their grammar and lexis than English does, indexing status and contact through verb morphology (Japanese) or choice of lexical items (in Javanese, for example, there are two or three words for every common English word, and you have to choose the appropriate one depending on tenor). English speakers express deference, for example, by favouring possibility as a modality (*possibly*, *maybe*, *may*, *might*), being indirect in commands (*Would you mind opening the door?* instead of *Open the door*), agreeing with their superiors, letting their superior initiate topics of conversation, avoiding affect and so on. Again, a full discussion of this matter depends on a detailed understanding of the lexico-grammatical resources of English uses in this area. The unifying theme of these resources is social distance. They show how close you feel to the person you are talking to – along the 'vertical' axis of power relations and the 'horizontal' axis of communality (Eggins and Slade 1997; Poynton 1985).

Before turning to another important semiotic parasite, genre, it might be instructive to stop and consider for a moment what life would be like if register did not exist. It is impossible to find examples of recognisably human activity without register, although people often fantasise about what life without register would be like, thinking in terms of some kind of heaven, utopia or nirvana. A world without field would be one in which people didn't do anything with their lives. They simply wander around, eating grapes and berries as they run across them, in a sort of never-ending picnic (without the picnic basket of course). Without tenor, everyone would have to be equal – you could never be sure who God was; that would spoil everything. And you would be on more or less friendly terms with everyone – no passionate loves or enemies. You'd wander around visiting everyone, randomly in turn (no friends, no strangers, all kin). Without mode there could be no media, not even writing of any kind. You would simply chat with your companions about what you were doing at the time – picking berries, eating fruit, taking a walk, whatever. Reminiscing or planning would just not be possible. Sound boring? A question of taste perhaps. Whatever the case, humans as we know them do not live in worlds of this kind. The closest they get is perhaps the odd moment, relaxing with a lover or close friend, job forgotten, kids asleep in bed, gender issues at rest, with memories of the past and fears for the future held in delightful abeyance. Transcendent moments to say the least; drug-induced reveries perhaps; musical interludes? Inevitably, life (i.e. register) sweeps us away.

Genre

What about this other parasite, genre? Like register, genre has no phonology of its own. It makes meanings by shaping register – by conditioning the way in which field, mode and tenor are recurrently mapped onto one another in a given culture. This mapping tends to unfold in phases, and gives rise to the distinctive goal-oriented staging structure of genres. Consider, for example, a service encounter in a small shop. To begin you exchange greetings with a salesperson who will offer to serve you. You will then state your needs, perhaps helping yourself, or getting the salesperson to satisfy your requirements. When you get what you need, you will be told how much it costs. You then pay your money, say goodbye and leave. These stages can be set out as follows (cf. Hasan 1977, 1984; Mitchell 1957; Ventola 1987), using '^' to indicate sequence:

> Greeting ^ Service Bid ^ Statement of Need ^ Need Compliance ^ Decision to Buy ^ Payment ^ Leave-taking.

Some elements may be skipped; some may recur; and they do not always occur in this order. The important thing is that you get what you were after, using language to work your way through whatever steps are necessary. Note that these stages are culturally specific. In many cultures, for example, the price of goods is not fixed and you would have to bargain to establish a fair price before deciding to buy (Mitchell 1957). This is something that many travellers find difficult, because bargaining for small goods is not a 'matter-of-fact' part of the culture from which they come.

Consider now how the values of field, mode and tenor change as you move through the phases outlined above. Suppose that the field involves a small greengrocer's shop. During the Service Bid and Payment the focus of the text will be on the activity of buying and selling. But during the Statement of Need, Need Compliance and Decision to Buy the focus will shift to the products the shop is offering. And the Greeting and Leave-taking are not really about anything at all. As far as mode is concerned, the text will tend towards face-to-face dialogue, language in action. But imagine that you are dithering over the avocados in the Decision to Buy stage. The greengrocer may well launch into a sales pitch, involving a more abstract monologic mode which reflects upon the merits of the avocados in question, speculates about how much you will enjoy eating them, makes suggestions for preparation and entices you with a special offer. A shift in tenor might be involved in this sales pitch as well, with the grocer carrying on as your trusted confidant. If you do buy, you are likely to leave the shop you entered as a customer feeling more like the grocer's mate. If you don't, you may leave feeling a little less friendly than when you came in – perhaps reluctant to return in future. The register values shift around as they do in reaction to your goals. This is what genre is set up to explain: how you accomplish things, on a day-to-day basis, in a culturally specific way.

Like register, genre is realised both probabilistically and indexically. Let's take an example of a genre of a different kind to illustrate this – a narrative (Labov and Waletzky 1967; Martin and Plum 1997). Two of the best known indexical realisations of narrative are the opening *Once upon a time* and the closing *And they lived happily ever after*. Once you hear these clichés, you know immediately what genre you are listening to (unless of course someone is playing a joke on you; the point is that you know it's a joke precisely because your expectancies are frustrated). Probabilistic realisations of narrative are also relevant. The Orientation which introduces the characters and sets the story in time and place will tend to include relational clauses (e.g. *Once upon a time there was a . . . He/she was a . . . the cottage faced . . .*) with associated circumstantial elements. The Complication will then tend to continue with a series of temporally relate material processes (*She did this and then she did this and then she did . . .*) leading up to something unexpected – a crisis. At this point the temporal unfolding may be suspended for a moment while the thoughts and feelings of the hero and perhaps another protagonist are explored (*He felt . . .*; *he thought . . .*; *he said: '. . .'*). Then the Resolution carries on, much like the Complication in its realisation until the problem set up in the story is resolved, for better or worse. Finally, the narrator may comment on the point of telling the story in a *Coda*, often using a demonstrative *that* to refer to the story itself along with some expression of attitude (e.g. *That was a really close call*). Note that since both genre and register are realised for the most part probabilistically, they allow the individual considerable freedom in determining just how they are to be realised. The patterns of selection by which we recognise a genre, or some field, mode or tenor, are distributed throughout a text; there are only a few local constraints.

This does not mean however that register and genre can be ignored. They cannot. You have to use enough signals of register and genre to ensure that your listener can see where you are coming from. Otherwise, you will simply not be fully understood. But the notion of probabilistic realisation over whole texts does mean that genre and register are not mechanical formulae, which stand in the way of an individual's creativity or self-expression. It is perhaps a truism to say that you can't write if you don't first know language. But it is equally true to say that you can't write if you don't control the appropriate register and genres. Unfortunately, control of these systems is something that educators have too often taken for granted.

Like all semiotic systems, genre involves choice, and these choices bundle together into groups oriented to relatable generic tasks. In our culture, for example, there are many different kinds of narrative. What they have in common is taking up a stance with respect to a temporally related series of events forming the backbone of the text. Perhaps the simplest form of narrative is the recount. In recounts, nothing really goes wrong, and this is what distinguishes them from narratives. Narratives are focused around relatively problematic or noteworthy events the narrator is making a point about. They may have a more developed beginning and end than recounts, with a more elaborate Orientation and a Coda which makes the point of telling the story explicit. This is because we usually tell recounts to people with whom we share a great deal of experience, whereas narratives are more public texts, needing to stand up in their own right. Labov and Waletzky (1967) suggest that one difference between narratives of personal experience (stories about something that happened to you) and narratives of vicarious experience (stories that happened to someone else or are made up) is that narratives of personal experience have some kind of evaluation at the crisis point, during which the listener is invited to identify with the narrator's feelings at this point in the story.

Specific kinds of narrative makes specific kinds of point (Martin and Plum 1997). The point of a fable is usually made explicit in a moral. Parables make their point metaphorically, though they may be embedded in a religious discourse whose message they serve to exemplify. While sharing many aspects of structure, each of these narrative types differs somewhat in the stages it goes through and the precise nature of the stages themselves. This is because each has a different, though relatable purpose in our culture. Recounts review activities, narratives proper entertain, fables and parables instruct, and more literary narratives function as highly valued displays of verbal art. In order to achieve these different goals, the structure of the texts themselves must differ.

As with register, research into genre from a linguistic point of view is still developing. (For recent developments see Christie and Martin 1997; Eggins and Slade 1997; Ghadessy

1999; Martin and Veel 1998.) The important thing as far as applied linguistics is concerned will be to determine which genres consumers of linguistics are interested in, and to begin working on these.

In summary then, as Malinowski argued more than fifty years ago, you cannot understand a text unless you know something about the context in which it occurs. Because we are social animals, this context is a social one. It involves people doing things with their lives (field), interacting with other people (tenor), and making use of one or another channel of communication and abstraction (mode) to do so. Beyond this it involves people engaging in purposeful goal-oriented activities (genre). The register categories of field, mode and tenor discussed here represent the attempt of one school of functional linguistics to come to grips with what Malinowski and Firth meant by context of situation. The discussion of genre represents a more recent attempt by students of the linguists working in this school to explore what Malinowski and Firth meant by context of culture. The strategy they are using is to interpret both register and genre as semiotic systems in their own right, but semiotics with the peculiar property of having no phonology of their own. Both depend on language's words and structures to making meaning. Interpreted in this light, linguistics is the foundation not only of the study of human communication, but of social science taken in a very broad sense. The functional linguists adopting this extroverted stance are attempting to provide a perspective on learning which both challenges and complements that drawn from cognitive psychology in educational research. (For recent reviews of their contributions see Christie 1992; Cope and Kalantzis 1993; Grabe and Kaplan 1996; Hasan and Williams 1996; Martin 1993, 1997, 1999.)

Note

An earlier version of this chapter was published in F. Christie (ed.) 1984 *ECT 418 Children Writing: A Reader*. Geelong, Vic: Deakin University Press.

References

Bazell, C.E., J.C. Catford, M.A.K. Halliday and R.H. Robins (eds) 1966 *In Memory of J.R. Firth*. London: Longman.

Bernstein, B. (ed.) 1973 *Class, Codes and Control 2: Applied Studies Towards a Sociology of Language*. London: Routledge and Kegan Paul (Primary Socialisation, Language and Education).

Biber, D. 1988 *Variation across Speech and Writing*. Cambridge: Cambridge University Press.

Biber, D. 1995 *Dimensions of Register Variation: A Cross-linguistic Perspective*. Cambridge: Cambridge University Press.

Biber, D. and E. Finegan (eds) 1994 *Sociolinguistic Perspectives on Variation*. Oxford: Oxford University Press.

Birch, D. and M. O'Toole (eds) 1988 *Functions of Style*. London: Pinter.

Christie, F. 1992 Literacy in Australia. *Annual Review of Applied Linguistics* 12: 142–55.

Christie, F. and J.R. Martin (eds) 1997 *Genres and Institutions: Social Processes in the Workplace and School*. London: Cassell.

Cope, W. and M. Kalantzis (eds) 1993 *The Powers of Literacy: A Genre Approach to Teaching Literacy*. London: Falmer (Critical Perspectives on Literacy and Education) and Pittsburg: University of Pittsburg Press (Pittsburg Series in Composition, Literacy, and Culture).

Culler, J. 1976 *Saussure*. London: Fontana Modern Masters Series.

Eggins, S. 1994 *An Introduction to Systemic Functional Linguistics*. London: Pinter.

Eggins, S. and J.R. Martin 1997 Genres and registers of discourse. In T.A. van Dijk (ed.) *Discourse as Structure and Process*. London: Sage (Discourse Studies: A Multidisciplinary Introduction, Volume 1), 230–56.

Eggins, S. and D. Slade 1997 *Analysing Casual Conversation*. London: Cassell.

Firth, J.R. 1957a *Papers in Linguistics 1934–1951*. London: Oxford University Press.

Firth, J.R. 1957b A synopsis of linguistic theory, 1930–1955. In *Studies in Linguistic Analysis* (Special volume of the Philological Society). London: Blackwell, pp. 1–31. Reprinted in F.R. Palmer (ed.) 1968 *Selected Papers of J.R. Firth, 1952–1959*. London: Longman, pp. 168–205.

Fries, P. and M. Gregory (eds) 1995 *Discourse in Society: Systemic Functional Perspectives*. Norwood, NJ: Ablex (Advances in Discourse Processes).

Gerot, L. 1995 *Making Sense of Text: The Context–Text Relationship*. Sydney: Antipodean Educational Enterprises.

Ghadessy, M. (ed.) 1988 *Registers of Written English: Situational Factors and Linguistic Features*. London: Pinter (Open Linguistics Series).

Ghadessy, M. (ed.) 1993 *Register Analysis: Theory and Practice*. London: Pinter.

Ghadessy, M. (ed.) 1999 *Context: Theory and Practice*. Amsterdam: Benjamins.

Grabe, W. and R. Kaplan 1996 *Theory and Practice of Writing*. London: Longman (Applied Linguistics and Language Study).

Gregory, M. 1967 Aspects of varieties differentiation. *Journal of Linguistics* 3: 177–98.

Gregory, M. and S. Carroll 1978 *Language and Situation: Language Varieties and their Social Contexts*. London: Routledge and Kegan Paul.

Halliday, M.A.K. 1973 *Explorations in the Functions of Language*. London: Edward Arnold.

Halliday, M.A.K. 1975 *Learning how to Mean: Explorations in the Development of Language*. London: Edward Arnold (Explorations in Language Study).

Halliday, M.A.K. 1978 *Language as a Social Semiotic: The Social Interpretation of Language and Meaning*. London: Edward Arnold.

Halliday, M.A.K. 1985 *Spoken and Written Language*. Geelong, Vic.: Deakin University Press. Republished by Oxford University Press 1989.

Halliday, M.A.K. 1994 *An Introduction to Functional Grammar* (2nd edn). London: Edward Arnold.

Halliday, M.A.K. and R. Hasan 1985 *Language, Context, and Text: Aspects of Language in a Social-semiotic Perspective*. Geelong, Vic.: Deakin University Press. Republished by Oxford University Press 1989.

Halliday, M.A.K. and J.R. Martin 1993 *Writing Science: Literacy and Discursive Power*. London: Falmer (Critical Perspectives on Literacy and Education).

Hasan, R. 1977 Text in the systemic-functional model. In W. Dressler *Current Trends in Textlinguistics*. Berlin: Walter de Gruyter, pp. 228–46.

Hasan, R. 1984 The nursery tale as a genre. *Nottingham Linguistic Circular* 13 (Special Issue on Systemic Linguistics), pp. 71–102. Republished in Hasan 1996, pp. 51–72.

Hasan, R. 1985 *Linguistics, Language and Verbal Art*. Geelong, Vic.: Deakin University Press. Republished London: Oxford University Press 1989.

Hasan, R. 1990 Semantic variation and sociolinguistics. *Australian Journal of Linguistics* 9(2): 221–76.

Hasan, R. 1996 *Ways of Saying: Ways of Meaning*, edited by C. Cloran, D. Butt and G. Williams. London: Cassell.

Hasan, R. and J.R. Martin (eds) 1989 *Language Development Learning Language, Learning Culture*.

Norwood, NJ: Ablex (Advances in Discourse Processes 27 – Meaning and Choice in Language: Studies for Michael Halliday).

Hasan, R. and G. Williams (eds) 1996 *Literacy in Society*. London: Longman (Applied Linguistics and Language Study).

Hjelmslev, L. 1961 *Prolegomena to a Theory of Language*. Madison, WI: University of Wisconsin Press.

Kress, G. and B. Hodge 1979 *Language as Ideology*. London: Routledge and Kegan Paul.

Labov, W. and J. Waletzky 1967 Narrative analysis. In J. Helm (ed.) *Essays on the Verbal and Visual Arts* (Proceedings of the 1966 Spring Meeting of the American Ethnological Society). Seattle: University of Washington Press, 12–44. Reprinted in *Journal of Narrative and Life History* 7(1–4): 3–38.

Leckie-Tarry, H. 1995 *Language and Context: A Functional Linguistic Theory of Register*, edited by David Birch. London: Pinter.

Malinowski, B. 1923 The problem of meaning in primitive languages. Supplement I to C.K. Ogden and I.A. Richards *The Meaning of Meaning*. New York: Harcourt Brace & World, pp. 296–336.

Malinowski, B. 1935 *Coral Gardens and their Magic. Vol. 2*. London: Allen and Unwin.

Martin, J.R. 1985 *Factual Writing: Exploring and Challenging Social Reality*. Geelong, Vic.: Deakin University Press. Republished by Oxford University Press 1989.

Martin, J.R. 1992 *English Text: System and Structure*. Amsterdam: Benjamins.

Martin, J.R. 1993 Genre and literacy – modelling context in educational linguistics. *Annual Review of Applied Linguistics* 13: 141–72.

Martin, J.R. 1997 Linguistics and the consumer: theory in practice. *Linguistics and Education* 9(3): 409–46.

Martin, J.R. 1999 Mentoring semogenesis: 'genre based' literacy pedagogy. In F. Christie (ed.) *Pedagogy and the Shaping of Consciousness: Linguistic and Social Processes*. London: Cassell (Open Linguistics Series), pp. 123–55.

Martin, J.R. and G. Plum 1997 Construing experience: some story genres. *Journal of Narrative and Life History* 7: 1–4 (Special Issue: Oral Versions of Personal Experience: three decades of narrative analysis; Guest Ed. M. Bamberg): 299–308.

Martin, J.R. and R. Veel 1998 *Reading Science: Critical and Functional Perspectives on Discourses of Science*. London: Routledge.

Mathesius, V. 1964 On the potentiality of the phenomena of language. In J. Vachek (ed.) *A Prague School Reader in Linguistics*. Bloomington: Indiana University Press.

Matthiessen, C.M.I.M. 1993 Register in the round: diversity in a unified theory of register analysis. In Ghadessy 1993: 221–92.

Mitchell, T.F. 1957 The language of buying and selling in Cyrenaica: a situational statement. *Hesperis* 26: 31–71. Reprinted in T.F. Mitchell 1975 *Principles of Neo-Firthian Linguistics*. London: Longman, pp. 167–200.

Painter, C. 1984 *Into the Mother Tongue: A Case Study of Early Language Development*. London: Pinter.

Painter, C. 1991 *Learning the Mother Tongue* (2nd edn). Geelong, Vic.: Deakin University Press.

Painter, C. 1999 *Learning through Language in Early Childhood*. London: Cassell.

Pearce, J., G. Thornton and D. Mackay 1989 The Programme in Linguistics and English Teaching, University College London, 1964–1971. In Hasan and Martin 1989: 329–68.

Poynton, C. 1985 *Language and Gender: Making the Difference*. Geelong, Vic.: Deakin University Press. Republished London: Oxford University Press 1989.

Rochester, S. and J.R. Martin 1979 *Crazy Talk: A Study of the Discourse of Schizophrenic Speakers*. New York: Plenum.

Rothery, J. 1996 Making changes: developing an educational linguistics. In Hasan and Williams 1996: 86–123.

Saussure, F. de 1915 *Course in General Linguistics*, edited by C. Bally and A. Sechehaye in collaboration with A. Riedlinger. New York: McGraw-Hill 1966.

Ure, J. and J. Ellis 1977 Register in descriptive linguistics and linguistic sociology. In O. Uribe-Villas (ed.) *Issues in Sociolinguistics*. The Hague: Mouton, pp. 197–243.

Ventola, E. 1987 *The Structure of Social Interaction: A Systemic Approach to the Semiotics of Service Encounters*. London: Pinter.

Chapter 10

Clare Painter

UNDERSTANDING GENRE AND REGISTER: IMPLICATIONS FOR LANGUAGE TEACHING

L EARNING A NEW LANGUAGE ALWAYS involves learning at least something
of the ways of operating in the society where that language is used. Most language
teachers have usually been very conscious of the need to take this fact into account in devis-
ing fruitful language-learning methodologies. To assist with this goal, it is helpful to have
ways of thinking about language that focus on its role in enabling the learner to participate
in the new culture. Two concepts which have proved very worthwhile in this endeavour are
those of *genre* and *register*, which derive from systemic-functional linguistics (SFL).

What is genre?

In the context of language education the term *genre* comes from a perspective on language
which sees it as a resource – a resource that we call upon in order to achieve our social
goals (see Martin, Chapter 9).

Any activity in the culture may to a greater or lesser extent involve language; for
example, booking a taxi, recounting an anecdote, holding a meeting, providing a record of
a meeting in minutes, making a social security benefits claim and so on. Neither the
activities themselves nor the way they are carried out will necessarily be uniform across
cultures. In many cultures, for example, any purchase of goods will require a stage of
bargaining in the process and an outsider who does not appreciate this will be unable to
operate effectively, however good their command of the grammatical patterns of the
language.

One way of viewing the culture for the purposes of language teaching, then, is in
terms of the totality of its purposeful activities of the kind mentioned above, and it is these
culturally specific, purposeful activities which are referred to as *genres*. Martin and Rothery
(1980–81) define genre as "staged, goal-oriented social process", emphasising therefore
the following three points:

1   Any genre pertains to a particular culture and its social institutions (hence "social"
     process).

2   Social processes are purposeful (hence "goal-oriented").

3   It usually takes a number of steps to achieve one's purpose (hence a "staged" process).

It may seem surprising that this definition makes no direct mention of language. But this allows us to recognise that some genres are more heavily dependent on language than others for their achievement. A genre like supermarket shopping is one where language plays little part, simply facilitating the social process in a minor way, while others, like formal meetings, insurance claims or career resumés, consist of nothing but language and cannot be achieved without it. It is these that are likely to be of most concern to the language teacher, for whom it may be most useful to think of a genre as a culturally specific text-type which results from using spoken and/or written language to (help) accomplish something.

Recognising genres

Most language teachers are familiar with the notion that we use language differently depending on our purposes. But since all the genres mentioned so far will use the same set of rules of English grammar, we need to clarify what it means to say the language is used differently in different cases. To elucidate this fully, we will need to bring in the additional concept of *register*, but at this point, purposeful language variation can be discussed in terms of two aspects. First, the overall shape or structure of the text may vary. This is because the structure is created by the particular steps we go through to achieve the goal. Second, if we think of a particular language as an array of possibilities, then the choices of vocabulary and grammatical patterns that are selected from the underlying system of possibilities will vary according to the purpose.

Let us look at one or two examples of familiar written genres to illustrate this, beginning with an example of what Rothery (1986) calls a *procedure*.

    Text 1   *Installing the ribbon cartridge*

1   Locate the ribbon knob on the ribbon cartridge and turn the knob clockwise to tighten the ribbon.

2   If the **ribbon cartridge deck** is off to the side, gently slide it toward the centre to give yourself some working room.

3   Lower the ribbon cartridge on to the deck. Make sure that the ribbon slips between the plastic **ribbon guide** and the clear **paper guide**.

4   When the ribbon is in position, gently press the cartridge between the two **cartridge support tabs**, so that the ribbon snaps into place. Make sure the ribbon is still positioned between the ribbon and paper guides.

5   Take any slack out of the ribbon by turning the ribbon knob clockwise.

6   Return the front cover to the printer by slipping the cover tabs into the receiving slots and pressing down on the cover.

    (Original text accompanied by illustrations, indicating boldface items.)

Genre: schematic structure – Procedure

The overall shape of the text is termed its *generic* or *schematic structure* (Martin 1984; also Chapter 9, this volume). A simple procedure is an instructional text which achieves its purpose in two main stages. First, there is a statement of the *goal* of the procedure, usually in a single sentence or simply a heading (as in Text 1). Then follows a specification of the *method* of arriving at the goal in the order in which the actions are to be undertaken. These two stages are "obligatory", while some kinds of procedural texts have an additional distinct stage where things required for the achievement of the goal are presented (e.g. the list of ingredients in a recipe or the labelled diagram of component parts accompanying self-assembly products).

Distinctive linguistic features – Procedure

Some of the linguistic choices that characterise a procedure are as follows:

1   There is clear temporal sequencing which is usually explicitly marked. The two most common ways for this to be done are by numbering the steps in the method, as in this text, or by using conjunctive links such as *first, second, then, next, finally*.
2   The use of imperative mood is typical, as in this text (*Locate the ribbon cartridge*, *lower the ribbon*, *press the cartridge*). Sometimes the generalised pronoun *you* is heavily used as well (*Make sure you do X and Y*, etc).
3   A further characteristic is the predominance of clauses with action verbs, such as *turn, slide, lower, press*.
4   Also typical are expressions of manner and cause as in Text 1 (e.g. manner: *gently, by turning, by slipping*; cause-purpose: *to tighten, to give yourself some working room, so that the ribbon*, cause-condition: *if the deck is off to the side . . .*).

Genre: schematic structure and linguistic features – Analytical exposition

By way of contrast, we now turn to a written text-type referred to by Martin (1985/1989) as an *analytical exposition*, the purpose of which is to explain some aspect of the world and bring the addressee to share the writer/speaker's point of view.

Text 2

Although earlier perspectives of standpoint theory certainly had limitations . . ., there are some basic premises worthy of consideration. One primary premise states that knowledge is socially situated. This seems particularly appropriate for my research proposal because it "sets the relationship between knowledge and politics at the center" (Harding 1993: 55–6). Harding (1993) noted another related assumption concerning the activities of those groups at the top (or centre) of the social structure which organize and set boundaries on what persons performing these activities can comprehend about themselves and their world. This implies that research that studies and works with the social members at the bottom (or exterior) of the social structure necessarily provides fuller understanding of the larger society. Their experiences would have implications for the whole society. Thus standpoint theory provides an understanding of why we must consult previously ignored persons and groups as sources of knowledge, and it problematizes seemingly innocent, meaningless events in daily life.

(DeFransisco 1997: 49)

There are three main steps to achieving a successful exposition. Initially the general position to be argued is presented in the *thesis* stage, as is done here in the opening sentence. Following the thesis, any number of *arguments* are provided in its support. In Text 2, there are two arguments offered in support of the thesis: *One primary premise . . . center'* and *Harding (1993) noted another related assumption . . . society*. Finally the thesis is represented as an outcome of the argument(s) in a *reiteration*, here *Thus standpoint theory. . . . daily life*. In a longer text, of course, the thesis might be accompanied by a *preview* of the ensuing arguments as well as being preceded by some orienting background material. In addition, each argument might be elaborated into a distinct paragraph or even several paragraphs, and the reiteration would include a summary of the main points of the argument stages.

The distinctive linguistic features of an analytical exposition include the following:

1   The things talked about in an analytical exposition, whether human or not, are predominantly generic rather than specific (e.g. *groups, persons, events*).
2   "Timeless" verbs are favoured (e.g. *organize, can comprehend, implies, problematizes*), except where specific events are described in elaborating an argument.
3   If the text is organised on a time line (e.g. with *first, second, finally*) it will be a rhetorical one, not an actual one as in a procedure. Alternatively, contrast or simply accumulation of points may organise the arguments with respect to one another, as here (*One primary premise . . . another related assumption . . .*). Often, the reiteration will be introduced with *thus, therefore* or some such rhetorical linker.
4   A written exposition will tend to use "abstract" and "nominalised" forms (e.g. *perspectives, limitations, consideration, assumption, implication*).
5   "Referring" words like *it* or *this* may well refer to longer parts of the text than just preceding nouns (e.g. *this seems . . . , this implies . . .* above).

The functionality of genres

Many teachers will recognise an extended analytical exposition as one kind of "essay" in terms of school or tertiary education, and familiarity with the essay as a "format" may make it less easy to focus on the key aspects of what is intended by the term *genre*. The most fundamental point here is to recognise that the schematic structure of a text is not a random, arbitrary one: it is one that has evolved over time in a particular culture because it has proved effective for its purpose. In this sense genres are *functional*. The purpose of a genre determines its shape (i.e. its schematic structure). Thus the structure is not so much an arbitrary prescriptive formula as a facilitating convention. This is why the labels used to describe the generic structure of a text are not terms like "Introduction", "Middle/Body" or "End", since such terms simply identify the parts of the text without suggesting their function. SF linguists prefer labels which suggest the function of the stages of the genre to highlight the fact that the text has identifiable parts precisely because these steps enable the interactants to achieve the social purpose.

Following from this, it is possible to address the worry that has sometimes been expressed (e.g. Richardson 1994; Sawyer and Watson 1987) that to teach genres is to force the potentially creative individual to conform to a restricting, constraining recipe. Yet if a genre is a kind of text which has evolved over time because that way of achieving the goal has worked well in the culture, then generic conventions are in principle functional and enabling, not arbitrary, prescriptive formulae (and should never be taught as if they were the latter!). Creativity can build on the fact that generic patterns are unconsciously expected by native speakers and hearers, making it possible to play with these patterns in various ways, to be ironic or outrageous and so on. Such effects are only possible against a background of what is expected, and are only possible from a speaker/writer who has good control of the predictable generic form.

Introducing an individual to the functions and forms of new genres takes nothing from their creativity. As anyone goes through life taking on new roles and using language for new purposes, they are learning new genres, but this does not mean that they lose the ability to operate in the old ones. Someone who learns to use the objective, impersonal language of a bureaucratic report, for example, does not thereby lose the ability to tell a funny or moving personal anecdote when this is functional in the context. Learning new genres is a matter of extending, not restricting, the individual's potential, and given our definition of genre as a *social* process it follows that new genres are not likely to come into being by being "invented" by individuals. There are of course literary artists like James Joyce who may be argued to have done just that, but even here it is clear that the creativity of a Joyce (or a Mozart) was not based on any ignorance of the artistic genres of their time; nor hampered by their expertise in them.

Generic forms and change

Genres have been described as culturally evolved goal-directed social processes which are "in principle" enabling and facilitative of some sociocultural purpose. But of course societies change, and generic forms that were once functional may become less so, or else may come to serve purposes no longer seen by all as appropriate. It is in these respects, and in relation to these kinds of tensions, that a familiar genre may be found genuinely constraining and restrictive rather than enabling. Let us take as an example two possible teaching genres within tertiary education: the monologic lecture and the interactive workshop.

First let us suppose a culture in which all higher education will be conducted by means of monologic lectures. This may have evolved as a functional genre for the following reasons:

1   It is economical – few teachers are available and only a low staff-to-student ratio is required.
2   It maintains considerable distance between teachers, who have an accepted high status, and students, who do not.
3   It is efficient – much information can be passed on in a short time and the accepted model of learning is one of the transmission of knowledge from the authoritative teacher to the ignorant learner.

On the other hand, it would probably be in the following rather different circumstances that the interactive workshop/seminar genre is functional:

1   Teacher availability and economic conditions allow for smaller groups of students per teacher.
2   An egalitarian ethic prevails promoting reduced social distance between teachers and students.

3   A relatively small amount of "content" may be addressed at any session and the accepted model of learning is one of critical enquiry and problem-solving, rather than knowing a recognised body of knowledge.

Clearly, which genre is most functional is not a matter simply to be prescribed by an individual. It depends on the economic circumstances, the social relations and the educational ideology prevailing in a particular culture. If learning is viewed as the memorisation of a large body of knowledge, then the interactive workshop is scarcely functional; and anyone implementing it without addressing the interactants' view of what education was would hardly be successful. But views on such matters are open to change, perhaps as part of wider changes in social relations, perhaps through challenging debate and discussion about the nature of education itself.

The point here, then, is that genres are not fixed and immutable any more than social institutions are. Where there are points of tension in those institutional arrangements and the social relations enacted within them, there may emerge dissatisfaction with existing genres. But when a genre ceases to be seen as ideally functional, changes in generic forms will not be achieved by leaving creative individuals "free" to "invent" new forms. To the extent that language is a tool for social change it is likely to be by harnessing those genres which function to persuade and inform that an individual may have an impact.

Genre in language teaching

Genre can be a valuable concept for English language teachers, whether involved in mother-tongue settings or teaching English as a second or foreign language. Depending on the homogeneity of the class and other circumstances, an awareness of genre is clearly relevant for designing curriculum in a way responsive to student needs. For example, if there are particular work-, school- or leisure-related purposes which all your students need spoken or written English to accomplish, then the English course can be oriented towards achieving control of the relevant spoken and written genres. Students will need to gain a clear understanding of the nature and stages of the social process under attention and how it is like or unlike comparable social processes in their own culture. This will provide the learner with insights into the English-speaking culture and opportunities to reflect on or contest its assumptions as well as to gain confidence and experience in using the language patterns that are particularly foregrounded in the genre. In this way students will gain choices about the extent to which they wish to operate in the ways of the new culture, and teachers will have a basis for designing clear outcomes for the language course or any part of it.

Text variation: taking account of situational context

While the concept of genre provides a valuable basis for a language curriculum oriented to engaging the learner in purposeful language activities, it needs to be supplemented by a framework that allows a more systematic and detailed consideration of the linguistic patterns relevant for different occasions of any genre. In particular, students need a flexibility in their language use that goes beyond an understanding of the schematic structure of different genres – crucial though that is. Such a flexibility will be enhanced by a closer consideration of the situational contexts in which language occurs and indeed by a closer consideration of the language itself.

Let us begin to do this by taking a short text fragment (Text 3) that has been disembedded from its context of occurrence.

Text 3

Well, let's reverse round this corner. The first thing we do is check our mirror to see if it's safe to stop. Take your car gently forward looking down here – there's nothing parked – and take up your first position three feet from the kerb, two car lengths – clutch down – brake to stop – clutch right down. Now then, put your handbrake on next, then into neutral. Right . . .

If we think about this piece of text in terms of genre, we might recognise it as (part of) a *procedure*, like Text 1. In other words it is an instructional text, where the goal is specified in a single clause *Well, let's reverse round this corner*, and the remainder of the text begins to detail the method in the order in which this is to be achieved, using imperative clauses *take your car . . ., take up your first position . . ., put your handbrake on*. As with Text 1, action verbs predominate (*reverse, do, take, take up, put*) and sequence is signalled explicitly (*the first thing, next, then*). Also like Text 1, there are expressions of cause (cause: purpose, *to see if it's safe to stop*) and manner (*gently forward*).

But clearly there are significant differences in the language used in the two cases as well, and these relate to differences in the nature of the situations giving rise to the texts. Coming to Text 3 without being given any information about the situational context in which it arose, any native speaker can readily see that what is going on is a driving lesson, that the words spoken come from the instructor to the pupil and that the text was originally spoken in a face-to-face situation. These aspects of the context are immediately obvious to us, but that itself is the interesting point. We infer these facts about the social context entirely from the language of the text. If it is possible, indeed easy, to do this, there must be something quite systematic about the way these aspects of the context are reflected in, or created by, the text.

Register

Exploring the relationship between situational contexts and the texts they give rise to is known within SFL as *register* analysis. It draws in particular on the work of M.A.K. Halliday (e.g. 1978a, 1985/1989), who suggests that any context for language in use be considered in terms of three components, known as *field*, *tenor* and *mode*. Field for Halliday in fact subsumes the notion of sociocultural purpose, which we have here treated separately so as to allow for a discussion and comparison of genres with a particular focus on schematic structure (following Martin's and Rothery's approach). Having begun by focusing on social purpose and genre, our attention will now turn to other aspects of *field* and to *tenor* and *mode*, three aspects of the context sometimes referred to as *register variables* (Martin 1997).

Field

The *field* of a spoken or written text can be viewed as the cultural activity or subject matter with which the writer/speakers are concerned: for example, gambling would be a field common to many cultures, though with variations in the subfields, such as racing (with its own subfields: horse, dog, camel . . .), lotto, raffle, cards (bridge, poker . . .), poker machines, keno, roulette, etc. Other examples of fields are nuclear physics, wine, travel, building construction, astrology, education, football. These are a random selection of fields within our culture and, of course, different members of a culture are involved in different selection from the totality of possible fields within their society.

One of the ways in which the two procedures, Texts 1 and 3, differed from each other was in their fields. While the first was concerned with setting up personal computer equipment, the other was concerned with driving a car. Consequently, despite the similarities we observed in overall structure and in some grammatical patterns, there were wide differences in the vocabulary drawn on and in the kinds of activities being sequenced.

Tenor

Tenor is a term for the social relations between the interactants in any discourse. The most obvious dimension of tenor concerns power relations, determined by the relative status of the interactants. Close friends may have equal status when they converse, but in other cases, one party to an interaction may be relatively more powerful because of their age (e.g. older to younger sibling), their position in an institutional hierarchy (e.g. senior executive to junior), their role (e.g. teacher to student, doctor to patient), their expertise in relation to the field, and so on. Conversely, speakers — whatever their institutionalised status — may be more or less interested in creating "solidarity" with the addressee and this too will have a bearing on the way they talk to each other, resulting in a more or less "personal" tone, the inclusion or exclusion of humour, expressions of feeling, and so on.

In terms of tenor, Texts 1 and 3 are largely similar. In both cases the text producer enacts the role of instructor, using the *imperative mood* to encode this role. In both texts there is an absence of humour or affective language, though the use, in Text 3, of the inclusive first-person pronoun *we* and *our* rather than the second person *yourself* of Text 1 is a minor difference attributable to a small effort at solidarity on the part of the driving instructor.

Tenor is a dimension of the context that second-language learners find it notoriously difficult to navigate, as is illustrated by Text 4, a note received by an English teacher from her adult ESL student:

Text 4

Dear Ms C

Please be advised that I will not be attending this today English class because I have to attend the 1 Day structure workshop conducted under the auspices of the ATS.

I hope the above explanation could merit your consideration why I will not be attending the days class.

Thank you.

Yours faithfully,

The intention of the writer of the note was to be courteous and respectful by explaining her absence, yet her opening strikes the wrong note. This is because she presents the information about her absence neither as a request for permission nor as an apology, which would be the two possibilities that would acknowledge the teacher as having more status than the student in this context. Instead she borrows bureaucratic phrasing and uses the imperative mood appropriate for a command. At the same time, everything in the brief note is expressed rather formally (e.g. *merit your consideration* rather than *you will accept*), which seem to deny the close personal relationships that had been built up between the teacher and her students during the course. Thus the tone was neither distant courtesy nor friendly familiarity, either of which would have constructed tenor relations with which the teacher would have been more comfortable.

Mode

Mode refers to the medium of communication, in particular whether it is spoken or written, which will have far-reaching effects on the language used. It also includes the channel of communication (face-to-face or via telephone, e-mail, broadcast or print) since whether or not there is visual and/or aural contact and whether feedback is ongoing, delayed or impossible must affect the language choices made. We could say that, whereas tenor is concerned with the social distance between interactants, mode considers the effect of physical distance. In addition, another dimension of distance may be included, which is the distance from the experience being talked about, a variable which may be useful to explain, for example, the difference between a running commentary on a football match and an account of the game recollected after the event.

Returning once again to our brief comparison of Texts 1 and 3, we can see that the difference in mode here – Text 1 being written and Text 3 spoken – accounts for further differences between the texts. The driving instructor needs to do a little work to maintain the floor in the face-to-face mode and uses "fillers" like *well*, *now then* and *right* to avoid handing over turns. The face-to-face mode also allows for greater inexplicitness – references to *this (corner)* or to *here*, as well as elliptical utterances (like *clutch down*) which arise because the language is ongoingly accompanying the pupil's actions.

Text 3 is embedded in the material situation and accompanies actual actions, while Text 1 is slightly more distanced from the activities described. Both can be compared with Text 2, where the experiences encoded in language are even more distanced – being generalised, hypothetical and divorced from any sequence of occurrence. The effect on the language is the use of typical features of academic written text, such as "abstract nouns", references to parts of the texts (*this [premise]*, *another assumption*), and "rhetorical" conjunctions like *thus*. It is in terms of mode as well as genre that Text 2 is most distinct from Texts 1 and 3.

The brief comparisons that have been made of Texts 1 and 3 have suggested, first, that since the texts were produced with a common social purpose – that of instructing, of laying out a procedure to achieve a goal – they share a common overall structure and certain key linguistic characteristics. They are the same underlying genre. Second, though, we have seen that a closer analysis of the specific contexts in terms of field, tenor and mode can be used to account for the differences in the language of the texts. The concepts of both genre and register are needed to give the most useful and revealing account of how we use language differently in different situations.

The theory of register is not simply, however, that every text embodies and reveals three different aspects of its situational context. Its further argument is that this is the case because particular areas of the language system are sensitive to particular aspects of the context. So let us turn finally to a closer consideration of the nature of the language system.

Model of language as sets of options

Building systematic links between contextual and linguistic parameters has been facilitated by the SFL approach to describing language. Rather than viewing a language as a finite list of rules, and language-learning as the "acquisition" of these rules, SFL models the language as sets of related choices or options, each of which is called a *system*. For example, the option of *declarative* (as in *he's coming*) is related to the option of *interrogative* (as in *is he coming?*) and the further option of *imperative* (as in *come!*) because all three are concerned with the role taken up by the speaker (giving or demanding information or action). These are options within the grammatical system of MOOD.[1] Similarly, the choice of *active voice* (as in *the boys broke the window*) is related to the choice of *passive voice* (as in *the window was broken [by the boys]*), since they represent alternative ways of sequencing the pieces of information in the clause. As can be seen, any particular such option, if actualised in a text, is likely to have some implication in terms of lexico-grammatical structure. On this view, any written or spoken text is an occasion of language in use, embodying in its words and structures particular selections from all the various sets of options that constitute the language system.

Groupings of options into metafunctions

When first elaborating all the sets of options that might describe English as fully as possible, Halliday noticed that some sets of options seemed to be closely interrelated, while others seemed to be relatively independent (Halliday 1978b: 46–7).

As an example, let us think about "question tags" in English, such as *does he?* at the end of the clause *he doesn't smoke, does he?* If we tried to specify which English structures might take a question tag, we would find that the possibility of "tagging" depends partly on the mood of the clause: it is not possible, for example, to add a tag to a *wh*-interrogative like *why does he smoke?* In addition, to work out what *kind* of tag is possible we would have to note the polarity of the clause: for example, negative imperatives like *don't smoke it* and positive interrogatives like *does he smoke?* can only have a positive tag added. In other words, we cannot specify the grammatical possibilities for tagging without reference to options in the mood and polarity systems. The three systems of MOOD, POLARITY and TAGGING are closely interconnected.

On the other hand, there are other grammatical choices – such as the choice between "intransitive" (*he slept*) or "transitive" (*he kicked the ball*) – which do not depend on choices of MOOD, POLARITY and TAGGING but on other systems in the grammar. In particular the choice of PROCESS-TYPE, revealed by the verb, is relevant. For example, a "material" type of process (*he kicked the ball*, *the ball rolled*) may be transitive or intransitive, while a "relation" type, encoding a state of being or possession (*the car is mine*), cannot be intransitive.

The important point for language teachers is that, when detailed descriptions of English are undertaken in this way, language systems appear to separate out into three groups, each relatively independent of the other two. More importantly still, each group of closely related systems is concerned with one particular area of meaning (Halliday

1978a; Halliday and Hasan 1985/1989). One set of systems involves what Halliday has called *ideational* meaning.[2] That is to say, it relates to the linguistic coding of the things and events of experience – to what we are talking about. Another set of systems (including MOOD, POLARITY and TAGGING) relates to *interpersonal* meaning; that is, to the speaker's stance, towards both the topic and the addressee. The third set of systems is concerned with making the text coherent by making connections with both the co-text and the physical context. This, Halliday termed *textual* meaning. These three main sets of inter-related meaning systems are known as *metafunctions* – that is, functions of language in terms of which the language system is organised.

Some examples of systems of options for meaning within each metafunction are given in Table 10.1.

Table 10.1 The metafunctions of English

Metafunction	Example of language system
Ideational:	PROCESS TYPE (material, e.g. *kick*; mental, e.g. *understand*; verbal, e.g. *say*; relational, e.g. *be*)
Expressing what is going on – the content of what is talked about	CIRCUMSTANCE TYPE (time/place/manner/cause, etc.)
	PARTICIPATION (transitive/intransitive) The above three systems are jointly known in SFL as TRANSITIVITY
	Patterns of lexical choice (vocabulary)
Interpersonal:	MOOD (declarative/interrogative/imperative)
Constructing the relationship between speaker/writer and addressee, expressing stance	MODALITY (degrees of probability and obligation: *must*, *should*, etc.)
	POLARITY (positive/negative)
	VOCATION (terms of address: *sir*, *darling*, *doctor*, *my dear*, etc.)
	PERSON (1st: *I, me, my, mine, we, us, our, ours*. 2nd: *you, your, yours*. 3rd: *he, him, his, she, her, hers, it, its, they, them, their, theirs*)
	SPEECH FUNCTION (statement, question, answer, command, compliance, offer, refusal, etc.)
	ATTITUDE (*unfortunately*, etc.)
Textual: Creating coherence: making links with co-text and context	THEME (ordering of elements: marked, e.g. *this, I don't need*; unmarked, e.g. *I don't need this*)
	INFORMATION FOCUS (at phonological level – placement of stress)
	REFERENCE (pointing words: anaphoric or "backward pointing", e.g. *John* . . . **he**; cataphoric or "forward pointing", e.g. *the best solution is **this*** . . . ; exophoric "beyond text", e.g. *He* – pointing at John)
	CONJUNCTION (linkers of time, causality, contrast, etc.)

Context and metafunction

So far we have identified three components of contexts (*field*, *tenor*, *mode*) and three metafunctional components of the language system (*ideational*, *interpersonal*, *textual*). The main claim of register theory, though, is that the contextual and linguistic components are in a systematic relationship to one another. It is through choices in the different metafunctions that the context is "created" by the language of the text and conversely, each of the register variables "activates" a different area of the semantics and grammar. Field influences experiential choices, tenor influences interpersonal choices and mode influences textual choices. Thus the relationship between context and text is systematic and it is two-way. For example, tenor (roles and relations between speakers) may influence the interpersonal language choices the speakers take up, but equally, the interpersonal language choices made by the speakers (re-)construct the tenor for that occasion. It is because of this relationship between register variable and metafunction that the predictability of context from text or text from context is possible (see Figure 10.1).

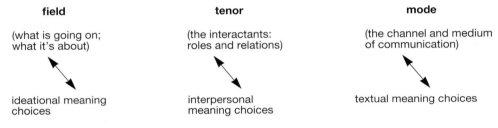

field

(what is going on; what it's about)

ideational meaning choices

tenor

(the interactants: roles and relations)

interpersonal meaning choices

mode

(the channel and medium of communication)

textual meaning choices

Figure 10.1 The relation of contex and metafunction

It is the functional relation between sociocultural purpose and generic structure and between the register variables and the metafunctional components of the linguistic system that make genre and register such useful concepts in language education. They can be used to analyse and make explicit to learners the sociocultural features of a particular text-type under attention and to prepare them for the particular linguistic choices that will be foregrounded.[3] In this way student language problems can often be recognised as stemming from failure to appreciate aspects of the tenor or mode that is expected, or lack of knowledge of the field in question. Alternatively, the learner may lack experience with the appropriate linguistic forms for actualising the perceived features of the context. This may stem from unfamiliarity with the culturally expected schematic structure, or from a lack of technical vocabulary for the field, or from an insufficient range of interpersonal linguistic forms to create the desired tenor, or from inexperience of the textual linguistic choices that are needed for a sophisticated "written mode". A consciousness of genre and register enables the teacher to identify and focus on whatever aspect of language in use the learner needs most help with. It also enables a teacher to readily and systematically control the difficulty of tasks; for example, by working on new genres in relatively familiar fields, or by encouraging students to rewrite a text varying the tenor or the mode only, and so on. Whether in the design of curricula, specific language activities or assessment tasks, a programme utilising the notions of genre and register will have a dual focus on the sociocultural and situational context and on the meaningful language choices that realise it. Students will thus be learning the ways and meanings of the culture as they learn the lexico-grammatical forms of the language.

Notes

1   It is a convention that names of "systems" or sets of options are written in small capitals.

2   Ideational meaning has two components, the *experiential* and the *logical*; the term *experiential* is therefore often used synonymously with *ideational*.

3   It is beyond the scope of this chapter to discuss classroom methodology, but the issue of the appropriate way to teach genre is one that has been explored in several papers, such as Feez in press; Gray 1987; Hammond and Macken-Horarik 1999; Hammond *et al.* 1992; Joyce 1992; Macken 1989; Macken-Horarik 1996). In particular, the issue of sharing the conceptual framework and the linguistic metalanguage with students is an important one (see e.g. Rothery 1989).

References

DeFransisco, V. (1997) "Gender, power and practice: or, putting your money (and your research) where your mouth is". In R. Wodak (ed.) *Gender and Discourse*. London, Sage, pp. 37–56.

Feez, S. (in press) "Heritage and innovation in second language education". In A. Johns (ed.) *Genres in the Classroom*. Hillsdale, NJ, Erlbaum.

Gray, B. (1987) "How natural is 'natural' language teaching – employing wholistic methodology in the classroom". *The Australian Journal of Early Childhood* v.12(4): 3–19.

Halliday, M.A.K. (1978a) "An interpretation of the relationship between language and social structure". In M.A.K. Halliday *Language as social semiotic*. London, Arnold, pp. 183–92.

Halliday, M.A.K. (1978b) "A social-functional approach to language". In M.A.K. Halliday *Language as social semiotic*. London, Arnold, pp. 36–58.

Halliday, M.A.K. (1994) *Introduction to Functional Grammar* (2nd edn). London, Arnold.

Halliday, M.A.K. and Hasan, R. (1985 / 1989) *Language, Context, and Text: Aspects of Language in a Social-semiotic Perspective*. Deakin, Deakin University Press, London, Oxford University Press.

Hammond, J. and Macken-Horarik, M. (1999) "Critical literacy: challenges and questions for ESL classrooms". *TESOL Quarterly* v.33(3): 528–44.

Hammond, J., Burns, A., Joyce, H., Brosnan, D. and Gerot, L. (1992) *English for Social Purposes*. Sydney, NCELTR.

Joyce, H. (1992) *Workplace Texts in the Language Classroom*. Sydney, NSW Adult Migrant English Service.

Macken, M. (1989) *A Genre-based Approach to Teaching Writing: Years 3–6* (4 vols). Sydney, NSW Literacy in Education Research Network (LERN) and the NSW Directorate of Studies, NSW Department of Education.

Macken-Horarik, M. (1996) "Literacy and learning across the curriculum: towards a model of register for secondary school teachers". In Hasan, R. and Williams, G. (eds) *Literacy in Society*. London, Longman, pp. 232–78.

Martin, J.R. (1984) "Language, register and genre". In *Children Writing: A Reader*. Geelong, Vic, Deakin University Press, pp. 21–30.

Martin, J.R. (1985 / 1989) *Factual Writing: Exploring and Challenging Social Reality*. Deakin University Press, London, Oxford University Press.

Martin, J.R. (1993) "Genre and Literacy – modelling context in educational linguistics". *Annual Review of Applied Linguistics*, 13: 14–172.

Martin, J.R. (1997) "Analysing genre: functional parameters". In F. Christie and J.R. Martin (eds) *Genre and Institutions: Social Processes in the Workplace and School*. London, Cassell, pp. 3–39.

Martin, J.R. and Rothery, J. (1980–81) *Writing Project Reports 1 & 2* (Working Papers in Linguistics). Department of Linguistics, University of Sydney.

Richardson, P.W. (1994) "Language as personal resource and as social construct: competing views of literacy pedagogy in Australia". In A. Freedman and P. Medway. (eds) *Learning and Teaching Genre*. Portsmouth, NH, Heinemann.

Rothery, J. (1986) "Teaching writing in the primary school: a genre based approach to the development of writing abilities". *Writing Project Report* (Working Papers in Linguistics no. 4). Department of Linguistics, University of Sydney.

Rothery, J. (1989) "Learning about language". In J.R. Martin and R. Hasan (eds) *Language Development: Learning Language Learning Culture: Meaning and Choice in Language: Studies for Michael Halliday* (Advances in Discourse Processes v.27). New York, Ablex, pp. 199–256.

Rothery, J. (1990) "Making changes: developing an educational linguistics". In R. Hasan and G. Williams (eds) *Literacy in Society*. London, Longman.

Sawyer, W. and Watson, K. (1987) "Questions of genre". In I. Reid (ed.) *The Place of Genre in Learning: Current Debates*. Geelong, Vic, Deakin University Press.

Chapter 11

M.A.K. Halliday

LITERACY AND LINGUISTICS: RELATIONSHIPS BETWEEN SPOKEN AND WRITTEN LANGUAGE*

A linguistic view of literacy

I N THIS CHAPTER I SHALL TRY to explore the concept of literacy from a linguistic point of view. By 'linguistic' here I mean two things: (1) treating literacy as something that has to do with language; and (2) using the conceptual framework of linguistics – the theoretical study of language – as a way of understanding it. More specifically, the framework is that of functional linguistics, since I think that literacy need to be understood in functional terms.

[. . .]

In many instances the term *literacy* has come to be dissociated from reading and writing, and written language, altogether, and generalized so as to cover all forms of discourse, spoken as well as written. In this way it comes to refer to effective participation of any kind in social processes.[1]

Having argued for much of my working life that we still do not properly value spoken language, or even properly describe it, I naturally sympathize with those who use the term in this way, to the extent that they are by implication raising the status of speaking, of the spoken language, and of the discourse of so-called 'oral cultures'. The problem is that if we call all these things literacy, then we shall have to find another term for what we called literacy before; because it is still necessary to distinguish reading and writing practices from listening and speaking practices. Neither is superior to the other, but they are different; and, more importantly, the interaction between them is one of the friction points at which new meaning are created.[2] So here I shall use literacy throughout to refer specifically to writing as distinct from speech: to reading and writing practices, and to the forms of language, and ways of meaning, that are typically associated with them.

[. . .]

1 Written language

As a writing system evolves, people use it; and they use it in constructing new forms of social action, new contexts which are different from those of speech. These contexts in turn both engender and are engendered by new lexicogrammatical patterns that evolve in the language itself. If we reflect on the lexicogrammar of written English, for example, we soon recognize features that are particularly associated with language in its written mode.

A great deal has been written, since the early 1970s, on spoken and written language; much of it purports to show that written language is more logical, more highly structured and more systematically organized than speech. This is the popular image of it; and it is very largely untrue – although you can readily see how such a picture came to be constructed. If you compare tape-recorded speech, with all its backtracking, rewording and periods of intermittent silence, with the highly edited, final form of a written text from which all such side-effects of the drafting have been eliminated; if you regard the overt intrusion of 'I' and 'you' into the text as making it less logical and less systematic; and if you then analyse both varieties in the terms of a logic and a grammar that were constructed out of, and for the purposes of, written language in the first place – you will have guaranteed in advance that written language will appear more orderly and more elaborately structured than spoken. And you will also have obscured the very real and significant differences between the two.

It is true, of course, that first and second person are much less used in written than in spoken texts. The system of person in the grammar construes a context which is typically dialogic, with constant exchange of roles between speaker and listener; this is not the pattern of written language, which is typically monologic and, except in a genre such as informal correspondence, does not accommodate a personalized reader as co-author of the text. (This is not to deny the role of the reader as an active participant in discourse, but the reader reconstitutes the text rather than sharing in its construction.) Hence there is less of a place for personal forms when making meaning in writing. And interpersonal meaning is made less salient in other ways besides; for example, there is much less variation from the unmarked choice of mood – most writing is declarative, except for compendia of instructions where the unmarked mood is imperative. The discursive relationship between writer and readers tends to be preset for the text as a whole. But it would be wrong to conclude from the absence of 'I' and 'you', and of interrogative clauses, that the writer is not present in the lexicogrammar of the written text. The writer is present in the attitudinal features of the lexis, in words which signal 'what I approve/disapprove of'; and, most conspicuously, in the network of interpersonal systems that make up modality. Modalities in language – expressions of probability, obligation and the like – are the grammar's way of expressing the speaker's or writer's judgment, without making the first person 'I' explicit; for example, *that practice must be stopped* means 'I insist that that practice is stopped', *it couldn't possibly make any difference* means 'I am certain that it doesn't make any difference'. Modalities never express the judgment of some third party. They may be presented as depersonalized, or objectified, especially in written language (e.g. *it seems that, there is a necessity that*); but all are ultimately manifestations of what 'I think'. The account given so far assumes that the clause is declarative. If, however; it is interrogative, the onus of judgment is simply shifted on to the listener: *could it possibly make any difference?* means 'do you think it possible that it makes some difference?'

However; a more significant feature of written language is the way its ideational meanings are organized. If we compare written with spoken English we find that written English typically shows a much denser pattern of lexicalized content. Lexical density has sometimes been measured as the ratio of content words to function words: higher in writing, lower in speech (Taylor 1979). But if we put it this way, we tie it too closely to

English. In a language such as Russian, where the 'function' elements more typically combine with the 'content' lexeme to form a single inflected word, such a measure would not easily apply. We can, however, formulate the content of lexical density in a more general way, so that it can be applied to (probably) all languages. In this formulation, lexical density is the number of lexicalized elements (lexemes) in the clause. Here is a sentence taken from a newspaper article, with the lexical elements in bold:

> Obviously the **government** is **frightened** of **union reaction** to its **move** to **impose proper behaviour** on **unions**.

There are nine lexemes, all in the one clause – lexical density 9. If we reword this in a rather more spoken form we might get the following:

> ||| Obviously the **government** is **frightened** || how the **unions** will **react** || if it tries to make them **behave properly** |||

There are now three clauses, and the number of lexemes has gone down to six – lexical density $6/3 = 2$.[3]

Needless to say, we will find passages of varying lexical density both in speech and in writing, with particular instances showing a range of values from zero to something over twenty. To say that written texts have a higher lexical density than spoken texts is like saying that men are taller than women: the pattern appears over a large population, so that given any text, the denser it is the more likely it is to be in writing rather than in speech. This explains the clear sense we have that a passage in one medium may be in the language of the other: someone is 'talking like a book', or 'writing in a colloquial style'.

How does the difference come about? It is not so much that when we reword something from a written into a spoken form the number of lexemes goes down; rather, the number of clauses goes up. Looking at this from the other end we can say that spoken language tends to have more clauses. But if one lexically dense clause in writing corresponds to two or more less dense clauses in speech, the latter are not simply unrelated to each other; they form hypotactic and/or paratactic clause complexes. Thus the spoken language tends to accommodate more clauses in its 'sentences'; in other words, to be less lexically dense, but more grammatically intricate. This may not emerge from averaging over large samples, because spoken dialogue also tends to contain some very short turns, and these consist mainly of one clause each. But given any instance of a clause complex, the more clauses it has in it the more likely it is to be found occurring in speech.

Most of the lexical material in any clause is located within nominal constructions: nominal groups or nominalized clauses. Thus in the example

> The **separable** or **external soul** is a **magical stratagem** generally **employed** by **supernatural wizards** or **giants**

there are two nominal groups, *the separable or external soul* and *a magical stratagem generally employed by supernatural wizards or giants*; and all nine lexemes fall within one or the other. But what makes this possible is the phenomenon of grammatical metaphor, whereby some semantic component is construed in the grammar in a form *other than* that which is prototypical; there are many types of grammatical metaphor, but the most productive types all contribute towards this pattern of nominalization. What happens is this. Some process or property, which in spoken language would typically appear as a verb or an adjective, is construed instead as a noun, functioning as head/thing in a nominal group; and other elements then accrue to it, often also by grammatical metaphor, as classifier or epithet or inside an embedded clause or phrase. In the following example the two head nouns, *variations* and *upheaval*, are both metaphorical in this way:

> These small variations of age-old formulas heralded a short but violent upheaval in Egyptian art.

How do we decide that one of the two variants is metaphorical? If they are viewed synoptically, each of the two is metaphorical from the standpoint of the other; given an agnate pair such as *her acceptance was followed by applause* and *when she accepted, people applauded*, we can say only that there is a relationship of grammatical metaphor between *her acceptance* and *she accepted*, but not – at least in any obvious respect – that one is metaphorical and the other not, or less so. If they are viewed dynamically, however, one form does turn out to be the unmarked one. Thus, in instances of this type, there are three distinct histories in which 'accept' is construed as a verb *before* it is construed as a noun:

1   diachronically, in the history of the language;
2   developmentally, in the history of the individual;
3   instantially, in the history of the text.

Thus (1) the noun is usually derived from the verb, rather than the other way round (the derivation may have taken place in ancient Latin or Greek, but that does not affect the point); (2) children usually learn the verbal form significantly earlier than the nominal one; (3) in a text, the writer usually proceeds from verb to noun rather than the other way round, e.g.

> She accepted the commission. Her acceptance was followed by applause.

In all these histories, the process starts life as a verb and is then metaphorized into a noun.[4]

One of the reasons why these nominalizing metaphors appeared in written language may be that writing was associated from the start with non-propositional (and hence non-clausal) registers: for example, tabulation of goods for trading purposes, lists of names (kings, heroes, genealogies), inventories of property and the like. But another impetus came from the development of science and mathematics, originating in ancient Greece, as far as the European tradition is concerned. To pursue these further we shall have to move 'up' one level, so as to take account of the contexts in which writing and written language evolve (see section 4 below). Meanwhile, we have now reached another step in our linguistic interpretation of literacy: literacy as 'having mastery of a written language'. In this sense, if we say that someone is literate it means that they are effectively using the lexicogrammatical patterns that are associated with written text. This does not imply that they are consciously aware of doing so, or that they could analyse these patterns in grammatical terms. But it does imply that they can understand and use the written wordings, differentiate them from the typical patterns of spoken language, and recognize their functions and their value in the culture.

I am not suggesting that written language is some kind of uniform, homogeneous 'style'. On the contrary, writing covers a wide range of different discursive practices, in which the patterns of language use are remarkably varied. But the fact that such practices are effective, and that such variation is meaningful, is precisely because certain 'syndromes' of lexicogrammatical features regularly appear as a typical characteristic of text that is produced in writing. This means, of course, that there are other combinations of features which do not appear; or appear only seldom, even though they would not be devoid of meaning: for example, we do not usually combine technical or commercial reports with expressions of personal feeling. But we could do; such gaps, or 'disjunctions', are not forced on us by the language, and with new developments in language technology there are already signs of change (cf. section 3 below).[5] By thinking about what does not usually occur, we become more aware of the regularities, of what is common to the varied forms of written discourse.

The value of having some explicit knowledge of the grammar of written language is that you can use this knowledge, not only to analyse the texts, but as a critical resource for asking questions about them: Why is the grammar organized as it is? Why has written language evolved in this way? What is its place in the construction of knowledge, the maintenance of bureaucratic and technocratic power structures, the design and practice of education? You can explore disjunctions and exploit their potential for creating new combinations of meanings. The question then arises: Are the spoken and written forms of a language simply variants, different ways of 'saying the same thing'? Or are they saying rather different things? This takes us to the next link in our exploratory chain.

2 The written world

I referred in the last section to the way in which metaphorical patterns of nominalization are built up in the course of a text. The example referred to in note 4 was a paper entitled 'The fracturing of glass', in *Scientific American* (December 1987); it contains the following expressions, listed here in the order in which they occur (in different locations spaced throughout the text):

1   the question of how glass cracks
2   the stress needed to crack glass
3   the mechanism by which glass cracks
4   as a crack grows
5   the crack has advanced
6   will make slow cracks grow
7   speed up the rate at which cracks grow
8   the rate of crack growth
9   we can decrease the crack growth rate 1,000 times.

Note how the metaphorical object *crack growth rate* is built up step by step beginning from the most congruent (least metaphorical) form *how glass cracks*.

To see why this happens, let us focus more sharply on one particular step:

> . . . we have found that both chemicals [ammonia and methanol] speed up the rate at which cracks grow in silica. . . . The rate of crack growth depends not only on the chemical environment but also on the magnitude of the applied stress. (p. 81)

This shows that there are good reasons *in the discourse* (in the 'textual' metafunction, in systemic terms). In carrying the argument forward it is often necessary to refer to what has already been established – but to do so in a way which backgrounds it as the point of departure for what is coming next. This is achieved in the grammar by thematizing it: the relevant matter becomes the theme of the clause. Here the theme *the rate of crack growth* 'packages' a large part of the preceding argument so that it serves as the rhetorical foundation for what follows.

When we look into the grammar of scientific writings we find that this motif recurs all the time. The clause begins with a nominal group, typically embodying a number of instances of grammatical metaphor; this summarizes the stage that has now been reached in the argument and uses it as the taking-off point for the next step. Very often, this next step consists in relating the first nominal to a second one that is similarly packaged, in a logical-semantic relationship of identity, cause, proof and the like. Thus a typical instance of this clause pattern would be the following:

> The sequential appearance of index-minerals reflected steadily increasing temperature across the area.

Here is a condensed version of the context in which this is built up:

> [Barrow] recognized a definite and consistent order of appearance or disappearance of particular metamorphic minerals (**index minerals**), across the area. . . . The differences in mineralogy observed by Barrow could not be due to chemical differences because the rocks all have similar bulk chemical compositions. The most likely explanation . . . is that the sequential appearance of index minerals reflected steadily increasing temperature across the area.
>
> (Clark and Cook 1986: 239)

In a study of the evolution of the grammar of scientific English from Chaucer to the present day (reference in note 5 above), I found that this clause pattern is already operational in Newton's writing (the English text of the *Opticks*), becomes well established during the eighteenth century, and has become the favourite clause type by the early years of the nineteenth century. Since this kind of nominalization is frequently objected to by stylists, it is valid to point out that, however much it may become ritualized, and co-opted for use in contexts of prestige and power, it is clearly discourse-functional in origin.

However, while these nominalizing metaphors may have been motivated initially by textual considerations, their effect in the written language – perhaps because they arose first in the language of science – has been to construct an alternative model of human experience. Spoken language is organized around the clause, in the sense that most of the experiential content is laid down in the transitivity system, and in other systems having the clause as point of origin; and this – since the clause construes reality as processes (actions, events, mental processes, relations) – creates a world of movement and flux, or rather a world that is moving and flowing, continuous, elastic, and indeterminate. By the same token the written language is organized around the nominal group; and this – since the nominal group construes reality as entities (objects, including institutional and abstract objects, and their quantities, qualities and types) – creates a world of things and structures, discontinuous, rigid, and determinate. Here experience is being interpreted synoptically rather than dynamically (Martin 1991).

This is the same complementarity as we find between the two different media. Spoken language is language in flux: language realized as movement and continuous flow, of our bodily organs and of sound waves travelling through air. Written language is language in fix: language realized as an object that is stable and bounded – as text in material form on stone or wood or paper. Thus the complementarity appears at both the interfaces where the discursive connects with the material (both in the meaning and in the expression); and both are significant for the social-semiotic functioning of language. If we use David Olson's distinction between communicative and archival functions (Olson 1989), spoken discourse is typically communicative, and becomes archival only under special conditions (e.g. a priesthood transmitting sacred oral texts); whereas written discourse is typically archival, a form of record-keeping, and hence can accumulate knowledge by constant accretion, a necessary condition for advancing technology and science.[6] On the other hand, those who are constructing scientific knowledge experimentally need to hold the world still – to stop it wriggling, so to speak – in order to observe and to study it; and this is what the grammar of written language does for them.

Thus the written world is a world of things. Its symbols are things, its texts are things, and its grammar constructs a discourse of things, with which readers and writers construe experience. Or rather, with which they *reconstrue* experience, because all have been speakers and listeners first, so that the written world is their secondary socialization. This is critical for our understanding of the educational experience. Despite our conviction that we as conscious subjects have one 'store of knowledge' rather than two, we also have the sense that educational knowledge is somehow different from 'mere' commonsense know-ledge; not surprisingly, since it is construed in a different semiotic mode. The language of the school is written language.

But, of course, educational knowledge is *not* constructed solely out of written language. Whereas our primary, commonsense knowledge is – in this respect – homo-glossic, in that it is construed solely out of the clausal grammar of the spoken language, our secondary, educational knowledge is heteroglossic: it is construed out of the dialectic between the spoken and the written, the clausal and the nominal modes. Even though the scientific textbook may be overwhelmingly in nominal style, provided we are reasonably lucky, our total educational experience will be multimodal, with input from teachers, parents and peers, from classroom, library, teachers' notes and handouts, all of which presents us with a mix of the spoken and the written worlds. At its worst, this is a chaos, but it does offer the potential for more effective participation in social-semiotic practices than either of the two modes can offer by itself.

Literacy, then, in this context, is the construction of an 'objectified' world through the grammar of the written language. This means that in at least some social practices where meanings are made in writing, including educational ones, the discourse will actively participate in an ideological construction which is in principle contradictory to that derived from everyday experience. To be literate is, of course, to engage in these practices, for example as a teacher; and to construe from them a working model to live with, one that does not deny the experience of common sense. Again, I would observe that, in order to turn the coin – to resist the mystique and the seductive appeal of a world consisting entirely of metaphorical objects – it is helpful to have a *grammatics*, a way of using the grammar consciously as a tool for thinking with. It seems to me that . . . the two worlds have been pushed about as far apart as they can go, and in the next period of our history they are bound to move together again. I think, in fact, they are already starting to do so, under the impact of the new forms of technology which are deconstructing the whole opposition of speech and writing. This is the topic we have to take up next, as the next link in the interpretative chain. But in doing so, we are back where we started, concerned once again with the nature of the written medium.

3   The technology of literacy

The critical step in the history of writing technology is usually taken to be the invention of printing with movable type. The significance of this from our present point of view is that it created maximum distance between written and spoken text. A written text now not only existed in material form, it could be cloned – it had become a book. Books existed in lots of copies; they were located in libraries, from which they could be borrowed for variable periods of time;[7] they could be possessed, and bought and sold, as property. Producing books was a form of labour; and created value: printing, publishing, bookbinding were ways of earning a living. The book became an institution (the book of words, book of rules), without thereby losing its material character; note the expression *they threw the book at me* 'quoted the authority of the written word'. With printing, language in its written form became maximally objectified; and this extreme dichotomy between speech and writing was a dominant feature of the five hundred years of 'modern Europe' from about 1450 to 1950.

We have seen how this object-like status of the written word is enacted metaphorically by the nominalizing grammar of the written language. Meanwhile, however, the technology has turned itself around. Within one lifetime our personal printing press, the typewriter, from being manual became first electric then electronic; and from its marriage with the computer was born the word processor. With this, in hardly any time, the gap between spoken and written text has been largely eliminated. On the one hand, whereas in the printing era the written text passed out of the writer's control in being transmitted, we now once again control our own written discourse; and since we have our own private means of transmission, the communicative function of writing has come to the fore, as people write to each other by electronic mail. And as the functional gap has lessened, so also the material gap has lessened, and from both ends. With a tape-recorder, speech becomes an object: it is on the tape; can be 'played' over and over again (so listening becomes like reading); can be multiply copied; and can be stored (and so used for archiving functions). With a word processor, writing becomes a happening; it can be scrolled up the screen so that it unfolds in time, like speech. The tape-recorder made speech more like writing; the word processor has made writing more like speech.

We have seen the effects of this in education. Teachers who favour 'process writing' are emphasizing the activity of writing as well as – and sometimes at the expense of – the object that results from it.[8] Children who learn to write using a word processor tend to compose their written discourse in a manner that is more like talking than like traditional writing exercises (Anderson 1985). What is happening here is that the consciousness barrier is disappearing. When the material conditions of speaking and writing are most distinct, the consciousness gap is greatest: speaking is unselfconscious, proceeding as it were from the gut, while writing is self-conscious, designed and produced in the head. (This is why the writing of a 6-year-old typically regresses to resemble the spoken language of age 3.) Although writing and reading will always be more readily accessible to conscious reflection than speaking and listening, *relatively* we now have more occasions for being self-conscious when we speak (international phone calls, talkback shows, interviews, committees and so on), and more chances of remaining unselfconscious when we write.

This suggests that the spoken and the written *language* will probably come close together; and there are signs that this is already beginning to happen. Not only textbook writers but also public servants, bankers, lawyers, insurers and others are notably uneasy about the 'communication gap'; they are even turning to linguists to help them communicate – note the success of the Plain English movement towards greater reader-friendliness in written documents. I have referred already to the scientists wanting a discourse of continuity and flow, and suggested that the way to achieve this is to make their technical writing more like speech, so that they are not cut off from the commonsense construction of experience. But we need to think grammatically about this. To the extent that written discourse is *technical*, to that extent it probably has to objectify, since most technical constructs are metaphorical objects, organized in paradigms and taxonomies.[9] Even non-technical writing has numerous functions for which a nominal mode seems called for. So it is not, I think, a question of neutralizing the difference between written language and spoken. What the technology is doing is creating the material conditions for interaction between the two, from which some new forms of discourse will emerge. Again, the effects are likely to be felt at both the material interfaces of language: new forms of publication, on the one hand, with (say) print and figures on paper combining with moving text and graphics on the screen; and on the other hand new ways of meaning which construe experience in more complex, and hence more 'realistic', ways arising out of the complementarities of the spoken and the written modes. Such a construction of experience would seem to call once again for the poet-scientist, in the tradition of Lucretius; I think Butt (1988a, 1988b) would say that Wallace Stevens is the first such figure in our own times, at least among those writing in English, but there are also scientists with the semantic prosodies of poetry, like Stephen Hawking. And if science is to technology as poetry is to prose, then the marriage, or perhaps *de facto* relationship, has already been arranged: in the post-industrial, information society the real professional is the semiotician-technician, for whom the world is made of discourse/information and the same meta-grammar is needed to construe both the grammar of language on the one hand, and the 'grammar' of the teleport, on the other.[10]

At this level, then, literacy is a technological construct; it means using the current technology of writing to participate in social processes, including the new social processes that the technology brings into being. A person who is literate is one who effectively engages in this activity (we already refer to people as 'computer-literate', a concept that is now much closer to literacy in its traditional sense than it was when coined). But – the other side of the coin again – I think that here, too, and perhaps especially in this context, we need the concept of literacy as informed defence. To be literate is not only to *participate* in the discourse of an information society, it is also to resist it, to defend oneself – and others – against the anti-semantic, anti-democratic 'technologizing' of that discourse. And here more than ever one needs to understand how language works, how the grammar (in its systemic sense of lexicogrammar) interacts with the technology to achieve these effects. If you hope to engage successfully in discursive contest, you have first to learn how to engage with discourse.

4 The frontiers of literacy

[. . .]

Malinowski gave us the concepts of 'context of situation' and 'context of culture'; we can interpret the context of situation as the environment of the text and the context of culture as the environment of the linguistic system. The various types of social process can be described in linguistic terms as contexts of language use. The principle of functional complementarity means that we can talk of the contexts of written discourse.

Certain contexts of writing are largely transparent: if we represent them in terms of field, tenor and mode then there is a fairly direct link from these to the grammar of the text. Such relatively homogeneous forms of discourse, like weather reports, sets of instructions (e.g. recipes), shopping lists and other written agendas, and some institutional discourses, can be specified so that we can construe them in either direction: given the context, we can construe the features of the text, and given the text we can construe the features of the context. To be literate implies construing in both directions, hence constructing a relationship between text and context which is systematic and not random.

Other written texts are not like this; they present a more or less discordant mix of multiple voices. These are texts whose context embodies internal contradictions and conflicts. As an example, one large class of such texts consists of those designed to persuade people to part with their money. The goods and services offered have to display all desirable qualities, even where these conflict with one another, as they often do; and to combine these with a price-figure that is in fact in conflict with their claimed value, and has to be presented as such but with the inconsistency explained away ('you'd never believe that we could offer . . . but our lease has expired and we must dispose of all stock', etc.). In the following example the text has to reconcile the 'desirable building land' with the fact that it is on a site that should never have been built on; the linguistic unease is obvious:

> . . . is a high quality bushland, residential estate which retains environmental integrity similar to a wildlife reserve.

Such features need, of course, to be demonstrated with full-length texts.

Another example is technocratic discourse, which, as Lemke (1990) and Thibault (1991) have shown, intersects the technical-scientific with the bureaucratic – the authority of knowledge with the authority of power – to create a contradictory motif of 'we live in an informed society, so here is explicit evidence; but the issues are too complex for you to understand, so leave the decision-making to us'; they go on to 'prove' that children who are failing in school do not benefit from having more money spent on them, or that the environment is not under serious threat. Reproduced below, however, is an example of a different kind (though not unrelated to these last). It is a party invitation addressed to tenants in a prestigious 'executive residence' (name withheld).

> Dear tenant
>
> IF YOU JUST WANNA HAVE FUN . . .
> Come to your MOONCAKE NITE THEME PARTY next Saturday.
> That's September 20 – from 7.30 p.m. until the wee hours!!
> A sneak preview of the exciting line-up of activities includes:

* Mr/Ms   Tenant Contest
* Find <u>Your</u> Mooncake Partner
* Pass the Lantern Game
* Bottoms Up Contest
* Blow the Lantern Game
* Moonwalking Contest
* DANCING
* PLUS MORE! MORE! MORE!

For even greater fun, design and wear your original Mooncake creation, and bring our self-made lantern passport!
But don't despair if you can't because this party is <u>FOR</u> you!
Lantern passports can be bought at the door.
Just c'mon and grab this opportunity to chat up your neighbour.
Call yours truly on <u>ext. 137</u> NOW! Confirm you really wanna have fun!! Why – September 20's next Saturday.
See you!

Public Relations Officer
P.S. Bring your camera to 'capture' the fun!

In the cacophony of voices that constitute this text, we can recognize a number of oppositions: child and adult, work and leisure, 'naughty' and 'nice', professional and commercial – constructed by the lexicogrammar in cahoots with the prosody and paralanguage. But this mixture of bureaucratic routine, comics-style graphic effects, masculine aggression, childism and condescension, straight commercialism, conspiratorialism and hype adds up to something that we recognize: late capitalist English in the Disneyland register. Presumably there are institutions in southern California where people who are being trained to 'service' business executives learn to construct this kind of discourse. The context is the disneyfication of Western man (I say 'man' advisedly), whereby the off-duty executive reverts semiotically to childhood while retaining the material make-up of an adult.

Literacy today includes many contexts of this contorted kind, where the functions of the written text have to be sorted out at various levels. To be literate is to operate in such complex, multiple contexts: to write with many voices, still ending up with a text, and to read such texts with kaleidoscopic eyes. Once again, the grammatics will help: it is the point about conscious knowledge again. And once again there is the other side of the coin, literacy as active defence: resisting the disneyfication, as well as more ominous pressures; probing the disjunctions, and extending the semogenic potential of the culture.

[. . .]

We are all familiar with the claim that linguistics has nothing useful to say on the subject of literacy. But it always seems to be a kind of linguistics very remote from life that is cited to justify the argument. It is a pity, because to reject linguistic insights seals off an important avenue of understanding. What I have tried to suggest here is that a functional linguistic perspective provides a valuable complementarity to the view from sociology and the philosophy of education.

Notes

1   The following is taken from *Australia Post*'s description of International Literacy Year 1990: 'Literacy involves the integration of listening, speaking, reading, writing and critical thinking; it incorporates numeracy. Literacy also includes the cultural knowledge which enables a speaker, writer or reader to recognise and use language appropriate to different social situations' (*Australian Stamp Bulletin* No. 203, January–March 1990, p. 10).

2   The situation is similar to that which arises with the term *language*. If we want to extend it to mathematics, music and other semiotic systems, in order to emphasize their similarities of form or function or value in the culture, then we have to find another term for language. The expression 'natural language' arose in response to just this kind of pressure. I am not aware of any comparable term for literacy in its canonical sense.

3   There are of course many possible rewordings. We might for example keep the word *move* and end with *if it moves so as to make the unions behave properly*; this adds two lexemes, *move* and *unions*, but it also adds one clause, a hypotactic clause of purpose, giving a ratio of 8/4, still = 2. Other variants would alter the lexical density; but it would be difficult to find a convincing 'spoken' version in which it was not significantly lower than in the written one.

4   For an instance of how grammatical metaphor is built up in the course of a text, see Halliday (1988).

5   See Lemke (1984) who introduces the notion of 'disjunctions' in the context of a general theory of language as a dynamic open system which provides an essential component of the present interpretation.

6   Note the apparent paradox that, in the archival function, written language becomes the dynamic member of the pair. The spoken archive (canon of sacred texts, traditional narrative and song, etc.) can *change* in the course of transmission, but it cannot grow – it cannot become a library of knowledge.

7   According to *The Return of Heroic Failures*, by Stephen Pile (Penguin Books, 1988), the most overdue book in the history of the lending library was borrowed from Somerset County Records Office, in England, by the Bishop of Winchester in 1650, and returned to the library by the Church Commissioners 335 years later, in 1985. The book in question was, appropriately, the *Book of Fines*.

8   This issue has been foregrounded in the 'genre debate' in Australia; see for example, Painter and Martin (1987) and also Moore (1990).

9   Martin (1990) has argued convincingly that the technicalization of discourse must depend on nominalization and grammatical metaphor. On the other hand, Whorf pointed out that the technical terms of Hopi metaphysics were typically verbs. (But probably not taxonomized?)

10 For an overview of the development and present state of information technology see Meadows (1989).

References

Anderson, J. 1985. *C.O.M.P.U.T.E.R.S in the Language Classroom*. Perth: Australian Reading Association.

Butt, D. 1988a. 'Randomness, order and the latent patterning of text', in David Birch and Michael O'Toole (eds), *Functions of Style*. London: Pinter.

Butt, D. 1988b. 'Ideational meaning and the "existential fabric" of a poem', in Robin P. Fawcett and David J. Young (eds), *New Developments in Systemic Linguistics, Vol. 2: Theory and Application*. London and New York: Pinter.

Clark, I.F. and Cook, B.J. (eds) 1986. *Geological Science: Perspectives of the Earth*. Canberra: Australian Academy of Science.

Halliday, M.A.K. 1988. 'On the language of physical science', in Mohsen Ghadessy (ed.), *Register of Written English*. London: Pinter.

Lemke, J.L. 1984. *Semiotics and Education*. Toronto: Victoria University (Toronto Semiotic Circle, Monographs, Working Papers and Prepublications).

Lemke, J.L. 1990. 'Technocratic discourse and ideology', in M.A.K. Halliday, John Gibbons and Howard Nicholas (eds), *Learning, Keeping and Using Language: Selected Papers from the Eighth World Congress of Applied Linguistics, Sydney 1987*. Amsterdam: Benjamins.

Martin, J.R. 1990. 'Literacy in science: learning to handle text as technology', in Frances Christie (ed.), *Literacy in a Changing World*. Melbourne: Australian Council for Educational Research (reprinted in M.A.K. Halliday and J.R. Martin, *Writing Science: Literacy and Discursive Power*. London and Washington, DC: Falmer Press, 1993).

Martin, J.R. 1991. 'Nominalization in science and humanities: distilling knowledge and scaffolding text', in Eija Ventola (ed.), *Functional and Systemic Linguistics: Approaches and Uses*. Berlin and New York: Mouton de Gruyter.

Meadows, J. 1989. *Infotechnology: Changing the Way We Communicate*. London: Cassell.

Moore, H. 1990. 'Process vs product, or down with the opposition', in M.A.K. Halliday, John Gibbons and Howard Nicholas (eds), *Learning, Keeping and Using Language: Selected Papers from the Eighth World Congress of Applied Linguistics, Sydney 1987*. Amsterdam: Benjamins.

Olson, D.R. 1989. 'On the language and authority of textbooks', in Suzanne de Castell, Allan Luke and Carmen Luke (eds), *Language, Authority and Criticism Readings on the School Textbook*. London: Falmer Press.

Painter, C. and Martin, J.R. (eds) 1987. *Writing to Mean: Developing Genres across the Curriculum*. Applied Linguistics Association of Australia, Occasional Paper No. 8.

Taylor, C. 1979. *The English of High School Textbooks*. Canberra: Australian Government Publishing Service (Education Research and Development Committee, Report No. 18).

Thibault, P.J. 1991. 'Grammar, technocracy, and the noun: technocratic values and cognitive linguistics', in Eija Ventola (ed.), *Recent Systemic and other Functional Views on Language*. Berlin: Mouton de Gruyter.

Chapter 12

Maree Stenglin and Rick Iedema

HOW TO ANALYSE VISUAL IMAGES: A GUIDE FOR TESOL TEACHERS

Introduction

READING TEXTS IS AN ESSENTIAL part of the teaching and learning activities that take place in all classrooms, especially TESOL classrooms. TESOL students are often asked to read a wide range of written texts such as newspaper and magazine articles, advertisements, procedural texts, tourist brochures, film reviews, community notices, etc. Visual images such as maps, diagrams, photographs, tables and drawings also increasingly accompany these texts. The texts which TESOL students are expected to be able to "read" are thus multi-modal. A multi-modal text is one in which a number of different modes (words in headings and headlines; images and the written texts themselves) are integrated to form a composite whole.

To prepare students for reading such complex multi-modal texts, TESOL teachers often begin by establishing a relevant context for the reading activity. They do this by firstly separating the different modes and then engaging students in a range of pre-reading activities. For example, a common pre-reading task involves the use of visual images such as photographs and drawings together with headlines or headings to prompt students to predict the content of the text they are about to read and involve them in discussing their prior knowledge and experiences (Hood *et al.*, 1996: 73–6). The rationale for these activities is that they encourage students to use their social knowledge to generate predictions about the written text which are later tested and either confirmed, or challenged, when the students begin to "sample" the actual text.

Implicit in this practice is the assumption that the meaning(s) of visual images are transparent, obvious and accessible to all students. However, Kress and van Leeuwen (1996) and Nichols (1981) have shown that visual images are socially and culturally constructed products which have a culturally specific grammar of their own. The most obvious example Kress and van Leeuwen (1996: 4–5) give is that in Western cultures, visual communication is deeply affected by the convention of writing from left to right. Thus in Western visual communication the information that is "known" or "assumed" is often placed on the left-hand side of the image and new information is placed on the right. For example, in dieting advertisements, photographs of the person looking overweight are placed on the left-hand side while photographs of the person looking slim are placed on the right. This practice contrasts with those cultures which have developed the reverse convention, i.e. they write from right to left and therefore "assign different values and meanings to these key conventions of visual space" (Kress and van Leeuwen, 1996: 3). In becoming literate, students thus need to acquire the ability to be able to "read" and access the culturally specific meanings inherent in both visual and written texts.

To assist students in acquiring these essential and complementary literacy skills, teachers themselves need to become aware of these issues. They also need to acquire the tools for informed visual analysis together with a language for discussing the meanings constructed in the visual learning materials with their students. In this chapter we aim therefore to do several things. First, to introduce TESOL teachers to some of the tools they can use to systematically explore and teach some of the meanings in visual images. Second, to demonstrate how these tools can be used for visual image analysis by applying them to a set of images. Finally, we will explore how the tools for visual image analysis can be used in practical ways to inform TESOL classroom teaching.

What tools can be used to analyse visual images?

Kress and van Leeuwen (1996) have extended the use of systemic functional linguistics (SFL) to the analysis of images and sound. In short, Kress and van Leeuwen propose a way of talking about visuals to bring out systematically what is communicated by means of images and visual design. They discuss three areas of representation. First, the structure of the visual image; second, the events and happenings in the world including the people involved in the events, and the circumstances associated with the events; and finally, the relationship "set up" between the image and the viewer. Each of these areas of representation will now be explained and exemplified using a six-step procedure for installing an iMac. This procedure can be used with elementary, intermediate or advanced students as exemplified in the teaching notes beginning on page 206 of this chapter.

Tools for analysing the structure of visual images

According to Kress and van Leeuwen (1996) there are four main tools that can be used to analyse the structure of visual images. They are the placement of elements on the horizontal axis (left to right); the placement of elements on the vertical axis (top to bottom); the framing of images; and the salience, that is to say, the prominence given to the images.

The way in which images are structured relates to the placement of elements in the image. Images can be divided in distinct ways. For example, the placement of some elements on the left-hand side of the image and some on the right is, as we shall see, a meaningful choice. Similarly, the placement of some elements in the top or bottom section of the image indicates another meaningful choice.

In Western images, the left- and right-hand sides complement each other. The left-hand side of the image will often be devoted to things with which we are familiar or which we are assumed to take for granted. This side can therefore be called the "Given". The right-hand side, by contrast, often displays new visual information. This side can be called the "New". For example, when we are shown "before" and "after" shots of house renovations or slimming diets, we often get the old version on the left, and the new version on the right.

In fact, Western newspaper and magazine publishers see their right-hand side pages as more prominent, and they believe these are read more carefully by their audiences than their left-hand pages. As a consequence, advertisers pay higher rates to have their ads printed on right-hand-side pages than on left-hand-side pages. While this kind of left–right division of meaning in Western images is quite common, it tends to be the reverse in non-Western kinds of representations (Opama, 1990).

Another important structural characteristic concerns the *opposition* between top and bottom. Higher up in images we tend to find what is positioned as "Ideal", the generalised, or the essence of something. Lower down we often find the "Real", the specific, or the instance. In advertisements, for example, one generally finds a photo of an attractive island, or a person, or a car, at the top, whereas the more factual information is generally found at the bottom. These contrasts are summed up in Table 12.1.

Table 12.1 Meanings of visual space

The Ideal/the Given: most highly valued medium salience	*The Ideal/the New:* most highly valued high salience
The Real/the Given: less highly valued low salience	*The Real/the New:* less highly valued medium salience

Some images are not so much geometric and organised in terms of left to right and top to bottom as they are circular or "concentric". These images do not divide their visual space into four quadrants as shown in Table 12.1, but instead have a clear centre. Women's magazine covers are a good example: the model's face occupies the central space on the page. Rather than left to right and top to bottom contrasts, such images oppose centre (e.g. the model's face) and periphery (e.g. magazine title, headlines and additional images).

A third issue concerns the framing of the image. As Figure 12.1 shows, images can be made to stand out by using strong outlines or be allowed to blend into their own surroundings. The trees on the left in Figure 12.1a are quite strongly separated off from the text. This is suggestive of an "ordered world". In Figure 12.1b the trees are less clearly separated from the text, suggesting a less ordered and less constrained world.

(a)

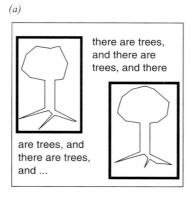

(b)

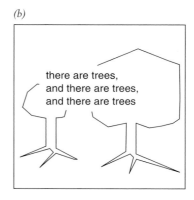

Figure 12.1 Framing and order

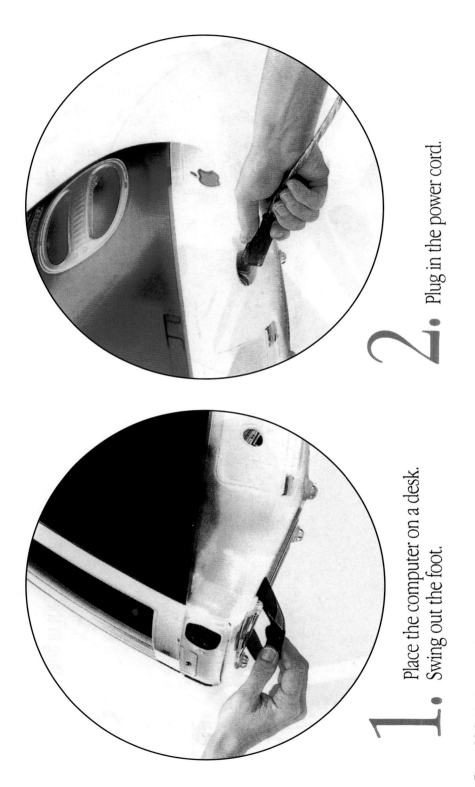

2. Plug in the power cord.

1. Place the computer on a desk.
Swing out the foot.

Figure 12.2 The iMac installation text
© Hunter Freeman 1999

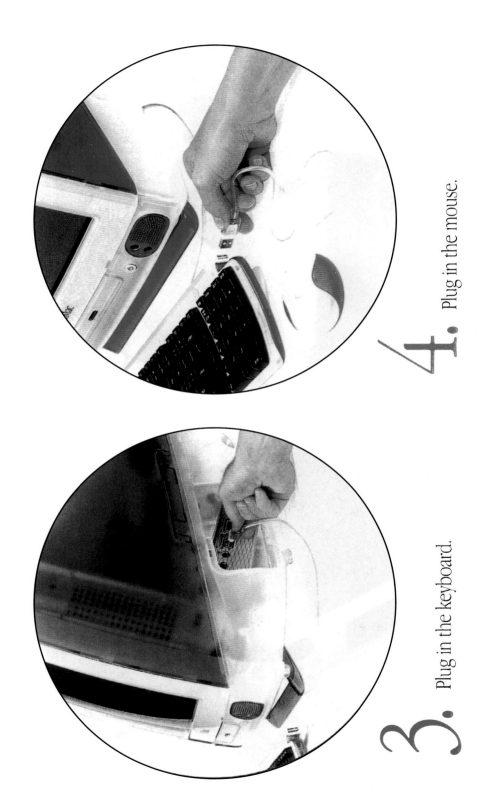

4. Plug in the mouse.

3. Plug in the keyboard.

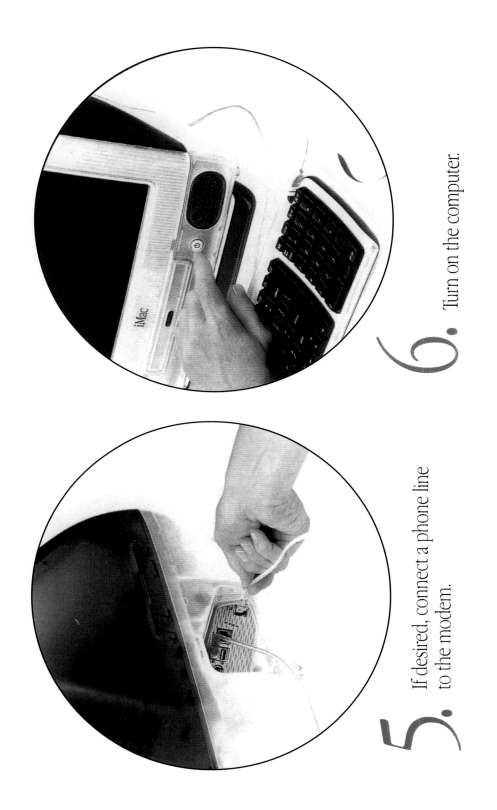

6. Turn on the computer.

5. If desired, connect a phone line to the modem.

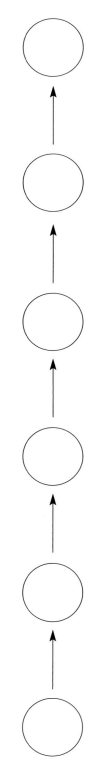

The iMac installation reading path

Framing and the placement of specific elements lead us to a final issue: that of salience or prominence. The stronger the framing and the more central the visual element, the more salient it is likely to be. At the same time, framing contributes to our sense of order and separation: it constructs a world where things are kept apart. Figure 12.1*a* shows how framing can contribute to the salience and separateness of visual elements. Figure 12.1*b* is an example where the relative absence of framing gives a sense of a world where things can freely intermix.

Analysing the structure of images in a procedure for installing an iMac

The iMac installation text shown in Figure 12.2 is a procedure, a text which enables people to do or make things. It is also a multi-modal text as it includes both written language and visual images. This particular text has been chosen because it is ideally suited for students learning about procedures. The images in this multi-modal procedure do not just illustrate the written instructions; rather they add new and crucial information to the instructions. This means there is a strong relationship of interdependence between the visual and written modes in this text. In other words, the images and the text do not "stand alone". Therefore, to read this multi-modal iMac text successfully, students need clear information about the structure and organisation of both the written text and the visual images accompanying it. We will begin the analysis by briefly explaining the purpose, structure and language features of procedural texts in Western cultures and then move on to ana- lysing the structure of the actual images and the nature of the interdependence relationship between the two modes in this text.

The purpose, structure, language features and visual design of procedures

First, procedures are important in Western societies, as well as others, because they are enabling texts. We encounter them in a variety of social contexts such as banks, post offices, workplaces, swimming pools and homes where they appear in posters, manuals, cookbooks, magazines and on forms. They are also often found on equipment such as fire extinguishers and public telephones. The social purpose of a procedure is to enable a sequence of actions to be carried out in order to achieve a particular goal. For example, the goal of the iMac procedure is the successful installation of the computer.

To achieve this social purpose, procedures move through two main stages: goal ^ (followed by) steps 1–n. The goal is usually the title of the text and gives the outcome of the procedure, while steps 1–n give the actions that need to be carried out to achieve this goal. In the iMac procedure the steps are numbered from 1 to 6. Numbering steps in this way is a common choice for ordering procedural texts.

Second, as procedures are texts which are to be acted on, the first word in each step is usually the verb, or in SFL terms, the material or action process. Some examples of action processes in first position in the steps of the iMac procedure are, *place*, *plug in*, *swing out* and *turn on*. However, many important meanings about these action processes also occur at the end of each step (Rothery, 1994: 186). These meanings give the reader vital and more specific information about the action processes, such as:

* when they are to happen (e.g. just before serving)
* where (e.g. in the centre of the bowl)

- how long for (e.g. five minutes/half an hour)
- what with (e.g. a metal spoon/toothpick)
- in what way (e.g. gradually, gently).

In SFL these meanings are referred to as circumstances. In order for a written procedure to be carried out successfully, the circumstances are essential. They need to be accurate, complete and easy to understand. Without them the reader would often be unable to follow the text successfully.

In terms of design, layout or visual composition, procedures are usually read from top to bottom and each step within the sequence is read from left to right. The predominance of this top to bottom reading path is related to the presentation of a procedure as a linear sequence of steps that needs to be followed, and acted on, in a set order. Finally, the steps in a procedure are often accompanied by black-and-white sketches or line drawings. Now let us see how these linguistic and visual conventions are realised in the iMac procedural text.

How are the images in the iMac procedure structured? What choices are made for Real–Ideal and Given–New?

The first thing we notice is that this multi-modal text does not follow the top to bottom visual convention for procedures and foregrounds a Given to New, or left to right, reading path. We predominantly engage with the text on the horizontal plane by beginning with the first image on the left-hand side (and its accompanying written text) and moving across the page until we reach the last step in the procedure. Our reading path can thus be represented as:

Figure 12.3 Reading path

To ensure that we follow this visual pathway, there is a number from 1 to 6 below each image in an extremely large and bold orange font. This prominent and sequential numbering system makes the horizontal and linear reading pathway of this multi-modal text explicit for readers. This sequence confirms that reading paths usually begin with the most salient elements. In this text the most salient elements are undeniably the images and their accompanying numbers. The large numbers on the page also serve another function in that, because of their size, they bridge the white space that lies between the image and the written text. They are thus connecting or linking the two modes on the page: the image and the written instruction below it. In doing so, they draw our attention to both. Note also how the images are tenuously framed with a fine black line so that they are not presented as a discrete unit, separate from the text.

With regard to salience, we can see how the prominence of the images is enhanced by the removal of all background visual details from the page. In particular, note how the white colour of the table on which the computer sits and the white background of the page focus our attention on the images.

This procedural text is also organised along the vertical axis. The upper section, which typically represents the promise of the product, contains all the visuals in this text. In Kress and van Leeuwen's terms it is the Ideal: it represents the fulfilment of the procedural goal, the successful connection of the computer. The lower section, which typically presents the factual, "down to earth" information, the Real, contains the written instructions in this text – the specific step-by-step actions that need to be carried out to achieve the goal.

Let us now take a closer look at the composition of the individual images. We notice that there is another order of Given–New operating in their organisation. In the first and last images, the hand operating the computer is placed on the left-hand side or in the Given position and the computer is the New. In the middle images, however, this placement is reversed. These choices can be explained with reference to the circumstantial elements that need to be visually communicated. When the user is required to be in front of the computer to connect something, the user's hand is in the Given position. It is thus taken for granted that we face the computer front-on when we are using it. However, when we have to connect cords to the side or back of the computer or the keyboard, we are not facing the computer in the usual front-on way. We are actually approaching it from a New and different angle and thus the hand in the middle images is placed on the right or in the new position.

By looking at the structure of visual images in this way students are learning how the written and visual elements relate to each other and how they are integrated into a compositional whole. They are also learning important cultural information about how the placement of the elements in the text (Given–New; Real–Ideal) gives them specific information values. Let us now move on to the next level of visual image analysis. This will involve us in looking at the way images construct events or happenings in the world.

Tools for analysing events or happenings in the world

In describing events or happenings in the world, Kress and van Leeuwen (1996) distinguish between two types of images: portraits or landscapes and snapshots or action shots. They refer to portraits or landscapes as *conceptual* images, and snapshots or action shots as *narrative* images. Conceptual images include those images which set out an object and its various parts, such as labelled diagrams; a range of related objects, such as taxonomies; or objects which are symbolically related, for example, a prisoner standing behind a barbed wire fence.

Narrative images show the represented participants engaged in either an action such as serving a ball on a tennis court or, through the direction of their glance engaged in reaction. Action images are realised by means of something that points, that is a *vector*. A vector is a line formed in the image by one or more of its participants or by their limbs. In reaction images this vector is realised by the direction of the glance, originating from a human being or animal, towards the phenomenon that is reacted to.

Analysing the "events" or "happenings" in the iMac installation procedure

These tools can illuminate some of the meanings being communicated in the iMac procedure. At a general or global level, the images show the actions that need to be carried out to install the computer. Each image in the sequence is therefore a narrative or action shot. Together the images form a cohesive sequence of actions or events that unfold over time and culminate in the successful installation of the computer.

According to Kress and van Leeuwen (1996: 56–7) narrative shots are made up of the following: participants and an action that is realised by a vector. Let us begin by identifying the participants. If we look closely at the text we can see two participants in each image; a hand and the object it is acting on. Typically in narrative shots, one of the participants has the role of actor who performs the action. In all of the iMac images the hand is the Actor involved in the process of connecting objects to the computer. This is in marked contrast to the written instructions where information about who needs to perform the actions is not specified. Therefore, in this particular text, information about the Actor is realised solely in the visual mode.

The other participant in narrative images is the goal or the "done to". In the iMac images the Goals are the objects being acted on. They include the power cord, the keyboard, the mouse and so on. We have already seen that the written instructions accompanying these images also contain the information about the Goals. In fact, Kress and van Leeuwen (1996: 44) point out that written text and visual images can have their own ways of realising similar meanings.

If we begin to act on the written text in this procedure, we soon realise two other things. First, that the written language in each step in the procedure has been condensed or distilled to its most skeletal elements, the "bare bones" if you like. Second, that the circumstances associated with the action processes are not included in the written text. Thus the written instructions generally do *not* tell us what to connect the various cables and cords to. However, we already know that, in order for a written procedure to be carried out successfully, accurate circumstances are essential. So where are the circumstances located in this text?

How circumstances are constructed in visual images

In steps 2, 3, 4 and 6 and the second instruction of Step 1, circumstances have been separated from the written text and transformed into visual information. In other words the circumstances have been placed *in* or close to the centre of the actual images. Thus the images in these steps show us where to connect the power cord, the keyboard and the mouse. They also show us where to find the foot of the computer and where to find the button that turns the computer on. The action processes and the circumstances in most of the steps have thus been separated from their normal semiotic mode (written language) and a new and strong semiotic relationship of interdependence has been set up. This interdependence is also reflected in the thin framing of the images.

There are, however, two exceptions to this trend. They occur in the first half of Step 1 and in Step 5. Step 1 contains two instructions. The first concerns the placement of the computer on a desk; the second is about swinging out the foot of the machine. The accompanying image does not illuminate both of the instructions in Step 1. For instance, it does not show the user where to place the computer; it only shows where the foot of the computer is located. Therefore the circumstantial information associated with the first instruction, where to place the computer, is missing and thus needs to be explicitly stated in the written text. Step 5 of the procedure relates to a new and innovative feature of the iMac: the inclusion of a modem which one connects to via a phone line. The modem is not only new but represents an optional feature of the computer. In other words, it is not imperative that the modem be used each time the computer is. For these reasons, both modalities are used to present the circumstantial information about the modem: image and written text.

As the identifying characteristic of a narrative image is the presence of a vector let us now identify the vectors in the images and the meanings they are making. Vectors function to create diagonal lines of action in images. In the iMac images, the hand is the initiating part of the vector that creates a diagonal line of action. More specifically, the direction of the vector is created by the position of both the hand and the fingers holding the object. In all of the images the vector is thereby pointing us to the circumstantial information we need to locate, that is *where* each object held by the hand needs to be connected to.

The next important point that we need to consider is *why* circumstantial information has been transformed from written text into visual images. Circumstantial information is often very complex, and hence extremely difficult to formulate accurately and succinctly in written language. It often makes the instructions very long, verbose and difficult to understand. By transforming circumstantial meanings into visual images, the designers of this text have chosen a simpler, more direct and economical way to communicate such complex information.

As the images now contain most of the circumstantial information crucial to the success of the procedure, the designers have had to ensure that these meanings are not lost. Thus they have not only used strong vectors to point us to the circumstances; they have also given the circumstantial information maximal salience within each image in two main ways. First, through the *size* of the images, and second, through the placement of circumstantial information in or near the actual *centre* of the image. In these ways the circumstantial information is made the prominent feature in this multimodal text.

One final and interesting point needs to be made in relation to the framing of the events in the images. Note that each image is presented in a round or circular frame. Kress and van Leeuwen (1996: 52) point out that circles are self-contained and complete in themselves. These images are thus signalling that each step in the procedure is a self-contained unit of information and, as we have seen, it is. It visually communicates the essential information we need to complete each step of the procedure: it shows us who the participants in each step are, what action they are involved in as well as providing us with circumstantial information.

Table 12.2 shows the similarities and differences in how events are constructed in the written and visual modes in this multi-modal procedure.

This summary draws our attention to several important points. First, that images and written text do not "stand alone", and second, that the written and visual modes do not always realise the same meanings. By understanding the way events are constructed in visual images students are learning about the interdependence between the visual and written semiotic modes in texts produced in Western societies. They are learning that images and written text do not "stand alone", how written and visual structures usually,

Table 12.2 Summary of meanings made in the written and visual modes

Events / happenings	Written steps	Visual images
Actors		✓
Action processes	✓	✓
Goals	✓	✓
Circumstances		✓

though not always, create similar patterns of meaning, and how this information can be made visually prominent. The final level of analysis will look at the relationships set up between the images and the viewer.

Tools for analysing the relationships "set up" between the images and the viewer

First, we can distinguish at least two types of relationships between viewers and images. For example, the subjects in some images enter into direct eye-contact with the viewer. In other images the subjects direct their gaze away from the viewer and present themselves for our contemplation. Thus images in which the subjects enter into direct eye-contact with us "*demand*" our visual engagement; images in which the subjects direct their gaze elsewhere "*offer*" themselves for a less engaged and more objective kind of observation.

Another important dimension of the social meaning of images is the type of "shot". For example, close shots (including head and shoulders) and very close shots (the head, or possibly an aspect of the face) suggest we have an intimate relationship with the visual subject (or object). Medium close shots (which cut off the subject at the waist) and medium shots (cut off at the knees) suggest social familiarity, but not intimacy. Medium long shots (full figure), long shots (the subject occupies approximately half the image), and very long shots (anything wider) suggest we have a public acquaintance with what is portrayed.

A third and very important aspect of the way relationships are set up between images and viewers is visual *modality*. Modality in visuals, just as in language, realises what "we" consider true or less true. Images are often interpreted as more or less "real", or more or less "credible". Modern music film clips, for example, have a different *modality* from standard television or feature film. The ingredients of modality are made up of colour (both that of black/white versus colour and level of colour saturation), focus (amount of detail both of subject and background), and speed (in the case of film). These features are collectively referred to as modality markers.

Kress and van Leeuwen stress that modality markers are often used in different levels of intensity. For instance, the colours in an image could be shown as naturalistic; the focus blurred; and the background details minimised or abstracted. This variation creates a "different modality", a different standard for adequately representing the world. In Kress and van Leeuwen's words, "visual modality rests on culturally and historically determined standards of what is real and what is not, and not on the objective correspondence of the visual image to a reality defined independently of it" (Kress and van Leeuwen, 1996: 168). For example, there is a general trend in modern film and imagery to use computer images to represent an enhanced view of reality by means of technographics. This trend may well be signalling how the prevailing "naturalistic" modality is giving way to a more abstract and "scientific" modality.

It must be stressed, however, that different social contexts dictate different kinds of modality. Very different ideas about what is a "truthful representation" prevail in areas like science and advertising. Whereas advertising tends to emphasise the sensory qualities of what is depicted by focusing on colour and texture, in areas of science far more abstract representations are accepted as representing reality.

Another important interactive meaning in images is the "point-of-view" dimension, or that of *perspective*. Images without perspective present a subjective or idiosyncratic view of the world. Perspectival images present a window of the world, as it were, which pretends to be an extension of the viewer's own space. Kress and van Leeuwen say that the introduction of perspective to the image "compels the viewer to become, together with the institution that has produced the image, an 'us' with respect to a 'them' or an 'it' – that is, with respect to the participants represented in the image" (Kress and van Leeuwen, 1990: 32).

Perspective necessarily involves some kind of "angle", the third important dimension of how we enact social relations using images. When we look at objects at our own level (the horizontal or level angle) they tend to admit a degree of social involvement. If we are positioned higher than what is displayed (the high angle) we tend to be in a position of superiority, while standing lower (the low angle) usually signals respect to what or who is observed. In addition, a frontal (or straight-on) point of view will tend to index that what is represented is part of our world, while an oblique (side-on) point of view indexes it as much less so.

Thus the interactive meanings in images are realised by Mood (offer versus demand); Distance (shot type); Modality (levels of "reality") and Perspective (subjective – involving angle – versus objective). The social relations constructed by visual images can thus be summarised in the following way.

Mood (I–you):

- demand (+ eye contact)
- offer (– eye contact).

Shot type – distance or "degrees of involvement":

- close shot (head + shoulders)
- very close shot (aspect of face)
- medium close shot (cuts off at the waist)
- medium long shot (full figure)
- long shot (subject is half the image)
- very long shot.

Visual modality:

- colour: degree of saturation
- focus: amount of detail of both subject and background.

Analysing the relationships "set up" between the images and the viewer

In analysing the relationships set up between the viewer and the images in the iMac text, three tools will be used. First, whether the images enter into a demand or offer relationship with us; second, the type of camera shot that has been used, and finally, the choices that have been made with regard to colour saturation, the sharpness of the focus and the inclusion of background details.

What relationship do the images set up with us?

The first issue we need to consider concerns the relationship set up between the images and the viewer/user of the iMac procedure. In other words, do the images "offer" something for our contemplation or do they enter into a "demand" relationship with us? As all the images show a hand and part of a user's arm in the process of acting on an object, that is connecting it to a computer, the relationship they set up is one of an "offer". In this instance each image is offering us *information* about what we must do, step by step, to successfully install the computer.

Do the images involve us?

Second, we need to look at the degree of our involvement with the images. This is determined by the type of camera shot. In the iMac text, each shot is a close-up of the hand and the specific part of the computer that the various attachments need to be connected to. This choice of shot functions to involve us with the images by bringing us into a relationship of familiarity with the computer, its attachments and its installation procedure. This high level of involvement also makes us feel comfortable about our ability to successfully carry out the procedure.

How "lifelike" are the images?

The third aspect we need to consider is modality. In other words, do the images present the steps in the procedure as though they are "real" or as though they are imaginings? As we have already discussed, Kress and van Leeuwen (1996: 163) stress that the dominant criterion for assessing how "real" an image is, depends on *how much* what we can normally see of an object corresponds with what we can see of it in a visual image. To determine this, we now need to look at the degree of colour saturation, the sharpness of the focus and the detail in the images. As already noted, these are collectively known as modality markers.

The most colourful elements in each image are undeniably the iMac computers. These computers are currently being marketed as "state-of-the-art" technology, not only in terms of their performance capacity but also in terms of their design. One feature of their design innovation is the bright range of colours they come in. Thus iMacs are available in grape (purple), blueberry (blue), lime (green), tangerine (orange) and strawberry (red). This means they can be easily colour co-ordinated to match one's office or home. It is not surprising then that the images show this colour range in its entirety and that the colour choice for the computer in each step is different. Nor is it surprising that the colour of each computer is presented in full saturation. These choices for "lifelikeness" or naturalistic representation are further enhanced by the sharp focus of the images. This sharp focus makes it extremely easy for us to identify the exact or precise location of the sockets we need to connect things to. Furthermore, the use of sharp focus in conjunction with close-up shots enables detailed visual information to be communicated very clearly in the text.

However, not all of the modality markers used in the images are "real" or "lifelike". Note for instance how the surroundings, such as the table on which the computers rest and the room in which they are located, are absent. The images thus lack a setting and this diminishes their naturalism. Once again this is a deliberate choice. By leaving out the setting in this way, the designers have concentrated our attention on the most essential items of information being "offered" to us in the image: the participants, the actions they are involved in and, most importantly of all, the location of the circumstantial information.

In summary, this text appears to represent a significant cultural shift in the design of multi-modal procedures, a shift that seems to be operating on a number of different levels.

First, there is a shift in reading pathways from vertical (top to bottom) to horizontal (left to right). Second, there is a shift in the degree of salience given to visual images in a procedural text. Another shift occurs in the circular framing of the images, a choice signalling that each image in the procedure is a self-contained unit of information. The final and most significant shift relates to the changing role of the visual images in communicating circumstantial information that is crucial to achieving the goal of the procedure.

How can this approach be used in TESOL teaching practice?

Contextualising the iMac procedure within a unit of work

The insights offered by the multi-modal analysis of the iMac procedure can be used in a range of reading activities with students at all levels of proficiency. Let us assume that elementary, intermediate and advanced level students are doing a unit of work on procedures and imperatives, and that the iMac text is one of the resources in that unit. Before the iMac text is introduced in the classroom, it is essential that all the students are familiar with the purpose and structure of procedural texts. Ideally, the students would have been involved in a range of activities requiring them to sequence pictures and/or steps from a number of procedural texts; discuss the top to bottom and left to right reading directionality; and identify what they consider the function of visual images in procedural texts to be. It is also essential, at some point, to discuss whether or not the students find procedures easy texts to follow successfully and why or why not.

All students, elementary, intermediate and advanced, should also be made aware of some of the language features of procedural texts, especially the tendency for action processes to come first within each step. Students should also be able to identify the object to be acted on in each step. For example, in the iMac procedure, these would be the computer, the foot (of the computer), the power cord, the keyboard, the mouse and a phone line. Intermediate and advanced students should also be familiar with the function and location of the circumstances in the steps.

Prediction activities for the iMac procedure

Before students are given the iMac procedure to read, the topic or field of computers should be introduced to students and computer-specific words from the iMac text such as *keyboard*, *mouse*, *power cord*, *cable*, *modem* should be pre-taught.

The iMac text should now be introduced through a series of prediction activities, ideally using overhead transparencies and an overhead projector. First, students should *only* be given the images to look at. The teacher could ask them what type of text they think these images come from (e.g. a newspaper story, a report, a procedure or a narrative). The teacher could then probe their understandings of left to right reading paths by asking them where they think one is expected to start reading this text and why.

Next, the numbers could be overlaid on the overhead projector (OHP). Students could now refine their earlier predictions about text type (e.g. a newspaper story, a report, a procedure or a narrative). They could then engage in a discussion about the function of the numbers. The teacher could ask them whether or not they think the numbers make the text easier to follow. This point could open up a discussion about left to right reading directionality in Western cultures.

Finally, the written text could be overlaid on the OHP and students could be asked how they would now read the text. They could draw arrows to show their reading pathway: top to bottom and left to right. Teachers could now ask the students why they think the visuals have been placed at the top and the written text below them. This could open up a discussion about the Real–Ideal placement of information in many Western texts. Teachers may also like to challenge advanced students to consider the function of the numbers on the page in bridging the written text and the visual images and why they think the images have been framed with only a fine black line. Advanced students could also be further challenged at this point to analyse the Given–New structure within each individual image and account for the differences in the placement of the user's hand.

Teaching the language features of the iMac text

Action processes and objects to be acted on

All students could be given a copy of the complete text to read. After they have finished, their attention could be drawn to the language features of the written text. The students could now be asked to underline the action processes in each step and then to circle the objects to be acted on.

Circumstances

Elementary students could then be asked to where they need to connect the cords/cables. Teachers could point out that in this procedure some of the information has been put in the images. They could then explain that users need to read *both* the visual images *and* the written text if they are to successfully connect their computer. This is probably as far as one would go with an elementary class.

Intermediate and advanced students could be asked to find the actual information in the written text that tells them *where* to connect the various cords/cables and then be directed to looking more closely at the visual images for this information. Their attention could also be drawn to the two exceptions to this trend in the first half of Step 1 and, in Step 5, where the circumstantial information is presented in written language. Students could be encouraged to speculate about why there are these two exceptions in the text.

It would also be interesting to discuss their views on why they think circumstantial information has been transformed into visuals in this procedural text and whether or not they think it makes the text easier to follow. Teachers could point out that one of the benefits of this approach is that it simplifies or reduces the written text to its "bare bones". One of the potential problems, however, is the risk that the circumstantial information may not be clear, obvious or easy for the reader to find. The designers have needed to use a number of strategies to make sure that the circumstances really stand out to the reader of the text. Students could be asked to brainstorm what they think these strategies may be.

Probing circumstantial meanings more deeply

Using their predictions as the springboard, intermediate and advanced students could now analyse some of the other strategies used in the text to focus the viewer's attention on circumstantial information in the visual images. For instance, they could consider the location of the circumstantial information within each image (near or close to the centre of each image) and why they think the circumstantial information has been placed in this central location (in order to give it maximal salience or prominence). They could also be asked why they think the photographer has chosen to use close up shots and sharp focus in each visual.

Finally, students could be asked to identify where the hand and fingers in each shot are pointing. They could then be introduced to the concept of a vector (diagonal lines of action). Teachers may like to explain the similarity in meaning between vectors in images and action processes in written language.

Advanced students could be extended even further. Their attention could be drawn to the white background of each image and the page in general. Students could be asked to speculate about why they think settings, such as the desk on which the computer is placed and the room in which it is located, are missing from the images. They could also be asked why they think only the fingers, hand and arm of the user are shown and why the user's face has not been included. Teachers could explain that this is because the images are offering us information and not demanding an interaction with us. In order to understand this point, students will probably need to see examples of images in which the subject looks directly at the viewer and to discuss the differences. Finally, students' attention could be drawn to the circular shape of the frames around each image and the cultural significance of round shapes (self-containment).

To round off the reading activity, students could be asked if they have seen any other procedural texts like this one and where they have encountered them (e.g. cookbooks, building manuals).

Conclusion

The perspectives opened up in this chapter offer teachers a set of tools to draw on in assisting students to develop competence in reading texts that are multi-modal. The benefits of using the three sets of tools we have described to analyse the structure of visual images, the way events or happenings are shown and the way relationships are set up with viewers are far-reaching. Students are learning how written and visual elements make patterns of meaning in multi-modal texts, how these elements relate to each other and how they are integrated to form a compositional whole.

This knowledge is crucial to students' understandings of how meanings are made in multi-modal texts. For instance, many native speakers find procedures extremely challenging texts to act on successfully and often make negative judgements about their own capacity if they experience difficulties following the instructions. Thus the more tools TESOL students have for understanding the information in the written text and in the visual images, the better equipped they will be to identify the problems they are experiencing. Failure to induct students into these understandings deprives them both of the cultural knowledge and reading strategies they need in order to access many of the essential and culturally specific meanings made in multi-modal texts such as this installation procedure.

References

Hood, S., Solomon, N. and Burns, A. (1996) *Focus on Reading*. Sydney: NCELTR, Macquarie University.

Kress, G. and van Leeuwen, T. (1990) *Reading Images*. Victoria: Deakin University Press.

Kress, G. and van Leeuwen, T. (1996) *Reading Images: The Grammar of Visual Design*. London: Routledge.

Nichols, B. (1981) *Ideology and the Image*. Bloomington: Indiana University Press.

Opama, R. (1990) Visual Semiotics: A Study of Images in Japanese Advertising. University of London, unpublished Ph.D. Thesis.

Rothery, J. (1994) *Exploring Literacy in School English*. Write It Right: Resources for Literacy and Learning. Sydney: Disadvantaged Schools Program, Metropolitan East Region.

PART FOUR

Analysing English: a clause perspective

Chapter 13

J.R. Martin

TECHNICALITY AND ABSTRACTION: LANGUAGE FOR THE CREATION OF SPECIALIZED TEXTS[1]

Specialized knowledge

AT THE COMMONWEALTH SCIENTIFIC and Industrial Research Organization (CSIRO) in Canberra, Australia, one section of the Personnel Management Manual admonishes administrators to avoid the use of the *passive tense* in their writing. As a writing consultant, I find what I suspect the author means poor advice – the passive is after all an important resource for organizing Themes in the development of an effective text. As a linguist, I find the advice simply amusing – because there is no such thing as a passive tense. There are present, past and future tenses, and active and passive voices. Presumably the would-be prescriptive grammarian who worked on that section of the manual intended the passive voice. But as the manual stands, the advice, poor though it is, does not really make sense.

In order to understand technical discourse, it is important to understand exactly what went wrong with this advice. To do this we need first to examine the nominal group **the passive tense**. In such groups the word **passive** sub-classifies **tense**. The same meaning can be re-expressed as a clause: **The passive is a kind of tense**. Technically words functioning like **passive** are called 'Classifiers' and the words they classify 'Things'. Here are some more examples (Classifiers in bold):

material process	**frying** pan
relational clause	**steel** wool
attitudinal epithet	**stone** wall
embedded clause	**red** wine
possessive pronoun	**lap** dog

Classifiers are nouns, verbs or adjectives and in English precede the noun they sub-classify. They are easily recognized because they are not gradable – that is, you cannot say ***a very possessive pronoun** (cf. **a very possessive parent**) or ***a more material clause** (see **a more material solution**). This is because Classifiers classify; they do not describe.

When we say Classifiers classify we mean that they refer to classifications of experience known as *taxonomies*. You may be familiar with these from biology, where living things are often presented in diagrams organized into species, genus, family and so on. When someone refers to the passive tense they are implying a taxonomy like that following:

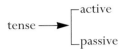

But this is in fact a confusion of two taxonomies, one for voice and another for tense. Linguists would organize English as Figure 13.1.

Figure 13.1 English systems for tense and voice

So when I wrote that there was no such thing as a passive tense, I meant that in the field of linguistics there are no taxonomies for English in which passive is a sub-class of tense.

Knowledge of this kind is admittedly specialized knowledge, although a generation ago it was not quite so specialized as it appears today!

Common sense

Common sense, like specialized knowledge, makes use of nominal groups (as illustrated above) and relational clauses (the 'being' clauses in the examples below) to classify experience. This is strikingly clear in the language of young children as they sort out the world (data from Clare Painter):

[3 years, 8 months]
(considering a jigsaw puzzle)
Child: There isn't a fox: and there isn't – Is a platypus an animal?

[3 years, 7 months]
(mother makes reference to her best boys)
Older brother: We have to be your best boys cause we're your only boys.
Child: And Daddy.
Older brother: He's not a boy, he's a man.
Child: He *is* a boy cause he's got a penis.

Here we see the child sorting out the world of living things, organizing animals and humans into common-sense taxonomies. Caregivers interact continually to guide the child into the common-sense organization of the adult world:

[3 years, 6 months]
Child: Mum, is grow mean move?
Mother: Well, it's not the same as move: it means get bigger, like when you blow a balloon up.

[3 years, 7 months]
Mother: Oh, we're drowned!
Child: What does drown mean?
Mother: Means we're all wet . . .
Child: Not drown; drown is go down to the bottom and be dead.

The main difference between common-sense taxonomies and specialized ones is that common-sense classification is based on what can be directly observed with the senses. Diseases for example are commonly classified according to symptoms and effects (see Figure 13.2).

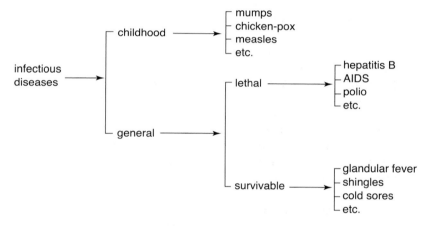

Figure 13.2 Common-sense taxonomy of diseases
Source: Courtesy of Joan Rothery

In the field of medicine on the other hand, diseases are organized according to their cause. Of the diseases noted above, cold sores, glandular fever, chicken-pox and shingles are all caused by the herpes virus, and chicken-pox and shingles are in fact caused by the same virus. So the specialized medical taxonomy differs from the common-sense one (see Figure 13.3).

Two important points about technical discourse should now be clear. The first is that technical terms cannot be dismissed as *jargon*. Technical terms organize the world in a different way than do everyday ones. Referring to a disease with respect to the simplex herpes virus is quite different to naming it cold sores. (Technical discourse can of course be used to exclude; and people are quite justified in complaining when it does so needlessly.) The second is that specialized knowledge is not just a set of technical terms. The terms imply taxonomies which organize reality differently to common sense. Understanding technical discourse means being familiar with these specialized taxonomies and the principles which led to their construction.

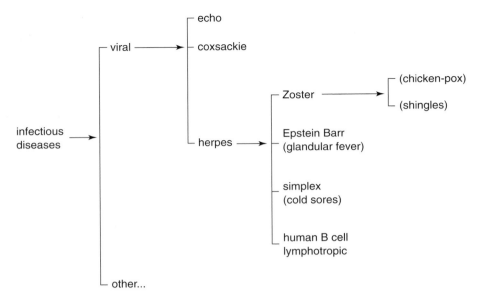

Figure 13.3 Medical taxonomy of diseases

Technical writing

Technical writing is most strongly associated in our culture with the various fields of science. In broad terms science is concerned with how the world is organized; and how it came to be that way. High-school textbooks deal with both these concerns.

The two most relevant genres will be referred to here as *report* (how the world is organized) and *explanation* (why it is organized that way). The main difference is that reports focus on things while explanations focus on processes. Science textbooks shift from report to explanation as appropriate when building up chapters.

Reports

Reports in science focus on classification and description. Consider the following section from *Our Changing World*, a geography textbook used in some Australian junior-secondary schools (generally Year 8) (approximately 13–14 years old).

> Fifteen per cent of the world's land area consists of deserts. The true **hot deserts** straddle the Tropics in both hemispheres. They are found on all continents between the latitudes of approximately 15 to 10 degrees, and they extend inland from the west coasts to the interiors of these continents. They are never found on east coasts in these latitudes as all east coasts receive heavy rains from either on-shore trade winds or monsoons.
>
> **Cool deserts** are found further polewards in the deep interiors of large continents like Eurasia or where mountains form **rain-shadows**, which keep out rain-bearing winds that might otherwise bring wet conditions.
>
> There are five major hot desert belts in the world (see fig. 3.2). The largest hot desert extends from the west coast of North Africa eastwards to Egypt and the Red

Sea – this is the great Sahara that covers 9 million square kilometers. The Sahara spreads eastward beyond the Red Sea into Arabia – a desert of 2.5 million square kilometers – and beyond the Persian Gulf in to Iraq and Pakistan (Thar Desert).

(Sale et al., 1980, pp. 45–6)

This report sets forth a classification of deserts, one of the world's major ecosystems. In this text technical terms are highlighted in bold face (**hot deserts, cool deserts, rain-shadows**). The taxonomy is being organized as in Figure 13.4.

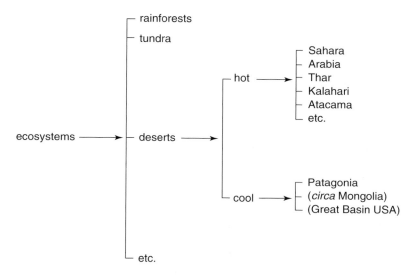

Figure 13.4 Taxonomy of ecosystems

So far we have only considered taxonomies which organize the world into classes and sub-classes, but reports are also commonly used to establish relations between parts and wholes. The following report examines the distinctive parts of cacti.

The conservers are those plants which store their own supplies of moisture for use during drought. These include the one thousand varieties of cactus and succulents. The cacti have extensive root systems spreading in all directions – sideways and downwards – to soak up as much water as possible when it does rain. They are able to swell to store water, and they then use this water over long periods of drought. A thick waterproof covering protects these desert water-tanks with their soft pulpy cells, and their leaves are often reduced to thorns to cut down on water-loss and protect the plant from animals that might otherwise eat it for its moisture (see fig. 3.21). The giant saguaro (pronounced say-w'are-oh) of south-west USA (see fig. 3.18) is a good example.

(Sale et al., 1980, p. 59)

As is the case with this report, part–whole relations are often illustrated with a labelled diagram. The relevant taxonomy is as in Figure 13.5.

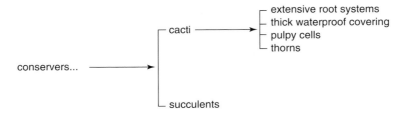

Figure 13.5 Taxonomy of conservers: cacti

Explanation

Explanations focus on processes – on how things come to be. In the geography text from which examples are taken here they tend to occur now and again in the middle of reports. Their purpose is not directly to classify phenomena but to outline an activity. The following paragraph illustrates the genre:

> We saw that **leaching** was a very prominent process in all hot, wet, forest lands; in deserts, because the rainfall is so low, it hardly occurs at all. Instead, a reverse process may develop called **calcification**. Water may soak into the ground after rains and dissolve mineral salts in the usual way, but as the surface dries out, this water is drawn upwards like moisture rising through blotting paper. The salts then accumulate in the surface soil as this moisture evaporates; thus desert soils are often rich in mineral salts particularly calcium, sodium and potassium. Provided the salts are not too concentrated (and their concentration is reduced under irrigation), they contain a plentiful supply of plant foods and can therefore be considered as fertile soils.
>
> (Sale *et al.*, 1980, p.55)

This explanation focuses on the technical process calcification, breaking it down into steps:

1   rain falls
2   water soaks into ground
3   water dissolves mineral salts
4   surface dries out
5   water drawn upwards
6   salts accumulate as moisture evaporates

In geography, phenomena may be classified according to the processes which gave rise to them. Desert landforms for example are organized as in Figure 13.6.

Explanations are very common when phenomena are classified in this way. Consider abrasion in the following explanation, noting once again the steps in the process:

> **Abrasion** occurs when lots of hard sand particles are carried by desert winds and are thrown with great force against all solid objects in their paths. Stones, rocky outcrops, and all natural and man-made objects are subjected to this **sand-blast** action. Within a metre or two of the ground, objects are cut, smoothed and polished

by abrasion. Where winds are funnelled through gaps and valleys, this sand blast action affects all rock surfaces. Stones and rocks have their sides smoothed and rocky outcrops gradually become honeycombed with sand blasted caves and **windows** during successive sand storms. **Mushroom rocks, window rocks** and **natural arches** are produced (see fig. 3.5).

(Sale *et al.*, 1980, p. 51)

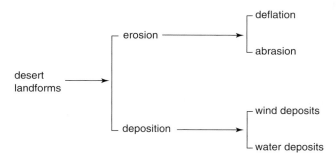

Figure 13.6 Taxonomy of desert landforms

The grammar of technicality

A brief note on the grammar of technicality is perhaps in order here. First, definitions. Definitions are a special type of relational clause which in effect translate common sense into specialized knowledge. Consider the following:

> **Precipitation** *refers to* all forms of water which fall (precipitate) from the sky.
>
> (Sale *et al.*, 1980, p. 44)

Here the technical term **precipitation** is related to its definition **all forms of water which fall from the sky** by the relational process **refers to**. These defining clauses are always reversible; in the passive clause the technical term comes last:

> When water falls to the earth, it must either soak into the earth or run off in creeks or rivers. The pattern which is made by these streams is called the **drainage system**.
>
> (Sale *et al.*, 1980, p. 44)

Common defining verbs include **be, call, mean, refer to, define, signify, represent, stand for, express**.

Definitions are important because they relate known common-sense terms or previously defined technical terms to new technical ones. Their limitation is that they do not relate the new technical terms to each other. This as we saw earlier is the job of another type of relational clause and of nominal groups. For example, when the child asked his mother 'Is a platypus an animal?' he was not trying to define a platypus, but was trying to find out how the platypus is related to other living things.

The relevant relational clause is not reversible. The sub-class comes first and is related to its superordinate, normally by the verb **be**: 'The Amazonian rainforest is a functioning ecosystem' (Sale *et al.*, 1980, p.24). Clauses such as these construct classifications. Where classifications have already been established, and simply need to be referred to, nominal groups are used (e.g. **the Amazonian rainforest ecosystem** following the above):

> The heavy rainfall totals of the Tropics are related to the constant heat which occurs near the equator. In these **low latitudes**, the noonday sun is almost directly overhead throughout the year, so the sun is very effective in heating land and sea.
>
> (Sale *et al.*, 1980, p. 10)

In this text the first sentence refers to latitudes near the equator; in the following sentence these are then picked up with a Classifier Thing structure: **low latitudes**.

Part–whole relations are also constructed through relational clauses, of the possessive type, with the whole before the part: 'The biosphere is made up of many hundreds of different **ecosystems**' (Sale *et al.*, 1980, p. 12).

Once constructed possessive nominal groups can be used to refer to a whole's parts: **the Amazonian ecosystem's biome**, **the biome's flora**, **the fauna's members**, etc.

In order to understand technical discourse both the definitions and the relationships among what is defined are critical. In geography, technical terms are highlighted as they are defined and commonly tested in homework, quizzes and examinations. Part–whole relationships are also commonly foregrounded in illustrations and diagrams. What tends to be backgrounded are the class/sub-class taxonomies reviewed above, although headings and subheadings often refer to global organization of this kind. These also lend themselves to the two-dimensional displays commonly used by linguists (as in the figures throughout this paper) and biologists and such presentations could be made more use of across science teaching than is presently the case.

The grammar of explanations depends much more on material (action) clauses than on relational clauses. Things happen and act on other phenomena. The actions themselves stand in an if/then relationship to each other. Accordingly we might re-express the calcification text as follows (logical relationships of implication are italicized and action processes appear in bold face):

1   *If* water **soaks** into the ground
2   *then* it will **dissolve** mineral salts.
3   *If* it does, *then if* the surface **dries out**
4   *then* the water is **drawn** upwards.
5   *If* it does, *then if* the water **evaporates**
6   *then* salts **accumulate** in the surface soil.

Abstraction

On 26 April 1986 an Australian newspaper the *Adelaide Advertiser* published reactions to Anzac Day (a public holiday commemorating all those who have served in Australia's armed forces) by two students, one aged 8, the other 16. The 8-year-old began as follows:

Today I watched the Anzac parade and I saw lots of brave men and women. Most of them had medals and wore uniforms. Some drove in cars because they were too sick to walk. There were lots of countries marching apart from Australia. There were bands and thousands of people watching and clapping.

The 16-year-old chose a more 'written' style:

The atmosphere at the dawn service was one of **solemnity**, as those who had first-hand **experience** of the **devastation** of war reflected on the past and remembered their friends and relatives who had lost their lives in **battle**. The gloomy atmosphere was emphasized by the dreary **drizzle**, drab attire and the long **silence**.

What is the difference between the two texts? Comparing clause Themes provides a partial answer:

Themes

8-YEAR-OLD	**16-YEAR-OLD**
Today	The atmosphere at the dawn service
and I	as those who had experience of the devastation associated with war
Most of them	The gloomy atmosphere
because they	
Some	
There	
There	

The 8-year-old uses simple 'spoken' Themes, organizing his text around people: **I, most of them, they, some** (of them). The 16-year-old uses more abstract Themes, organizing her paragraph around a description of the atmosphere at the service. In order to do this she makes use of words like **solemnity, experience, devastation, battle, drizzle** and **silence** which are referred to as nominalizations. If we remove these from the text it becomes much more 'spoken:

People were solemn at the dawn service as those who had experienced first-hand how devastating war can be remembered their friends and relatives who had lost their lives fighting. It was drizzling, people wore drab attire and they were silent for a long time, all of which made me feel even more gloomy.

And the text has in fact been reorganized as well. It no longer focuses on *the atmosphere* as Theme. People, rather than abstractions, are the point of departure for most clauses. Comparing the 'spoken' and 'written' versions of the 16-year-old's text is a useful point of departure in interpreting the function of abstraction in writing across subject areas.

Christie and Rothery (1989) point out the connection between choice of Theme and improving a text's interpretative focus. Each of the Themes they suggest involves abstract language. Note the nominalized language in their examples (nominalizations in bold face; Theme in italics):

The **desire** *to be a member of a prestige group* often influences adolescent **behaviour**.

Peer group **pressure** affects young people like Debby.

Experimenting *with drugs* is a dangerous thing.

Abstraction in science

As noted above, technical language enables scientists to reclassify the world. The taxonomies they establish in fact organize all phenomena as if they were things – because it is things rather then processes which lend themselves most readily to categorization as classes and sub-classes and as parts and wholes. So when processes are being classified they are nominalized and organized as things. The taxonomy cited above related to desert landforms illustrated this point; nominalizations involved included **erosion**, **deposition**, **deflation** and **abrasion**.

Somewhat ironically then, although science does concern itself with processes, analysing them in explanations, in the end it interprets processes as things. Technical verbs are very rare, and those that exist are seldom used; for example, **precipitation** is much more common than its verbal form **precipitate**:

> **Precipitation** refers to all forms of water which fall (precipitate) from the sky.
> (Sale *et al.*, 1980, p. 44)

Aside from facilitating classification, technical terms for processes function as a kind of shorthand. It is quicker to refer to **leaching** and **calcification** by name than to run through the processes to which each refers. In science then nominalization is used to facilitate classification. The vast majority of technical terms are nouns, and when processes are classified (e.g. **leaching** and **calcification**) or used as a classificatory principle (e.g. **deflation** and **abrasion**) nominalization is used.

Abstraction in the humanities

Unlike science, disciplines like English and history are not very technical. They do not have as their main function reclassifying experience. And so technical terms do not present much difficulty. But abstraction in the humanities can be very challenging. Literary criticism and historical interpretation may in fact be much more heavily nominalized than scientific writing, and so no less of a problem for students to learn to read and write. For many students abstraction probably forms more of a problem than technicality, since science teachers do teach the concepts and terms that make up scientific discourse whereas English and history teachers do not focus explicitly on nominalization as their main interpretative tool.

It should be noted however that science teachers make much more use of talk than writing to unpack technicality. In general science students write many more short single sentence definitions than reports or explanations, although they must certainly learn to read the latter where textbook material is used.

The result in English, history and the humanities-oriented parts of social science is that many students continue to write as they talk. The following text was written in year 10 (approximately 15–16 years old) by a student whose writing does not sound much more mature than that of the 8-year-old quoted above.

> I think Governments are necessary because if there wasn't any there would be no law people would be killing themselves. They help keep our economic system in order for certain things. If there wasn't no Federal Government there wouldn't have been no one to fix up any problems that would have occured in the community. Same with the state Government if the SG didn't exist there would have been noone to look after the school, vandalism fighting would have occurred everyday. The local Government would be important to look after the rubbish because everyone would have diseases.

If pressed, most teachers would probably criticize this text for its spelling, punctuation and grammatical usage alongside a general comment on 'poor ideas'. In fact editing the spelling, punctuation and usage does not transform the text into a mature piece of writing in Year 10 geography:

> I think Governments are necessary because if there weren't any there wouldn't be any law: people would be killing themselves. They help keep our economic system in order for certain things. If there wasn't any Federal Government there wouldn't be anyone to fix up any problems that occur in the community. It's the same with the State Government – if they didn't exist there wouldn't be anyone to look after the schools. Vandalism and fighting would occur everyday. The Local Government is important to look after the rubbish, because otherwise everyone would have diseases.

Organizing exposition

To effect a real transformation we need to organize the 'spoken' text into exposition, highlighting its thesis, setting forth the arguments and possibly summing up. And to do this we need abstract language – of the kind underlined in the next version of the text below – along with appropriate linking words (i.e. **to begin**, **similarly**, **finally**):

> I think Governments at *different levels* are necessary *for a number of reasons*. They make laws, without which people would be killing themselves and help keep our economic system in order.

> To begin, the Federal Government fixes up problems that occur in the community.

> Similarly, the State Government looks after schools, preventing vandalism and fighting.

> Finally the Local Government is important to look after rubbish; otherwise everyone would have diseases.

> *As a result of these and other factors*, Governments at several administrative levels are necessary.

This text still has a long way to go – as a next step its central paragraphs need developing. But the basic scaffolding is there. In a sense what we are looking at here is a movement from what Christie and Rothery (1989) call judgments – a movement from personal feelings and their motivation to public positions and their rationale.

Exposition is an important tool in interpretation in the humanities. A mature form, taken from Simmelhaig and Spenceley, a progressive Year 10 history text, is presented below (in the following texts nominalizations are in bold face to highlight the abstract language used):

> Wars are costly **exercises**. They cause **death** and **destruction** and put resources to **non-productive uses** but they also promote **industrial and technological change**. This **benefit** does not mean that war is a good thing, but that sometimes it brings **useful developments**.
>
> The Second World War further encouraged the **restructuring** of the Australian economy towards a **manufacturing basis**. Between 1937 and 1945 the value of **industrial production** almost doubled. This **increase** was faster than otherwise would have occurred. The **momentum** was maintained in the post-war years and by 1954–5 the value of manufacturing output was three times that of 1944–5. The **enlargement** of Australia's steel-making capacity, and of chemicals, rubber, metal goods and motor vehicles all owed something to the **demands** of war. The war had acted as a hot-house for **technological progress** and **economic change**.
>
> The war had also revealed **inadequacies** in Australia's scientific and research **capabilities**. After the war strenuous **efforts** were made to improve these. The Australian National University was established with an emphasis on research. The government gave its **support** to the advancement of science in many areas, including agricultural production. Though it is difficult to disentangle the **effects** of war from other **influences**, it is clear that future generations not only enjoyed the security and peace won by their forefathers but also the **benefits** of war-time **economic expansion**.
>
> (Simmelhaig and Spenceley, 1984, p. 121)

The first paragraph articulates the Thesis – that wars promote industrial and technological change. Then two Arguments illustrating this are presented in paragraphs two and three: restructuring towards a manufacturing basis and efforts to improve scientific and research capabilities. Both Arguments are introduced with a topic sentence and then elaborated. The exposition ends with a Reiteration, summing up the position: the benefits of war-time economic expansion.

This text is heavily nominalized, and its organization into Thesis–Argument–Reiteration depends on abstract language:

- *Thesis* – but they also promote **industrial and technological change**.
- *Argument 1* – The Second World War further encouraged the **restructuring** of the Australian economy towards **a manufacturing basis**.
- *Argument 2* – The war had also revealed **inadequacies** in Australia's scientific and research **capabilities**.
- *Reiteration* – it is clear that future generations not only enjoyed the security and peace won by their forefathers but also the **benefits** of war-time **economic expansion**.

Abstract reports

Reports are an important feature of writing in the humanities as well as in science. But the reports are much less technical, having the function of making generalizations about generic classes of participants. They vary in the amount of nominalization they use. The following report, which discusses three major roles of Vietnamese women soldiers, is relatively concrete:

> It was mainly after 1965 when the US sent troops into the south on a massive scale, that the movement to have women join the army increased. Women became full-time members of the armed forces in the south. Many of them held leading positions. About 40 per cent of the regimental commanders of the PLAF were women. These were troops who dealt with the American mobile reserves, initiated offensive operations and attacked major US concentrations. All were volunteers who received no salary and when not in combat, helped in harvesting, building homes and schools and administering free medical care and medical training.
>
> Women also formed a major part of regional guerilla forces, full-time fighters who operated in the region where they lived. They engaged US forces in the same area by ambushes, encircled bases and attacked posts.
>
> Women in local self-defence units, or militia women, were not full-time soldiers but fought when their area was attacked, pinning down local forces and keeping their posts permanently encircled.
>
> A higher percentage of women were in the local militia and regional guerilla units than in the PLAF. The local militia kept villages fortified with trenches, traps and spikes. These defences were decisive in wearing down the morale of Saigon and US troops.
>
> (Simmelhaig and Spenceley, 1984, p. 172)

The report classifies the women into three groups: PLAF, guerilla units and local militia; but it does not set up technical terms for these. It is basically concerned with describing the habits of each group.

Much more abstract reports are commonly found, both in primary and secondary sources. In history, the most abstract secondary reports function as introductions – to chapters or to collections of primary-source material. The following is taken from Allport and Allport, a progressive senior-secondary text. It discusses Masters and Servants legislation:

> However, there was **uncertainty** in some quarters concerning the **regulation** of free labour. British law was applicable but colonial **regulations** were considered necessary to clarify the position. In 1828 the first Master and Servants **legislation** was enacted. This did not solve the problems of **control**; labour was still scarce and the legal system and the **policing** of its **regulations** was still at a rudimentary **stage**. By 1845 the **growth** of many working class **organizations** – **benefit** societies, trade societies, craft unions and political organizations such as the short-lived Mutual Protection Association – stimulated the **revival** of a system of **control**. All previous Masters and Servants Acts were thus superseded by the 1845 Act. The 1845 Masters and Servants Act originally aimed to provide more severe **penalties** for

breaches of work **contract**; yet due largely to public **pressure** by the working class the bill was amended to eliminate the sections to which the workers objected.

(Allport and Allport, 1980, p. 8)

Some of the most incongruent report writing in fact occurs in primary sources where various forms of bureaucratic writing are introduced. Writing in administrative contexts, with an eye to social control, is the source of much of the most heavily nominalized discourse in Western culture.

The following resolutions were carried at the Australasian Conference of Employers held in the Sydney Chamber of Commerce, 10–13 September 1890.

That this Conference reaffirms the principle of '**freedom of contract**' between individual employers and employees, and asserts that any **infringement** of that principle is not only destructive to **commerce** but is also inimical to the best **interests** of the working classes.

That any **attempt** to force, or **threat** of **force**, or any **persuasion** other than that permitted and defined by law to men who are not unionists, or any other form of **boycotting**, should, in the **opinion** of this Conference, be resisted by **united action**.

This Conference is of the **opinion** that employers should declare that they will not be coerced in the **dismissal** of any labour that has taken **service** with them in the present **emergency**; and in the **event** of any **attempt** being made to coerce such labour to join any trade organization or to interfere with them in the **discharge** of their daily **work**, the combined Associations represented at this Conference will take all possible **means** to insure their personal **safety**.

That this Conference declares that to maintain **discipline**, and thus protect life and property, owners of **shipping** in the coastal and intercolonial trades should not engage or retain in their **employ** any captains or officers who may be members of a Union affiliated with any labour organizations.

(Alcott and Alcott, 1980, p. 65)

Texts such as these raise the question of whether nominalization is a question of function or status. It does not seem to be used to organize the report in ways similar to the ways it organizes exposition as outlined above. And one might argue that nominalized language is simply a symbol of literacy and thus education and thus power in our culture. So for resolutions to sound credible, they must be written in language of this kind. This would imply that if we translate written resolutions into spoken English, nothing but status is lost. The problem can be exemplified by taking the second resolution from the text above and asking whether a 'Plain English' translation means the same thing:

This Conference thinks that people should act together to stop unionists attempting to force or threaten to force or illegally persuade non-unionists (to join unions?) or boycotting (businesses employing non-unionists?).

This is a difficult issue which cannot be fully resolved here. It would involve for example looking in detail at *theme* and *information* structure in the English clause, at nominal group complexes, at nominalization and implicitness, at ideology and text structure and so on. But it is important not to lose sight of the instrumental role of abstraction in interpretation. Consider the following passage from Kress (1988b) who is critiquing a recently released Australian *Writing K-1* syllabus (for primary-school level):

> It is here where that peculiar theoretical/ideological **mix** of Process Writing in its Australian **manifestation** that I described earlier leads to **inevitable** and **insoluble** problems for a writing curriculum. The **mix** of West Coast psychology ('**ownership**', peer group **work** in the form of '**conferencing**'), romantic liberal/**individualism** (writing as personal '**expression**'), and of a late Leavisite **elitism** (high cultural literary forms as implicit or explicit models of eventual goals, the diary both as **confessional** and as autobiography, the personal narrative as short story or novel, etc) has as its real content the **training** of an individual student subject with a certain kind of **sensibility**. The **view** of **writing** put forward in the document is a view of writing merely as a vehicle for individual **expression**.
>
> (Kress, 1988b, pp. 14–15)

In the second sentence Kress distils an ideological profile of Process Writing in terms of a mix of West Coast psychology, romantic liberal individualism and late Leavisite elitism. Each of the three ingredients is unpacked to a certain degree in parentheses. But the job of explaining each is really the work of an educational historian. And without abstract language it would be impossible for the historian to range over and make generalizations about the human experience which has been drawn together and interpreted in these terms. Nor could Kress have brought these themes so efficiently to bear on the syllabus without language of this kind. The main point as far as education is concerned is that students need to learn to read abstract discourse if they are to be functionally literate in our culture and write abstract discourse if they are to interpret their world in a critical way.

The grammar of abstraction

What exactly does it mean to make abstract writing 'plain'? Essentially what we are looking at is the relationship between semantics and grammar – between meaning and form. In 'plain' English there is a 'natural' relationship between the two. Actions come out as verbs, descriptions as adjectives, logical relations as conjunctions and so on. These correspondences are outlined below:

SEMANTICS	GRAMMAR
participant	noun
process	verb
quality	adjective
logical relation	conjunction
assessment	modal verb

In the plain English translation of the second resolution given above, for example, the processes are realized as verbs. But in the original all these processes except **resisted**, **permitted** and **defined** were coded as nouns:

PROCESS	VERBAL FORM	NOMINAL FORM
"attempt"	attempting	attempt
"force"	to force	force
"threaten"	threaten	threat
"persuade"	persuade	persuasion
"permit"	permitted	permission
"define"	defined	definition
"boycott"	boycotting	boycott
"opine"	thinks	opinion
"resist"	resisted	resistance
"unite"	united	unity
"act"	act	action

The same text includes qualities coded as nouns:

QUALITY	ADJECTIVE	NOUN
"free"	free	freedom
"safe"	safe	safety

and logical relations are expressed in nominal and verbal form: cf. **in the event of** vs. **if**; **insure** vs. **so that**.

WRITTEN
. . . and in the event of any attempt being made to coerce such labour . . .

SPOKEN
. . . if they try to coerce such labour . . .

WRITTEN
. . . the combined Associations represented at this Conference will take all possible means to insure their personal safety.

SPOKEN
. . . the combined Associations represented at this Conference will do everything they can so that they will be safe.

The last example also contains an assessment of ability, in adjective (**possible**) and modal (**can**) form.

Overall, the effect of abstraction in the grammar of a text is to foreground relational clauses at the expense of material ones and to at the same time foreground nominal groups at the expense of clause complexes. The text itself then codes reality as a set of relationships between things. By way of illustration consider the nominal groups in the Kress passage quoted above:

that peculiar theoretical/ideological mix of Process Writing in its Australian manifestation that I described earlier

inevitable and insoluble problems for a writing curriculum

The mix of West-Coast psychology ('ownership', peer-group work in the form of 'conferencing'), romantic liberal/individualism (writing as original personal 'expression'), and of a late Leavisite elitism (high cultural literary forms as implicit or explicit models or eventual goals, the diary both as confessional and as auto-biography, the personal narrative as short story or novel, etc.)

its real content

the training of an individual student with a certain kind of sensibility

The view of writing put forward in the document

a view of writing merely as a vehicle for individual expression

As far as relational clauses are concerned, the first nominal group *leads to* (causes) the second, the third *has* (as a part) the fifth, in the role of the fourth, and the sixth *is* (a kind of) the seventh. Kress's critique is formulated as relationships of cause, componence and sub-classification among processes dressed up as things. This brings out the essential continuity between humanities and science as far as interpreting the world is concerned. Both use writing as a tool to analyse the world as if it was simply a collection of thing-like phenomena with various sorts of relationships among them. But whereas the humanities tend to take this process only as far as the interpretations coded in the discourse patterns of the texts, science goes one step further and technicalizes the phenomena and their relationships, translating common-sense understandings into specialized ones. One might say, in summary, that for the historian texts *interpret* the world from a nominal point of view, while for the scientist they *reconstruct* the world as a place where things relate to things.

Note

1   This chapter is taken from *Writing in Schools: Reader* (1989a), School of Education, Deakin University, Geelong, Victoria, Deakin University Press, chapter 2.3.

References

Allport, G. and Allport, C. (1980) *Working Lives*, Sydney, Methuen.

Christie, F. and Rothery, J. (1989) 'Exploring the written mode and the range of factual genres', in Christie, F. (ed.) *Writing in Schools*, Geelong, Victoria, Deakin University Press (B.Ed. Course Study Guide), pp. 49–90.

Kress, G. (1988) 'Barely the basics? New directions in writing', *Education Australia*, Term 1, pp. 12–15.

Sale, C., Friedman, B. and Wilson, G. (1980) *Our Changing World. Book I: The Vanishing Natural Ecosystem*, Melbourne, Longman Cheshire.

Simmelhaig, H. and Spenceley, G.F.R. (1984) *For Australia's Sake*, Melbourne, Nelson.

Chapter 14

Eleanor Er

TEXT ANALYSIS AND DIAGNOSTIC ASSESSMENT

Introduction

GENRE-BASED APPROACHES TO TEACHING writing have been increasingly adopted in adult migrant classes in the Australian Adult Migrant English Program (AMEP). Central to such approaches is the analysis of model texts. Using discourse analyses through systemic-functional grammar theory, teachers can make explicit to learners the patterns of language choices made by native speakers for specific writing purposes.

Teachers have found the notion of the generic staging of texts particularly accessible and very teachable in terms of focusing attention on the organisation and structure of whole texts. Learners can be assisted by the teacher in the joint construction of a similar text before constructing their own individual texts independently

In this chapter, I will show how analysis of a learner's text can be used for diagnostic assessment and to inform further teaching directions. It is my contention that in the adult TESOL context, when learners have completed their first drafts, they need explicit teaching of specific features of the English lexicogrammatical and discourse systems, so that approximation towards control of the genre can be broadened to approximation towards control of the second language.

The classroom context

The text to be analysed was written by Dorota, a student in an AMES class of intermediate fast-paced learners. The text was the result of teaching which was directed towards the writing of a specific genre, the film review. Prior teaching involved the use of a sub-titled film to stimulate discussion, in order to develop prediction learning strategies and to extend vocabulary. The text was developed through focusing upon a variety of genres which the film review encompassed (dramatic monologue, narrative, etc.). In the previous lesson, a film review from *The Sydney Morning Herald* newspaper was used as a model for studying the language of film reviews and for discussing their social purpose.

The text

The original text produced by Dorota is presented below (Figure 14.1).

> „ Moon Sickness" is made by Italian director .
> It is a psychological and a little bit fantastic film.
> This film is set in a small village in Sicilly at
> the turn of our century . In general „ Moon Sickness'
> tells us about human feelings, temptations, emotions
> and sympathy to others. The film is about life
> of a poor familly who lives in a dry and craggy
> country. We can observe how their life is changing
> of a strange sick of one of them . Motivations
> of their behaviours are coming from general rules
> of life in a small village.
> Actors play in a very convincing way. They
> create very realistic individual persons.
> A very important part of this film is a music.
> It describes a gloomy and foreboding atmosphere
> In „ Moon Sickness"
> To express more a mood of film director uses
> a moon as a reason of drama and landscape.
> Yellow and red are dominants colours of
> the film.
> In comparison with other films of the same
> subject „ Moon Sickness" is more realistic and
> probably that this story could happen.

Figure 14.1 Text 1: Sample of student writing from review writing genre

Figure 14.2 presents the same text broken down into clauses and indicating the structural stages.

The text shows a clear understanding of the purpose of the genre, which is a type of report. It is "thing focused" on the film, and it is a "generalised" rather than a "particular-ised" response which is required. However, the purpose of the report does require a personal assessment on the part of the reviewer. But the interpersonal distance between the writer and the readers requires that the personal assessment is given in generalised rather than personal language. Not all students grasped this quite complex piece of interpersonal positioning, as evidenced by this extract from another student text:

> This simple story of peoples characters living in the hardest conditions *I've ever seen.*

Dorota, however, has a clear understanding of the generic structure of the review. The text appears logically organised and well structured. The generic structure can be glossed as:

> Introduction ^ Story Orientation ^ Summary of Film as Message ^ Analysis of Film as Art Form ^ Assessment.

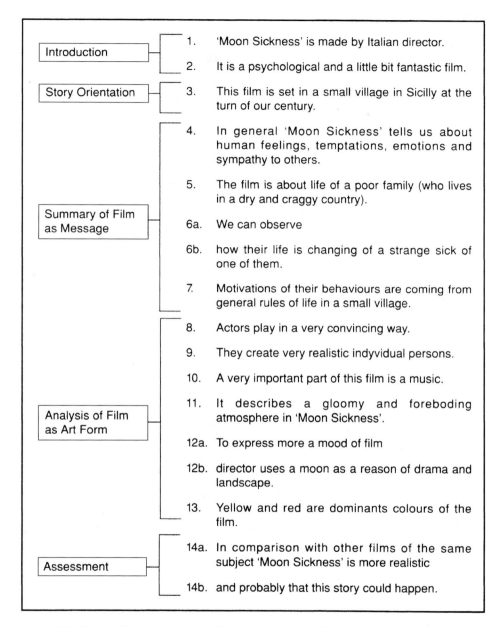

Figure 14.2 Text 2: Clause breakdown of student writing sample

Paragraphing coincides with elements of the generic stages, which contributes to the organised effect of the text.

This was a first draft and clearly using a genre approach has been effective in giving the student an understanding of the purpose of the writing, its overall generic structure and the appropriate elements of this type of report writing. But where does the teacher go from here? How can the student be helped to develop her writing? Further text analyses can identify ways in which the teacher can extend the student's language development.

Thematic development

In terms of generic staging, the text appears to be well developed and organised in that generic stages are evident and logically sequenced. A more detailed analysis of thematic progression, however, would be useful in showing the student how text cohesion could be improved. Halliday (1985: 38) points out that English clauses are ordered as "message" with Given Information serving as the "point of departure" of the message presented first (Theme). The remainder of the message presents New Information (Rheme). An analysis of Theme–Rheme structure in Dorota's text indicates a method of development which makes a series of seemingly unrelated points about the film (Figure 14.5).

The analysis of Theme-rheme patterns indicates that there is one dominant theme, the film itself (T1, T5, T9). The first five themes are identical (T1) so that the ideas of the first five clauses occur in a parallel type of thematic progression (Figure 14.3).

Figure 14.3 Thematic progression

At only three points in the whole text is New Information cited in the Rheme taken up in the following clause Theme and developed (T3 = R5, T6 = R9, T7 = R10). The overall effect therefore is of a stream of disconnected ideas, few of which are developed in any way.

Fries (1983: 124) makes the point that this type of thematic progression, with a high incidence of cross-referential links from Theme to Theme, is more likely to be found in narrative-type texts because narratives tend to relate a sequence of events involving a common character. Academic texts, on the other hand, correlate with thematic progression which shows a high incidence of cross-referential links from the Rheme of one sentence to the Theme of the next. This, he says, is because scholarly texts present complex arguments in which each successive idea is an expansion of "and dependent on" an idea in the previous sentence, as illustrated in Figure 14.4.

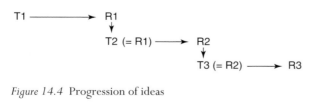

Figure 14.4 Progression of ideas

In Dorota's text. there are only three instances of this second type of progression (clauses 7, 11 and 12) and these are not handled confidently. This contributes significantly to the sense that the text is lacking in the development of ideas.

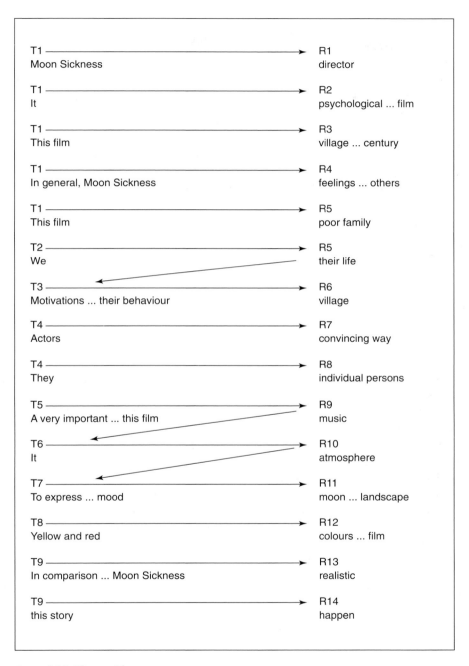

Figure 14.5 Theme–Rheme structure

Through explicit teaching of the information structure of English clauses, the selection of Theme and the way thematic development helps to structure ideas and arguments, this student could be assisted to produce more effective reports. For example, she can be shown that the first two sentences present two separate, unconnected pieces of information about the film:

"Moon Sickness" is made by Italian director.

It is a psychological and a little bit fantastic film.

She could be guided to take up the New Information in clause 1 and to incorporate it in the Theme in clause 2. In this way the two separate ideas are linked and developed to read:

"Moon Sickness" is made by the Italian director, Taviani.

What Taviani presents us with is a psychological study of human emotions with a touch of fantasy.

(See italicised text in *Text 3* on page 238 for further examples.)

Conjunction

Conjunction refers to the semantic connection between clauses. The most remarkable feature of this text is that there are virtually no conjunctively related units. Together with the way in which Theme development is realised, this explains the "feel" that the text lacks cohesion.

There are no conjunctive relations set up to tie the different parts of the text together and organise the text as message. So whilst the generic stages of the film review are clearly present and logically ordered, the lack of cohesive ties adds to the sense of a lack of cohesion in the development of ideas.

Furthermore, there are few conjunctions to structure the "goings-on" external to text organisation. The explicit "In general" (clause 4) could have been exploited to provide cohesive links with following clauses. However, successive clauses relate instead to specific elements of the storyline, leaving it to function in a more limited way as equivalent to the adverb, "generally".

In clause 14, the prepositional group "In comparison with other films," gives an indication that the student has an understanding of how to reorganise experience to suit text purposes. The process "compare" is realised as a prepositional group for the purpose of organising the text as message in an example of textual metaphor.

It would not be beyond this student to learn how to organise and link ideas through the resources of conjunction. For example, clauses 8 to 13 are experientially linked as participants/component elements in film-making to create specific effects upon the audience. The resources of conjunction could therefore be exploited in internal, additive relationship to develop ideas and to create a sense of textual cohesion, for example:

An important part . . . (actors)
Another element . . . (music)

Additionally/Further . . . (the moon, landscape, colours . . . to create mood and drama)
Overall . . . (effect on audience).

Logical relations

In addition to the lack of development of ideas through Theme–Rheme patterns and the lack of conjunctively related units between clauses and text parts, few complex sentences are used to set up logical relations between clauses within the sentence boundary. Of fourteen sentences, eleven are single clauses or simple sentences and this also adds to the impression that there is a lack of development of ideas in the text.

The student has used three clause complexes indicating a readiness to explore ways of linking ideas within the sentence boundaries, that is, in clause complex logical relationships. Clause 6b, "how their life is changing of a strange sick of one of them", is a mental projection of the main clause 6a, "We can observe". In clause 12a–b, "To express more a mood of film" enhances the main proposition in the dominant clause, "director uses a moon as a reason of drama and landscape". And in clause 14a–b, the second clause 14b elaborates on the statement made in 14a, "In comparison with other films of the same subject "Moon Sickness" is more realistic and probably that this story could happen."

The student needs to be made aware of ways to link and develop ideas using clause complex structures. This would help her to develop the logico-semantic organisation of ideas at sentence level, that is, beyond the presentation of single ideas in a series of clause simplexes. This would further encourage elaboration of her ideas and promote language development. For example, clauses 6 and 7 could be developed into a complex clause so that two separate ideas are logically developed, increasing the meaning potential, for example, "As his/her illness progresses, the behaviour of the villagers . . .".

[. . .]

Reference

Reference is the system for tracking participants through a text. It constitutes an important grammatical resource for maintaining text cohesion. Grammatically, it is realised largely through pronoun and definite/indefinite article systems. An analysis of reference chains reveals a very sparse use of this resource to create text cohesion. The one main reference chain relates to the film. This reflects the pattern of thematic development discussed earlier and the reliance on the film as point of departure for ideas (Figure 14.6).

While pronoun and demonstrative pronoun reference is fairly well handled, error analysis indicates that the student's control of reference is tentative. In particular, the use of the definite article in instances when reference assumes membership of a shared context of culture (homophoric reference) is problematic. There are five instances of homophoric reference errors in the text. They involve the omission of the definite article or the substitution of either indefinite article or pronoun:

- (clause 3) "the turn of *our* century" (substitution of "our" for the definite article "the" in homophoric reference used to assume shared membership of the cultural context, mankind; cf. "the turn of *the* century";

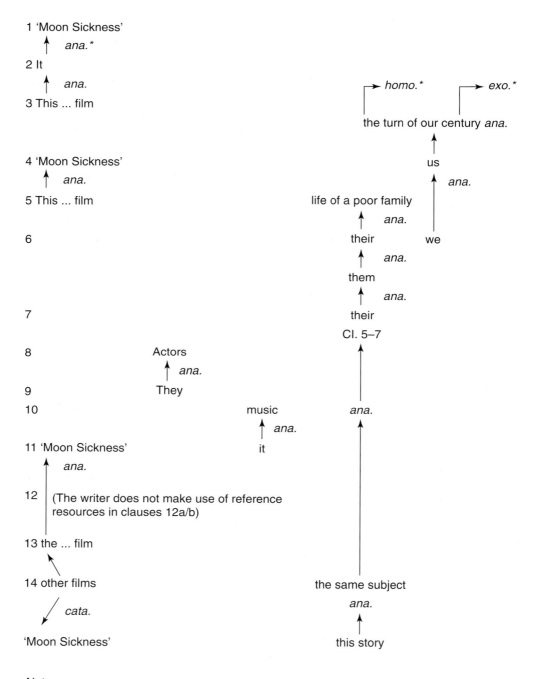

Figure 14.6 Reference chains

- (clause 12b) "director uses *a* moon" (substitution of indefinite article "a" for the definite "the" in homophoric reference to assume shared membership of the cultural context, world; cf. "the director uses *the* moon".

Three errors relate to the use of the indefinite article to assume shared membership of the film-going community:

- (clause 10) "A very important part of this film is *a* music". (Substitution of indefinite article "a" for definite article "the".)
- (clause 12a) "*a* mood of film". (Substitution of indefinite article "a" for definite article "the".) The omission of the definite article in the nominal group "the film" shows the lack of control of anaphoric reference, where reference refers back to mention of the film earlier in the text.
- (clause 12b) "director uses a moon" (omission of definite article, "the" director, relating to anaphoric reference assuming shared membership of the film-going community).

Omission of the definite article in esphoric reference (forward reference within the same nominal group) occurs in three instances:

- (clause 5) This film is about life of a poor family;
- (clause 7) . . . from general rules of life in a small village;
- (clause 13) Yellow and red are dominant colours of the film.

Generally nonphoric participants, that is, participants not previously mentioned in the text, are handled more confidently although the indefinite article in the presenting nominal group in clause 1 is omitted:

- (clause 1) " 'Moon Sickness' is made by Italian director".

The tentativeness of Dorota's control of English phoricity systems is reflected also in her reliance on the marked demonstrative, "this film" (clauses 3, 5, 10) over the unmarked "the film".

The above analyses have been particularly revealing in uncovering the problems which Dorota and, I would suggest, most adult ESL learners have with the definite and indefinite articles. The above analyses reveal that this learner has special problems with homophoric reference relating to shared context of culture as well as with forward esphoric reference.

Most grammar books require several pages to outline the seemingly idiosyncratic rules of usage of the definite and indefinite articles in English. For example, Murphy (1985) takes from Units 71 to 77 (142–54) to cover this point of language use. For teachers who have ever struggled (as I have) to help learners with this aspect of reference, error analysis which pinpoints the source of difficulty in this way can simplify both teaching and learning considerably.

Second draft reorganisation

Dorota's first draft of a written film review is a good attempt by an adult learner at gaining control of a second-language written genre. By working on *thematic development* (italicised in Text 3 below) and **conjunctive relations** (in bold face in Text 3 below), to improve text cohesion and on the areas of reference and the lexico-semantic reorganisation of ideas, a second draft could be something like the following:

Text 3: Second draft reorganisation

"Moon Sickness" is a film by the Italian director, Taviani. *What Taviani presents us with* is a psychological study of human emotions with a touch of fantasy.

The film is set in a small village in Sicily at the turn of the century. *In studying the lives of a poor family who live in this dry, craggy country, we* observe how their lives change as one of them falls ill with a strange sickness. *How they behave, their feelings and temptations*, is largely motivated by the unwritten rules of life in a small village.

The actors are convincing and they create realistic characters.

Another element which plays an important part in this film is the **music**. *Through the music*, a gloomy and foreboding atmosphere is built up.

Further, the director uses the moon and the landscape to heighten the mood and intensify the drama.

Finally, his use of yellow and red as dominant colours contributes to the special effect this film casts on the audience.

Overall, in comparison to other films on the same subject, "Moon Sickness" is more realistic: this story could happen.

Tenor and effect on reader

Clauses 8 to 13 of Dorota's text, describing the participants and elements of film-making which create special effects (the film as art form), fail to realise the interpersonal potential which can be opened up. That aspect of Tenor, the writer-reader relationship which relates to affect or the writer's attitude, is not taken up.

By reorganising thematic development and conjunction, the second draft provides greater potential for these clauses to be developed along a more dynamic prosodic structure, piling up the special effects through the resources of amplification.

Dorota shows good evidence of understanding the development of intensity realised through epithets: "gloomy, foreboding, dominant, special . . ." and through nominal-isations: "music, atmosphere, mood, drama . . .".

However, by reorganising thematic development, she could be shown how intensity adjuncts realised incongruently as relational processes can be exploited to pile up, or amplify the effect, as demonstrated in the reorganised version in Text 3: "heighten, intensify, build up, contribute . . .".

Macro-genre development

What we have in this text is an "elemental" film review. To develop it beyond its one page length, a further elaboration of ideas needs to be worked in to build up what Martin (1992) refers to as a "Macro-genre". That is, by engaging the ideational, interpersonal and textual resources of the grammar, elemental genres such as this can be expanded to the text lengths that are expected when writing such genres.

The introductory thesis/opinion can be developed through elaboration and tied into the conclusion. The overall text structure can in this way be strengthened, giving the whole text a periodic structure moving from thematic prediction ("a psychological and slightly fantastic film") to accumulating new information ("realistic . . . could happen").

In the first draft form of the text, generic stages consist of little more than "topic sentences". These need to be elaborated into paragraphs, extending the experiential content of each topic sentence and accumulating supportive argument for the opening thesis/opinion.

Conclusion

The learner has made an outstanding effort in a first attempt at a written film review. Using generic staging to scaffold the text, she has produced a very creditable first draft. The teacher was understandably pleased at the success of the written results achieved.

However, though impressive in terms of the writer's English language proficiency and her brief exposure to English language learning, the text would still fail to be valued highly by native speaker examiners or professional colleagues. The student needs to be helped with further attention to grammar and discourse features. Teachers can apply the tools which systemic-functional linguistics provides to lead the student beyond an initial attention to generic staging and lexis. Otherwise the implementation of genre-based literacy pedagogy could become what Martin (1990: 48) calls a reductivist, "prescriptive concern with experientially derived part-whole staging".

Taking whole texts as the basic unit of language, the insights and analyses provided by systemic-functional linguistics can be effectively applied in classrooms for the diagnostic assessment of students' language weaknesses and to show students how their writing can be improved.

References

Fries, P.H. 1983. On the status of theme in English: arguments in discourse. In Petofi, J.S. and E. Sozer (eds) *Micro and Macro Connexity of Text*. Hamburg: Helmut Buske Verlag.

Halliday, M.A.K. 1985. *Introduction to Functional Grammar*. London: Edward Arnold.

Martin, J.R. 1990. Macro-genres: the ecology of the page. Department of Linguistics, University of Sydney.

Martin, J.R. 1992. *English Text: System and Structure*. Amsterdam: Benjamins.

Murphy, R. 1985. *English Grammar in Use*. Cambridge: Cambridge University Press.

Chapter 15

Beverly Derewianka

PEDAGOGICAL GRAMMARS: THEIR ROLE IN ENGLISH LANGUAGE TEACHING

Introduction

THE TEACHING OF GRAMMAR HAS been surrounded by controversy for several decades. Should it be taught explicitly? Should we simply raise students' awareness? Should it be taught systematically or at the point of need? Should it be taught at all? It is not the intention of this chapter to attempt to answer such questions. Rather, its purpose is to provide an overview of the most influential grammatical paradigms in second and foreign English language teaching for those teachers wishing to make an informed choice about an appropriate pedagogical grammar for their particular context. While the description of the different grammars is ordered chronologically, this does not imply that each has in turn fallen from use. All are still exerting some degree of influence in language teaching contexts internationally and it is therefore important that teachers of English be familiar with their basic principles and how they might be drawn upon for language teaching purposes.

What is grammar?

The first hurdle is how to define the term "grammar". Here we are immediately confronted by the different ways in which the word is commonly used. "Grammar" can refer to a particular component of the language system that all native speakers intuitively employ in communication. "A grammar" can also be used to refer to a particular description of this component, as in a "traditional grammar" or a "functional grammar". Following from this, the term is often used to refer to a textbook on grammar or part of the English curriculum.

Different linguistic schools will define grammar in different ways depending on their particular field of interest:

- A traditional grammarian might see grammar as the "parts of speech" together with a set of rules governing how they can be combined, often accompanied by pointers as to what is considered "correct" and "incorrect" usage.
- A structural linguist might see grammar as the sum total of sentence patterns in which the words of a particular language are arranged.

- A philosophical/cognitive linguist might see grammar as our innate knowledge of the structure of language.
- A functional linguist might see grammar as a resource used to accomplish communicative purposes in specific contexts.

All of these definitions are quite appropriate. Different descriptions of grammar provide particular tools for doing particular jobs.

A further complication is where to draw the boundaries. Is grammar a discrete component of language, restricted, for example, to the description of how a sentence is structured (syntax)? Or is it at the heart of the language system, mediating between the construction of meaning (semantics) and the sound system (phonology)? Some will want to differentiate between grammar (the "function" words) and lexis (the "content" words) while others find difficulty drawing such a clear distinction. Some will want to include features such as punctuation and spelling in grammar (and in some cases there will be certain connections). From another angle, some will distinguish between grammar (the system of language) and usage (the prevailing standards of acceptable use in a community). And again, others will dispute this dichotomy.

Defining grammar, then, is not a straightforward matter and it is important to clarify how the term is being used in any particular context. For our purposes here, the following very basic definition might be sufficient:

> Grammar is that dimension of the language system that is concerned with words and how they can be combined in various ways.

What is a pedagogical grammar?

The term "pedagogical grammar" does not refer to any particular type or school of grammar. Rather it refers to the objective of the author and the audience for whom it is intended. It is often a simplified version of a more theoretical grammar. A pedagogical grammar is the result of a process of filtering and interpretation at different levels:

- The descriptive or theoretical linguist writes for other linguists in highly specialised language, attempting to convince them of the validity of a particular grammatical theory or aspect of a theory.
- The applied linguist or educational linguist will look at how these insights can be used to explore real-life questions such as "how do different communities use language?" or "how do we learn language?"
- The teacher educator and syllabus developer will interpret the work of the theoretical and applied linguists for the teaching profession, often making the concepts and terminology more accessible and identifying how they might be of use in teaching.
- The textbook writer and the teacher will further "pre-digest" the description of language for the students by selecting and sequencing those features which may be relevant to a particular group of learners and by making decisions about the most appropriate form of presentation.

The term "pedagogical grammar" refers to the kind of knowledge about grammar needed by the teacher and the way this is made available to the student in the form of lessons or materials (descriptions, explanations, examples and exercises). Dirven (1990, p. 1) defines pedagogical grammar as "a cover term for any learner- or teacher-oriented description or presentation of foreign language rule complexes with the aim of promoting and guiding learning processes in the acquisition of that language".

A pedagogical grammar differs from theoretical or descriptive grammars in terms of such aspects as:

- the degree of technicality
- the scope, selection, sequencing and presentation of material
- the relevance to teaching and learning.

Whereas the descriptive grammar will relate to one particular view of language, the pedagogical grammar can be eclectic, drawing on more than one theory. Whether the pedagogical grammar is in the teacher's head or in a textbook, the sources of the knowledge are often not explicit and can be hard to trace back to a single, "pure" theory of grammar. The concern of a pedagogical grammar is not so much theoretical consistency as accessibility, efficiency and usefulness.

> The authors [of pedagogical grammars] specifically reject the notion that they are trying to teach linguistic theory. Indeed, they admit that the theoretical framework they adopt may be open to criticism for that reason. They accept that it may be necessary, for pedagogical purposes, to be eclectic in their theoretical orientation. They take the point of view that these considerations override theoretical coherence.
>
> (Corder 1973, p. 326)

While recognising the pragmatic nature of pedagogical grammars, it is obviously preferable that they reflect as closely as possible the basic principles and objectives of the theoretical grammars on which they draw. Pedagogical grammars are often reduced to mere caricatures of the grammatical theory they purport to represent.

Grammatical paradigms

We can identify numerous types of grammatical description in current use, each based on different principles and approaches to language. To make things more manageable, however, we will limit ourselves to a handful of broader grammatical paradigms that have had a significant impact on language teaching over the years:

- traditional grammar
- structural grammar
- transformational generative grammar
- functional grammar.

It is possible to look at these paradigms and imagine that they are all quite distinct from each other and that each has arisen quite independently "from nowhere". In reality, however, there is a great deal of overlapping and their histories have been intertwined over the centuries. So before we look at each of them in detail, let's spend some time considering where they have come from.

The Western heritage

Roger Bell (1981) usefully cautions that we should not see the above list of grammars as representing some sort of chronological sequence. Popular belief often has it that the term "traditional grammar" refers to the model developed by the Ancient Greeks and Romans which held sway until the early twentieth century, to be followed by structuralism, which was supplanted by transformational grammar, which in turn has been superseded by functional grammar. Bell, however, prefers to talk about "the Western tradition" which, over the centuries, has spawned many different approaches to grammatical description, providing the foundations for most of our "modern" grammars (one of which we know as "traditional grammar").

Halliday (1977) maintains that throughout Western history there have been two major approaches to grammar: the formal and the functional. He does not see these as being contradictory, though they are often made to appear so, particularly in the past couple of decades. Each has assumed prominence at different periods. With Aristotle (384–322BC) we have the beginnings of a formal approach. He saw language as a set of constituent classes: syllables, affixes, articles, nouns, verbs, conjunctions, and so on, with rules for their combination. As a philosopher, he was concerned with truth value and logic. The early sophists in Ancient Greece, on the other hand, viewed language from a functional perspective. They were concerned with meaning and saw language as a communicative resource. Their interest was in the rhetorical function of language as a mode of action and as a means of putting ideas across to others.

> We can follow these two strands throughout the subsequent history of ideas about language in the west. The one stems from Aristotle; it is "analogist" in character, based on the concept of language as rule, and it embeds the study of language in philosophy and logic. The other has, for us today, less clearly defined origins, but it can probably be traced to Protagoras and the sophists, via Plato; it is "anomalist" in character, and has a marked element of Stoic thought in it. It is not philosophical (the Stoics were the earliest scholars explicitly to separate linguistics from philosophy, and grammar from logic) but rather descriptive or, to use another term, ethnographic; and the organising concept is not that of *rule* but of *resource*.
>
> (Halliday 1977, p. 36)

The philosophical strand tended to dominate in certain periods. It reappeared in the thirteenth and fourteenth centuries with the theories of the Modistae, who laid the foundations of formal syntax. In the seventeenth century, the Aristotelian scholastic tradition was further developed by the French "rationalist" school of Port-Royal and the English school of universal semantics. In the twentieth century it surfaced in American structuralist linguistics and in the transformationalist grammar of Chomsky.

In the footsteps of the ancient rhetoricians, the functional strand developed in parallel with the philosophical. There has always been a tradition of learning languages informally for the purpose of communicating with native speakers. From this perspective, language was seen as "a human artifact which had arisen from social and individual needs" (Bell 1981, p. 79). Ethnographers in the eighteenth century became interested in describing the vernacular languages of Europe and the New World and by the nineteenth century this had gained prominence. In the early twentieth century, the ethnographic tradition was taken up by the Prague school and the London school in Europe and by the anthropological linguists such as Boas and Sapir in America. Today we see its influence in the work of scholars such as Firth and Halliday.

Traditional grammar

The term "traditional grammar" is generally used in a rather loose way to refer to a number of grammars that are primarily concerned with language as a set of rules. The basic terminology and system of classification was based on the work of early philosophers such as Aristotle and Dionysius Thrax. We still draw on insights developed by these ancient linguists such as the notion of active and passive voice; tense; subject and object; subject-verb agreement, and so on (Bloor and Bloor 1995).

In the Middle Ages, the vernacular languages were starting to be used for writing and learning instead of Latin and attention turned to developing a grammatical description of English. The earliest important English grammar was written by Ben Jonson, a contemporary of Shakespeare.

Grammarians of the time took the classical grammars as the norm:

> During the Middle Ages, and well into the modern period, Latin was highly regarded as a language of special excellence. It was widely believed that Latin was ideally suited to expressing logical, abstract thought. At the same time it was felt that the various national languages were not so well suited for such purposes. The national languages, like humankind itself, seemingly had fallen from a state of original grace and were somehow corrupt and degenerate versions of what they might have been. This attitude had much less to do with the intrinsic merits of individual languages than with the fact that Latin had always been used for scholarly purposes while the others had not.

> But it was also true that Latin had a formal grammar, available in textbooks, while the national languages did not. It was commonly thought, because of this, that Latin was an "organised" language while other languages were not. The simple truth was that scholars had not troubled to compose grammars of languages other than Latin.
>
> (Pearson 1977, p. 22)

During the reign of Queen Elizabeth I of England, there was nationalistic fervour as the British Empire expanded. The English language was viewed as a symbol of nationalism, and there was a bid to establish the "purity" of the language and to define "correct" English in terms of an immutable set of rules based on the prestige of the classical grammars. Normative grammars were written which attempted to set the standards.

By the eighteenth century many grammars had been produced, most of which were concerned with codifying the principles of English and reducing it to rules. The middle class was concerned with matters of correctness and order and had a passion for precise-ness. Grammar became a factor in judging a person's status. Grammarians looked to the prestigious Latin for the rules and when a Latin rule didn't fit, a new rule was concocted (Savage 1973). Perhaps the most influential of the early traditional grammars were those written by Lowth (*Short Introduction to English*, 1762) and Murray (*English Grammar*, 1794).

Nineteenth-century grammarians were still quibbling over the number and names of grammatical classes, varying between three (nouns, verbs and particles) and ten (article, noun, adjective, pronoun, verb, participle, adverb, conjunction, preposition and inter-jection) (Marckwardt 1966). The late nineteenth century also saw the production of a number of comprehensive scholarly grammars of English, such as those by Jespersen and Sweet. These were not strictly in the "traditional" mould and paved the way for the modern grammars of the twentieth century. Jespersen's eight-volume grammar (*A Modern English Grammar*, 1909–49) dedicated the first volume to English pronunciation, an area relatively neglected in previous grammars. Jespersen also recognised the inadequacy of the formal distinction between different parts of speech and instead referred to primary words (e.g. noun: "weather"), secondary words (adjuncts, e.g. adjectives: "hot") and tertiary words (e.g. adverbs like "extremely").

The grammar that most people have in mind when they use the term "traditional" is the "school grammar" of the nineteenth and early twentieth centuries. This is a somewhat impoverished pedagogical version of the rich scholarly grammars. It names the "parts of speech" and sets out rules of how they fit together, drawing on the often ill-fitting Latinate models.

Beyond their modest descriptive goals, pedagogical traditional grammars also generally include a prescriptive element, appealing to the community's concern for "standards" by specifying rules of usage. Students of English are warned that they should not, for example, split the infinitive, end sentences with a preposition, or say "It's me".

The resultant model of traditional grammar taught in schools is often inflexible and unable to cope with the realities of English in use:

> School grammar is closed. By various devices it excludes from view all unsettled and unsettling questions. It gives artificially unambiguous answers to the questions it can accept as appropriately grammatical and no help at all with others.
>
> (Gleason 1973, p. 122)

While the pedagogical version of traditional grammar may be limited in scope and awkward in its adaptation of Latinate rules, it is still probably the most commonly used grammar in second and foreign language teaching worldwide.

Analytical tools

Traditional grammar divides sentences into parts and labels the parts. At the level of the word this is called "parsing" and at the level of the sentence it is called "analysing".

The words, or "parts of speech", are generally divided into:

- nouns
- verbs
- pronouns
- adjectives
- adverbs
- prepositions
- conjunctions
- miscellaneous

Table 15.1 Parsed sentence

Word	Part of speech	
Police	*noun*	*third person; plural; nominative; simple; common gender; common*
searched	*verb*	*third person; plural; simple; past tense; finite; active*
the	*article*	*definite*
neighbourhood	*noun*	*third person; singular; accusative; compound; neuter gender; common*
for	*preposition*	
several	*adjective*	*numerative (cardinal)*
hours	*noun*	*third person; plural; accusative; simple; neuter gender; common*

Table 15.1 shows one way of parsing the sentence: "Police searched the neighbourhood for several hours."

Sentences are generally analysed into subject and predicate:

Police	searched the neighbourhood for several hours.
subject	*predicate*

Implications of traditional grammar for teaching

In the field of second and foreign language teaching, the teaching approach generally associated with traditional grammar has been the Grammar-Translation Method. The ultimate goal of the method is the study of the literature and culture associated with the foreign language, resulting in a broad humane understanding of life. This is sometimes referred to as the "Classical Method".

The Grammar-Translation Method was developed primarily for the teaching of reading and translation. Oral work is generally reduced to a minimum – usually the drilling of rules and the reading aloud of a written text to demonstrate proficiency in pronunciation. Students studying the classics are not expected to be able to compose original texts, so writing is not encouraged.

While there is no explicit "theory of language learning" associated with Grammar-Translation, the methodology regards the language as an object to be studied rather than as a tool to be used. Students are generally led chapter by chapter through the textbook. They learn the rules (and the exceptions to the rules), learn lists of vocabulary and the translation of each vocabulary item, memorise grammatical patterns (e.g. I am, you are, he/she is, we are, you are, they are), and translate sentences and passages from one language to the other.

Various versions of the Grammar-Translation Method are still used in many countries throughout the world today as the main language teaching method.

Benefits of traditional grammar

- It provides students with a basic way of talking about language using common terminology which is still used to varying degrees in most contemporary descriptions of language (including many communicative grammars).

- It allows students to identify the basic parts of the sentence.
- It enables students to be efficient by learning a set of relatively simple rules from which they can generalise.
- It has links with a long tradition of scholarly grammatical work.
- It is often valued as a mental discipline and respected as a tradition.
- For many EFL students in particular, it builds on what they already know about English grammar and meets their expectations.
- It enables students to work with most EFL and ESL textbooks, which assume a general familiarity with the traditional terminology.
- It is easy for the teacher with limited English and not much time or training who simply wants to follow a textbook and have the reassurance of clear-cut answers.

Drawbacks of traditional grammar

- The Latinate framework does not reflect the realities of the English language.
- The parts of speech are defined inconsistently, i.e. nouns, verbs and interjections in terms of meaning ("a verb represents an action or state"); adjectives and adverbs in terms of function ("an adverb modifies a verb"); other words in terms of structure ("a conjunction comes at the beginning of a clause").
- Rules of usage tend to reflect preferences for fossilised forms of a previous era.
- There is little acknowledgement of English as a dynamic, changing language.
- It fails to adequately take into account varieties of English other than the "standard".
- It is limited in its scope, emphasising form over function and meaning.
- The written mode is privileged.
- It operates only at the level of the sentence and below.

Structural grammar

In the 1930s the fledgling discipline of linguistics recognised that traditional grammar lacked the rigour required for scientific respectability. Structuralist grammarians sought to describe English afresh in terms of objective, detailed and systematic observation from ethnographic studies. They would often go and live in a remote community in order to document the native (usually oral) language. When they turned their attention to familiar languages such as English, they again adopted these empirical, scientific practices. Charles Fries, for example, recorded and transcribed many hours of telephone conversations and based his analyses on these instances of authentic language use.

While traditional grammar provides an abstract, idealised set of rules derived from Latin, structuralists are more concerned with patterns of language in use – observing and describing what actually happens when people use the language in their everyday lives. Rather than impose an inappropriate Latinate structure on the description, the linguists sought to describe each language on its own terms – from the sound system through to whole utterances. Their approach gave rise to the school known as "structuralism", which developed somewhat differently in Europe and America.

The fundamental principles of structuralism, as outlined by W. Nelson Francis, include:

- A language constitutes a set of behaviour patterns common to the members of a given community. It is part of what anthropologists call the culture of the community. Its phenomena can be observed, recorded, classified and compared.

- Each language or dialect has its own unique system of behaviour patterns. . . . There is no such thing as "universal grammar", or at least, if there is, it is so general and abstract as to be of little use. . . . The grammar of each language must be made up on the basis of a study of that particular language – a study that is free of preconceived notions of what a language should contain and how it should operate.
- The analysis and description of a given language must conform to the requirements laid down for any satisfactory scientific theory: simplicity, consistency, completeness, usefulness.

(Nelson Francis 1973, p. 137)

Analytical tools

Whereas traditional grammar dealt only with the written language, the structuralists saw speech as primary. Between 1933 and 1957, structural grammarians placed great emphasis on analysing the sound system. The most influential figure of the period was Leonard Bloomfield, whose book *Language* (1933) included a precise description of phonemes – the distinctive individual sounds of the language. The simple vowel phonemes were described in terms of where and how they were produced in the mouth: the height of the jaw, the position of the tongue, and so on.

The structuralists then turned their attention to words, breaking them down into their component parts. These parts are called morphemes. The word "disconnected", for example, consists of three morphemes: "dis-" (negative meaning), "connect" (base word), "-ed" (action in the past).

Whereas traditional grammar often defined the parts of speech in terms of meaning ("A noun represents a person, place or thing"), the structuralists felt that meaning was too subjective and unscientific. Parts of speech were therefore defined quite differently – not in terms of "meaning" but in terms of where they are located in the structure of a sentence (e.g. "the" is a word which comes before a noun) and its structural characteristics (e.g. "wounded" is a verb because it contains the suffix "-ed").

In fact, Fries avoided terms such as "noun" and "preposition". Rather he referred to "form words" and "function words". He nominated four classes of form words:

Class 1	Words that pattern like "boy", "concert", "building", etc.;
Class 2	Words that pattern like "run", "see", "seem", etc.;
Class 3	Words that fit the pattern: e.g. The *white* boat is *fast*;
Class 4	Words that fit the frame: e.g. The boy runs *quickly*.

Similarly there were a number of groups of function words:

Group A	Words that pattern like "a" and "the" in English sentences;
Group B	Words that pattern like "is" (auxiliary) . . . and so on.

Words were classified, then, in terms of their structural properties. A noun, for example, is a word that can be preceded by an article and which can be made plural.

Having analysed the smaller units – phonemes, morphemes and words – the structuralists moved on to looking at the larger units: how these smaller units were arranged to form phrases, clauses and sentences. Sentence patterns are important in structural grammar: how do native speakers of the language arrange words in a particular order? In analysing the sentence, they used a process called immediate constituent analysis (IC analysis). The sentence is divided into its parts – one cut at a time – until the process cannot be continued any further and the fundamental building blocks of the sentence have been reached (Table 15.2).

Table 15.2 Sentence broken down into its parts

1	Police	searched		the	neighbourhood		for	several	hours	
2	Police	searched		the	neighbourhood		for	several	hours	
3	Police	searched		the	neighbourhood		for	several	hours	
4	Police	searched		the	neighbourhood		for	several	hours	
5	Police	searched		the	neighbourhood		for	several	hours	
6	Police	searched		the	neighbourhood		for	several	hours	
7	Police	searched		the	neighbourhood		for	several	hours	
8	Police	search	ed	the	neighbourhood		for	several	hours	
9	Police	search	ed	the	neighbour	hood	for	several	hours	
10	Police	search	ed	the	neighbour	hood	for	several	hour	s

At this level, the unit of analysis is the tagmeme – a unit of grammatical arrangement that can be described in terms of slots (grammatical functions or positions within a sentence) and fillers (the class of items grammatically acceptable in each slot).

Implications of structural grammar for teaching

While the origins of structural grammar were in anthropology, its potential was seized upon by the teaching profession. The mid-twentieth century was an era of mass education. The study of languages was no longer seen as an élite prerogative but was opened up to all students, many of whom had no interest in obscure rules and painstaking translation. It was also an era of mass travel, where new means of transportation meant that people could readily visit hitherto inaccessible and "foreign" places. There was a great demand therefore for language courses that gave quick access to the spoken language for purposes of communication with native speakers. The Second World War also required soldiers who were able to communicate fluently in foreign languages. Finally, it was an era when educators, impressed with the new learning theory of behaviourism, were looking for a complementary linguistic description – a description that derived from real-life behaviour, that dealt with aspects of oral language, that outlined patterns and structures that could be drilled and manipulated without recourse to rules or translation. Structural grammar provided just what was required.

The "slot and filler" descriptions provided the basis for exercises that involved the manipulation of a particular structure. Some of these exercises are referred to as substitution tables or pattern drills, where students are provided with a basic structure and are required to change certain elements (Table 15.3).

Programmes are designed so that they start with the "easiest" structures and work up towards the more complex. The lessons develop in manageable steps with no great

Table 15.3 Pattern drills

The boy	kicked	the ball
The girl	kicked	the ball
The children	kicked	the ball
The boy	*kicked*	the ball
The boy	*hit*	the ball
The boy	*caught*	the ball

challenges to the students so that they are not led to make any errors. If errors do occur they have to be eliminated immediately so that they do not become entrenched. The use of the students' first language is discouraged along with any explicit explanation of underlying rules. The pedagogical grammar is therefore not explicit, but informs the construction of habit formation exercises based on sentence patterns, particularly common in the teaching methodology referred to as "audiolingualism".

Until the 1970s, structural syllabuses were central to all language teaching and it is still not uncommon to find pattern drills and substitution tables being used to reinforce a particular structure.

Benefits of structural grammar

- It brought a fresh perspective to the teaching and learning of languages.
- It includes an emphasis on oral language.
- It deals with the complexity of language-in-use more so than does traditional grammar (though the analysis is still simpler than the reality).
- It attempts to describe each language on its own terms rather than impose an inappropriate Latin template.
- It provides a detailed description of the phonology and morphology of English.
- It shifts the focus from the individual word to combinations of words in patterns.
- It approaches the study of language from a more rigorous, scientific perspective.
- It uses authentic language as its database.
- It provides the basis for exercises involving the learning of grammatical patterns.

Drawbacks of structural grammar

- There is a tendency for a complex, dynamic system to be reduced to rigid, simple patterns.
- It does not recognise that the analysis of a relatively small sample of instances of language cannot account for the entire language system.
- It does not differentiate between sentences that have the same structure but different meaning (e.g. he was killed by midnight; he was killed by the enemy).
- It does not deal well with the syntax of complex sentences.
- There is a lack of integration between levels of description (e.g. intonation and syntax).
- It emphasises structure at the expense of other aspects (e.g. function, meaning).

- Though derived from authentic data, the teaching examples are generally idealised in order to present a typical pattern.

Transformational generative grammar

At the height of the structuralist movement Noam Chomsky published a damning critique, claiming that structural grammar dealt only with the surface features of language. It allowed you to analyse the language into its constituents and to label those parts in an objective way, but it didn't explain the relationship between structures. On the surface, for example, the following phrases have the same structure:

the growling of lions
the raising of flowers.

While the surface structure of these is the same, their underlying deep structure is quite different. "The growling of lions" can be derived from "lions growl". "The raising of flowers", however, cannot be derived from a similar base structure: "flowers raise". Rather, it has a different derivation: "they raise flowers" (Marckwardt 1966).

According to Chomsky, the structuralists, in describing "what has been observed" in terms of a specific language, ignored the underlying rules that specify the set of grammatical sentences associated with a particular deep structure. The deep structures are seen as universal to all languages and are said to be genetically programmed in the human brain. These abstract deep structures are transformed into the surface structures that characterise particular languages. This model is referred to as transformational generative grammar (commonly shortened to TG or TGG).

The learner's innate knowledge of the universal rules of language is referred to as the learner's "competence". When a learner is exposed to a particular language the deep underlying rules enable them to quickly pick up the specifics of that language. This is said to explain how children are able to learn so swiftly the complexities of their mother tongue. The language that the learner actually uses is referred to as "performance". A learner's performance is often seen as somewhat degenerate and untidy when compared with the idealised competence. (More recently, Chomsky prefers the terms I-language (internal) and E-language (external) to competence and performance.)

In summary, Chomsky's ideas contradicted many of those of the structuralists:

- Rather than seeing each language as unique, Chomsky believes that all languages share key characteristics – a universal grammar.
- Rather than seeing language as a list of surface structures, Chomsky has sought to identify the relationship between the surface structures and the underlying deep structures.
- Rather than seeing language as a form of physical behaviour, Chomsky sees language as an innate mental phenomenon.

Since its dramatic introduction in the 1960s and 1970s, the theoretical base underpinning transformational generative grammar has continued to develop and diversify. In the late 1970s and early 1980s Chomsky presented a revised version of TGG which he called government and binding theory. Related theories such as phrase structure grammar and relational grammar also emerged. While these are of great interest to syntactic linguists, they have had little or no direct impact on second and foreign language teaching. There is promising work being carried out in the field of second language acquisition that draws on the insights of universal grammar. This might become significant for the syllabus designer or textbook writer, but does not as yet have the characteristics of a pedagogical grammar.

Analytical tools

Chomskyan syntactic theory has evolved over the past few decades to a point where it is highly complex and abstract and of less obvious relevance to second language teaching. The analysis below illustrates the analytical tools which are characteristic of the period when TGG was seen as being a potentially significant influence on classroom practice.

Following the structuralists, TGG would analyse a sentence into its constituents (Figure 15.1).

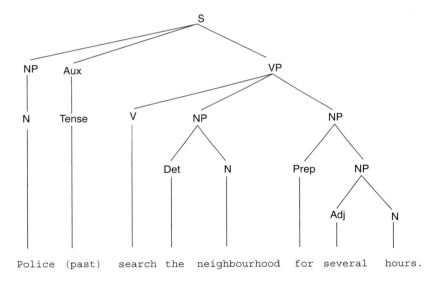

Figure 15.1 Tree diagram of sentence

The tree diagram can also be represented in the form of a phrase-structure rule. At the broadest level, we have the rule:

S → NP VP

indicating that a sentence (S) has two main constituents, the noun phrase (NP) and the verb phrase (VP). (There is also an indication of tense: Aux.) We can go into further detail by examining the constituents of the verb phrase, in this case:

VP → V NP PP

Here, the verb phrase consists of a verb (V) plus a noun phrase (NP) and a prepositional phrase (PP). The noun phrase in turn consists of a determiner (Det) followed by a noun (N) and the prepositional phrase consists of a preposition (Prep) and a noun phrase (NP). This noun phrase in turn can be divided into an adjective (Adj) and noun (N).

The following are some basic phrase-structure rules:

$$S \rightarrow NP \quad VP$$
$$NP \rightarrow (Det) \quad (ADJ) \quad N \quad (PP)$$
$$VP \rightarrow V \quad (NP) \quad (S) \quad (PP)$$
$$PP \rightarrow Prep \quad NP$$

(The brackets indicate that the constituent is optional.)

One transformation we could perform on the above sentence is to make it passive. In this case, the key features we would need to consider are the NP (police), the VP (searched) and the second NP (the neighbourhood). We could also indicate the tense (past). Other information is not relevant and can be referred to simply as X and Y.

The rule for the active voice would look something like the following:

1	2	3	4	5	6
X	**NP**	**Aux**	**V**	**NP**	Y
θ	**police**	**past tense**	**search**	**the neighbourhood**	for several hours

In transforming this into the passive, we need to follow the following transformation rule:

1	5	3	4	(by 2)	6
X	**NP**	**Aux**	**V**	**(NP)**	Y
θ	**the neighbourhood**	**past tense**	**search**	**(by police)**	for several hours

This gives us a regular formula for describing how the passive is formed in English.

In later versions of TGG a semantic element was included. The word "policeman", for example, could be defined in terms of its semantic attributes:

POLICEMAN $\rightarrow$
+ Noun
+ Countable
+ Animate
+ Human
+ Male
+ Adult

Implications of TGG for teaching

Chomsky's theory of language acquisition has had a profound influence in the field of second language learning. His arguments against structuralism and behaviourism rocked the language education field, challenging the dominant language teaching approach to its core. He argued that rather than learning language through the repetition of structures until they became automatic and error-free, language was learned by being immersed in "language in use". This activated the language acquisition device in the learner's brain, enabling the learner to draw upon the innate rules of language and to hypothesise about how this particular language "worked", based on the evidence supplied in the context of hearing and using the language. The learner became an active, creative processor of language rather than merely passively mimicking sounds and structures.

Chomsky, however, insisted that his theory of grammar had little direct classroom application:

> My own feeling is that from our knowledge of the organization of language and of the principles that determine language structure one cannot immediately construct a teaching programme. All we can suggest is that a teaching programme be designed in such a way as to give free play to those creative principles that humans bring to the process of language learning, and, I presume, to the learning of anything else. I think we should probably try to create a rich linguistic environment for the intuitive heuristics that the normal human automatically possesses.
>
> (Chomsky 1968, p. 690)

Because the deep structure rules represented the speaker's competence – already inherent in the learner – there was therefore no point in teaching these rules explicitly. Instead it was more important to create a context where the rules could be activated through exposing the learner to comprehensible, meaningful input that is appropriately graded and relevant to the learner (Krashen 1983). This insight underpins much communicative, learner-centred methodology, particularly as developed in the United States.

Although Chomsky's ideas remain very influential, particularly in the United States, they have also provoked negative reactions. The dichotomy between "competence" and "performance" in particular has been the subject of strong criticism. Lewis (1993), for example, refers to Chomsky's competence as "an idealisation, untarnished by the messiness of real language use. Performance became a rag-bag term for all the untidy aspects of language which are evident if we examine real language data" (p. 15).

> Nowadays, for most linguists and methodologists, it is largely discredited. Many objections can be made. Widdowson has pointed out that the concept of "native speaker competence" is not well-defined. Which native speakers? There are, in the real world, no idealised speaker-listeners and no homogeneous speech communities.
>
> In order to defend the competence/performance dichotomy, it was necessary to ignore huge amounts of language actually produced by native speakers. If the evidence supported the theory, it was used; if the evidence contradicted the theory, the evidence was dismissed as "degenerate". Competence, by definition, could not be empirically investigated. Its existence was merely asserted.
>
> (Lewis 1993, p. 11)

In Halliday's view, Chomsky took an extreme position and unnecessarily polarised the discipline of linguistics:

If Chomsky had admitted that he was building on the work of his predecessors, the ensuing dialogue between philosophers and ethnographers of language could have been very fruitful and rewarding. Instead he presented his theories in the form of a violent polemic aimed directly at those whose model of language he was taking over; in the course of this he so misrepresented the work of his other contemporaries and forerunners that for the following decade and more it was impossible for the two groups to engage in any dialogue at all. Probably never before in the history of ideas about language have the two views, of language as resource and language as rule, been made to seem so incompatible. . . . It soon came to be realized that the price to be paid for the Chomskyan type of formalism was much too high; it required a degree of idealization so great as to reduce natural language back to the status of an artificial syntax. Once its claims for psychological reality could no longer be sustained, transformation theory lost its original glamour; and today we are witnessing a retreat from these extreme positions and an attempt to reconcile the philosopher's demand for being explicit with the ethnographer's demand for being relevant.

(Halliday 1977, p. 45)

Finally, Bell (1981) points out that Chomsky argued so effectively against the shortcomings of structuralist grammars that they were discredited and virtually abandoned. TGG, however, didn't provide a robust alternative for language teaching, leaving a void and a sense of disillusionment among language teachers. Despite "the intellectually exciting nature of the ideas and hypotheses embodied in TG, most applications of it to teaching have been no more than misunderstandings or trivializations" (Bell 1981, p. 107).

Benefits of TGG

- It provides a framework for relating mind and grammar, going beyond surface structures.
- It offers a more accurate and complete conception of the system of language, building on both traditional and structural models.
- It emphasises universal characteristics of language, an important factor in translation, contrastive analysis, and positive transference from the students' first language.
- It clarifies how certain syntactic structures and complex sentences are formed (e.g. passives, negatives, questions).
- It provides the basis for analysing the nature and degree of learner errors, which are viewed positively as indications of the learner's current hypothesising about how the language works.
- Recent work in second language acquisition suggests a principled basis for the introduction of certain structures at particular stages of learning.

Drawbacks of TGG

- Transformational linguists themselves did not encourage the use of TG grammar in language teaching.
- It emphasises the ideal speaker/listener's competence at the expense of actual performance and the ability to use language appropriately in acts of communication.

- It privileges form over function.
- It does not take social and cultural differences and context of use into account.
- It operates at the level of the sentence and below.
- The theory is seen as too abstract and remote for teachers so there is a tendency to either ignore or trivialise the theoretical underpinning and to misrepresent it as empty formalism.

Functional grammars

Transformational generative grammar focused on the speaker's competence. Chomsky's narrow definition of competence, however, was disputed by those who saw it as more than grammatical competence. In the 1980s there were attempts to extend the notion of competence to what Hymes called "communicative competence". Canale (1981) described communicative competence as including:

- linguistic competence (grammatical correctness in terms of the forms, inflections, and sequences used to express the message);
- sociolinguistic competence (knowledge of how to express the message in terms of the person being addressed and the overall circumstances and purpose of the communication);
- discourse competence (the selection, sequence and arrangement of words and structures as a clear and effective means of expressing the speaker/writer's intended message);
- strategic competence (strategies to compensate for any weaknesses the speaker/ writer has in the above three areas).

Educators started to turn to grammar with a more functional orientation to seek answers to questions about how language operates to create meaning in social contexts.

Systemic functional grammar

There are a number of functional grammars. One which has had a significant impact in the field of language education is that developed by Michael Halliday and colleagues, referred to as systemic functional grammar (SFG). Halliday's approach has been to develop a model of grammar which provides a clear relationship between functions and grammatical systems. He describes language in terms of three "macro-functions" (which he refers to as "metafunctions"):

- Using language to represent our experience of the world (the *ideational* meta-function). Language can be used, for example, to construct familiar worlds, imaginative worlds, scientific worlds, religious worlds, concrete worlds, abstract worlds, and so on.
- Using language to interact with others (the *interpersonal* metafunction). Language can be used to create and maintain different kinds of roles (e.g. expert, novice, parent, child, teacher, student) and relationships (e.g. affection, hostility, neutrality).
- Using language to create coherent and cohesive texts, both spoken and written (the *textual* metafunction). Certain features of the language system function to organise the flow of information in an accessible way or to make links between ideas.

Each of these metafunctions is related to a particular grammatical system. Whenever we use language, we draw on certain grammatical resources to represent ideational meanings ("what is this text about?"), other grammatical resources to express interpersonal meanings ("what is the nature of the interaction?"), and yet other grammatical resources to develop the textual quality ("how does this text hang together?").

Halliday's model also emphasises the relationship between grammar and context. At the broader level, we need to consider the relationship between language and its cultural context. Grammatical systems (and vocabulary) evolve within a particular culture to enable humans to achieve their social purposes. Different discourse communities in a culture will use language in different ways. Our use of language both reflects the context of culture and helps to shape it.

At the more specific level, we need to consider the use of language within a particular situation. There are features in each situation that will influence the kinds of grammatical and lexical choices we make, including such variables as

- the subject matter or **field** of discourse ("what is being spoken about")
- the roles and relationships or **tenor** of discourse ("who is involved in the interaction")
- the channel of communication or **mode** of discourse ("the part language is playing").

A particular combination of these three variables (field, tenor and mode) is referred to as the register. If we know the register, then we can generally predict the kind of grammatical resources that will be used in any given text.

For a representation of Halliday's model see Figure 15.2, which attempts to demonstrate how a particular text is embedded within a cultural context. Within that culture, the particular situation will have an impact on the choices made from the language system.

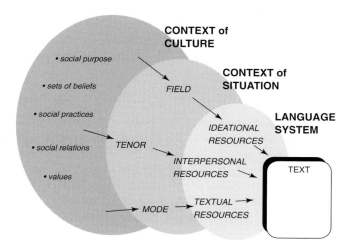

Figure 15.2 A Hallidayan model of language

Analytical tools

Because systemic functional grammar is concerned with meaning in context, analysis generally involves looking at the whole text and the lexicogrammatical features which are characteristic of that kind of text. (Halliday uses the term "lexicogrammar" because it is difficult to separate out lexis (vocabulary) from grammar.) In the following text, the social purpose is to relate an incident in the form of a newspaper story. It is therefore organised in a particular way: the first part of the text introduces the incident, those who were involved, and the time and location. This is followed by an elaboration on different aspects related to the incident and, as is typical of such stories, it finishes with a projection into the future.

> A 65-year-old man was found stabbed to death in his bed, and his son bleeding from several wounds in the kitchen, in a bizarre stabbing in Russell Hill near Greensvale yesterday.
>
> The son's pet border collie dog was also found stabbed to death in a bath.
>
> Neighbours said that they had seen a suspicious-looking person wearing sunglasses and a dark jacket lurking near the house.
>
> Police searched the neighbourhood for several hours. They believe the suspect might still be in the area.
>
> The injured man was in a critical condition at Greensvale hospital last night. It will be several days before police can interview him.

If we look at the field, we will be able to predict certain lexicogrammatical features. The story is about a murder in the suburbs. The field involves a range of participants, both human (*a 65-year-old man, his son, neighbours, police, etc.*) and non-human (*the son's pet border collie dog, Greensvale hospital, the neighbourhood, etc.*). The participants engage in a variety of processes: they carry out actions (*was found, searched*); they use their senses (*had seen*); they say things (*said*); they use their cognition (*believe*), and so on. Some of the participants are initiators of the actions and others are receivers. Many of the processes are surrounded by different kinds of circumstances: Where? (*in his bed, in Russell Hill near Greensvale, in a bath, near the house*); When? (*yesterday, for several hours, last night*); Why? (*from several wounds*); How? (*in a critical condition*).

So far we have used semantic (or functional) terms to characterise the field: various types of participants, processes and circumstances. We could also, however, look at the grammatical categories that typically realise these. Participants are generally realised by the grammatical category of the noun group; processes are generally realised through the verb group; and circumstances are generally realised through adverbs and prepositional phrases. So in Halliday's grammar, there is one set of terminology to talk about meaning and function and another set to refer to the grammatical classes that realise those meanings. This is important because there is no one-to-one correspondence between meaning and grammatical class.

Turning to the tenor, we note that the relationship is one of tabloid journalist writing for a not-too-discerning audience. He does not engage with the readers overtly by giving commands or asking questions, by addressing them personally or using in-group jargon. He does, however, provoke interaction through the choice of emotive and evaluative vocabulary: *stabbed to death*; *a bizarre stabbing*; *suspicious-looking*; *lurking*. He also includes the sensational: *The son's pet border collie dog was also found stabbed to death in a bath*. The use of the modal *might* also introduces a degree of uncertainty that invites the reader to speculate. There is a range of lexicogrammatical systems that we can use to realise interpersonal meanings: the mood system, polarity, attitudinal lexis, modality, vocatives, speech role pronouns, and so on.

The mode is written. We would therefore expect features typical of the written mode: lengthy noun groups to compact the information (*the son's pet border collie dog*; *a suspicious-looking person wearing sunglasses and a dark jacket*); using the beginning of sentences to focus attention on how the topic (or theme) is being developed (*A 65-year-old man > The son's pet border collie dog > Neighbours > Police > They > The injured man*); the use of the passive to organise the flow of information (*was found*); linking devices to make the text cohesive, such as pronouns (*A 65-year-old man – **his** bed – **his** son*) and synonyms (*his son – the injured man*).

It is of course possible to undertake a detailed analysis at the level of the individual clause and its components. If we were to look at our model sentence ("Police searched the neighbourhood for several hours"), a functional analysis would reveal the following:

- In terms of its **ideational** meaning, the sentence represents a "slice of experience" involving the activity of searching (a "material" process as opposed, for example, to a "mental" process). The participants in this process are the police, who initiated the activity (the "actor"), and the neighbourhood, which is on the receiving end of the activity (or "goal"). There is also an indication of how long the activity lasted: or several hours (a circumstance of time).
- In terms of its **interpersonal** meaning, it is engaging with the reader by presenting a statement of fact (realised in the grammar by the structure "subject + finite"). A different way of interacting would have been to ask a question (*Did police search the neighbourhood?*) or by a command (*Search the neighbourhood*).
- In terms of its **textual** meaning, the writer has chosen to place "Police" at the beginning of the sentence. In English we use the beginning of a sentence as a position of prominence to indicate how we are developing the theme or topic focus. The writer could have chosen instead to use "the neighbourhood" as theme by using the passive. So while a TGG analysis would focus on how the passive is formed, a functional analysis also considers the rhetorical effect of choosing the passive – its function in organising the flow of information in the text.

We could represent this analysis diagrammatically (Table 15.4). Note that the sentence performs all three functions simultaneously. The sentence is part of a larger text which is situated in a particular cultural context so the analysis would ultimately need to be related to how this sentence contributes to the meanings being developed by the text as a whole and how the text is culturally situated. Any functional analysis is most revealing when used to make a comparison with other texts that construct different meanings through making different grammatical choices.

As you can see, any model of language that tries to incorporate meaning, function, context and grammatical categories is bound to involve a great deal of complexity. Halliday

Table 15.4 Diagrammatic analysis of sentence

	Police	searched	the neighbourhood	for several hours
Ideational	*Participant* *(actor)*	*Process* *(material)*	*Participant* *(goal)*	*Circumstance* *(temporal)*
Interpersonal	*Subject*	*Finite*		
Textual	*Theme*	*Rheme*		

himself describes his grammar as "extravagant". Language is a rich, dynamic, open-ended system and cannot be represented faithfully by a simplistic grammar. It is possible, nevertheless, to focus initially on certain aspects of Halliday's functional grammar that are quite accessible without trying to deal with the model as a whole.

Implications for teaching

The growing emphasis in the 1970s and 1980s on what people need to *do* with language and what *meanings* they want to express led to the development of more functionally oriented syllabuses.

A major impetus for the development of such a syllabus came from changing educational and commercial realities in Europe and the need for people to communicate in the various languages spoken in the European Economic Community. Following an analysis of the needs of adult European language learners, the British linguist, D.A. Wilkins, prepared a preliminary document which described the sorts of communicative meanings which learners would need to be able to make. These communicative meanings were grouped into *functional* categories and *conceptual* categories.

Functional categories refer to the social purpose of an utterance – what job the language is being used for in a particular context. Was the speaker offering to help? requesting a service? giving a command? Wilkins (1976) describes six broad functions:

- judging and evaluating (e.g. appreciation, condemnation, approval)
- persuading (e.g. advice, commands, cautions)
- arguing (e.g. informing, denying, supporting)
- reasoning (e.g. hypothesising, justifying, explaining, generalising)
- expressing personal emotions (e.g. pleasure, surprise, shock)
- formulaic expressions (e.g. greetings, sympathy, gratitude).

Conceptual categories, on the other hand, refer to the "content" of the utterance, including such notions as:

- time (e.g. point of time, duration, frequency, sequence)
- quantity (e.g. countable, uncountable, numerals)
- space (e.g. dimensions, location, motion)
- roles (e.g. agent, initiator, object, instrument)

as well as modal meanings:

- degree of certainty (e.g. possibility, probability, doubt)
- degree of commitment (e.g. intention, willingness, obligation).

So while the function might be "inviting", the conceptual notions might be "a friend", "to dinner", and "on Sunday". (We must remember that here we are talking about syllabuses and not strictly pedagogical grammars.)

The functional-notional syllabus has had a significant influence on second language teaching. The work of British applied linguists such as Wilkins, Widdowson, Littlewood, Brumfit, Johnson and others (many of them influenced by Halliday) have emphasised language as a social phenomenon that occurs within specific contexts. The language needed by an itinerant worker in order to operate in a factory context is quite different from the language needed by a businessperson to chair a meeting. This recognition has led to the development of English for Specific Purposes (ESP) – custom-designed courses catering for the particular needs of different groups, primarily adults. Thus we find such courses as:

- English for the Oil Industry
- English for Writing Lab Reports
- English for Childbirth
- English for the Coffee Break
- English for Library Research
- English for Phone Conversations
- English for Panelbeaters.

At the beginning of the twenty-first century, Halliday's functional grammar is having an impact in the field of language education in many parts of the world, aside from its influence on functional-notional syllabi. In Australia, for example, it has been adapted for a range of pedagogic contexts and informs syllabus and materials development from primary school through to adult education. Halliday's metafunctions provide second language teachers with a useful way of identifying language development in their students and of planning for continuing development:

- What linguistic resources do students have for representing the world – the world of everyday experience, the world of the imagination, the technical world of the scientist, the abstract world of the historian, the workplace world, the world of the mathematician, and so on?
- What linguistic resources do students have for interacting in the world in culturally appropriate ways: asking questions, proffering opinions, requesting services, offering to do things, moderating their assertions, and so on?
- What linguistic resources do students have for constructing texts which are coherent and cohesive?

The emphasis is not so much on the correction of grammatical errors or on syntax for the sake of syntax, but on extending the learners' ability to use language effectively and appropriately in a variety of contexts.

Benefits of a functional grammar

- It places the emphasis on using language to achieve real-life purposes.
- It identifies the grammatical features that are relevant to achieving those purposes.
- It deals with language in use, not idealised rules.
- It is interested in variation in language, not simply the "standard" variety.
- It recognises the relationship between language use and context.
- It operates at the level of the text and below.
- It encompasses spoken as well as written language.
- Systemic functional grammar in particular provides a principled and systematic description of the relationship between function, meaning and grammar.

Drawbacks of a functional grammar.

- The sequencing and grading of functions and notions cannot be controlled as easily as with a form-oriented grammar.
- Systemic functional theory can be seen as too complex and inaccessible in its raw state for teachers to utilise.
- SFG requires investment on the part of the teacher and a willingness to re-think language and grammar.

Summary

Table 15.5 summarises some of the key features of the grammatical paradigms we have been reviewing. Because it is simply an outline, it cannot do justice to the fullness of each model and the various schools within each tradition.

Other recent developments

While we have focused on the major grammatical paradigms that have given rise to most pedagogical grammars currently in use, language educators need to be alert to other developments in the field that could inform their practice. Here we will mention only two: corpus-based descriptions and lexical approaches.

Corpus-based descriptions

The tradition of gathering authentic language data from language in use within the language-speaking community is continued today by many of those involved in corpus studies. With the advent of the computer, enormous amounts of language used in various contexts (newspapers, novels, magazines, textbooks, transcripts of various types of oral interaction, and so on) can be collected, entered, stored, organised into categories, processed and made accessible for analysis in various ways. In this way, a "grounded theory" of English can be developed, where the description starts from the evidence rather than from imposing some theoretical model.

One of the most famous of the corpus collections is the COBUILD corpus ("The Bank of England"), which has amassed some 200 million words of "raw", naturally occurring data. If you are interested in the use of any particular word, you will be presented with all the instances of that word as it occurs in the context of its surrounding text.

the city	*of*	*York*
the art	*of*	*painting*
the age	*of*	*eight*
the problem	*of*	*unemployment*
a price increase	*of*	*15 per cent*
some fool	*of*	*a boy*
the back	*of*	*the van*

Corpus studies are starting to provide evidence of language use that has the potential to overthrow many of our cherished beliefs about how we use English.

> Analysis of extended naturally-occurring texts, spoken and written . . . has revealed quite unsuspected patterns of language. Traditional descriptive frameworks are normally not able to account for or accommodate such phenomena, and new approaches are required.
>
> (Sinclair 1991, p. xvii)

Lexical approaches

Another challenge to our common understanding of pedagogical grammars is an approach that puts lexis at the heart of language learning rather than grammar. Lewis, for example, argues that "language consists of grammaticalised lexis, not lexicalised grammar". Using lexis (including "chunks" of language) as a starting point rather than grammar "represents a radical change to the status quo" and "a major shift with profound theoretical and practical implications" (p. 95).

What does Lewis mean by "lexis"? Unlike vocabulary, which is seen as a collection of individual words, lexis may consist of multi-word units. Many of these units are formulaic and are the basis of much of the language used by native speakers in everyday use. Multi-word units can be produced and processed more rapidly as they are perceived as single, unanalysed wholes. In our conversations, we don't generate each sentence "from scratch" by combining a number of individual words into unique utterances. Rather, "users rely on a vast store of fixed phrases and pre-patterned locutions by which they routinely manage aspects of interaction" (p. 90).

Even though much of the language used by native speakers consists of idiomatic formulaic expressions, in traditional ESL programmes these expressions are generally left to the more advanced stages, while beginning and intermediate students learn "the basics". Lewis suggests that we should in fact be exposing students to idiomatic chunks from the beginning. He describes an idiomatic expression as one where the meaning of the whole is not immediately apparent from an examination of the constituent parts. Such expressions often involve metaphor:

I see what you mean.
The damage is already done.
We're not out of the wood yet.

Table 15.5 Key features of grammatical paradigms

	Traditional	Structural	Transformational	Functional
View of language	Sees language as a set of rules	See language as a set of habits	Sees language as characterised by rule-governed creativity	Sees language as a system of meanings
View of grammar	Rules of formation and usage	Building blocks which combine in various structures	An innate device in the human mind	A resource for making meaning in social contexts
Derivation of description	Derived from ancient Greek and Latin models	Derived from recording of actual samples of spoken English	Derived from theorising about universal principles of language	Derived from observation and analysis of what people do through language
Related disciplines	Philosophy	Ethnography/behaviourist psychology	Philosophy/cognitive psychology	Sociology, anthropology
Form vs. function / meaning	Primarily concerned with form though traces of function	Entirely focused on structure with little reference to meaning or function	Emphasis on syntactic form with more recent interest in semantics	Principled relationship between form and function
Degree of similarity between languages	Languages are different but can be made to conform to classical grammatical descriptions	Each language is unique and must be described on its own terms	All languages have in common an underlying universal grammar	Certain principles are universal but language use varies according to context

Table 15.5 Continued

	Traditional	Structural	Transformational	Functional
Mode emphasis	A grammar of the written mode	Language is speech not writing	Not concerned with mode	Shows how we draw differently on the language system in speaking and writing
Unit of analysis	Parts of speech and their combination	Phonemes, morphemes and relatively simple syntax	Phonemes through to complex syntactic forms	Text, clause, group, word, phoneme
Key figures	Dionysius Thrax, Bishop Lowth	Bloomfield, Fries	Chomsky	Halliday
Classroom implications	Overt teaching of rules, often as an end in themselves	No overt discussion of grammar but teacher's knowledge of grammar guides selection of structures	Teacher's knowledge of acquisition sequence guides selection of input/data from which students hypothesise	Discussion of relevant grammar point in context to heighten language awareness and appropriate use

Lewis refers to similar work by Nattinger and De Carrico (1992), who state that:

> One common pattern in language acquisition is that learners pass through a stage in which they use a large number of unanalysed chunks of language in certain predictable social contexts. They use, in other words, a great deal of "prefabricated" language. Many earlier researchers thought these prefabricated chunks were distinct and somewhat peripheral to the main body of language, but more recent research puts this formulaic speech at the very centre of language acquisition and sees it as basic to the creative rule-forming processes which follow.
>
> (Lewis 1993, p. 95)

This suggests a methodology which is in opposition to structuralist practices where language is divided into individual components or "building blocks" which are then pieced together to form larger chunks. A lexical approach would stress the introduction of meaningful, pre-assembled chunks of language, which can ultimately be expanded on, played with, combined, and even analysed where useful.

Lewis rejects the structural and Chomskyan models of language as being overly concerned with the production of well-formed sentences. Rather, he stresses that the language which we actually use in our everyday lives is "the real thing", not simply a degenerate version of some idealised competence. Lewis makes the distinction between "correct" language (which often doesn't resemble the "natural" language) and "successful" language (which achieves the purpose at the time).

In order to account for successful language in use, we need observations of real data rather than some theoretical construct of what language should look like. Lewis points to the work of discourse analysts and corpus studies as providing us with increasingly accurate descriptions of how English is actually used in the real world.

In summary, Lewis states:

> It is difficult to grasp immediately the enormity of the changes implied by the perception of lexis as central to language. It is much more radical than any suggestion that there are a few multi-word items which have in the past been overlooked. The primary perception is that historically we have studied language by breaking it into the wrong bits – words and structures. . . . The ability to chunk language successfully is central to the theoretical understanding of how language works.

Which grammar?

Having surveyed the most commonly used grammars in second and foreign language teaching, we might still be tempted to ask: "Which grammar is best?" As always there is no simple answer.

"It all depends"

Your choice of pedagogical grammar might be influenced by a number of considerations.

Contextual variables such as:

- the model of grammar favoured by the educational authorities and the community;

- the model of grammar used in the school's textbooks and syllabus;
- availability of textbooks and other teaching resources which espouse any particular approach to grammar;
- the model of grammar underpinning assessment activities (especially external examinations);
- the objectives and nature of the teaching programme (e.g. emphasis on receptive or productive skills; "survival" or academic; ESL or EFL);
- the role played by grammar in the curriculum.

Learner variables such as:
- the model of grammar the students are already familiar with;
- the age of the students;
- their level of proficiency in English;
- their reasons for learning English;
- their educational background and learning style;
- their literacy in L1.

Teacher variables such as:
- proficiency in English;
- familiarity with a particular grammar;
- willingness to learn about a different grammar;
- teaching style;
- beliefs about learning and how any particular model of grammar might complement those beliefs.

An eclectic approach

Obviously, no model of grammar is inherently "better" than any other. In making decisions about which grammar best meets the needs of their students, teachers need to be aware of what the different grammars can offer. Quite often, the teacher will find that no single grammatical description will meet all needs equally well in all contexts at all times. One response is to draw on a number of models simultaneously (Dirven 1990). A possible scenario might be as follows.

A class of advanced second language learners from Korea are studying English for Academic Purposes. The teacher might draw on her knowledge of **functional** grammar in planning a particular unit of work: identifying a particular purpose for which they need to use language (e.g. to write an argumentative essay); analysing the way in which such a genre is organised; selecting key characteristic lexico-grammatical features of such a genre to focus on (e.g. abstract and technical terminology; nominalisations; evaluative lexis; discourse markers; the passive voice). At a point in the unit where the teacher needs to explain the syntax of the passive, she might draw on her knowledge of **transformational generative** grammar in order to clarify the process by which an active statement can be transformed into a passive one. If a group of students is still having difficulties remembering the passive structure, she might provide a few **structural** drills using substitution tables to impress it on their memories. She might also use structural grammar to contrast the formation of the passive in English and Korean. And because the students are familiar with **traditional** grammar, she might use traditional terminology as far as possible in the classroom.

Some grammar reference books for teachers attempt to combine functional descriptions with more traditional terminology and categories so that the reader can see the potential for working with meaning, but can feel comfortable with the traditional terms, especially when dealing with issues of syntax and accuracy (e.g. Derewianka 1998; Leech and Svartvik 1975). Others provide an outline of English structure and syntax and then incorporate a section on "pragmatics" or "English in use" (e.g. Finegan and Besnier 1989).

Even back in the 1980s, Brown (1980, p. 243), however, was cautioning against uninformed eclecticism:

> It is easy to claim to be an eclectic, and dip haphazardly into every attractive aspect of every conceivable method or approach, and then jumble everything together. It is quite another task to practice "enlightened" eclecticism — that is, to engage in an intelligent use of selected approaches built upon and guided by an integrated and broadly based theory of second language acquisition.

Conclusion

Although the introduction to this chapter vowed to avoid the numerous issues surrounding the teaching of grammar, let us briefly return to them here in the light of what we have discussed. One of the perennial questions in language teaching relates to both the teacher's and the students' knowledge of grammar: What, if any, value is there in knowing explicitly about how language works?

As far as the student is concerned, the results of studies are inconclusive. Much more research needs to be conducted into a variety of teaching contexts using different grammatical models and teaching approaches before we can say anything definitive about its usefulness or otherwise.

In terms of the teacher's knowledge of grammar, however, it is generally agreed these days that this is one of the core components of a language teacher's expertise. Grammar is at the heart of language teaching. An understanding of grammar can assist teachers in:

- identifying the needs of their students, including specific grammatical needs;
- developing appropriate programmes to meet those needs (ranging from the explicit teaching of grammatical concepts and terminology through to a more implicit "language awareness" approach);
- responding to students' queries about aspects of grammar and knowing how to simplify the explanation to suit the age and proficiency level of the student;
- assessing particular aspects of students' language use in terms of effectiveness and accuracy;
- understanding how the grammar of the students' mother tongue might influence the learning of the target language;
- evaluating, selecting and developing teaching materials.

The teacher is the interface between linguistic theory and the learner and therefore needs to become as familiar as possible with a variety of descriptions of grammar in order to be in a position to evaluate their usefulness for various teaching contexts. While it might be unrealistic to expect that every language teacher will have the time and inclination to come to a full understanding of a number of different grammatical paradigms, they should nevertheless be able to participate in the discourse of their profession, to read the relevant literature in an informed way, and to draw on their developing knowledge appropriately.

References

Bell, R.T. (1981) *An Introduction to Applied Linguistics: Approaches and Methods in Language Teaching*, New York: St Martin's Press.

Bloomfield, L. (1933) *Language*, New York: Henry Holt.

Bloor, T. and Bloor, M. (1995) *The Functional Analysis of English: A Hallidayan Approach*, London: Edward Arnold.

Brown, H.D. (1980) *Principles of Language Learning and Teaching*, Englewood Cliffs, NJ: Prentice-Hall.

Canale, M. (1981) "From communicative competence to language pedagogy", in J. Richards and R. Schmidt (eds) *Language and Communication* (pp. 2–27), London: Longman.

Chomsky, N. (1968) "Noam Chomsky and Stuart Hampshire discuss the study of language", *Listener*, May, pp. 687–91.

Collins COBUILD (1990) *Collins COBUILD English Grammar*, London: Collins.

Corder, P.S. (1973) *Introducing Applied Linguistics*, Harmondsworth: Penguin.

Derewianka, B. (1998) *A Grammar Companion for Primary Teachers*, Sydney: PETA.

Dirven, R. (1990) "Pedagogical grammar", *Language Teaching*, January.

Finegan, E. and Beonier, N. (1989) *Language: Its Structure and Use*, San Diego: Harcourt Brace Jovanovich.

Gleason, H.A. (1973) "What grammar?" in J. Savage (ed.) *Linguistics for Teachers: Selected Readings*, Chicago: SRA.

Halliday, M.A.K. (1976) *System and Function in Language: Selected Papers*, London: Oxford University Press.

Halliday, M.A.K. (1977) "Ideas about language", *Aims and Perspectives in Linguistics* (ALAA).

Halliday, M.A.K. (1978) *Language as Social Semiotic: the Social Interpretation of Language and Meaning*, London: Edward Arnold.

Krashen, D. and Terrell, T. (1983) *The Natural Approach*, California: The Alemany Press.

Leech, G. and Svartvik, J. (1975) *A Communicative Grammar of English*, Harlow, Essex: Longman.

Lewis, M. (1993) *The Lexical Approach: The State of ELT and a Way Forward*, London: Language Teaching Publications.

Marckwardt, A. (1966) *Linguistics and the Teaching of English*, Bloomington: Indiana University Press.

Nattinger, J.R. and DeCarrico, J.S. (1992) *Lexical Phrases and Language Teaching*, Oxford: Oxford University Press.

Nelson Francis, W. (1973) "Revolution in grammar" in J. Savage (ed.) *Linguistics for Teachers: Selected Readings*, Chicago: SRA.

Pearson, B. (1977) *Introduction to Linguistic Concepts*, New York: Alfred A. Knopf.

Savage, J.F. (1973) *Linguistics for Teachers: Selected Readings*, Chicago: SRA.

Sinclair, J. (1991) *Corpus, Concordance, Collocation*, Oxford: Oxford University Press.

Wilkins, D.A. (1976) *Notional Syllabuses*, Oxford: Oxford University Press.

Index

Abercrombie, D. 11
abstraction 4, 218–27; abstract reports 223–5; grammar of 225–7; in the humanities 220–1, 227; in science 220, 227
academic discourse communities 67–72, 73–4
academic writing 101
accent (pronunciation) 12, 60–1
access, privileged 69–70
Achebe, C. 84
action, conversations for 43–4
action calls 40
action clauses 218
action images 199, 201
action processes 197–8, 206
action/reflection scale 158–9
actors 201
Adams, J. 9
adjacency pairs 133–4
Adult Migrant English Program (AMEP) 97
affect 127–8
airline reservations 39–41
Amsterdamska, O. 68
analytical exposition 169–70, 221–2
anecdote 126, 127
Apple Computer 39
appropriateness 19–20
archival functions 187
argument 222
argumentative text structure 118–19
Aristotle 243
Asia 30
assessment, diagnostic 4, 229–39
Austin, J. 135–6
Australia 96–8
authentic spoken texts 124–5
authority 68
autonomy 44–5

Baldwin, J. 84
Bamgbose, A. 18
Barton, D. 107, 108
Basic Law 71–2
Bazerman, C. 75
Bell, R.T. 243, 255
Berkenkotter, C. 73
Berry, M. 129–31, 132
'best practice' 62–3
Bhatia, V.K. 113
bilinguals' creativity 17–18
Bloomfield, L. 248
Bock, M. 101
Britain's economic advantage 28–9
British Council 82–3
broadcasting 27
Brown, H.D. 268
bureaucratic writing 224
Burton, D. 132

Canale, M. 256
centralization 44
Chamorro 80
channels of communication 157–8
children's writing 154–5
Chomsky, N. 74, 251, 253–4, 254–5
Christie, F. 219–20
circles model 13–14
circumstances 198, 206–7; construction in visual images 200–2
citations 68
Clark, R. 101
classification 211–18
classifiers 211
clause 94–5, 186
COBUILD corpus 262–5
codification 16–17
collocations 12

colonialism 84–5
common sense 212–14
communicative competence 19–20, 256
communicative functions 187
communicative meanings 260–1
communicative resource 96, 243–4
competence 251, 254; communicative 19–20,
    256
complexity of generic forms 66–7
comprehensibility 21–2
computer interface 38–9
computer technology 33–4, 38–49
concentric images 196
conceptual categories 260–1
conceptual images 199
conjunction 234
connotative semiotics 155
contact 127–8, 160
context 95, 151, 163, 190–1, 257; of culture
    116, 151–2, 163, 257; genre and 111–12;
    and metafunction 178; of situation 116,
    151–3, 163, 172–8, 257
contextual variables 266–7
contrastive rhetoric (CR) 115–19; main aim
    115; outline of theoretical approach 115–16;
    value for analysing written language 116–19
control 43–4; hegemony and world Englishes
    74–5; legislative context 71–2
conversation analysis (CA) 132–5, 142, 144
conversations for action 43–4
cooperative principle 136
Coordinator, The 43–4
Corder, P.S. 242
corpus-based descriptions 262–5
Coulthard, R.M. 129
counter-discourse 83–6, 87
creativity, bilinguals' 17–18
critical discourse analysis (CDA) analysing
    spoken discourse 138–40, 142, 144; main
    aims 99; outline of theoretical approach
    99–100; written language 99–102
critical literacy (CL) 102–7; main aim 102–3;
    outline of theoretical apporach 103–4; value
    for analysing written language 104–7
critical reading 101–2
Crystal, D. 18
culture 19–20; context of 116, 151–2, 163,
    257; formalising the relationship of language
    and culture 153–4

Day, R. 80
decision-support systems 46–7
deep structure rules 251, 254
definite articles 235–7
definitions 217
deixis 159

demand for English 32–3
depth 14–15
Desai, A. 17
descriptive characterizations/analyses 13–22
diagnostic assessment 4, 229–39
dialects 10, 20, 54, 60
diasporas 10, 15
Dirven, R. 242
discourse: counter-discourse 83–6, 87; orders of
    discourse 100; and positioning 103
discourse analysis: critical discourse analysis
    see critical discourse analysis; spoken
    discourse 123–48; written language
    93–122
discourse communities 67–72, 73–4
discourse competence 256
diseases, taxonomies of 213, 214
Disneyfication 190–1
dispreferred responses 134
distance learning 42
diversity 60–1
'Dowry system' 117–18
Durkheim, E. 149

eclecticism 267–8
economic advantage 28–9
economic inequalities 81–3
economic modernisation 34
editorial intervention 68
Eggins, S. 127–8
electronic mail (e-mail) 43–4
embedding 68–9
engco model 30–1, 32–3, 36
English as an International Language (EIL)
    78–80
English for academic purposes (EAP) 112–13
English for Specific Purposes (ESP) 112–13, 261
English in the workplace (EWP) programme
    97–8
English language family 53–4
ethical framework for ELT 35–6
ethnographic methods 112
ethnomethodology 132–3
Euro-English 57
events 199–202
exchange structure analysis 129–32
executives 45–7
exemplum 126, 127
expanding circle 13–14
explanation 214, 216–17
exploitation 72–3
exposition 169–70, 221–2

face-saving 45–6
Fairclough, N. 68, 69, 99, 100, 138
Feak, C.B. 114

field 126, 143–4, 152–3, 156–7, 173–4, 257, 258; and ideational meaning 154, 178
Firth, J.R. 151, 152
flexibility 60
form words 248
formal grammar 243
framing 196–7
Freedman, A. 113
Freire, P. 104
French Academy 16
Freud, S. 149
Fries, C. 247, 248
Fries, P.H. 232
function words 248
functional categories 260
functional grammars 243–4, 256–62, 263–4; analytical tools 258–60; benefits 262; drawbacks 262; implications for teaching 260–1
functional tenor 155
functionalist perspective 19, 79–80, 86–7
functionality of genres 170–1
future: of Englishes 3, 53–64; English as a transitional phenomenon 32–5; linguistic change 53–9; managing the future 35–6; pedagogy 59–63; rival languages 29–32; role of English 2, 26–37; world English 26–9

Garfinkel, H. 133
gate-keeping 132, 139–40; discourse communities 73–4; English and 81–2
Gates, W.H. (Bill) 43
Gee, J.P. 103
generic integrity 66, 68
genre 3, 3–4, 65–77, 160–3, 167–72; approaches to written language 108–15; complexity of generic forms 66–7; ESP 112–13; functionality of genres 170–1; generic forms and change 171–2; generic staging of texts 229–39; generic structure analysis 126, 127, 142; manipulation 72–3; new rhetoric studies 111–12; organizational preferences and generic controls 67; politics of 72–5; power of 67–72; provisional nature of genres 112; recognising genres 168–70; SFL and 109–11; teaching and 75–6, 172; value in analysing written language 113–15
Gilbert, P. 103
given-new 195–6, 198–9
global influence 30–2
global spread of English 9–10, 78–80, 86–7; see also world Englishes, worldliness of English
goals 200, 206
Gollin, S. 140
Goodrich, P. 65
grammar 12; of abstraction 225–7; corpus-based

descriptions 262–5; defining 240–1; functional grammars 243–4, 256–62, 263–4; grammatical paradigms 242–62, 263–4; lexical approaches 265–6; pedagogical grammars 4–5, 240–69; selection for pedagogical grammar 266–8; structural grammar 247–51, 263–4; of technicality 217–18; traditional grammar 244–7, 263–4; transformational-generative grammar 251–6, 263–4; Western heritage 243–4
Grammar-Translation Method 246
Grice, H.G. 136

Halliday, M.A.K. 1–2, 19, 173, 254–5; formal and functional grammars 243; meaning and metafunctions 153–4, 176–7; SFL 94–6 passim, 150–1, 256–7
happenings 199–202
health, language 61
hegemony 74–5
hierarchy of language 32
Hong Kong 71–2
Huckin, T.N. 73
human development index (HDI) 31
humanities, abstraction in 220–1, 227
hybrids 32, 55–7

ideal-real 196, 198–9
'idealised' spoken texts 124–5
ideational meaning/metafunction 153–4, 177, 178, 182–5, 256–7, 259, 260
identity 18, 53–4
ideology 99
iMac installation procedure 197–9, 199–202, 203–7
images, visual 4, 194–208; analysing events or happenings in the world 199–202; analysing relationships between images and viewer 202–5; analysing structure 195–9; using iMac procedure in TESOL teaching practice 205–7
immediate constituent analysis (IC analysis) 249
indefinite articles 235–7
indexical realisations 157, 158–9, 160, 161–2
inequalities, global 81–3, 85–6
information technology 33–4, 38–49
inner circle 13–14
innovation 68–9, 72–3
input 15; types of 18
insider information 69–70
instance 95–6
institutional stature 47
intelligibility 20–2, 53–4
interactional interactions 127, 128
interactions, types of 127–8, 143
interdisciplinary critique 104–7

international academic relations 82
international norm 58–9
Internet 34–5
interpersonal meaning/metafunction 153–4,
    177, 178, 182, 256–7, 259, 260
interpersonal motivation 127, 128
interpretability 21–2
interpretation process 99–100
IRF structure 129
Ivanic, R. 101

Janks, H. 101
Jespersen, O. 245
Johnson, B.M. 45
Jonson, B. 244

Kachru, B. 79
Kachru, Y. 116, 117–19
Kenya 81
Knobel, M. 104
knowledge: common sense 212–14; shared
    69–70; specialized 211–12, 213
Kress, G. 73, 139, 225; images 194–5, 199,
    200, 201, 202–3

Lankshear, C. 102–3, 104–7
leading-edge technology 33–4
learner variables 267
left-right axis 194–5, 195–6, 198
legislation 70–2
Lewis, M. 254, 265–6
lexical density 182–4
lexicogrammatical analysis 110–11, 258–60
lexis 12; field and lexical items 157; pedagogical
    grammars 265–6
Leydesdorff, L. 68
lingua franca 3, 27–8; rival languages to English
    29–30
linguicism 82
linguistic competence 256
linguistic diversity 60–1
linguistic genocide 80–1
linguistic imperialism 82, 84
literacy 4, 181–93; frontiers of 190–1; linguistic
    view of 181; as social practice 103;
    technology of 188–9; written language
    181–5; written world 185–8
literacy studies 102–8; critical literacy 102–7;
    main aims 102; new literacy studies 107–8
logical relations 226, 235
Luke, A. 104

macro-genre 238–9
macro-level approaches 104
Malinowski, B. 151–2, 155
Mandarin 30

manipulation, genre 72–3
market share 33
Martin, J.R. 94, 109, 167–8, 169
material clauses 218
Mazrui, A. 84–5
Mboya, T. 85
McArthur, T. 55, 56
meaning 85, 260–1; options for 176–7, 178,
    259, 260; potential 116; see also
    metafunctions
media texts 104–7
medical taxonomy of diseases 213, 214
metafunctions 153–4, 176–7, 256–7, 259, 260;
    context and 178
metaphors 183–4, 185–6
Microsoft Corporation 43
migration 81–2
mindset, change in 62
minitexts 118
mixing 68–9
modality 182; visual 202, 203, 204–5
mode 126, 144, 152–3, 157–9, 175–6, 257,
    259; and textual meaning 154, 178
modernisation, economic 34
monolingualism 17–18, 28–9
mood 153–4, 176; visual images 202, 203–4
Moore, S. 61
morphemes 248
multi-modal texts 194, 197; see also images,
    visual
multi-word units 265
Mukherjee, B. 17
Myers, G. 65

narrative 126, 127, 161–2
narrative images 199–200
native speakers 15, 22
natural spoken texts 124–5
needs, unmet 46–7
Nelson Francis, W. 247–8
new Englishes 84–5
new-given 195–6, 198–9
new literacy studies (NLS) 102, 107–8
new rhetoric studies (NRS) 111–12, 113
Ngugi wa Thiong'o 81
nominal groups 218, 226–7
nominalization 183–4, 185–6, 224–5
norm, international 58–9
novel hybrids 56–7

objects to be acted on 200, 206
office automation 44–5
official language status 11–12
options, set of 176–7
order 196–7
orders of discourse 100

organizational preferences 67
outer circle 13–14

paradigmatic relations 151
paradigms, grammatical 242–62, 263–4
parsing 245–6
participatory design 45
passive tense 211–12
passive voice 253
pattern drills 249, 250
Pearson, B. 244
pedagogical grammars 4–5, 240–69; defining
    241–2
pedagogy *see* teaching
pedestrian crossing 150
peer review 68
performance 251, 254
personal computers 46
personal tenor 155
perspective 202–3
Phillipson, R. 82–3
philosophy 243
phonemes 248
pluricentric languages 9
polarity 176
political inequalities 81–3
politics 103; of genre 72–5; new Englishes and
    84–5
positioning 103
potential calls 40
power 153, 160; of genre 67–72; language,
    ideology and 99; spoken discourse 127–8,
    139–40
pragmatic motivation 127, 128, 130
pragmatics 135, 136–7, 142, 144
prediction activities 205–6
predominant paradigm 78–80
preferences, organizational 67
preferred responses 134
presupposition questions 40
printing 27, 188
privileged access 69–70
probabilism 111
probabilistic realisations 157, 158–9, 160,
    161–2
problem-solution analysis 118–19
procedures 97–8, 168–9; iMac installation
    procedure 197–9, 199–202, 203–7;
    purpose, structure, language features and
    visual design 197–8
process writing 188, 225
production process 99–100
professional communities 70–1
prominence 197, 198
pronouns 235–7
pronunciation (accent) 12, 60–1

Quirk, R. 20–1, 79

range 14–15
Rao, R. 17
reaction images 199
reading 101–2
reading paths 198
real-ideal 196, 198–9
received pronunciation (RP) 11, 60
recount 126, 127, 162
reference 235–7
references 68
reflection/action scale 158–9
regional languages 30
register 3–4, 152–3, 154–60, 173–8, 257;
    analysis of spoken discourse 126, 130, 142,
    143–4; *see also* field, mode, tenor
reiteration 222
relational clauses 217–18, 226–7
relationships between images and viewer 202–5
relevance, maxim of 136–7
reports 214–16; abstract 223–5
research articles 68, 114–15
resource, language as 96, 243–4
responses 134
rheme 232–4
Rice, D.E. 45
rival languages 29–32
Rothery, J. 110–11, 167–8, 219–20

Sacks, H. 133
salience 197, 198
Saussure, F. de 149
schematic structure 109–10, 168–9
school grammar 245
science 187, 189; abstraction in 220, 227
scripted dialogues 124–5
Searle, J. 135–6
second draft reorganisation 237–8
semantics 225, 253
semiotic systems 150, 155
sentence patterns 249, 250
shared knowledge 69–70
Shor, I. 107
shot type 202, 203, 204
Sinclair, J. 129, 265
single world standard English 26–8
situation, context of 116, 151–3, 163, 172–8,
    257
skills: for future workers 47–8; transfer 34
Slade, D. 126
Smith, L.E. 21–2, 28
social change 171–2
social distance 160
social facts 149–50
social inequalities 81–3

social role relationships 127–8, 130
sociolinguistic competence 256
solidarity 70–1
sophists 243
South Africa 101
Soyinka, W. 17
Spanish 30, 31
speakers of English, number of 78
specialized texts 4, 211–28; abstraction 218–27; common sense 212–14; specialized knowledge 211–12; technicality 214–18
speech act theory 135–6, 137
speech community 15–16
spoken language 3, 96, 123–48; bringing together analytical tools for language teaching 140–5; conversation analysis 132–5, 142, 144; critical discourse analysis 138–40, 142, 144; exchange structure analysis 129–32; relationships with written language 4, 181–93; SFL 126–9, 130; speech act theory and pragmatics 135–7; spoken texts and the language classroom 124–6; typology of interactions 127–8
sportswriting 41–2
standardization 39–41
standards/standard English 10–11; and codification 16–17; future of Englishes 57–9; single world standard English 26–8
status 153, 160
story-telling genres 126, 127
strategic competence 256
Street, B. 107–8
Strevens, P. 27–8
structural grammar 247–51, 263–4; analytical tools 248–9; benefits 250; drawbacks 250–1; implications for teaching 249–50
structure of visual images 195–9
substitution tables 249, 250
Swahili 81
Swales, J.M. 114
system 95–6
systemic functional grammar (SFG) 154, 256–62, 263–4
systemic functional linguistics (SFL) 1–2, 3, 4, 94–8, 150–3, 176–8; and concept of genre 109–11; main aims 94; outline of theoretical approach 94–6; and spoken language 126–9, 130; value for analysing written language 96–8

tagging 176
tagmemes 249
Tanzania 81
taxonomies 211–18
teacher variables 267
teaching: distance learning 42; ethical

framework for ELT 35–6; future of Englishes 59–63; genre and 75–6, 172; grammatical paradigms and 246, 249–50, 253–5, 260–1; images and procedures 205–7; spoken texts and 124–6; types of input 18; worldliness of English 86–7
technical efficiency 46–7
technicality 4, 214–18; grammar of 217–18; reports 214–17
technocratic discourse 190
technology 2–3, 27, 33–4; language and work 38–49; of literacy 188–9; transfer 34
Technology Bill of Rights 48
tenor 126, 130, 144, 152–3, 159–60, 174–5; dimensions of 127–8; and effect on reader 238; and interpersonal meaning 154, 178; SFG 257, 258–9
text 94–5; analysis and diagnostic assessment 4, 229–39; variation 172–8
textual meaning/metafunction 153–4, 177, 178, 256–7, 259, 260
theme 153–4, 219–20; development 232–4
thesis 222
threat, English as 80–1
Tirkkonen-Condit, S. 118–19
traditional grammar 244–7, 263–4; benefits 246–7; drawbacks 247; Grammar-Translation Method 246
transactional interactions 127, 128
transformational-generative grammar (TGG) 251–6, 263–4; analytical tools 252–3; benefits 255; drawbacks 255–6; implications for teaching 253–5
transitional phenomenon 32–5
transitivity 153
turn-taking 133, 134–5
turn types 133–4, 135

unconscious rules 149–50
units of work 205
universal grammar 251–2
unmet needs 46–7
users, types of 13–14

van Leeuwen, T. 194–5, 199, 200, 201, 202–3
variation: generic 74–5; text 172–8; types of 13–14; varieties of English 10–13, 20, 54–7, 60–1; see also world Englishes
vectors 199, 201
vertical axis 196, 199
viewer-image relationships 202–5
visual images see images, visual

Wallace, C. 101–2
Western heritage 243–4
Widdowson, H. 99

Wilkins, D.A. 260
word processor 188
work councils 45
workplace 2–3, 38–49
Winspisinger, W.W. 48
world Englishes 2, 9–25, 26–9; characteristics
    of 10–13; communicative competence
    19–20; global spread of English 9–10,
    78–80, 86–7; hegemony and 74–5;
    intelligibility 20–2; issues 13–22;
    monolingual attitudes and bilinguals'
    creativity 17–18; native speakers 15; range
    and depth 14–15; speech community 15–16;
    standards see standards/standard English;
    types of input 18; types of variation and
    types of users 13–14
'world' languages 30–2

World Standard Printed English (WSPE) 57–8
World Standard Spoken English (WSSE) 57–8
worldliness of English 3, 78–89; critical views
    on English in the world 80–3; discourse,
    counter-discourse and the world in English
    83–6; English teachers and 86–7;
    predominant paradigm 78–80
writing 153
written language 3, 93–122, 181–5; contrastive
    rhetoric 115–19; critical discourse analysis
    99–102; genre approaches 108–15; literacy
    studies 102–8; relationships with spoken
    language 4, 181–93; systemic functional
    linguistics 94–8; see also text
written world 185–8

Xerox 39